MW01030715

THE CREATIVE WRITER'S CRAFT

THE CREATIVE WRITER'S CRAFT

Lessons in Poetry, Fiction, and Drama

Richard Bailey
William Burns
Linda Denstaedt
Claire Needham
Nancy Ryan

New York, New York   Columbus, Ohio   Chicago, Illinois   Peoria, Illinois   Woodland Hills, California

Sponsoring Editor: Marisa L. L'Heureux
Product Manager: Judy Rudnick
Design Manager: Ophelia Chambliss
Interior and cover design: Ellen Pettengell
Production Manager: Margo Goia

Acknowledgments begin on page 371, which is to be considered an extension of this copyright page.

 **Glencoe**   The **McGraw·Hill** Companies

Copyright © 1999 The McGraw-Hill Companies, Inc. All Rights reserved. Except as permitted under the United States Copyright Act of 1976, no part of this publication may be reproduced or distributed in any form or by any means, or stored in a database retrieval system, without prior written permission of the publisher.

Send all inquires to:
Glencoe/McGraw-Hill
8787 Orion Place
Columbus, OH 43240

ISBN : 0-8442-5716-8
Printed in the United States of America
   8 9 10 113 08 07

Library of Congress Cataloging-in-Publication Data

The creative writer's craft : lessons in poetry, fiction, and drama /
   Richard Bailey . . . . [et al.].
      p.   cm.
   Includes index.
   ISBN 0-8442-5716-8
   1. English language—Rhetoric.   2. English language—Rhetoric—
Problems, exercises, etc.   3. Creative writing—Problems,
exercises, etc.   4. Creative writing.   I. Bailey, Richard, 1952-

PE1408.C7143   1998
808'.042'076—dc21   98-23827
                                                                                      CIP

Contents

Preface xiii

 Writing Creatively 1

chapter 1 Writing the Creative Way 2
Generating Raw Material 4
Freewriting from Memory, Direct Observation, and Reading 5
Expanding the Good Stuff: Fictionalizing and Exploring 7
Composing and Structuring 9
Experimenting with the Techniques and Structures of Published
Works 9
Discovering the Best Structure for the Subject 11
Revising and Developing Meaning 13
Discovering Meaning: Listening to Feedback in Writer Response
Groups 13
Developing Meaning Through Revision: Transforming,
Rearranging, Expanding 15
Editing and Proofreading 16

Creating Poetry 21

chapter 2 Narrating a Simple Conflict: Dramatic Situation, Meaning, and Verb Usage 22

Exploring Dramatic Situation 24

Experimenting with Dramatic Situation 26

Writer's Practice 2.1: Dramatize an Event 27

Writer's Practice 2.2: Create a Dialogue 28

Writer's Practice 2.3: Narrate a Memory 29

Exploring Meaning 31

Experimenting with Meaning 33

Writer's Practice 2.4: Write a Narrative Poem 34

Writer Response Groups 35

Revising Verbs to Reduce Wordiness 36

Writer's Practice 2.5: Create "Muscular" Verbs 36

Examining Student Poems 38

chapter 3 Drawing an Unusual Comparison: Metaphor, Simile, Extended Metaphor, and Stanza 42

Exploring Metaphor and Simile 45

Experimenting with Metaphor and Simile 46

Writer's Practice 3.1: List Wild Comparisons 46

Exploring Extended Metaphors 47

Experimenting with Extended Metaphors 49

Writer's Practice 3.2: Extend a Comparison 49

Writer's Practice 3.3: Form Your Freewrite 51

Writer Response Groups 53

Revising for Stanzas 53

Writer's Practice 3.4: Revise to a Fixed Stanza Length 54

Examining Student Poems 56

chapter 4   Writing from Daily Life: Imagery, Direct Address, and Free Verse 59

Exploring Imagery 61
Experimenting with Imagery 63
   Writer's Practice 4.1: Collect Daily Images 64
   Writer's Practice 4.2: Reflect on Your Own Observations 65
   Writer's Practice 4.3: Write a Daily Life Poem 66
Exploring Meaning and Direct Address 68
Experimenting with Meaning and Direct Address 69
   Writer's Practice 4.4: Add Direct Address 69
Writer Response Groups 71
Exploring the Free-Verse Poem 72
Revising to Create a Free-Verse Poem 73
   Writer's Practice 4.5: Make Stanza and Line Decisions 73
Examining Student Poems 75

chapter 5   Mining the Memory: Memory and Imagination, Imagery, and Diction 80

Exploring Memory and Imagination 82
Experimenting with Memory and Imagination 84
   Writer's Practice 5.1: Loosen Memory and Imagination 84
Exploring Imagery 87
Experimenting with Imagery 90
   Writer's Practice 5.2: Craft an Imagery Poem 90
Writer Response Groups 92
Revising with a Careful Eye on Diction 92
   Writer's Practice 5.3: Create an Emotional Experience 93
Examining Student Poems 95

chapter 6   **Creating the Illogical World: Imagination, Third-Person Point of View, and Line Break   100**

Exploring Imagination   102

Experimenting with Imagination   104

Writer's Practice 6.1: Write a Collaborative Poem   105

Writer's Practice 6.2: Generate a Dreamlike Freewrite   106

Exploring Third-Person Point of View   108

Experimenting with Third-Person Point of View   110

Writer's Practice 6.3: Expand a Narrative with Details, Action, and Dialogue   110

Writer Response Groups   112

Revising for the Poetic Line   112

Writer's Practice 6.4: Shape Your Poem with Line Breaks   114

Examining Student Poems   116

chapter 7   **Creating from Sentences and Words: Sentence Control, Diction, and Cutting   120**

Exploring Sentence Control   123

Experimenting with Sentence Control   126

Writer's Practice 7.1: Surprise Yourself   126

Writer's Practice 7.2: Invent from Sentence Frames   129

Exploring the Impact of Diction   130

Experimenting with Diction   132

Writer's Practice 7.3: Do Diction Research   132

Writer's Practice 7.4: Expand Using Diction Research   133

Writer Response Groups   134

Revising: Cutting for Emphasis and Clarity   135

Writer's Practice 7.5: Cut Extraneous Detail   135

Examining Student Poems   137

Creating Fiction 143

chapter 8 Talking on the Back Porch: Leads, Conflict, First-Person Point of View, Dialogue, and Repetition 144

Exploring the Powerful Lead to Establish Conflict 149

Experimenting with the Powerful Lead to Establish Conflict 150

Writer's Practice 8.1: Write a Powerful Lead 150

Exploring First-Person Point of View 152

Experimenting with First-Person Point of View 153

Writer's Practice 8.2: Create an Honest or Dishonest Voice 154

Exploring Characterization Through Dialogue 156

Experimenting with Characterization Through Dialogue 159

Writer's Practice 8.3: Tell a Tale of Trouble 159

Writer's Practice 8.4: Create a Closing Conversation 163

Writer's Practice 8.5: Assemble the First Draft 164

Writer Response Groups 166

Revising with Repetition to Create Meaning 167

Writer's Practice 8.6: Insert Repetition 168

Examining Student Stories 170

chapter 9 Transforming Memory to Fiction: Setting, Movement, and Theme 174

Exploring Setting 177

Experimenting with Setting 178

Writer's Practice 9.1: Describe a Place 178

Exploring Movement 180

Experimenting with Movement 181

Writer's Practice 9.2: Move the Action 182

Writer's Practice 9.3: Move Back in Time 184

Writer's Practice 9.4: Assemble the First Draft 186

Writer Response Groups 189

Revising for Meaning and Theme: The Recurring Image 189
Writer's Practice 9.5: Repeat an Image 190
Examining Student Stories 193

chapter 10 Keeping Your Distance: Third-Person Objective Point of View, Suspense, and Tone 196

Exploring Third-Person Objective Point of View 201
Experimenting with Third-Person Objective Point of View 202
Writer's Practice 10.1: Maintain Your Distance 203
Exploring Suspense 205
Experimenting with Suspense 206
Writer's Practice 10.2: Complicate the Situation 206
Writer's Practice 10.3: Seek a Resolution 210
Writer's Practice 10.4: Assemble the First Draft 212
Writer Response Groups 216
Revising Your Story for Tone 216
Writer's Practice 10.5: Adjust the Backdrop 217
Examining Student Stories 223

chapter 11 Moving Inside a Character: Psychological Conflict, Flashback, and Imagery 227

Exploring Psychological Conflict 231
Experimenting with Psychological Conflict 232
Writer's Practice 11.1: Disturb Your Character's Peace 232
Exploring Flashback 234
Experimenting with Flashback 236
Writer's Practice 11.2: Replay a Scene 236
Writer's Practice 11.3: Assemble the First Draft 239
Writer Response Groups 241
Revising for Imagery 242
Writer's Practice 11.4: Invest an Image 243
Examining Student Stories 247

chapter 12 **Revisiting Your Craft, Repeating Your Story: Conflict, Repetition, and Theme 250**

Exploring Conflict and Character 255

Experimenting with Conflict and Character 256

Writer's Practice 12.1: Tell the Tale 256

Exploring Repetition 258

Experimenting with Repetition 258

Writer's Practice 12.2: Tell the Tale a Second Time 259

Writer's Practice 12.3: Tell the Tale a Third Time 260

Writer's Practice 12.4: Tell the Tale a Fourth Time 263

Writer's Practice 12.5: Assemble the First Draft 265

Writer Response Groups 269

Revising for Theme 270

Writer's Practice 12.6: Connect Your Imagery and Theme 271

Examining Student Stories 278

Creating Drama 283

chapter 13 **Exploring the Elements of Plays: Dramatic Characters, Dialogue, Structure, Conflict, and Action 284**

Exploring Strong Characters and Dramatic Dialogue 291

Experimenting with Strong Characters and Dramatic Dialogue 292

Writer's Practice 13.1: Record a Conversation from Memory 293

Writer's Practice 13.2: Record a Conversation from Direct Observation 294

Exploring the Actions of a Play 295

Experimenting with the Actions of a Play 297

Writer's Practice 13.3: Compose Parenthetical Actions 297

Exploring Dramatic Structure and Two-Character Conflict 298

Experimenting with Dramatic Structure and Two-Character Conflict 300

Writer's Practice 13.4: Create the Beginning of a Play 301

Writer's Practice 13.5: Intensify the Conflict 303

Writer's Practice 13.6: Find a Resolution and End Your Play 305

Exploring Stage Directions 306

Experimenting with Stage Directions 308

Writer's Practice 13.7: Add Stage Directions 308

Writer Response Groups 310

Revising for Consistency in Characterization 310

Writer's Practice 13.8: Revise for Character Consistency 311

Examining Student Plays 315

chapter 14 **Expanding Dramatic Possibilities: Three-Character Conflict, Twists and Turns, and Discovery or Reversal 324**

Exploring Three-Character Conflict 337

Experimenting with Three-Character Conflict 339

Writer's Practice 14.1: Record a Conversation 349

Writer's Practice 14.2: Construct a Scene 341

Exploring Twists and Turns 344

Experimenting with Twists and Turns 345

Writer's Practice 14.3: Change a Character's Behavior Using a Twist or Turn 345

Exploring a Discovery or Reversal 348

Experimenting with a Discovery or Reversal 349

Writer's Practice 14.4: End Your Play Using a Discovery or Reversal 349

Writer Response Groups 352

Revising Stage Directions 353

Writer's Practice 14.5: Reconsider Stage Directions 353

Examining Student Plays 360

Acknowledgments 371

Index 373

Preface

The Creative Writer's Craft: Lessons in Poetry, Fiction, and Drama offers you the opportunity to explore and develop crafting skills for writing various types of poems, short stories, and one-act plays. Some people who take creative writing courses nurture romantic images of becoming the kind of admired writers they love and try to emulate. They imagine how it would feel to be recognized wherever they go. They picture themselves writing bestsellers in exotic locations—a mountain resort in Colorado, a beach on a Caribbean island, an outdoor cafe in Paris. They focus on the rewards of writing and not on the writing itself. While we can't guarantee fame and fortune, we do have every confidence that this book will help you to establish a solid foundation for writing creatively and becoming the kind of writer you want to be. The lessons and writing activities herein encourage you to develop a writer's attitude—an attitude embracing the writing process rather than the final result.

The structure of the chapters are based on the habits and routines of real writers—writers who practice their craft and publish their works. On the surface, the writing practices of such writers are highly individualized and varied, but when their processes are observed and described, it is apparent that most share similar "stages" of writing: generating raw material, expanding, assembling drafts, revising, and preparing a finished manuscript. All too often, novice writers focus on the last stage and pay little attention to the creative process, jumping directly to the finished product as though speed is the goal. It is the final product that gets all the attention, after all. It is the final product that is evaluated and graded. And the ability to write a quality, error-free first draft for impromptu essay assignments and written exams has always been rewarded. This book attempts to reverse this inclination. It invites you to slow down and deliberately savor the creative process by exploring and experimenting with the elements of poetry, short stories, and plays. This book encourages you to embrace the journey, not the final destination.

The lessons and writing assignments in this book were tested in many classrooms. The varied readings and models have been chosen from a wide range of authors whose writings have proven to be motivational and inspirational to a broad range of students. Most of them, selected from a variety of recently published literary journals and anthologies, serve to exemplify writing approaches and practices currently sought by editors and readers alike. You are encouraged to turn to published pieces such as these to emulate techniques and to solve problems, to become attuned to the methods writers use to accomplish their art.

Organization of the Text

Chapter 1, "Writing the Creative Way," explores the stages of writing and provides a rationale for the flow of the exercises and the structure of the instructional chapters that follow. As the title of this book reveals, the instructional chapters are divided into three genres: six poetry chapters, five fiction chapters, and two drama chapters. The beginning chapters of each section focus on basic and essential crafting skills, and the later chapters increase in complexity as the more advanced skills are introduced. Each chapter explores two or three crafting skills, includes a professional model with a discussion of how the model serves to exemplify the skills being taught, and provides a series of writing activities that lead to a finished product.

Features of the Instructional Chapters

The following features, reflective of the creative writing process, form the structure of the instructional chapters of the book:

- The introduction to each chapter announces the new crafting skills to be taught and previews which skills from previous chapters will be revisited; the introduction also introduces a professional model, which is followed by questions related to the topic of the chapter.
- "Exploring" sections discuss and illustrate various creative strategies and explain how the professional model exemplifies those strategies.
- "Experimenting" sections include how-to instructions for the *Writer's Practice* assignments, the writing activities that accompany each chapter. A series of such assignments will lead to a finished product at the end of each chapter. Each *Writer's Practice* is illustrated by the work of a practicing writer and an explication of that work.

- "Writer's Response Group" sections include suggestions for small groups of students to discuss each other's first drafts, with an emphasis on the skills being taught.
- "Revising" sections introduce a variety of revision strategies—effective methods for re-seeing and rewriting first drafts. These sections include revisions of the work of the same practicing writer who provided the examples for the "Experimenting" sections.
- "Examining Student Samples" include student work written in response to the *Writer's Practice* assignments in each chapter.

Acknowledgments

The authors wish to thank their editor, Marisa L. L'Heureux, for her patience and encouragement during the writing of this book, as well as for her guidance and shaping of the finished product. They are also very indebted to their mentor, Stephen Dunning, who contributed the model story, "Choking on Love," to Chapter 8 and whose teaching inspired the approaches and lessons in this book.

A special thanks to Aaron Stander who brought the authors together and started them out in the right direction.

The authors are especially thankful to the instructors who used the chapters in their classrooms and contributed valuable feedback: Lori Buchholz, Tina Chambers, Sharry Doty, Susan Golab, Ann Serra Lowney, Cheryl Miller, Kris Nemesi, Nancy Nankervis, Richard Porritt, Richard Swartout, and Greg Warner.

We are also grateful to the reviewers who read and critiqued the final manuscript: Patricia Bridges, Anne Calcagno, Scott M. Fisher, and Suzanne Greenberg.

And, finally, the authors thank the many students who diligently worked through the exercises and contributed feedback. We would like to extend a special thank you to the following students:

Jacob Adkins
Nancy Alborell
Timothy Barrette
Todd Bauer
Genevieve Benson
Ruth Bonser
Heather Brown
Heidi Brown
Jason Busher
Sarah Butzine

Chas Claus
Lisa Davis
Geoffrey Denstaedt
Andy Dixon
David Dixon
Michael Flanigan
Beth Forbes
Jordan Fox
Michael Gay
Angela Goodrich

Regina Gregoroff
Brent Griffith
Ashley Halleran
Adam Hamilton
Kathy Julian
Jennifer Kerney
Patrick Killoran
Liz Koblinski
Stephanie Kotula
Brennan Krengel
Molly Lane
Bonnie Licari
Rebecca List
Amber Mitchell
Youssef Mosallam
Felicia Nelson
Megan O'Brien
Holly O'Connor
David Oliver
Polly Opsahl
Jill Orler
Meghan Pocs

Chris Prysok
Emily Regnier
Laura Richardson
Kelly Robinson
Peter Rynders
Lateece Scrivens
Walter Seitz
Matthew Sisco
Trevor Sisk
Meghan Sitar
Jamie Smith
Kimberly Stachulski
Kyle Stout
Jim Territo
Chip Thomas
Holy Traywick
Dana Wall
Brian Witkowski
D'Anne Witkowski
Jennifer Yeager
Lindsay Zebkar

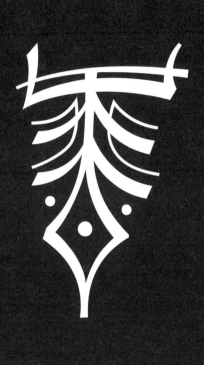

Writing
Creatively

chapter 1

Writing the Creative Way

It is not my intent to teach you how to raft, for only the river
is the true teacher, of which we are each forever a student.

-JEFF BENNETT,
The Complete Whitewater Rafter

How do real writers work? Movie scenes showing writers at work tend to paint a false picture of how writers actually function. In fact, most of these scenes can be classified into one of two stock types. The first shows a writer sitting in front of a typewriter. We see her thinking, but we don't know what she's thinking about. Then her fingers start moving. The camera zooms in on the typewriter, and we see a title appear. The carriage returns, and then the first half of the first sentence appears: "When the morning sun announced a new day. . . ." The writer looks confident. The scene fades from the screen, and we are left with the impression that she will continue typing straight through to the end of the work without hesitation or fumbling. She *is* a great writer, after all.

The second stock writer-at-work scene shows a writer who is perplexed and is struggling to make his words flow. We see him seated at his typewriter, looking extremely frustrated. He types frantically for a moment, then yanks the paper out, crumples it into a wad, and hurls it toward a wastebasket. He misses. This sequence is repeated, and then the camera zooms in on the wastebasket and the littered floor. The scene fades to indicate the passage of time. The next camera close-up shows a large pile of wadded papers scattered around the wastebasket and a frazzled writer. If the writer in the movie is a man, he will be unshaven. If the writer is a woman, she will have tousled hair and be wearing a comfortable old terry-cloth bathrobe. The scene fades, and we are left with the impression that the writing process is an agonizing ordeal.

Of course, both scenes are misleading. Few professional writers can create a perfect work of art at the first time attempt, or even expect to do so, and few think of rewriting as a waste of time. Words do not come to writers in any mysterious or magical way. In fact, what writers do is probably impossible to show on a movie screen. Writers explore impulses and hunches. They experiment with ideas. They play around with words. They make choices. They compose drafts. They rewrite and reflect and compose again. They repeat the steps they rely on to create a work of art.

Creative writers can be compared to white-water rafters—giving up control, riding the currents, unleashing the creative "river" hidden within. A creative writer navigates this river like a rafter, speeding up, slowing down, turning, occasionally steering for branches, exploring uncharted tributaries, running white water, and sometimes capsizing. The writer is a "pilot" making conscious decisions about the direction to take. Yet, there is the river's current to deal with—the pleasing but sometimes confounding pull that the pilot doesn't fully understand. As writers, we think we can control the composing process, when, in fact, letting the current have its pull and learning to detect and yield to its subtle tug is what we're about as writers. Yes, some piloting is necessary, but the current suggests that deep, intuitive right-brain aspect of writing. In white-water rafting there are levels of predictability and strategy, but, always, the river can be greater and wilder than the rafters know.

The writing process described in this chapter is based on the practices and methods of professional "pilots"—writers who are currently publishing poems, stories, and plays. Although these writers develop personal ways of working, the majority practice variations of the following stages of the creative process:

Generating Raw Material
- Freewriting from memory, direct observation, and reading
- Expanding the good stuff: fictionalizing and exploring

Composing and Structuring
- Experimenting with the techniques and structures of published works
- Discovering the best structure for the subject

Revising and Developing Meaning
- Discovering meaning: listening to feedback in response groups
- Developing meaning through revision: transforming, rearranging, expanding

Editing and Proofreading
- Cutting needless words and passages
- Line editing, reviewing word choice, and proofreading for errors

The outline above should not be thought of as a lockstep process, but rather as a convenient way to describe the common moves writers make. In practice, writers tend to blend steps or repeat them, looping backward whenever a work underway demands it. Sometimes, however, a writer might move through each major step in the process, exhausting the activities in each for an entire work before moving on to the next step.

This chapter discusses the importance and nature of the creative writing process and provides examples written by a student. Because the first step, "Generating Raw Material," is essential to the creative process, more space is devoted to it than to the other steps. The discussion focuses on techniques and procedures that typically are ignored or dismissed by beginning writers of poems, short stories, and plays. Beginners often try to think of interesting ideas or stories before they start writing, relying on subjects they have been thinking about for some time. Then they try to write from beginning to end, hoping to produce a finished product with one draft. But if the beginning writer is lucky, that won't happen. Most literature is *discovered* by its creator. In the act of writing something else, a writer discovers, expands, develops, and nurtures.

Generating Raw Material

Ask published writers where they get their ideas and most will answer, "From my writing." Most writers start writing about something small—an object, a person, a memory, an incident—and, in the process, they discover the subject for a story, a play, or a poem. This is what the preliminary stage of writing is all about—collecting hastily written chunks describing one's thoughts, fears, desires, memories, dreams, or the passing scene. The discovery process begins with these seeds for stories and poems.

What bits of writing should you collect? We offer specific suggestions in the exercises and assignments to come, but many writers try to capture

- gifts of the mind—details of memories, dreams, imagined experiences;
- scenes directly observed—sights, sounds, smells, things, people, conversations;
- ideas and passages found in print—newspapers, journals, anthologies, novels.

Begin a system for keeping the raw material that you generate. Collect your writing in a journal, notebook, or folder. Some writers carry a journal around with them and jot down thoughts as they occur or record interesting incidents when they happen. Other writers prefer to schedule a regular writing period each day and restrict their writing to that time. Try different methods and choose the one that is most comfortable for you.

Freewriting from Memory, Direct Observation, and Reading.

Generating raw material is enhanced by what is called *freewriting*. You may be familiar with such predrafting activities as listing, brainstorming, and clustering, activities that help writers generate ideas and subject matter through free association. Freewriting can, at times, be very similar to these activities, but in this book it refers to *all* writing activities connected to the early stages of drafting. This includes free associations; focused writings; recordings from direct observation, memory, and dreams; expansions; imitations; experimental renderings; and even, at times, first drafts.

About Writer's Block

What exactly is writer's block? Almost every writer goes through periods when writing doesn't come easily. A variety of unavoidable occurrences, such as family tragedies, job stress, or ill-health, can take a writer's attention away from her writing.

Another type of writer's block—when a writer just can't find anything to say—is easier to deal with. Freewriting on a regular basis will bring ideas to even the most "stuck" writer. So, if you ever feel frustrated while in the midst of a poem, story, or play, often the best course of action is to begin working on an entirely new poem, story, or play. While working on something new, you might just come upon some fresh ideas for a stalled piece.

For many writers, having a few pieces of work going at one time is the best way to prevent writer's block.

Freewriting is best done quickly. Speed is especially important in the early stages of creating poems, stories, and plays. Writing quickly forces you to let go and surrender control. In letting the river carry you, you allow it to bring up the wealth of memories, images, and feelings that are stored in your subconscious mind. Your task in freewriting is to record everything that crosses your mind. Creative writing is primarily a right-brain activity. This creative side of the brain thrives on speed; the faster we write, the more active it becomes. In turn, the more active the right side of the brain becomes, the faster we must write in response.

During this early stage in the creative process, novice writers have more to lose from overcontrol than from a lack of it. The left brain—the logical, critical part of our minds—can interfere with right-brain operations if we write too slowly. Questions and doubts keep popping into mind: "Is that the right word?" "This is no good." A writer needs to bypass the left brain, giving no time for doubts or criticisms to be conceived. Resist the inclination to slow down to tinker with a phrase, because the more time you invest in doing so, the more you become attached to your words and ideas, making it difficult to modify or eliminate them later.

Note that freewriting is not composing or drafting or creating a wonderful work of art. It is simply an effective method of producing raw material. Think of yourself as a video camera, recording the images and scenes flashing in front of your mind's eye. Write as fast as you can, capturing the details, descriptions, conversations, and ideas involved. Try not to miss anything, but leave all judgments behind. Write everything, because later you will cast out the ideas you dislike, like a prospector panning for gold nuggets buried in debris.

When freewriting from memory focus on something specific, such as a recent incident or something memorable from childhood. Don't begin by *explaining* what was going on, but focus on a small detail—a facial feature, an expression, something someone said, or an object that was in the scene. Write about this detail, letting the rest of the story come out haphazardly.

Freewriting from direct observation involves writing descriptions of a place that it is possible to observe while writing. An example is a specific room at home, at school, or in another public building. Besides describing visible details—decorations, furnishings, and the people there—include descriptions of the overall atmosphere of the place, its sounds and smells, and the actions and conversations of the people involved.

Newspapers and magazines can also stimulate raw materials. Scan newspapers for interesting articles such as human interest stories or the strange and unusual. Copy passages that are particularly interesting and then write plot ideas that come to mind: "Snake charmer dies from ninety-fifth bite." Then, as needed, freewrite visual details that are not found in the article, such as descriptions of the place or the person involved.

The following example, a freewrite from recent memory, was written by a student named Laura. She wrote it in one short burst, writing as quickly as she could, completely disregarding spelling, punctuation, neatness, or rules about writing in complete sentences. Some writers prefer to do their freewriting in longhand, using a large, scrawling script two or three lines high. Other writers opt to use a computer keyboard for fast typing. Laura does her freewriting in longhand first, then types it on a computer later:

> The lady's mouth is clamped shut she's so angry. She's wearing a scarf. Looks like silk. Red white and blue. She has it tied under her chin. I'm standing behind her in the checkout line at the supermarket and this lady takes a year to pay her tab—pulling coupons out of her purse and squinting at them. Then she's got to pay the bill with the exact change—taking a month to fish out the pennies. The clerk scans the coupons and hands one back—says it was out of date. The

woman upset and says "Stupid!" I don't know if she means the clerk or the coupon. The clerk says "sorry" several times—but the woman doesn't seem to notice and finally takes her groceries and leaves in a huff. I roll my eyes to let the clerk—I think her name tag said "Gloria"—rolled my eyes to let her know I side with her. There's a sticker on her blouse above the name tag that says "Have a nice day!" She shrugs her shoulders as if to say all in a day's work. Nothing new. The woman's purse had one of those clasps at the top that "snap" when you close them.

Notice the features of Laura's freewrite. The typed version that you just read is identical to the original. Because it was written quickly, it has the typical characteristics of freewriting:

- It lacks conventional punctuation and sentence structure. In fact, Laura used the dash for all internal punctuation, a technique that helps increase speed because it eliminates the need to stop and ponder about which punctuation is appropriate. Some of the sentences are fragments.
- The account of the incident is disorganized—things that happened early in the scene are reported later, and vice versa.

The potential value of a freewrite is its specific, concrete details: the woman's mouth, her scarf, the things that were said, the nonverbal communication between the "I" and the clerk, the actions of the woman shopper, the detail about her purse. For example, does the snap of its clasp at the end of the freewrite echo the woman's mouth clamped shut at the beginning?

Expanding the Good Stuff: Fictionalizing and Exploring

Expanding involves selecting the most interesting details, passages, and ideas from collected pages of raw material and writing more about them. How? With more freewriting, but with freewriting that is more focused and more useful than initial freewrites. It is in the act of expanding—fictionalizing beyond initial details, images, incidents, and scenes—that a writer tends to discover real subjects, stories, and meanings. The exercises in this book will give you experience in using two different techniques to expand freewriting. These techniques include imagining beyond the reality of things written about and imitating the prose or poetry of published writers.

The fictionalizing and imagining process begins with questions such as *What if . . . ? What happens next? What else can I write about this? What would Dad say about this?* Ask questions of your best passages or paragraphs and freewrite the answers. *What if the outcome were different? Then what would happen?*

The content of most initial freewrites is drawn from observations or memories that are reality-based. During the expansion process many writers begin fictionalizing, imagining the results if circumstances had happened differently. For example, if Laura had chosen to expand the passage about the angry woman in the supermarket checkout line, she might ask herself *What if the clerk had not been so easygoing? What would I have said if I were the clerk? What would happen next? What would Grandma say about the situation?* Laura explored some of these questions below.

> Mouth like a slash in a child's cartoon sketch. Her dentures seemed to move when she talked, clicking together like the jaws of a Jurassic Park dinosaur feeding on plants or people: chomp chomp.
>
> The clerk rang up the woman's groceries: over twenty items.
>
> The woman's purse, average size on the outside, looked like a filing cabinet on the inside. She thumbed through dozens of coupons, apparently arranged by categories, and pulled one out for the cereal. It had a picture of the box on it.
>
> The clerk looks at it, squints, then says, "Sorry, this is expired."
>
> "What?" the woman says, her teeth clicking. "How can it be expired?"
>
> "It says right here," the clerk said, pointing at the small print at the bottom of the coupon.
>
> The woman didn't really look where the clerk pointed. She grabbed the coupon and pushed it back into her cavernous purse. "Stupid!"
>
> "I'm not the stupid one here, lady!" the clerk says loudly. "The expiration date's right here at the bottom. Can't you read?" She has a superior, I gotcha look on her face.
>
> The woman doesn't or can't say anything and just stands there with her mouth opening and closing for a few moments. Then she starts sputtering, "You! Miss snotty mouth! How dare you! I'll have you fired!" The woman looks at me for support, but I just roll my eyes and shrug my shoulders.
>
> "I don't make the rules around here, Lady," the clerk says.
>
> "Stupid!" the woman says and then clamps her mouth shut.
>
> The manager comes walking over. "Is there a problem here, Gloria?"
>
> "She cheated me," the woman says. She tightens the scarf's knot under her chin. Babushka. That's what grandma would call a scarf like that.
>
> "Gloria?" the manager says and then looks at me like I'm some kind of judge or something.
>
> All three of them look at me, waiting for me to say something.
>
> I look back at them, shrug my shoulders.

What Laura managed to do in the expansion of her freewrite was to bring the conflict out in the open by verbalizing it. This created drama and excitement—basic ingredients of storytelling. The clerk's response is perhaps a bit harsh for the situation, but it permitted the writer to extend the original incident into a scene upon which a short story, a play, or even a poem can be built.

Composing and Structuring

While composing the first draft of a work, professional writers continue to reshape the plot, the response of characters to the action, conflict resolution, theme, symbols, and metaphors. Many writers who have an ending in mind when they begin a story or poem may change it completely during the writing process. In fact, it is not uncommon for them to eventually cut the images or characters upon which they based their initial drafts.

Novice writers may feel uncomfortable without a clear direction, plot, or structure during this process, however. These writers may avoid following their impulses and inclinations to try a different direction. The two techniques discussed in the following section are especially effective for providing a structural road to follow, while at the same time promoting the discovery of new ideas and directions. Both of these techniques are built into many of the exercises and assignments in the chapters to come.

Experimenting with the Techniques and Structures of Published Works

Writers are perceptive, discerning readers. When they read poems and stories they enjoy or admire, they take note of how the author structured the work. For example, perhaps there is an unusual arrangement of the stanzas in a poem or the sequence of events in a story. By deliberately using the structural frameworks of published pieces, writers get valuable practice in writing within given structures, as well as in inventing new possibilities and directions. An exercise such as this can help you discover just how to construct your own poem or story. By focusing on how professional writers construct their works, you acquire organizing techniques of your own. Laura began drafting her story by imitating the first three and a half paragraphs of Stuart Dybek's "Insomnia," a section of a story titled "Nighthawks." Here is the portion of Dybek's work that Laura examined:

> There is an all-night diner to which, sooner or later, insomniacs find their way. In winter, when snow drifts over curbs, they cross the trampled intersections until they come upon footprints that perfectly fit their shoes and lead them there. On nights like this in summer, the diner's lighted corner draws them to its otherwise dark neighborhood like moths.
>
> They come from all over the city and beyond—from farm towns in Ohio, Iowa, and Indiana, crossing the unlit prairie, arriving at vacant train stations and bus terminals, then making their way toward that illuminated corner as if it's

what they left home to find—a joint that asks no questions and never closes, a place to sit awhile for the price of a cup of coffee.

From the size of the two nickel-plated urns, the place must serve a lot of coffee. And yet it looks almost deserted now—only a couple, stretching out the night, at one end of the counter, and Ray, the blond counterman, bending to rinse out a cup, and a guy in a hat sitting alone with his back to the window. It never gets crowded. They file in and out—the night shifts, cabbies, drunks, sometimes a cop, loners mostly—there's never telling who might step through the door.

Earlier this evening, when most of the stools were taken, a woman in heels and a summer dress stopped outside and stood peering in as if looking for someone. At least it seemed that way at first, before it became clear that she'd only stopped to fix her makeup in the reflection of the plate glass. There were mostly men at the counter, and they pretended not to watch as she stroked a comb through her hair. She seemed so unconscious of their presence that watching her would have been like spying on a woman before her own bedroom mirror. Yet, though they didn't stare, the men on the other side of the glass wondered about her; they wondered who it was she had stopped to make herself still prettier for, or if she'd just been with someone and was on her way back to someone else. When she stepped away from the window, the reflection of the lipstick she'd applied seemed to remain hovering on the glass like the impression of a kiss. The men in the diner pretended to ignore this too, although in its way the reflected kiss was no less miraculous than the tear rolling down the cheeks of the parish church's plaster Virgin, that crowds will line up for blocks to see. The woman stepped beyond the light of the diner and disappeared down a street of shadowy windows. . . .

—Stuart Dybek

The manner in which Dybek manages time determines the structure of this piece. The phrases "On nights like this in summer" and "it looks almost deserted now" in the first and third paragraphs establish the time frame of the story: the action is happening *now*, on *this* summer night. The fourth paragraph opens with "Earlier this evening." Here Dybek records very recent and specific history. It is this structure that Laura imitates while composing the first draft of her story about the incident in the supermarket checkout lane. Also, Dybek narrates his story from an eagle's vantage point, looking at it from above, strictly as an observer. This is called the third-person omniscient point of view. Laura does the same, departing from her use of the first person *I* point of view in her freewrites and expansions. This allows her to constantly shift the focus from character to character. Did Laura imitate other features of Dybek's story?

Since most people buy their groceries for an entire week, the line at the supermarket's express lane tends to be short. But during weekday lunch hours like this, the line stacks up with people from nearby stores, office buildings, and the high school across the street, rushing in to grab a few items for lunch and then making their way to the express lane as fast as possible, eager to be out the door.

At twelve-fifteen the line is at its longest. People wind around the magazine rack and up Aisle 8. No one's smiling except Gloria, the checkout clerk who is doing her best to keep the line moving, her hands in constant motion as she scans and bags people's items.

Things go briskly until an old woman wearing a dark coat and a babushka pushes a cart into the lane and unloads it, plopping a larger than usual number of items onto the belt. Her face is heavily caked with makeup, and her lipstick matches the orange tint of her dyed hair. She has a fake pearl necklace looped around her neck. Gloria senses the impatience of those next in line, a high school girl wearing a varsity jacket, a stylish woman with a Cleopatra hairdo, and a balding man wearing a blue suit. They all start shifting from one foot to the other and staring at the woman's groceries, silently counting. The one with the Cleopatra hairdo starts tapping a foot. The man cranes his neck, looking down the row of checkout counters, hoping to find an empty lane.

Fifteen minutes earlier, when the express line was still short, the manager comes out of hiding and does his mid-day inspection. Gloria does her best to impress, her hands flying in constant motion, scanning, bagging, making change.

The manager looks at Gloria when he gets to her lane, but he doesn't smile. "Keep the line moving, girls. Keep the line moving."

As Dybek did, Laura structures her story around present tense time references in her first and second paragraphs: "during weekday lunch hours like this" and "At twelve-fifteen the line is at its longest." Then, like Dybek, she opens her fourth paragraph with a reference to recent history—"Fifteen minutes earlier"—and records what happened then.

Like many writers, Laura initiated her story by modeling, that is by using techniques she researched from a published work. Then, from that starting point, she took off in a new direction, letting her material suggest its own structure. The process that she used is described in the following section.

Discovering the Best Structure for the Subject

Another creative approach involves piecing a draft together from freewrites and expansions, and then writing new passages to fill in gaps. Here's the procedure: Spread out all of the raw material that you created for a work. Try different arrangements of the material, looking for patterns of development such as time sequence, flashback, general to specific, or inside to outside. You might consider a "patchwork"—putting sections together with no transitions. Allow the patchwork to suggest its own connections, directions, and structure. In other words, give up control and let the material speak to you. As before, you should work quickly and ignore spelling and grammar issues for a while.

This is the procedure that Laura followed when she assembled the first draft of her supermarket story. She started her draft with the beginning she modeled after Dybek's "Insomnia." She assembled the rest of the story using her accumulated freewrites and expansions and wrote new material to fill in and make connections as needed. She made changes to help the pieces mesh. Laura chose to include most of the material from that earlier expansion: the expired coupon, the name-calling, the clerk's defense, the customer's threat, and the manager's response. In the draft, Laura has the manager try to solve the problem by giving the woman credit for the coupon. The following section illustrates some of the new material Laura created to complete her story.

> After Gloria subtracts the fifty-cent credit, the woman's bill comes out to twenty-three dollars and thirty-three cents. The woman fishes through her purse, finds her wallet, and pulls out a ten and counts out thirteen singles—one at a time—smoothing each one out on the counter. She looks defiantly at the teenager as she does this. Then she goes digging for coins. "Mind if I get rid of some pennies?" she asks Gloria, then looks back at the teenager, smiling sweetly.
>
> The teenager glares.
>
> "You'll just have to wait," the woman says as she counts out eighteen pennies, making a small pile on the counter, then added a dime and a nickel.
>
> The girl remembers the water pistol in her jacket pocket and touches its cool handle. She'd taken from her kid brother that morning, the pistol her mother kept on top of the refrigerator to use on Molly, the family cat, when she jumped up on the counters. Her mom called the pistol a "behavior modifier."
>
> "You young people are just too impatient," the woman scolds.
>
> The girl wraps her fingers around the water pistol's handle and caresses the trigger with the tip of her index finger. Tommy'd tried to squirt her when she was leaving for school, and she pocketed it simply as a way to protect herself. Now its coolness gives her a reassuring, quiet feeling. "Take your time." The girl's voice is calm. "I'm in no hurry." She smiles her menacing smile—the edge of her top lip lifting in a slight sneer—a look she has practiced many times in the mirror.
>
> "You don't frighten me!" the woman says.
>
> When the girl pulls the water pistol out of her pocket, Gloria's heart does a flip-flop; the pistol's black color looks metallic, and for a moment she thinks it's a real gun.
>
> The manager is opening his office door when he hears the woman shriek. Up until that moment he was thinking about the plate of roast beef, mashed potatoes, and gravy on his desk, hoping it was still warm.

If you compare Laura's initial freewrites and expansions with the story above, you will notice that she arranged her material in a time-sequence pattern, relating details and actions in the order they happened. Notice, too, the changes she made and the new material she created during the composing process—details that contribute to the story's plot and conflict. The expansion of the manager's character, the addition of the teenage girl's water pistol, and the added dialogue are some examples of Laura's changes.

Revising and Developing Meaning

The goal of revision is to improve a story, poem, or play. How does revising help to accomplish this goal? There are numerous approaches, including developing the suspense, intensifying the conflict, changing the point of view or tense, expanding characterizations, and altering structure. These techniques are discussed in the chapters to come. A more immediate problem many writers might face when confronting this stage of the writing process, however, is pinpointing a work's strengths and weaknesses. Writers tend to love *everything* when they first create it, and until they can distance themselves from their writing, they resist making any kind of significant change to their work. This was the case with Laura and her supermarket story. Until she read it aloud to a group, she was convinced it couldn't be improved.

Discovering Meaning: Listening to Feedback in Writer Response Groups

Nothing can help a writer gain the necessary distance from her work as effectively as listening to readers discussing its strengths, structure, meaning, and vision. Hearing others respond to your writing will give you the kind of feedback that leads to effective revision. The feedback process described in this section is based on procedures developed by Stephen Dunning. The best size for a response group is four or five students. If each group member is limited to two poems or two pages of prose, each person will be able to read and to receive six to eight minutes of discussion during one class period. Reading and responding to longer pieces, such as a complete short story, may take up to twenty or twenty-five minutes per writing sample. The feedback process works as follows:

1. All group members create a piece of writing to share. Readers provide photocopies of their work so that each group member can see as well as hear the text.

2. The first person reads her work aloud while group members follow along on their copies. Group members mark places about which they have questions or comments, but they do not verbalize anything until the reading is completed.

3. A few moments of silence are allowed after the reading is concluded to let participants collect their thoughts and review the work. Group members then respond to the reading, using nonjudgmental language to talk to each other. To promote this kind of discussion, group members should begin their comments with phrases such as "I notice," "I wonder," "I

think," "What if," "I feel," and "This reminds me of." Time is tracked so that everyone receives an equal amount of feedback.

Initial comments should focus on what group members feel are the work's strengths. Then the conversation should address the meaning of the work, aspects that are confusing, areas that can be expanded, and incidents or passages that seem out of place or irrelevant. Although strategies for improvement and revision can be suggested, the point of the discussion is the conversation concerning content, theme, organization, and meaning—not the fix for weaknesses.

The group members converse about the work with one another, not the writer. During their discussion, the writer takes notes on what is said, but he does not participate in the discussion. Only after the group has established what are the work's strengths and its meaning does the writer have the opportunity to ask his own unanswered questions.

4. The writer thanks the readers and the group moves on to consider another group member's work until all have received feedback.

Titleless?

Writers usually consider several different title ideas before choosing titles for their works. They look within their poems, stories, and plays for title ideas. A phrase or a portion of a quotation that suggests what the work is about may serve as a good title. Titles may also come from the images, themes, and metaphors found in a work.

Specific titles say more about a work than abstract ones and thus often make better title choices. For example, a specific title such as "Choking on Love" describes Stephen Dunning's story in Chapter 8 much better than an abstract title such as "Choked" would. On the other hand, short, intriguing titles such as Stuart Dybek's "Insomnia" and Laura's "Incivility," both found in this chapter, are also effective.

New writers may think that they need titles for their poems, stories, and plays before bringing them to a writer response group. This is not the case. In fact, the writer response group process and its focus on content and meaning often help generate title ideas.

Laura read her supermarket story in a group and received many ideas for revision. Although the group members were very enthusiastic about the story—its characterizations, descriptions, conflicts, and humor—they agreed that the point of view was confusing. Simply put, Laura was trying to emulate Dybek's third-person omniscient point of view, shifting from one character to another. In her story she focused more on Gloria's perceptions than on those of the other characters; however, when Laura did slip into the minds of other characters, it seemed peculiar. Therefore, the group suggested that Laura abandon Dybek's third-person omniscient point of view and use instead the third-person *limited* point of view, which focuses on the thoughts and perceptions of one character, in this case Gloria, the checkout clerk.

Developing Meaning Through Revision: Transforming, Rearranging, Expanding

Once a writer becomes aware of the range of possibilities and meanings of a piece, rewriting is required to achieve its maximum effectiveness and quality. Keep in mind that some changes are more radical than others:

- expanding existing sections from within by adding specific and concrete detail
- adding new sections or stanzas and deleting others
- restructuring or altering stanzas or plot sequence
- changing point of view and tense

Less radical, but nonetheless important, changes would be those that develop cohesion and heighten meaning.

We recommend that you revise in several short work periods rather than trying to do everything in one sitting. A revision spread over three twenty-minute sessions will tend to be more effective than a single one-hour session because the first fifteen or twenty minutes of a work period tend to be the most efficient time for such work.

Also, we recommend that you work on only one thing at a time. Address the most drastic changes first. In fact, the most basic big change for both prose and poetry may be to expand the work by adding specific and concrete detail. A common weakness of a beginner's first draft is that it is too abstract and expositional to involve readers. Reading a poem or story developed with abstractions or general terms is like entering a room in which the furniture is covered with white sheets. You can tell that you're looking at a chair, for example, but you can't see beyond its basic shape. You can't see its detail and texture. As a writer, you want to invite the reader into the room to sit in a chair that she can see and feel.

Look at the following sequence of images and notice the progression from the abstract to the concrete:

Abstract terms:
man
an old man
an old, retired man
an old, retired man who is a grandfather

A specific term:
an eighty-year-old, retired salesman with a granddaughter

A concrete description:
Mort Johnson, who used to sell cars at Chance's Used Cars on Telegraph Road, is so thin he needs suspenders to keep his pants up. He carries his tray to the nearest available table, his granddaughter leading the way.

Which written image draws in the reader most effectively? Undoubtedly, most would say that the concrete description above is most inviting to the reader. To improve the concreteness of a work, read it slowly, preferably aloud, looking for opportunities to shift from abstract images to concrete ones. As you read, jot down substitutions and additions. If you need more room, freewrite revisions in open spaces on your manuscript or on a separate sheet of paper.

Although Laura's group thought her story exhibited many concrete details, she still made additions and changes as she groomed her story. Look for these additions when you read the finished version of Laura's story included at the end of this chapter.

Editing and Proofreading

The assignments in the following chapters do not include specific lessons on editing and proofreading. However, these last-minute touches a writer makes before turning her work over to a teacher or publisher are very important. Here are some tips for the editing and proofreading process:

- Use your first editing session to cut needless words, lines, sentences, and passages. If you are working on a poem, you may become involved with this activity in earlier stages of the poem's creation. For most short stories, however, the best time to cut is after you have completed all expansions and revisions.

- Use your word processor's spelling check feature, but keep in mind that it has limitations. Not every word will be in the feature's dictionary—people's names, for example—and it cannot distinguish incorrect usage of correctly spelled words such as *then/than*, *two/too/to*, and *they're/their/there*.

- Ask another writer to proofread your work and offer your proofreading services in return. You will improve with practice.

- When proofreading your own work, remember to focus on one aspect at a time and to work slowly. When you work on word choice, for example, ignore punctuation. When editing for punctuation, ignore the appropriateness of descriptive imagery. Also, reading your work aloud will help to slow down your reading, making it easier to notice punctuation errors, confusing wording, and the like.

For the writer who is generating raw material, as discussed earlier, we stressed the importance of speed as a method of combating interference in the creative process by the left brain. In this stage of the writing process, however, the opposite is true. If a writer tries to refine, edit, and proofread her finished work too quickly, the right brain can interfere with what should be a left-brain process.

The following demonstration simulates a proofreading task. Below you will find a long sentence. Neither the meaning of the sentence nor its construction is important here. Your task is simply to count the number of times the letter *f* appears in the sentence shown. Don't continue reading until you have completed your count.

The Department of Labor discovered that a number of companies who offer its workers optional insurance policies do little to inform them of their differences.

If you are like most readers, chances are that you did not find all of the *f*s in the sentence. Most people count five *f*s the first time through, including the two in the word *offering*, two in the word *differences*, and one in the word *inform*. Five, correct? Wrong. There are actually eight *f*s used in the sentence. Did you count the ones in the words *of*? Probably not. Even though you were told to ignore the meaning of the sentence, it is likely that you paid attention to what it says. Because *of* is a structure or function word, not a "meaning" word, you probably didn't even see it when it appeared in the sentence. Responding to the meaning of written language is a right-brain activity. Checking the spelling of written words is a left-brain activity. If you didn't count the correct number of *f*s, it was because your right brain interfered with a left-brain task. There are two things you can do to help eliminate this kind of interference:

- Work slowly when you are involved in proofreading and editing tasks. The more slowly you work, the more proficiently your left brain functions.
- Focus on one proofreading or editing task at a time. When you edit for word choice, for example, ignore spelling and punctuation. Work on those issues in separate sessions.

Following is the finished, edited draft of Laura's story. As discussed earlier, Laura worked on changing the first draft's point of view from third-person omniscient to limited. When she completed her final edit to get the story ready for this chapter, she ruthlessly cut needless words and sentences, reducing the story from fifteen hundred words to eight hundred.

Incivility

One to ten items, cash only. Lunch hour. The lane's already stacked up with people as impatient and restless as short-fused wasps, swarming in from nearby stores, offices, and schools to grab a few items for lunch—the women tossed salads, the men preheated chicken or salami, the teenagers candy and pop.

Twelve-fifteen. People wind around the magazine rack and up Aisle 8. No one's smiling except Gloria, second week on the job, doing her best to keep the line moving, her hands in constant motion scanning, bagging, counting out change.

Then Mrs. Liz Claiborne Summer Smock shows up with a load. Face heavily caked with make-up, hair tinted orange. A fake pearl necklace looped around her neck.

Those next in line getting nervous: a school girl wearing a varsity jacket two sizes too large, a woman with a Cleopatra hairdo, a balding man wearing glasses. The others Gloria can't see. They're all shifting from one foot to the other and staring at the woman's groceries, silently counting. The teenager's lips move. Cleopatra starts tapping a foot. Baldy cranes his neck, hoping to find an empty lane.

At twelve o'clock, when the express line was still short, Mr. Manager made his midday inspection tour. Gloria did her best to impress. Hands in constant motion. Smiled.

"Keep it moving, girls. Keep it moving." He got to her lane and pivoted, then headed toward his office and his lunch, a pile of spaghetti cooling on his desk.

Two weeks, you learn about a place.

Now, this woman, Mrs. Summer Smock. Bright red lipstick.

Gloria scans her groceries: over twenty items. "This lane is limited to ten things," she says, but the woman ignores her.

"Not so fast! I have coupons!" Mrs. Smock snaps her purse open. A filing cabinet. Thumbs through, finds one, hands it over. It has a picture of the box: Fruit Loops.

Gloria takes it and squints. "Sorry, this is expired."

"What?" the woman's teeth click. "How can it be expired?"

"Says right here." Gloria points at the small print.

The woman doesn't really look. "Stupid girl," she says, grabbing the coupon and stuffing it back into her purse.

"I'm not the stupid one here, lady!" Gloria says loudly. "Can't you read?"

Mrs. Smock can't say anything and just stands there with her mouth opening and closing. Then she starts sputtering, "You! Miss Snotty Mouth! How dare you! I'll have you fired!" The woman looks at the teenager for support.

The girl shrugs her shoulders. "I'm going to be late for a class."

Most of the people in line give up and head for more promising lanes down the way. Only the teenager remains.

"I don't make the rules around here," Gloria says.

The manager, probably just settling down to eat his spaghetti when the commotion starts, comes hurrying over. "Problem here, Gloria?" He's a plump man wearing a white shirt decorated with a black bow tie and a name tag—*Hello! My name is Fred.*

"It's her coupon. It's out of date," Gloria says.

Fred turns to Mrs. Smock. "Well?"

Fingers fiddle with the necklace. "How can people read such small print?"

"The coupon's value?" Fred asks Gloria.

"Fifty cents. It was for the Fruit Loops."

Fred to the rescue. "Gloria, give this woman a cash credit for fifty cents." He stands there a moment, waiting for a response, but Mrs. Smock is in her purse thumbing through coupons again. Fred shrugs and heads back to lunch.

After the fifty-cent credit, the woman's bill is twenty-three dollars and thirty-three cents. The woman produces her wallet, pulls out a ten, and counts out thirteen singles—one at a time—smoothing each one out on the counter. She smiles sweetly at the teenager as she does this. Then she goes digging for coins. "Mind if I get rid of some pennies?"

The girl glares.

"You'll just have to wait!" Mrs. Smock says, a mother talking to a child. She counts out a pile of pennies, then adds a dime and a nickel.

"It's an important class," the girl says loudly. "But take your time. I'm in no hurry." She smiles, but it's a menacing smile—the edge of her top lip lifting in a slight sneer.

"You don't frighten me!" the woman says.

When the girl pulls a water pistol out of her coat pocket, Gloria's heart does a flip-flop. For a moment she thinks it's a real gun, and when the woman shrieks, time seems to come to a stumbling halt. Gloria sees everything around her frozen like a series of paintings in a modern art gallery—the look of total satisfaction in the teenager's eyes, the streaks of mascara running down the woman's drooping face, the rigid back of Mr. Manager stalled halfway through his office door, the plate of spaghetti on his desk getting colder.

This story, the result of the creative process described in this chapter, exhibits the features that readers demand: an abundance of concrete details, action and conflict, strong characterizations, and theme. The story's subject matter, announced by the title "Incivility," is exhibited by the characters waiting in line, especially by Mrs. Smock and the girl. The theme of the story is implied by the actions of the manager. When keeping the line moving is the ultimate value of the managing segments of a business, the satisfaction and contentment of its customers suffer. Laura's drastic cutting of her story at the end of the creative process, yielding a fragmentary style, helps to create the sensation of speed that is in keeping with present-tense action. It also helps to produce the illusion of "real time." In addition, the writing style evokes a fragmentary, stream-of-consciousness quality that firmly plants the point of view in Gloria's mind. Notice these features in the comparison of the first and finished drafts of the opening paragraph below. Although the finished draft has a shorter beginning paragraph, it contains more details and subject matter than that of the first draft. Nothing of importance was lost by cutting so extensively.

First Paragraph from Draft One
   Since most people buy their groceries for an entire week, the line at the supermarket's express lane tends to be short. But during weekday lunch hours like this, the line stacks up with people from nearby stores, office buildings, and the high school across the street, rushing in to grab a few items for lunch and then making their way to the express lane as fast as possible, eager to be out the door. [74 words]

First Paragraph from Finished Story
   One to ten items, cash only. Lunch hour. The lane's already stacked up with people as impatient and restless as short-fused wasps, swarming in from nearby stores, offices, and schools to grab a few items for lunch—the women tossed salads, the men preheated chicken or salami, the teenagers candy and pop. [52 words]

Although Laura's efforts resulted in a short story, the creative process for writing effective poems and plays is the same. In fact, it should be noted that Laura could have used the same materials for either a poem or a play. Some writers will experiment with all three types of literature before deciding on one.

Many students take a creative writing course hoping to write wonderful poems or stories that their friends will love and their teachers will praise. Although the assignments in this text may lead to such results, that is not the goal of this book. The goal is not the "good" poem or story; the goal is to learn about what it is to be a writer. It's about the creative writing process and the navigation. Because, like whitewater rafting, creative writing isn't so much about reaching the final destination, but about making the trip.

Creating
Poetry

chapter 2

Narrating a Simple Conflict: Dramatic Situation, Meaning, and Verb Usage

Advice to young writers who want to get ahead without any annoying delays: don't write about Man, write about a man.

-E. B. WHITE

Poets can learn a lesson from storytellers. Storytellers know an audience is drawn to a good story and that it cares about people's daily struggles. Beginning poets, on the other hand, may be lured to write the abstract poem that details an emotion or outlines a philosophy. The result is a poem that fails to connect with readers because the generalities in the poem are confusing. However, poets who concentrate on the simple details of a story and worry less about deep meaning are more likely to write an engaging poem.

This chapter will teach the basic elements of the narrative, or story, poem. Narrative poetry contains a clear speaker, a distinct setting, and a conflict, and it tells the story of an event or series of events. These elements comprise the dramatic situation of poetry and combine to create the meaning or theme of a poem. Another important element in poetry—using muscular verbs—is discussed at the end of this chapter.

The poems of Sharon Olds and Yusef Komunyakaa contain clear dramatic situations, meanings that are easy to access, and powerful verbs. Each poem's story is told by a speaker personally involved with the events. These speakers narrate simple stories attached to powerful emotions. The power of a good story is not always in the events being told: a poet does not have to create high drama with drastic consequences. The power of a good story is creating an emotional experience that is accessible to the reader. What emotional connections do the following narrative poems create for you?

Milk Bubble Ruins

SHARON OLDS

In the long, indolent mornings of fifth-grade
spring vacation, our son sits with the
tag-ends of breakfast, and blows bubbles in his milk
with a blue straw, and I sit and watch him.
5   The foam rises furiously
in a dome over the rim of his cup,
we gaze into the edifice of fluid,
its multiple chambers. He puffs and they pile up,
they burst, they subside, he breaths out slowly, and the
10   multicellular clouds rise,
he inserts the straw into a single globe
and blows a little, and it swells. Ten years ago
he lay along my arm, drinking.
Now, in late March, he shows me
15   the white light
pop and dissolve as he
conjures and breaks each small room of milk.

Questions

1. Who is the speaker? Be as specific as the poem allows.
2. What is the setting? When does this take place?
3. What conflict is revealed by the speaker's brief memory?
4. Why does the speaker tell us this simple story?

My Father's Loveletters

YUSEF KOMUNYAKAA

On Fridays he'd open a can of Jax,
Close his eyes, & ask me to write
The same letter to my mother
Who sent postcards of desert flowers
5   Taller than a man. He'd beg her
Return & promised to never

Beat her again. I was almost happy
She was gone, & sometimes wanted
To slip in something bad.
10   His carpenter's apron always bulged
With old nails, a claw hammer
Holstered in a loop at his side
& extension cords coiled around his feet.
Words rolled from under
15   The pressure of my ballpoint:
Love, Baby, Honey, Please.
We lingered in the quiet brutality
Of voltage meters & pipe threaders,
Lost between sentences . . . the heartless
20   Gleam of a two-pound wedge
On the concrete floor,
A sunset in the doorway
Of the tool shed.
I wondered if she'd laugh
25   As she held them over a flame.
My father could only sign
His name, but he'd look at blueprints
& tell you how many bricks
Formed each wall. This man
30   Who stole roses & hyacinth
For his yard, stood there
With eyes closed & fists balled,
Laboring over a simple word,
Opened like a fresh wound, almost
35   Redeemed by what he tried to say.

Questions

1. Who is the speaker? Be as specific as the poem allows.
2. What is the setting?
3. What does the father want? What does the speaker want?
4. Why does the speaker tell us this story?

Exploring Dramatic Situation

Dramatic situation is achieved when a writer crafts details, actions, and thoughts into a story with conflict and meaning. The meaning arises from the interaction of the events of the story. However, dramatic situation in poetry focuses more on the moment. The poem cannot take on the whole history of a conflict. The poem can only successfully relate a detailed moment. Both Sharon Olds and Yusef Komunyakaa detail moments between a parent and child. One is told by the parent; the other is told by the child; but in their telling, the stories suggest a larger truth about life. This is the beauty of the narrative: a moment in time passes, the storyteller gains perspective, and the story is retold. This happened to me, the storyteller says, and now I know what it means. Let me show you.

To put it more simply, narrative poets must connect with their readers on two levels: on the concrete level of plot and on the more abstract level of theme. The plot contains the answers to the basic questions of who, what, where, and when:

- *Who* is speaking?
- *What* is happening, and *what* is the conflict?
- *Where* do the events occur?
- *When* do the events occur?

The answers to these questions clarify the *dramatic situation* of a poem. The dramatic situation must be clear to the writer and to the reader before questions of theme—essentially questions of *why*—can be answered.

To understand this, consider the analogy between going to a party and reading a poem. Both occur within a certain place and time; both are full of possibilities. At a party, you first notice who is present, who is talking to whom, what food is being served. Then you settle in and make conversation. Only later are you able to consider what the party meant and whether the experience was good or bad. A poem is entered in a similar fashion. Oh, you say to yourself as you begin reading, this poem takes place in a park, in late fall, and the person telling me about it is a woman who has just lost her watch in the river. At last I can move on to why she's telling me this.

Now, think of a poem with a foggy dramatic situation as a party you must enter blindfolded. It would take you a long time to figure out who is there and what there is to eat, and in your confusion you might mistake a birthday party for a garage sale or a dance. When you consider what the party meant to you, you will primarily remember your confusion—not the more subtle conversations or conflicts.

The poet's first task, then, is to build a foundation of basic, concrete details to orient the reader. In "Milk Bubble Ruins," the clarity of speaker, setting, and conflict are clear after the first reading. To illustrate, answer the questions to identify the dramatic situation.

- *Who* is speaking? A parent of a fifth-grader, probably his mother.
- *What* is happening? A boy is blowing bubbles into his milk with a blue straw. His mother sits and watches him and remembers when he was an infant.

- *Where* and *when* does this event take place? The setting is a table, possibly in a kitchen or dining room. It occurs in the morning during spring vacation after breakfast. Then the time and place shift, first to the mother's memory of her infant son and then back to the present time and place. Notice the transitional words that alert the reader to these shifts and clearly signal the movement from action to memory: "Ten years ago" and "Now."

This poem is rooted in the world of speaker, place, and time, while still being about something bigger. That something bigger, the theme, will be considered later.

Let's ask the same questions of "My Father's Love Letters."

- *Who* is speaking? A child, it seems. How do we know the speaker is a child? He or she complies with the father's wish, week after week, to write love letters to the mother. A teenager or adult would probably refuse. The word choice also reveals youth: the speaker wants to slip in something "bad" about the father, to keep the mother away, and "bad" is a child's word.

- *What* is happening? Every Friday the father, who is illiterate, recites the words for his child to write love letters to the mother who has left the father and the child. The father used to beat her, and now regrets what he has done and wants the mother back.

- *Where* does this occur? In the tool shed, surrounded by extension cords, pipe threaders, and wedges.

- *When* does the story take place? On Fridays, in the evenings, with a "sunset in the doorway."

In both poems, the concrete, sensory descriptions answer the questions of the dramatic situation and make the readers feel as if they are present for the story.

Experimenting with Dramatic Situation

The secret to writing powerful narratives is achieving a voice. Voice in writing means that the speaker's personality emerges to create a tangible character. A distinct voice helps a reader sense that a real person is telling the story. The reader becomes engaged with this real person and begins to relate to the story. Thus, it is voice that creates the connection between reader and poem. Therefore, creating a speaker with a unique voice may be the most important task of the poet. As you experiment with dramatic situation, imagine you are sitting with a close friend. Imagine you are talking to her, and she is listening intently. Keep that image in your mind as you write.

Who Am I Writing To, Anyway?

A secret to writing with a clear, distinct voice is to direct your writing toward a person who would understand your poem. In "Milk-Bubble Ruins," for example, Sharon Olds seems to write to fellow mothers who might understand the mixed feelings she has for her son. These fellow mothers are the understanding audience for this poem.

So as your write, ask yourself, "Who understands this conflict?" Although you may not read your poem directly to this person or group of people, knowing who the understanding audience is will help you to write it.

Complete Writer's Practice 2.1, 2.2, and 2.3 to invent a brief narrative moment. Write all three freewrites at one sitting. Each freewrite should take approximately ten to fifteen minutes to complete, so set aside a total of forty-five minutes for these writing assignments. By writing the three freewrites in a single writing session, your work will gain depth and unexpected connections.

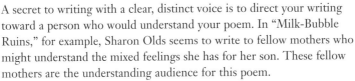

Writer's Practice 2.1 *Dramatize an Event*

Begin with E. B. White's advice: ". . . write about a man." Focus this advice even more: write about yourself. This may sound threatening—you may not like to write about your own life. You may think your life is boring, but remember, the narrative poem is not about high drama. You may think your life has no interesting meaning, but meaning comes from the simple human experience reflectively explored.

So, use your own life. Imagine a place you visit regularly, even daily. Select a place where you felt a small tension between you and another person. Do not reach for a dramatic conflict, such as a major fight; rather, search for a place with tension, something that might occur in anyone's life. Avoid high drama. Sharon Olds used a kitchen and a child blowing bubbles in his milk; Yusef Komunyakaa used a tool shed and a child writing a letter.

- Consider places where tension occurs frequently: a communal room in your home, such as the kitchen, bathroom, or family room; a room or place at school or work; a restaurant or vacation spot.
- Describe the place. What do you see? What do you hear? What do you smell? Include specific descriptions of objects or people. Include colors.
- Insert a real or imagined person into the place. Include an action for this person that explains what he or she is doing in this place. Do not explain the person's presence: the action will accomplish the explanation for you.
- Allow yourself to slip into reflection: the and-now-I-know-what-it-means aspect of the poem. Accomplish this by rereading your concrete

description of the place. Then consider why you selected this place. Add a sentence or two reflecting on the possibly hidden importance of selecting this place. Begin this part of the freewrite with the pronoun "I." Remember you are talking to a friend. Tell your friend something about yourself. Attempt to speak some simple truth the place generates.

Begin writing if you feel you are ready, or examine our writer's model and explication. Write one hundred to two hundred words describing a place, inventing a person with whom the speaker feels tension, and reflecting on the setting and tension.

Our Writer

The parking lot at school is dark and cold. The lights glow with an orange fluorescence. Parents drive their kids up to the front door; the kids get out before the car stops, slam the door, the next car pulls up . . . an endless cycle. Everyone seems grumpy. They hurry into the building in silent clumps, pulling on backpacks and straining under armfuls of books. There's cold spilled French fries on the pavement. The snow banks pile up around the perimeter. They are frozen and slick. I'm carrying too many bags, hot coffee, my lunch. Sarah is up ahead, I yell hello, she yells back, doesn't wait for me to catch up. I was always the slow one. Walking home as a kid, I'd dawdle, especially in the spring, when the roads were still dirt and the melting snow made rivers down the sides of the road. I'd walk home, slowly, eyes on the ground, smelling the wet earth, happy to be alive.

The freewrite stays very much on task, almost following the list of suggestions. Your freewrites may be looser and longer. Allow stray thinking to happen, but try to address the list of suggestions as completely as our writer did. Notice that concrete details of the place, sounds, and sights are closely described. They invent a busy high school parking lot that is probably typical of any high school parking lot at the beginning of the school day. Notice the reflection contains concrete description as well. However, it leaves the school and attaches itself to the feeling of being left behind by Sarah. This tension helps the writer find a simple truth: "I was always the slow one." This feeling statement leads to the memory of walking home from school.

Writer's Practice 2.2   *Create a Dialogue*

Stay in the setting you created in Writer's Practice 2.1. Now, write a short imaginary conversation between you and the real or imagined person with whom there was tension. In this real or imaginary conversation, speak your heart. Say what it is you want from this person, or what you believe is at the heart of the tension. Ask these questions to get started: What is at the root of our tension? What do I want from this person? What do I want for myself?

- Try to make the language sound like real people speaking. Use short phrases and sentences.
- Remember, write fast.
- Indicate speaker changes with the letters "A" and "B." Use "B" to represent the speaker, which is you. Use "A" to represent the real or imagined person created in Writer's Practice 2.1.
- Try to write five exchanges—five lines from you, five lines from the other person.

Begin writing if you feel you are ready, or examine our writer's model and explication. Write fifty to one hundred fifty words of dialogue. Attempt to explore the emotional tension generated in Writer's Practice 2.1.

Our Writer

A: Hey! Wait up!

B: I'm late, I can't. You're late, too.

A: How long can it take to wait for me to catch up? I feel like I'm always chasing you, always the one to make you stop what you are doing.

B: What do you want from me?

A: I don't know. Not much, now that I think of it. I want you to slow down . . . I want to slow down. I don't want the world and everyone in it, especially you, to rush by me without appreciating it.

B: I know what you mean.

A: It's so cold and dark. I could use a little beauty.

B: Me, too.

A: Have you seen the comet?

B: I haven't had time.

Notice that this is not an argument, although it could have been. The speaker tells of a desire or a wish that she has, not just for the other person but for people in general. She wants to slow down; she wants Sarah to slow down; she wants time to appreciate beautiful things. This wish appeared in the reflective portion of Writer's Practice 2.1 and then was explored in Writer's Practice 2.2.

Writer's Practice 2.3 *Narrate a Memory*

Writer's Practice 2.2 may have helped you get deeper into an emotion. Our writer explored feeling burdened and rushed, as well as wishing to slow down. If you have not identified an emotion, do so now. Determine what is causing the tension between the speaker (you) and the other person invented for the poem. Name it.

In Writer's Practice 2.3, you will work deeper into the emotions of the poem by inventing a memory tied to the poem's emotional tension. This can be based on a real memory, but do not stay loyal to the past. If you cannot remember the details of the memory, or if the facts of the real memory get in the way, feel free to invent new facts and details.

- Begin with the words "I remember."
- Write about a memory that may or may not be related to the place invented in Writer's Practice 2.1. Trust yourself. Do not go searching for a memory that is the perfect fit. Instead, describe whatever memory comes to mind. Be sure to include setting details, names of people, dialogue, and actions. Do not be loyal to the truth.
- Work for a simple moment. Avoid high drama memories.

Write one hundred to two hundred words in paragraph form. Since you are beginning with the pronoun "I," you will be writing in first person. First person allows a story to be told through the sensibilities of the speaker. The speaker is telling his or her own story, which enables the poem to be more personal. Use first person and past tense. Past-tense verbs will signal a shift into the past and indicate a memory. Write the memory as if you are speaking to a trusted friend. Begin writing if you feel you are ready, or examine our writer's model and explication.

Our Writer

I remember sitting with my uncle Joel on the steps of my grandma's farmhouse when I was ten. Us looking at the stars, him telling me about how the sky went on forever. There, it seemed to. All dark and then brilliant stars. He said the universe went on into infinity, and I said it must end somewhere. He said, if there's a wall at the end of the universe, then what's on the other side of the wall? I remember the smell of the farm—cows, corn, rich earth. The sound of the trucks on the two-lane highway roaring past us, whooooosh, the sound of destination, many miles. I remember sleeping in the bedroom above the garage at grandma's, the deep sleep of one who knows the sun will come up through that window and begin a day without much to do but poke around and see what the world had to offer that day. I leaned against Uncle Joel as he pointed at the Big Dipper.

Here, our writer remembers a time when life was slow. She trusted herself to deliver a memory and many parallels appeared. She remembers a night scene when the sky is visible and brilliant, which parallels the night scene in Writer's Practice 2.1. The intimacy of the childhood memory contrasts the lack of intimacy in Writer's Practice 2.1. The deep sleep available to the speaker in the memory contrasts the tiredness of the speaker in Writer's Practice 2.1. The warmth of the night, the rich farm fragrances, and the pleasant and enticing sounds of traffic also contrast the parking lot in Writer's Practice 2.1. This close paralleling is not unusual if the three freewrites are written within the same time span. Now our writer has many opportunities as she moves on in the exercise.

Exploring Meaning

A good story has its own meaning, just like a good joke. If you do not laugh at a joke, the explanation does not help to make it funnier. Meaning springs from the well-told joke much like it springs from the well-told story. Your job as writer is to connect with the reader so the story is clear. Use the following statement as a rule of thumb with narrative poems: If I have to tell the reader the meaning, then I haven't done my job as storyteller.

Who Makes Meaning?

Do readers make meaning? Or do writers make meaning? Both do.

Most poets begin with an experience, emotion, or image in mind and then write in order to see what else might lurk in their memories or imagination. They often rely on writer response groups to help them understand what they have written and to see if their intended meaning is clear. They may then revise with that meaning in mind.

Readers make meaning, too, by carefully reading the details of a poem and making sense of the patterns they see. Good readers ask themselves questions and then read for the answers. As they do so, a poem may trigger similar experiences or emotions and thus take on a deeper, more personal level of meaning for the reader.

Once the dramatic situation is clear to the reader, then answers to more complex questions can be determined.

* *Why* does the speaker speak?
* *Why* is the setting important?
* *Why* is the conflict created?

The answers to these questions help the reader construct the meaning or theme of the poem.

Return again to Sharon Olds's poem. It contains the simple story of a moment shared between mother and child. But does it mean anything? To see, answer the *why* questions:

- *Why* is the speaker watching her son?
- *Why* is this story told?
- *Why* would a mother have conflict watching her son blow bubbles?

Perhaps the speaker wants companionship. It is vacation, and the slow pace allows for a moment of togetherness. The use of the word "we" in line seven binds parent and child together. Perhaps the speaker wants to appreciate her son's creativity: Olds devotes eight lines of the seventeen-line poem to the son's careful blowing and popping of the milk bubbles. Perhaps the parent watches for a third reason. The blowing of the bubbles calls to mind an earlier time with the son, when he was an infant and nursed in his mother's arms. Now, however, the son is an individual; he breaks the bubbles as easily as he breaks his ties to his mother. Perhaps the speaker wants to have her son both ways: as an infant who is dependent and as a boy who is his own person. The speaker, then, watches the son for multiple reasons—reasons that are rich and complex and perhaps without end. But we could not have reached these conclusions without putting the concrete details of the story together.

Now examine "My Father's Love Letters," answering the *why* questions:

- *Why* does the speaker tell the story of these Friday nights?
- *Why* is the speaker conflicted about writing the letters?

This poem more clearly answers the *why* questions. The speaker seems troubled by many conflicting issues that appear each Friday night. While the speaker is happy the mother escaped, the mother is also missed. Also, the child is conflicted toward the father; this man is, after all, someone who beat his wife, stole flowers, and can barely write. Yet this man is also a skilled laborer, a man who struggles to reach his wife and apologize, a man who is deeply lonely. In some strange way, the act of writing the weekly letters changes the child's vision of the father. Writing the letters almost allows the child to forgive the father for driving the mother away.

Each poem's meaning is embedded in the details of each speaker's story. Yet each poem has two things that help create the meaning of the story: (1) the title, and (2) a single sentence that draws the story to a close and, at the same time, makes a subtle comment on the story's action. These two elements tie both the subject and the speaker's story together. Both poems benefit from the combination and do not rely on telling the reader the meaning.

In Sharon Olds's poem, the last lines make the connection between the title, the subject, and the story's details:

Now, in late March, he shows me
the white light
pop and dissolve as he
conjures and breaks each small room of milk.

Olds prepares the reader for a deeper meaning with her title: "Milk Bubble Ruins." The word "Ruins" suggests destruction, a pretty powerful word in combination with making milk bubbles, which have a very brief existence. No one would naturally lament the popping of a milk bubble. However, the speaker feels a sense of loss remembering her son's infancy at the same moment he breaks the bubbles. The speaker's metaphor "each small room of milk" indicates mixed feelings about her son growing up.

In Komunyakaa's poem, the last lines also make the connection between the title, the subject, and the story's details:

Laboring over a simple word,
Opened like a fresh wound, almost
Redeemed by what he tried to say.

The title, "My Father's Love Letters," tells the reader the significance of the story from the beginning. The reader understands that the speaker is helping the father write love letters to a wife who ran away. As the story unfolds, the reader may side with the mother. However, the last three lines create a momentary tender and vulnerable view of the father, and the child's momentary and partial acceptance of the father's pain. The simile "like a fresh wound" reveals the pain the father feels each time he struggles to write the letters. The words "almost / Redeemed" suggest the flickering moment of forgiveness in the heart of the child.

Experimenting with Meaning

Crafting meaning means taking your foot off the gas pedal. You may have discovered lots of things to say in your earlier writes. You may have unknowingly created threads of meaning or concocted an intricate tale with a deep and valuable memory. Like our writer, you have a poem just bursting at the seams with meaning. However, remember that the meaning comes from combining a simple, detailed story, a title, and a single sentence that draws the narrative to a close to make a subtle comment on the story's action. Consider imitating the light-handed approach of Olds and Komunyakaa.

Writer's Practice 2.4 *Write a Narrative Poem*

Return to Writer's Practice 2.1, 2.2, and 2.3 and select details or moments that illuminate the tension or conflict you have discovered in the writing. It is not necessary to include all of the three freewrites.

- Begin the poem with a word such as "When," which forces you to continue by telling the story.
- Write a sentence that places the speaker in a clear setting and introduces the conflict.
- As you work your way through the story, use words to signal shifts in time, such as "Years ago," "Later," or "Now." Or use words that signal shifts in place, such as "Outside," "In the kitchen," or "Nearby."
- Write in first person and present tense.
- In the final three or four lines, attempt to insert a detail, metaphor, or simile that connects the story to a larger meaning.
- Then look into the poem for a phrase that might help connect the story's details and the final lines. Use those words for the title.

Begin writing if you feel you are ready, or examine our writer's model and explication. Write a sixteen- to twenty-five-line poem that tells a story. Remember to focus on creating a clear story with a clear speaker.

Our Writer

Reading Whitman

When Sarah walks ahead of me in the parking lot
in the morning, I want to yell to her,
to stop, turn around, look at me. Papers
spill from my bag, ice covers the lot,
5   I could use a hand.
Better yet, we could look for the comet
those two observers found that same night.
Years ago, my Uncle Joel and I sat
on Grandma's front step one August night
10   and breathed in quiet.
He told me the universe went on without end.
Inside, the lights are going on,
the school is filling up.
Today we are reading Whitman,

15   and secretly, we will all want
       to be born again, but
       not now, we're too tired.
       From the beginning I've only wanted
       to take my time home from school,
20   watch the muddy rivers in the spring.
       Now you stop, turn, walk in without me.
       The sky lightens, and the stars are going out.

Our writer blended the three freewrites into a twenty-two-line poem. She used the memory to deepen the wish to get closer to nature, rather than simply slowing down. Our writer selects the title "Reading Whitman" to allude to the poet Walt Whitman's desire to avoid the technical and scientific view of life and to return to a simple, natural view. The story of the event is clear, but the tension between the speaker and the other person in the parking lot is less important. The dialogue work is not really included. It is not necessary to include all of the freewrites, and our writer elected to use only the emotion that emerged from the freewrite in Writer's Practice 2.2.

 ## Writer Response Groups

At this point, you have a sixteen- to twenty-five-line poem that tells a brief and simple story. You have created a clear story including the *who*, *what*, *where*, and *when*. You have crafted the *why* of the story by connecting a title and the final lines to the detailed story. Now form a response group. Examine each other's poems, reading for the following elements:

Essential Elements

- What is the poem about?
- Who is the speaker?
- How is the poem organized?

Craft

- How is the emotional tension of the poem created?
- Are the action and events of the poem clear?
- Do the parts of the poem connect to create meaning?

Revising Verbs to Reduce Wordiness

Poets face the challenge of writing with fewer words. This means every word must count. A common and persistent problem facing all poets is wordiness. How do you address the problem? Certainly, reducing repetition of unnecessary detail and cutting information that takes the poem in a wrong or confusing direction are obvious solutions. A less obvious solution is to change your verbs. This solution should not only be the first strategy for reducing wordiness, but it should be applied to all the poetry revision you do.

Writer's Practice 2.5 *Create "Muscular" Verbs*

Review your verbs and revise your poem. Cut unnecessary details as you revise your sentences.

- First, circle your verbs. Are they active and muscular? Notice Olds's verbs in her description of the son's bubble-blowing: *puffs, burst, subside, rise, swells, pop, dissolve, breaks.* Most of these verbs contain a single syllable, and in some cases they sound like what they are doing: *puffs, burst, pops.* Are your verbs similarly effective?
- Second, eliminate as many verbs of being as possible. Verbs of being include *is, am, are, was, were, have, had, would.* If you have a verb of being, you most likely have a wordy sentence. Changing the verb will force you to cut the sentence. Sometimes, the powerful verb is buried at the end of the sentence.
- As you revise your verbs, cut at least twenty words. The finished poem should be sixteen to twenty-two lines.

Begin revising if you feel you are ready, or examine our writer's model and explication. Your Writer Response Group may have suggested additions or clarifications that make your poem longer, so look closely to find repeated and unnecessary details or empty phrases that do not contain detail.

Our Writer

Two Scientists

When you walk ahead of me
in the dark school parking lot,
kids streaming past,
our bags spilling out quizzes and papers,
5   I want you to stop, turn,

look at me, say, let's just stand
here a minute. Then
I could show you the comet
two quiet observers found one night.
10   I could tell you: *Years ago,*
my uncle Joel sat with me
on Grandma's step,
a deep August night
and we said nothing. Just breathed
15   *the smell of corn and cows and*
sky without end.
Inside the school is filling up.
In each of my classes someone will read
"When I Heard the Learn'd Astronomer,"
20   and we will all wish
to glide toward some night sky.
But you turn, smile, walk in without me.
With each step forward more windows flicker on.
The sky, too, lightens.

Notice the clarity of the dramatic situation. The reader is ushered through the story with words shifting the poem's focus: "When," "Then," "Years ago," "Inside," and "But." The first few lines establish the scene as a dark parking lot and the speaker as a busy teacher watching kids streaming into the building. This teacher wants contact with her friend walking ahead of her. The poem has cut the details about the ice-covered lot and the wish for help that distract the current focus: wishing to connect with a friend and enjoying the night sky, which is quickly disappearing. The poem shifts to a memory the speaker imagines will help the friend understand the importance of this quiet moment. A second shift brings the poem and speaker back to the present and ends with the friend walking into school, missing the encounter. The speaker is left with the image of the school windows flickering on and the sky lightening. The poem ends without a resolution to the problem; rather, there is an acceptance that this is the way things are.

Notice many interesting and beautiful details have been removed from the poem: the wisdom of Uncle Joel and the second memory of walking home along muddy rivers in the spring. By cutting even beautiful images, the poem has gained a focus on the present moment and the importance of the speaker's wish to connect with another person and nature in a less hectic way. Our writer has also included the title of a Whitman poem, "When I Heard the Learn'd Astronomer," which is about a man who grows tired of the facts and figures of an astronomy lecture and escapes outside to the perfection of the night sky. She connects the story's details to this poem by titling it "Two

Scientists," which suggests the friends might be caught up in the details of the day and be missing the beauty of the moment.

Examining Student Poems

Inventing from narrative allows a poet to focus on a simple story. Creating a dramatic situation from the small tensions in life requires a poet to avoid high drama and to find meaning in the details of the small moment. A poet achieves the narrative poem with simple tools: a first-person narrative voice; attention to details, dialogue, and memory; meaning connected to the details through a title and a metaphorical close; and close attention to verb usage. The student poems that follow illustrate the importance of a first-person voice, a detailed story, and meaning created through connecting a title, a well-told story, and a metaphorical closing. Each poet used the lessons in this chapter to create a distinctly different poem.

At the Bridge

KRIS NEMESI

Our walk home usually extends through the woods,
the long way, well beyond the busy school parking lot.
Good exercise, we both claim, to justify our habit.
Today, Grandma stops at the bridge on the footpath,
5   leans on the wooden rail and looks down.
Below, a dried brook's bed is strewn
with brown September leaves and twigs.

"I hate to see summer end," she says.
She looks away, and her breath is short.
10   "I dread the long, dark winter."
I help her with one arm of her sweater, then the next.
"As a child, fall meant school, a new start," she says.
"But not now." She pulls her sweater close.

Two girls walk down the path toward us.
15   They lean together and giggle. When I step forward
to say hello, they don't look up. I see one hides
a cigarette cupped in her palm so I step back
as they pass, keeping their secret in teenage unity.
But Grandma stares with big-eyed delight.

20   "I smoked my first cigarette in my friend's shed
after school one day," she says. "She had a stash

in a coffee can. Of course I choked, and coughed.
I felt very guilty. But we laughed together all afternoon,
bonded by our small rebellion." She winks at me.
25 "Are you shocked?"

I picture Grandma, then sixteen, red-haired,
skinny like me, laughing as she holds her first cigarette.
I lock my arm in hers and smile. We turn
in time to watch gold leaves fall from trees.
30 Fall colors in the brook's bed
suddenly look deep and rich and important.
We start for the woods.
"Any more rebellions?" I ask.

Kris's poem contains an imagined memory at the end of the story. The speaker pictures her Grandma as a girl, like herself, and realizes the poignancy of aging. The deep rich colors of the woods, the dried brook, and the old bridge suggest the passing of time. The title, "At the Bridge," suggests that the speaker has bridged a space between herself and her grandmother: they are not so different after all.

Out Too Late

BRENT GRIFFITH

When I come home late at night,
after dinner, I think I should have
phoned, said why I was late,
stopped your worry. Lumpy potatoes fill
5 my plate, alone at the table,
growing colder.
Undone homework, littered
across the living room floor,
I turn and half smile, hoping
10 dad will understand,
thinking we'll talk tomorrow.
Years back, he and I talked all the time
time, while we watched our bobbers
floating, listening to Grandpa quietly ramble on
15 about the big fish he caught.

I break the silence,
"I didn't know it was. . ."
Dad's icy glare cuts me short.

Tough love he calls it, and
20 I wish I'd come home,
earlier. I know I've done it now,
once too often. Finally,
he shakes his head and goes upstairs.
Thunderous silence shakes the room
25 harsher than words.
I fear this time I've sunk the boat.

Brent retells the story of a guilty teenager returning home to a father's disappointment. The issues of silence and talk reappear in the poem a few times: both father and speaker do not talk to each other, unlike earlier days when there was a comfortable chatter between the two of them while they fished. The description of the lumpy, lonely potatoes and the undone homework on the floor emphasize the teenager's neglect of his responsibilities and the resulting guilt. The title reflects the concrete reason for the guilt as well as a deeper sense that the relationship with the father is beyond repair. The sunken boat in the last line suggests a loss of the easier, more intimate days of fishing shared with the father.

Glass Girl

Genevieve Benson

He walks around the room
examining things on oak shelves.
He picks up a figurine,
a girl curtsying in a pale blue dress,
5 roses blooming in her cheeks.
He marvels at her
vacant eyes and glossy lips,
holds her up to the light
so he can see through her.
10 She gives him her sparkling smile.
I sit on the couch,
hugging a pillow,
watching him delight in his glass girl,
and I feel five again,
15 watching my parents,
enchanted by the new baby.
Sitting against a wall,
I fingered a shag carpet while
they cradled her,

20   hovered over her,
       touched her face like
       she'd shatter and break,
       as if she were that glass girl
       he smoothes his fingers over now.
25   I wish I were that girl.

Genevieve uses a childhood memory to parallel her feelings about the boy's involvement with the glass figurine. The concrete description of the glass girl makes the boy's fascination with its transparent beauty seem more like a betrayal than an admiration of art. The memory deepens the sense of betrayal, since the speaker passively sits and watches, feeling as disconnected from the boy as she did from her parents when they brought home "the new baby." Genevieve did not use dialogue in her poem, depending more on description and powerful verbs. The power of the narrator's experience is reinforced in the final line, which expresses her conflict: she wanted to be the center of attention as a child, and now she wishes to be the center of attention with the boy.

chapter 3

Drawing an Unusual Comparison: Metaphor, Simile, Extended Metaphor, and Stanza

In a novel you get the journey. In a poem you get the arrival.

-MAY SARTON

The mind cannot invent anything entirely new. Every idea, theory, or invention is a combination of familiar pieces twisted or combined in a new way. The resulting combinations are often astounding. Poets seek to articulate the astounding by combining familiar details in new ways. In Chapter 2, you learned that meaning springs from a simple, concrete story, a title, and a single closing sentence.

In this chapter, you will find that meaning comes from a different combination of elements. You will build on details to create metaphors and similes, which are the poetic terms for comparison. Metaphors and similes articulate what is difficult to understand through literal language. For this reason, science makes frequent use of metaphor to explain what is difficult to see or conceive. Black holes, for example, are like a magnet or a whirlpool; an organic cell is like a factory or an engine.

Even those of you who do not consider yourselves poets or scientists use metaphor. For example, say your friend's father is a merchant marine who pilots a freighter around the Great Lakes. When he returns to port, you ask him: "What is it like, steering a huge boat from lake to lake?" Even if your friend's father is not a poet, he will be able to provide you with a useful metaphor so that you can understand his summer job: "It's like driving a Cadillac through the desert," he may say; or "It's like living inside a whale." He compares something unknown—piloting a freighter ship—to something more familiar or imaginable—Cadillacs and whales. To put it another way, he is comparing x, the unfamiliar, to y, the familiar. The comparative devices of metaphor, extended metaphor, and simile are explored in this chapter. Stanza decisions will also be explored.

Sylvia Plath and Richard Wilbur use metaphor to articulate a speaker's emotions about a significant person. Plath uses a series of comparisons in a two-stanza poem. Wilbur uses two extended metaphors in a twelve-stanza poem. How do the comparisons in the poems articulate what might be difficult to understand?

You're

SILVIA PLATH

Clownlike, happiest on your hands,
Feet to the stars, and moon-skulled,
Gilled like a fish. A common-sense
Thumbs-down on the dodo's mode.
5   Wrapped up in yourself like a spool,
Trawling your dark as owls do.
Mute as a turnip from the Fourth
Of July to All Fools' Day,
Oh high-riser, my little loaf.

10   Vague as fog and looked for like mail.
Farther off than Australia.
Bent-backed Atlas, our traveled prawn.
Snug as a bud and at home
Like a sprat in a pickle jug.
15   A creel of eels, all ripples.
Jumpy as a Mexican bean.
Right, like a well-done sum.
A clean slate, with your own face on.

Questions

1. Who is the "you" the speaker addresses?
2. What is the speaker's attitude toward this "you"? Name two or three comparisons that suggest this attitude.
3. What shift in attitude occurs between the two stanzas?

The Writer

RICHARD WILBUR

In her room at the prow of the house
Where light breaks, and the windows are tossed with linden,
My daughter is writing a story.

I pause in the stairwell, hearing
5   From her shut door a commotion of typewriter-keys
Like a chain hauled over a gunwale.

Young as she is, the stuff
Of her life is a great cargo, and some of it heavy:
I wish her a lucky passage.

10   But now it is she who pauses,
As if to reject my thought and its easy figure.
A stillness greatens, in which

The whole house seems to be thinking,
And then she is at it again with a bunched clamor
15   Of strokes, and again is silent.

I remember the dazed starling
Which was trapped in that very room, two years ago;
How we stole in, lifted a sash

And retreated, not to affright it;
20   And how for a helpless hour, through the crack of the door,
We watched the sleek, wild, dark

And iridescent creature
Batter against the brilliance, drop like a glove
To the hard floor, or the desk-top,

25   And wait then, humped and bloody,
For the wits to try it again; and how our spirits
Rose when, suddenly sure,

It lifted off from a chair-back,
Beating a smooth course for the right window
30   And clearing the sill of the world.

It is always a matter, my darling,
Of life or death, as I had forgotten. I wish
What I wished you before, but harder.

Questions

1. In stanzas 1–3, to what is the daughter's writing indirectly compared?
2. In stanzas 6–11, a second comparison is extended. To what, now, is the daughter's writing compared? What words suggest this comparison?
3. What is suggested about the nature of writing with these two comparisons?

Exploring Metaphor and Simile

Comparison is one of the most natural human impulses. Comparative devices such as metaphor and simile are probably the most often used device for crafting poems. These two devices fall under the category of figurative language, as opposed to literal language. Literal language is words and phrases that mean exactly what they say. If you told your friend that you were tired because you slept only two hours last night, you would be speaking literally, giving your friend the facts. However, if you said the same thing figuratively, you might say: "I'm dog tired today." The comparison between you and a dog more clearly describes how tired you are. Simile and metaphor are examples of figurative language.

A *simile* is a direct comparison, where the similarity between the two objects is expressed using words or phrases such as *like, as, than,* or *seems.* Sylvia Plath uses a list of comparisons, most of them similes, in her poem "You're" to suggest her satisfaction and wonderment with her unborn child. She writes that the *you*—her child—is "Gilled *like* a fish," "Mute *as* a turnip," "Snug *as* a bud." These comparisons are wild, unusual, and precise. They all suggest that the child is a mystery, but that it is itself, through and through, and is just right. It would not be possible to elicit the exact combination of emotions—curiosity, wonderment, and satisfaction—Plath felt without combining her descriptive lists of comparisons.

While simile directly states a similarity, *metaphor* implies similarity. In metaphor, intermediate linking words such as *like* or *as* are not used; rather, the reader must infer the comparison through the word choice and description. Some metaphors are plain; it is easy to see that Plath is comparing the unborn child to bread when she writes, "Oh high riser, my little loaf." Other metaphors are mere suggestions. Richard Wilbur implies a comparison between his daughter's struggle to write and a dazed starling trapped in the same room two years earlier. When he describes the bird as "humped and bloody" he is echoing an earlier description of his daughter's writing as a "commotion of typewriter-keys" and a "bunched clamor of strokes."

Experimenting with Metaphor and Simile

Using similes and metaphors in your writing is tricky. As discussed earlier, these devices are naturally poetic, since they may be unusual, wild, and evocative. On the other hand, they can be overdone. Too many metaphors in a poem can leave readers feeling as if they have eaten too much sugar. Therefore, it's best to let metaphors spring up where they seem to fit, rather than "inserting" many of them into a poem. As starting places for poetry, however, the *x* is *y* formula works well to stimulate the emotions and the imagination.

Plath and Wilbur built their poems around a significant person. It is no surprise that in both cases these significant people were their children. Children evoke strong emotional responses from their parents, and poetry is powerful when directed from the heart. You will eventually write a poem using an important "you" as a subject.

Writer's Practice 3.1 *List Wild Comparisons*

Looking for the original comparison is the goal of any writer. Since comparison is used so often, the world is full of obvious, overused comparisons. This activity will encourage you to push for the unusual, wild comparison that will enhance your poem and possibly set you on an unusual course.

Choose as a subject a person who evokes strong feeling in you. Consider someone to whom you have not fully spoken your mind or your heart, someone you want to understand. Then begin exploring comparison. It may help you to close your eyes and picture this person before or even while you are writing. However, don't ponder too much. Write down the first thing that comes to mind. You will find that the faster you write, the more your imagination is activated.

- Write a list of five metaphors, using the *x* is *y* formula. The person you selected will be the *x* and the wild comparison will be the *y*. You will finish this sentence: "You are. . . ." Do not use the words *like, as, seems,* or *than.* Do not be literal: *You are a mother, you are an accountant.* You are comparing your "you" to something unusual. Number these metaphors 1–5.

- Now write a list of five similes for the same person. Finish this sentence: "You are like. . . ." Number these similes 6–10.

- When you are finished, reread your list for any connections or repeated ideas.

Begin writing if you feel you are ready, or examine our writer's model and explication.

Our Writer

1. You are a flute, singing in the night when all the lights are out.

2. You are a dark flower opening for an hour once a year.

3. You are a mouth almost speaking.

4. Your hair is a dark bird's wing.

5. You are the skin on a hand that's holding a brush that's painting in small, straight strokes the grass in front of a barn.

6. You are like the egg that fell on the floor and loosened but didn't break.

7. You are like silver.

8. You are like the one dream I have over and over but cannot remember.

9. You are like cake and ice cream.

10. You are like the Irish linen in Grandmother's house, folded away in the dark drawer.

Notice that most of these are illogical. Numbers 3 and 5 are especially strange. Notice, too, that 6 and 10 are extended and explained, but 3, 4, 7, and 9 are short and specific. All of these types, wild and ordinary, short and long, are acceptable for this exercise.

Notice which images or ideas repeat themselves in the list. The notion of delicacy, for example, reoccurs in the images of the bird's wing, the skin on the hand, and the linen in the drawer. The ideas of articulation and memory are also repeated in the flute that sings, the mouth that almost speaks, and the dream not quite remembered. When you reread your list, be open to finding connections between similes, even if they are loose connections.

Exploring Extended Metaphors

When a poet creates a metaphor and then continues to use that comparison throughout a poem, the poet has created an *extended metaphor*. Richard Wilbur uses two separate extended metaphors in his poem "The Writer." His

first occurs in stanzas one through three, where he compares writing to a
journey on a ship:

> In her room at the prow of the house
> Where light breaks, and the windows are tossed with linden,
> My daughter is writing a story.
>
> I pause in the stairwell, hearing
> From her shut door a commotion of typewriter-keys
> Like a chain hauled over a gunwale.
>
> Young as she is, the stuff
> Of her life is great cargo, and some of it heavy:
> I wish her a lucky passage.

His word choice suggests these comparisons. The daughter is at the "prow"
of the house, which is the front of a ship; light "breaks," as water does upon
the sides of a ship; the subject of her writing is "cargo"; the typing makes the
sound of a chain hauled over a "gunwale," which is the side of a ship. In comparing writing to a rough journey at sea, Wilbur suggests the wild, difficult,
even dangerous nature of the artist.

The second half of the poem shifts to a memory of a bird trapped in a room.
This memory becomes the second extended metaphor for the nature of writing:

> I remember the dazed starling
> Which was trapped in that very room, two years ago;
> How we stole in, lifted a sash
>
> And retreated, not to affright it;
> And how for a helpless hour, through the crack of the door,
> We watched the sleek, wild, dark
>
> And iridescent creature
> Batter against the brilliance, drop like a glove
> To the hard floor, or the desk-top,
>
> And wait then, humped and bloody,
> For the wits to try it again; and how our spirits
> Rose when, suddenly sure,
>
> It lifted off from a chair-back,
> Beating a smooth course for the right window
> And clearing the sill of the world.

The starling's journey and the writer's journey are compared through Wilbur's word choice. The starling is "sleek," "wild," and "dark," as the daughter's writing is a "commotion," and the house, which becomes a ship, is caught in a storm. Later, the starling must set a right "course" for the right window, as the daughter must set a right course as she writes.

The last stanza switches perspective as the speaker draws the two extended metaphors together. He addresses his daughter directly: "It is always a matter, my darling, / Of life or death, as I had forgotten. I wish / What I wished you before, but harder." With these last lines, the speaker connects the two extended metaphors. He is also revealing something about himself: he knows something about the pain of writing and living, and therefore his wish that his daughter will have an easier time of it becomes more poignant. These two extended metaphors allow Wilbur to draw writing, the struggle for life, and journeys together to describe his feelings for his daughter. These metaphors create a meaning richer and more luminous than narrative or description could accomplish.

Experimenting with Extended Metaphors

When you wrote your fast list of metaphors and similes, you may have felt the urge to extend some of them, drawing out the comparisons. Not only is your aunt like a lake, she's like a lake that's frozen over, her children ice-skaters circling her surface, never disturbing her resolve. You could go on, exploring, directly or indirectly, the many ways your aunt is like a frozen lake. Extending a metaphor allows you to clarify and explore the intent lurking behind the original comparison. Our writer wrote that her sister was *like silver*. How so? Our writer herself might not know until she plays it out, describing the aspects about both that are similar.

Writer's Practice 3.2   *Extend a Comparison*

Chances are that one or two of your comparisons from the first writing assignment strike you in some way. Perhaps you love the sound of the words, or you are curious to see why you wrote what you did. This next step will require you to choose a metaphor or simile that provokes you, and then to extend it in order to find meaning.

Use one of your intriguing comparisons as the first sentence of a freewrite. Once you have recopied this comparison on a fresh sheet of paper, continue it.

- Extend it by comparing the many ways your *x*, the you, is like the *y*.
- Do not name the person. Instead, use the extended comparison to illustrate that person. Refer to the person as "you."

- Allow both the ordinary and the strange to come up. Do not choke or edit yourself. Write whatever comes to mind—quickly!

- Start a fresh comparison whenever you get stuck and don't know where to go, or when it seems natural and right to make a comparison.

- Write for five to ten minutes. Some of your earlier comparisons may sneak in—that's fine. Or you may discover new comparisons as you write.

- Near the end, begin a new line with "For me" or "I see." In this way you are drawing yourself to the subject, as Plath did implicitly in her last line and Wilbur did explicitly in his last line.

- When you are finished, look over your extended metaphors and see what repeats. If there is nothing specific, is there an overall impression of this person that seems to emerge from this freewrite?

Begin writing if you feel you are ready, or examine our writer's model and explication. This extended comparison should be between two hundred and three hundred words.

Our Writer

You are a flute, playing in the darkness. You play for your sister who cannot sleep. She can't hear you but she knows you play in your dreams, for your mouth is open, like you're going to speak, but can't. You are playing the flute in your dreams and I, your sister, watch you because I cannot sleep. I can never sleep once you go to sleep first. In the daytime after school you play piano and I lay on the green carpeting in the window's sun and listen to you play Mozart's "A Little Night Music."

You kept all of your sheet music in the piano bench, even after you moved out. Now you cannot find it. Today, visiting at mother's, you look for it again, like the bird looking for the roost that was destroyed or blown away, the way we all look again and again for what we have loved but can't believe is gone. You look for the music. It is always gone. Your hands open the bench. You say you can't buy new music—you can only play what you have already learned, for the memory stays in the hands.

For me memory is in the eyes. All those years of no sleep made me a seer. For you, sleep was your art. There you entered the dark waters of music and played for yourself, and played for your sister so she could sleep.

Notice that several of the original similes or images made their way in here: the mouth that's open, the dreams, the bird, the idea of articulation, music, speech, and sight. At the end, the writer makes a statement about the difference between the "you" and the speaker. The "you" and the "I" make sense of the world differently—the "I," the speaker, with her eyes, and the "you," the sister, with her voice.

Writer's Practice 3.3 *Form Your Freewrite*

Extending a metaphor creates resonance in your poem. It brings the reader back to a powerful and unusual comparison. An extended metaphor can be powerful with only a few extensions. For example, you need not feel compelled to think of *all* the possible ways your brother is like a car. Comparing his logical nature to the transmission, which enables the car to go in only one direction at a time, you might use the words *forward*, *reverse*, *overdrive*, and *neutral*. It might be overkill, however, to continue the comparison with other aspects of a car. Extended metaphor can weaken a poem if it is overdone, ordinary, or too obvious.

- Return to Writer's Practices 3.1 and 3.2 and select the metaphors, similes, or extended metaphors that surprise or please you.
- Write a thirty- to fifty-line poem describing some aspect of a person who is important in your life. Select one of two options:
  - a series of one- or two-line metaphors or similes to flesh out your subject, or
  - one or two extended, implied metaphors, in which you compare your subject directly to something else.

Why Is the Narrator So Important?

The narrator of a poem conveys the story or feeling of that poem. If the narrator changes, the meaning changes, and the details must change as well.

Look at a poem you are currently writing and ask yourself the following questions: Have I chosen the right person to tell the story or feeling of the poem? Does the story match the narrator's beliefs and values? Does the reader get enough information from this narrator to understand the meaning of the poem? Is the narrative voice consistent throughout the poem?

Begin writing if you feel you are ready, or examine our writer's model and explication. Whichever option you choose, make sure that the last few lines connect the important person and the speaker.

Our Writer

> Most schoolnights you fell asleep before me.
> Downstairs Mother and Father placed
> glasses in the sink, closed drawers,
> climbed the stairs and shut the door, while
> 5   I lay and watched your dark
> hair and white face.
> In the moonlight I saw your mouth purse
> as if you might sing,
> play your flute or speak to me.
>
> 10   Some afternoons you played the piano,
> and I listened to you, the spell of
> dust, sun, and "A Little Night Music"
> finally putting me under.
>
> Years later you visit Mother and search
> 15   again for the music in the piano bench.
> Someone—the maid? The movers?—misplaced it.
> Today your mute hands look for it,
> birds looking for the nest that blew away.
> You can only play what you have learned,
> 20   for the music is in the hands.
> I help you look, for your music sings to my eyes,
> and only then do I know I am not alone.

This poem is focused on developing a single comparison, that of the sister's music to her true voice. This comparison is developed with a few metaphors: the sister's music is compared to a spell; her hands without music are mute and restless birds. The lines about the speaker's poetry were cut because they took attention away from the central metaphor of the sister's music. The last line of the poem clarifies the importance of the sister's music to the speaker: it allows her to hear her sister's true voice. This comforts her and allows her to sleep.

This poem is quite similar to the freewrite from Writer's Practice 3.2. It does begin differently by setting a scene, but the rest of the poem then uses roughly the same organization and images from the previous freewrite. Of course, this may not be true for your draft. Yours may have kept only one or two key comparisons.

Writer Response Groups

At this point, you should have a poem draft with a significant person as its subject. The poem describes, defines, and characterizes through metaphors, similes, or extended metaphors, but it might not name the significant person. In addition, it connects this characterization to the speaker. Now form a response group of four or five writers. Examine each other's poems, reading for the following elements:

Essential Elements

- What is the poem about?
- Who is the speaker?
- How is the poem organized?

Craft

- What meaning do the metaphors, similes, and extended metaphors create?
- What if a single comparison was extended? What if some comparisons were cut?
- What is the relationship between the speaker and the significant person, and is this relationship clear?

Revising for Stanzas

As you wrote your poem, you probably paid attention to organization without realizing it. Perhaps you grouped lines together according to their mood, time period, or subject. In poetry, these groups of lines are called *stanzas*.

Stanzas are used to indicate a shift in time, place, or subject or to create a consistent pattern. Both Plath and Wilbur use a consistent number of lines in all of their stanzas—Plath has two stanzas of nine lines each, and Wilbur has three lines in each of his stanzas—but a consistent number of lines per stanza is not required in poetry. Many poems contain stanzas with varying lengths, although some kinds of poems have a consistent form as a requirement, such as sonnets and sestinas. All stanza breaks indicate a shift or change, however.

Plath's poem shifts in mood from stanza one to stanza two. The first stanza is full of concrete images, but the second stanza begins with uncertainty. The "you" is no longer like a turnip or a loaf of bread, but "Vague as fog and looked for like mail."

Wilbur also uses stanzas to group like actions or ideas together and to signal shifts. His consistent use of three-line stanzas, or tercets, brings attention to another interesting decision: sentence length. Stanzas 1–3 are a single sentence each and contain a single action. However, as the poem continues, the sentences become longer and carry over from stanza to stanza. One sentence is extended over stanzas 4–5. Then the sentence length increases in stanzas 6–10, the section describing the action of the starling. These five stanzas contain a single long sentence. The last stanza is a single short sentence again.

Why would Wilbur organize his sentences and stanzas this way? The reasons are to establish pace and to create tension. Stanzas introduce white space into a poem, which causes the reader to pause. Pausing slows the pace of the poem. Tension is also increased, especially when a reader must read for several stanzas before the end of a sentence is reached.

Writer's Practice 3.4 *Revise to a Fixed Stanza Length*

Committing to a stanza length can force you to reconsider a poem. Details that you love may not fit the prescribed length, and in reconsidering those details, you may also discover they are unnecessary. How could this be true? Isn't cutting what you love destructive to your poem? Not necessarily. Sometimes we hang onto a line or stanza because we love the way it sounds, or because it is clever. But that beloved detail may confuse the reader or be unnecessarily repetitious. Therefore, any activity that forces the poet to examine every word for its precision and meaning will improve the poem. This is your opportunity to re-see your poem, using an artificial and, in some ways, arbitrary decision.

Prose, Poem, or Both?

Because they lack the visual line breaks of most poetry, prose poems often appear to be regular prose paragraphs rather than poems. However, prose poems are actually poetry in prose format. They have the characteristics of poetry—such as compression, figurative language, repetition, and rhythm and movement—but not the line breaks.

The prose-poem format offers fluidity to the poet, allowing her to write in longer rhythms and motions. Prose poems can be narrative, but they are also often lyrical, creating surreal or dream landscapes and making wild or witty associations.

If you are working on a poem but cannot seem to find its shape, try giving it breathing room with the longer lines of a prose poem.

Examine your work from Writer's Practice 3.3. Just for the experience, for you may always change it later, organize your poem into stanzas. This work is best done on a computer, where you can more easily rearrange lines using the cut and paste feature. Make the stanza length consistent; for example, two stanzas of seven lines each, or twelve three-line stanzas, or three stanzas of four lines each. The number of stanzas and the length of the stanza are not as important as the commitment to make your current draft fit. Some tips to make the most of stanza usage:

- Focus each stanza around a single action or subject.
- Make shifts in time, place, or subject at the stanza break.
- Extend a single sentence across the stanza break to speed the pace of the poem or create tension.

Revise your metaphor draft using stanza decisions to clarify the poem as well as cut it. At this point, you may wish to name the "you" in this draft. By naming this significant person, your poem may become more personalized, especially if the person is someone close to the speaker, or if the relationship between the speaker and the unnamed "you" is unclear.

Begin revising if you feel you are ready, or examine our writer's model and explication.

Our Writer

Sleep Song

Downstairs Mother and Father placed
glasses in the sink, closed cupboards,
climbed stairs and shut their door

while I lay and watched you sleep.
5   In the moonlight I saw your mouth purse
as if you were calling to me

from across the sleepy waters
that divided us come
ten o'clock and all lights out.

10   After school you practiced piano
in the green living room while I
lay on the warm wool carpet, slept

and dreamt of waves of violet flowers
opening their throats to
15   notes warm as rain.

When you and I visit Mother, years later,
Your sheet music is gone.
Someone—the maid? the movers?—misplaced it.

So your mute fingers hover above the keys
20   white cranes awkward on the shore
as I root through every paper for your voice.

Adhering to a consistent line length forced our writer to focus each image and comparison. She added a new image, comparing the piano music to warm rain opening the throats of flowers. She cut lines that didn't create an image, such as the last two lines that stated directly the importance of the music. She replaced them with a comparison between the sister's voice and sheet music, a physical thing that is lost but can be found. Using tercets forced the poet to make her images more concrete. Each stanza, except for the last, is now a complete sentence, or else a complete action or idea. The first stanza, for example, describes the actions of the parents downstairs. The sentence carries into the second stanza, but the setting changes to the girls' bedroom with the speaker and the sister. This draws the two events together while still separating them as distinct events.

Notice, too, that the language is tighter. The first line has been cut—it wasn't needed. Words such as "like," "the," and "and" have also been cut, as well as a few descriptions—the white face and the dark hair in the moonlight, for example, which seemed mundane and ordinary.

Examining Student Poems

Comparison functions to explain things that are difficult to articulate. However, effective comparison poems make use of the unusual. The student models that follow all use metaphor to speak to an important person but do not rely solely on the comparison to convey meaning. In addition, all of the models make use of stanza breaks to create pauses and transitions between ideas or moods.

Anytime

LAURA RICHARDSON

You are leaving me. An imaginary
time keeper whispers:
"Time to go."

And you revolve lifetimes away
5   to learn about infinity and
all night parties.

You will turn strangers into new friends.
Noodles and toothpaste will sustain you.
All without a sister.

10   When I told you I would miss you,
you told me I could visit.
         Anytime.

I bet I'll never go.
I never thought I'd care about
15   early morning cartoons or

neighborhood night games.
Tree forts and sand tunnels,
escape routes and cement dungeons.

I waited too long to get to know
20   you. A priceless time
piece stolen with my eyes open.

The speaker addresses her brother as "you." She relates her brother to images and aspects of time: there is an imaginary timekeeper; it is time for him to go; the brother says she may visit anytime. At the end she draws these aspects of time together with a comparison of her brother to a stolen time-piece. Her three-line stanzas focus each comparison.

Gone Fishin'

DAVID DIXON

Before,
you were that
new house by the river with the
crazy roof and fancy windows. You were that
5   dog named Sport who always leaped
ten miles straight up when I
called her name or beckoned her to come closer.
You were the flashy red kayak no one believed
could win the April competition.

10   But ever since,
you have been that small delicate cabin
that kept to itself and seemed asleep every
time we spied it from the woods.
Now you are the docile dog Spot with
15   white rings around her eyes.

> The dog who never looked up
> when I called.
> You are that clumsy, frozen fishing shanty Grandpa used in January.
> Ever since the night you went alone—
> **20**   the night we found your life jacket silently floating in the darkness.

David chose to use a series of metaphors to characterize a person before and after a death. In the first stanza, the person is compared to wild, lively, unique things: a house with a crazy roof, a dog, a red kayak. In the second stanza, the parallel comparisons are to things withdrawn, quiet, and still: a quiet cabin, a docile dog, a frozen shanty. The two separate stanzas indicate a shift from life to death.

Mirror

ADAM HAMILTON

> I hate it when you say I'm just like him
> because I now see myself in the mirror of example
> when he embarks on a fit of rage
> like a time bomb
> **5**   erupting in my face.
>
> His words, brutally honest:
> "Why does this always happen?"
> "Why don't you ever listen?"
> "I give up!"
> **10**   They are a mirror to my faults.
>
> Why can't he understand?
> I fear the inevitable.
> I will grow to be the man I hate,
> I am a reflection of his past,
> **15**   as he is a reflection of my future.

Adam chooses a mirror as a metaphor to demonstrate how similar the speaker is to his father. This is a painful realization for the speaker. The father is compared to a time bomb, after all, about to explode with anger and disappointment at his child. Adam chooses three five-line stanzas to move from the speaker's thoughts to the father's actions back to the speaker's thoughts.

chapter 4

Writing from Daily Life: Imagery, Direct Address, and Free Verse

Young poets, young writers [need] to look into their own lives for material. I call this "working life." I know it is hard for many who are young to see that there is value in their lives, that there are moments in their lives that are worth reporting through writings. If they can take a slice of life and be able to focus on that piece, that makes for the better poem. What we like to hear are the really intimate details of all our lives. If younger writers could just adjust their focus from this wide-lens view to a focused-lens view, the writings would be powerful.

-GARY SOTO

Y ou probably pass by several worthy poems a day, but you are blind to them. Instead, you see the routine details of living: the same tree, cat, or sleepy face in the mirror. Maybe you imagine poems must be about big ideas or dramatic events, and the events of your daily life seem uninspiring. However, a poem that captures the daily details of living does not have to be mundane. In Chapter 2, you examined dramatic situation in Writer's Practice 2.1. You learned the importance of a speaker and how to access memory in Writer's Practice 2.3. You wrote a story or narrative poem capturing and inventing interesting events and experiences. The power in this poem came from carefully chosen detail or a clear conflict. These techniques helped you enter the poem and make decisions to craft your stories and feelings. Next, in Writer's Practice 3.1 and 3.2, you learned how to use comparison to enhance your stories and personalize a metaphorical connection to create meaning.

This chapter explores Gary Soto's advice: write a poem that "works life." You may be unaware that your life is full of poems. The seemingly insignificant tasks of living, such as making a trip to the grocery store, can offer several poems to a writer with an introspective nature. In addition, in this chapter you will experiment with first-person point of view, creating a speaker who talks from the heart with honest vulnerability. Also, you will learn how to improve your poetic lines.

Gary Soto and Mary Oliver create poems from observing daily experiences. Both of the following poems use carefully chosen detail, an unusual comparison, and a strong personal voice achieved through a first-person point of view. In addition, each poem rises from the poet's introspective nature. How does first-person point of view create meaning in a poem about a small observation or ordinary event?

Behind Grandma's House

GARY SOTO

At ten I wanted fame. I had a comb
And two Coke bottles, a tube of Bryl-creem.
I borrowed a dog, one with
Mismatched eyes and a happy tongue,
5   And wanted to prove I was tough
In the alley, kicking over trash cans,
A dull chime of tuna cans falling.
I hurled light bulbs like grenades
And men teachers held their heads,
10   Fingers of blood lengthening
On the ground. I flicked rocks at cats,
Their goofy faces spurred with foxtails.
I kicked fences. I shooed pigeons.
I broke a branch from a flowering peach
15   And frightened ants with a stream of spit.
I said, *"Chale,"* "In your face," and "No way
Daddy-O" to an imaginary priest
Until grandma came into the alley,
Her apron flapping in a breeze,
20   Her hair mussed, and said, "Let me help you,"
And punched me between the eyes.

Questions

1. How does the narrator begin his story?
2. List three to five details that characterize the narrator. What type of person is he?

3. Why are the Grandmother's actions surprising?

4. Why does the speaker feel the story is significant? What significance does it have for you?

Milkweed

MARY OLIVER

The milkweed now with their many pods are standing
like a country of dry women.
The wind lifts their flat leaves and drops them.
This is not kind, but they retain a certain crisp glamour;
5   moreover, it's easy to believe
each one was once young and delicate, also
frightened; also capable
of a certain amount of rough joy.
I wish you would walk with me out into the world.
10   I wish you could see what has to happen, how
each one crackles like a blessing
over its thin children as they rush away.

Questions

1. To what is the milkweed being compared?

2. What words make this comparison effective?

3. Who is the narrator speaking to in lines 9–12?

4. This poem is not a story: it expresses a feeling and attitude toward life. What feeling and attitude are expressed?

Exploring Imagery

Recognizing the poem breathing next to you is as important as knowing how to craft it. Novice writers may discover that finding a poem is as easy as focusing on small but important experiences in daily life. Consider this: you are eating dinner at a local restaurant. In the next booth, a gray-haired man hunches over a tape recorder, listening to the same song over and over as he slowly spoons soup into his mouth. When the song ends, he rakes his fingers through his hair and presses stop . . . rewind . . . stop . . . play. You reach for your date's hand and gently squeeze it. Or, consider this: you finish brushing your teeth, lean into the mirror, and clench white rows together. You turn your head and smile as if you are speaking to the person across the aisle in math class. You practice "Hi, hello, hey," each time adjusting your voice. These are poems waiting to be written.

To mine your daily life for experiences, keep a journal. Although stopping to write notes on an interesting event, sight, or piece of overheard dialogue may seem awkward, commit to doing it. If a journal is inconvenient to carry, put a piece of paper and a small pen or pencil in your pocket or purse. Write the concrete details using your senses: taste, touch, sight, smell, and hearing. These details create imagery—the sensory description of a place, object, or person. Poets rarely use a single sense to create their images, so don't rely simply on sight. While generating, always stretch yourself and include as many of the senses as possible. By pushing to describe difficult senses, you may discover an unusual perspective or feeling. And if you cannot describe a sense, then make a comparison. Practice gathering small events, not big ones, that seem meaningful to you in some way. Use a slice of your life to capture feelings, thoughts, or actions. You can use these events to show readers something simple about yourself and perhaps to help them understand something about themselves, as well.

Intensify the reader's connection to the poem by creating what Gary Soto calls the focused-lens view. His poem unapologetically tells the brief story of a ten-year-old boy's bold confusion in an alley and his grandmother's unexpected aid. The incident may have taken five or ten minutes. The speaker frames the experience with the first line, "At ten I wanted fame." Then a variety of images focus the view and build a tangible picture of a ten-year-old who wants to look "bad." When the Grandma appears and helps, readers laugh and feel a kinship with the experience. Notice Soto uses two senses predominately: sight and hearing. He shows the reader the contents of the speaker's pockets: "a comb" and "a tube of Bryl-creem." He shows the reader what the speaker carries: "two Coke bottles." He shows the reader the speaker's companion: "I borrowed a dog, one with / Mismatched eyes and a happy tongue." Then the reader hears the speaker's actions:

In the alley, kicking over trash cans,
A dull chime of tuna cans falling.
I hurled light bulbs like grenades

Soto continues listing actions and details so the reader can see the event vividly. When the grandmother enters the poem, the speaker and reader see "Her apron flapping in a breeze, / Her hair mussed."

Mary Oliver's poem creates an even tighter focus. She describes a milkweed, dried and ripe with seeds, and compares the milkweed to women. The speaker and reader see "The milkweed now with their many pods" and that "The wind lifts their flat leaves and drops them." The speaker and reader hear that "each one crackles like a blessing." The close link to the reader's senses creates a frame for the comparisons that make the observation meaningful. After Oliver observes the milkweed plants and suggests a comparison, she extends her comparison using sensory word choice.

> This is not kind, but they retain a certain crisp glamour;
> moreover, it's easy to believe
> each one was once young and delicate, also
> frightened; also capable
> of a certain amount of rough joy.

Words like "crisp" and "delicate" remind the reader that the speaker still is talking about milkweed plants. Even when Oliver describes the "thin children," the reader is aware that the children are the delicate seeds of the plant. Close observation creates opportunities, and Oliver utilized them to craft her poem.

Experimenting with Imagery

"Working life," as Gary Soto refers to it, requires you to develop a writer's eye for opportunities, but recognizing the small moment that can be turned into a poem takes practice.

Creating images is like capturing the senses in writing, to show the reader the experience. Imagery is the basic tool of a focused-lens view.

Adding Fictional Details

Poems capture the stories and feelings of everyday life, and the poet's task is to create the "Oh, yes, I know this feeling" effect. This means that remaining 100 percent truthful may not always be possible or desirable. Did Gary Soto's grandmother really punch him between the eyes? We doubt it, but that exaggeration creates surprise and engages readers.

Poets choose to add fictional details for other reasons as well. For one thing, they may not remember the actual details. Or they may not feel comfortable sharing them.

So don't be afraid to add details, action, dialogue, and thoughts that didn't actually occur. If you can't remember the details, make them up. Can you exaggerate the details? Sure. Engaging your reader is more important than remaining steadfast to the truth.

Writer's Practice 4.1   *Collect Daily Images*

On a single day, collect three to five moments in a focused-lens view. Observe yourself and others and use your senses to describe your observations. Try to use all five senses to collect information. The following suggestions will help you:

- Don't be picky about the moments. Take what the day offers you.
- Describe the observations using imagery that captures the senses.
- Include actions, feelings, thoughts, specific description, and bits of dialogue.
- Make comparisons using metaphors or similes.

Begin writing if you feel you are ready, or examine our writer's model and explication.

Our Writer

11:00 A.M.—A chipmunk streaks across the lawn ducking into the cover of a spruce tree then rushing to the next tree. Behind it, the orange cat bounds. At first, it looks like the chipmunk will beat the cat to the logs, but then the cat leaps onto it. Mom yells for my brother. He's in his room, probably playing Nintendo. "What!" he yells back. "The cat got a chipmunk. It's out here killing it." He doesn't respond or come to see the battle. As if this were a cartoon, the chipmunk slips out of the cat's grasp spurting from between her paws like a bar of slippery soap, but she reaches past its meager attempt to escape and paws it to the ground. Both are quiet as she bites the chipmunk again and again before she unexpectedly releases it. It lies still. "Oh, she killed it," Mom shrieks. "Ya think," I say but continue watching. Uninterested now, the cat steps back, an uninvolved spectator, as the chipmunk wiggles under the closest spruce tree. I can tell by its sideways and confused movement that the cat has done serious damage. Worse, she follows it. Mom shouts, "You fool, don't go under the tree. The cat. The cat will get you again."

2:30 P.M.—"I finished blowing the choke cherries off the driveway. I'll be home at 5:00," I shout to Mom.
   "Wait. Let me check." The drive is dotted with cherries. "You call that clean?"
   "I used the blower and the broom. They're stuck on." I am making up excuses but I'm late. I didn't really try very hard. I hate sweeping the choke cherries, they always stick to the asphalt.
   "Where's the broom?" Mom looks around the garage. "The big one."
   "Over there."
It is under the racks in the back corner of the garage. I never used it. I'm sure she'll ground me. I say nothing. She says nothing, just demonstrates how to

brush the cherries using short bursts on the broom. The cherries roll under the pressure. Then she says, "You call that stuck on? Then why can I get them off? Did you really use the broom?"

I hesitate, then say: "Yes."

She pauses, stares at me, broom in hand. "Well, use it again."

"Can I do it when I get back? I'll be late."

"Late for what? You're just going to run."

"I'll be late, that's all."

3:30 P.M.—I sprint up Pine Trail watching my feet. Gold shoes slap against black asphalt. Slap, slap, slap, slap. There's a rhythm to it. My shadow runs ahead of me, smaller, crouched, blurred. I try to beat it, knowing it will always win. I imagine it is Suzanne. Her blonde hair flipping and I run faster. Although I'm late, I could still catch her in town. She's been running the same route as me, maybe we could keep these accidental meetings going until she asks me out. Then I turned the corner of Pine Trail and Snowapple. The sun gleamed through a red maple. It looked like those night lights made of stained glass. Each leaf lost in the blaze of crimson. You could never be afraid if such a tree guarded you each night. I stopped dead to watch it. That was when Suzanne appeared next to me. She startled me, and my first thought was she must have changed her route, and we stood there together watching the tree glow. She had sweat beads on her nose, and one drop rolled along her face down her neck. Her bangs were wet and stuck to her forehead. They looked so brown. As we stood there, my feet tapped on the ground as if they wanted to talk. I wanted to know how she found me, if it was an accident, if she looked for me. Then she said, "Wanna get an ice cream?"

5:30 P.M.—A neighbor runs through my yard. He is carrying a brown grocery bag tightly shut. He grasps it by the rolled down top, his left hand supports the bottom. It appears to contain something square, possibly a box. He looks around, rolls the top tighter, and then turns his head sideways as he shoves the bag deep into the center of the biggest pine. He looks up. No one is outside. He runs off. I wonder: What is in the bag? Should I look? Why would he hide it? I remember the time someone stole my tennis shoes at school and hid them behind the heater. I don't know this boy very well, but I know he's always getting into trouble. His father is a minister. You'd think he'd be better behaved.

Writer's Practice 4.2 *Reflect on Your Observations*

Let your observations from Writer's Practice 4.1 rest for a day or two, then reread them. Look for feelings or ideas buried in the observations and reflect on your collection by freewriting for five to ten minutes. Ask yourself these questions:

- What significance do these moments have in my life?
- What current struggles of mine seem to be related to these moments?
- Does the moment reveal some truth about me?

Conclude your freewriting by asking yourself a question or by making a statement. Use the question or statement to pinpoint the central issue in the reflection.

Begin writing if you feel you are ready, or examine our writer's model and explication.

Our Writer

Reflection: I didn't realize that if I wrote down pretty insignificant things and tried to describe them that I could find a poem so easily. I've heard about people that keep journals and always thought it was a waste of time. For me, poems just come or more often don't come. So this made writing pretty painless. I realized that all the writes had something in common: I don't seem to be too interested in things; I didn't really care about the cat and the chipmunk even though my mother was all upset, even yelling at the stupid chipmunk. I didn't care too much about the neighbor boy, and I don't do much about the fact that I like Suzanne. I didn't realize that I was waiting for her to make the first move and I was making excuses. I was rushing with the choke cherries because I didn't want to miss her, but I didn't have to miss her, all I had to do was ask her to meet me. The truth it reveals is that I'm pretty laid back. I don't take action. I didn't really try to do a good job sweeping the choke cherries, and I didn't want to take a risk with Suzanne. Maybe I'm too shy; maybe I'm afraid I'll be ignored.

Writer's Practice 4.3   *Write a Daily Life Poem*

Reread your observations and your reflection, then select a single moment from your observations and show the reader the moment. Use imagery and comparisons to describe the setting, your actions, and the actions of others.

- Use sight, sound, smell, taste, and touch to describe the setting.
- Use active verbs to describe your actions and the actions of others.
- Use the first-person point of view.
- Include dialogue.
- Invent additional images, actions, or sensory description.

Write in stanzas, even though you will be adding to this work in Writer's Practice 4.4. Select an ordinary event, then use details to make the experience meaningful for the reader.

Begin writing if you feel you are ready, or examine our writer's model and explication.

Our Writer

> I leave pools of burgundy choke cherries,
> shout: "Be back at five."
> But mom says: "You call this clean?"
> "I'll be late," I plead.
> 5   "Late for what?"
> I look down and can't confess I'm only
> hoping to meet a girl accidentally, maybe.
> She points at the broom. I sweep
> knowing I'll never see Suzanne now.
>
> 10   I sprint up Pine Trail sure I've missed her.
> I turn up Snowapple and a brilliant red maple blinds me.
> It looks like it is on fire. Then I hear a runner behind me,
> and Suzanne's voice: "Hey, change your route?"
> I face her. Sweat beads up on the bridge
> 15   of her nose, and her bangs are matted brown.
> "Look at this tree," I say and feel stupid.
> But she says, "Yeah." And we stand
> wordless until the sun disappears.
>
> "Wanna have an ice cream?" she says.
> 20   "Sure." I slip my fingers into hers as we stroll
> past the post office like we have never seen it before.
> At Miller's Dairy, I order double fudge almond, and
> Suzanne orders chocolate chip cookie dough,
> and we silently lick the cones smooth.

Our writer tells the story of meeting Suzanne, including dialogue, the metaphor of the tree glowing, and the sensory description of Suzanne. The poem draft is more like a story written in the form of a poem, but it captures a simple truth that our writer discovered from his four freewrites: he is shy and does not assert himself. In his poem, he takes parts from two freewrites to get his point across. He creates the awkward dialogue with Suzanne at the tree, which was not included in the freewrite, and he adds details about their walk to the dairy as well. The conversation emphasizes the difficulty of expressing feelings of fondness or love. There is always the fear of looking stupid, and this fear keeps the speaker from asserting himself. Even though Suzanne invites the speaker for ice cream, there is a sense that she also has difficulty expressing herself, too.

Exploring Meaning and Direct Address

Although creating meaning may seem like a weighty task, it is really not so, because meaning will spring from the moment itself. In Writer's Practice 2.4, you discovered meaning can spring from the well-told story, and you crafted that meaning in writing a narrative poem. In Writer's Practice 3.2, you used extended metaphors to create meaning, and you crafted a comparison poem.

Meaning can also result from human interaction. The human brain is always constructing meaning, sorting feelings, and trying to make sense of information. Humans are naturally introspective and sharing introspective discoveries with other people is another natural impulse. Similarly, the best poems share introspective discoveries, such as human frailties—the honest discoveries people make about themselves and others.

In his poetry, Gary Soto explores human discoveries, beginning his poem with "At ten, I wanted fame." This short sentence helps readers make sense of the details, actions, and words that illustrate how impulsive the speaker was at age ten. Soto clarifies the actions and details with another honest statement: "And wanted to prove I was tough." These two statements by the speaker help the reader understand that the boy's actions are prompted by his desire to be recognized and to prove his masculinity.

Mary Oliver takes a step toward honest vulnerability in a different way. She creates meaning when her speaker talks directly to another person in the poem. From her focused observation and comparison of milkweed plants, Oliver shifts and speaks to an unidentified "you":

I wish you would walk with me out into the world.
I wish you could see what has to happen, how
each one crackles like a blessing
over its thin children as they rush away.

Who is "I"? Who is "you"? Neither person is clearly defined in the poem, and the reason the "I" tells the "you" the wish is never stated. Viewing the intimate details of this weed prompts the speaker to wish the "you" could see and understand what the "I" sees and understands about milkweed, and about other unspoken things as well. Paraphrasing the passage, the speaker might be saying: "I wish you could enjoy the simple things in life with me. I wish you could see the inevitable changes that must take place and enjoy these changes as I do." Although she does not name the listener, Oliver addresses him or her in a direct fashion, stating her wishes. The impulse to be heard and to share an understanding connects the observation to its meaning.

What is the meaning of Oliver's poem? Some may read it and believe that it is about women and the plight of women in the world today. Others may believe it is about the difficulty of letting children go and the necessity of doing just that. Still others may believe it is about a dissolving relationship. Readers might point to specific lines to support their beliefs, but the meaning is less complicated than those views and is stated clearly by the speaker: "I wish you could see what has to happen. . . ." The poem is about the way things are, the way things have to happen, and the ability to accept and possibly enjoy the unchangeable realities. And though it may have other, more abstract significance as well, readers must first recognize the simple truth that the speaker of the poem is offering.

Experimenting with Meaning and Direct Address

Direct address in a poem gives a sense of personal urgency. By stating the name of the listener, the poet creates a personal conversation that readers are allowed to hear. Further, direct address places a poem at a vulnerable and honest level. It can take the form of a statement or question or be a familial label such as *mother, grandmother, father, sister,* and *brother.* Labels such as these may broaden the meaning of a poem since all people have family and can relate to family issues. But be careful! These words also carry strong emotional baggage, which can add to or detract from a poem's meaning. And consider the following direct address: "Sister, forget history's hold on us." This statement speaks about the larger issue of the sisterhood of all women, rather than two female siblings only.

Writer's Practice 4.4   *Add Direct Address*

As you reread your focused-lens view and your reflection, imagine a friend to whom you would like to speak. He or she should be someone you trust who is willing to listen to you. What will you tell your friend about your focused-lens view? What do you see and understand that you want your friend to see and understand? Be honest, and reveal something about your feelings. Your reflection may help you develop the urgent message you want to speak to this friend. Create a direct address. Determine who is speaking and to whom the direct address will be spoken to. Begin the direct address by stating the person's name. Then, with a sense of urgency, deliver the truth that you want to share. Determine the placement of the direct adderss in the poem as you revise.

Combine the focused-lens view and this honest statement of a truth to clarify the narrative or description in Writer's Practice 4.3. Feel free to insert fictional details. Imagine the poem has two parts: (1) See this, which is the focused-lens view; (2) Understand this, which is the direct address. As you write, decide where to place the direct address:

- Open the poem with it to grab the reader's interest.
- Insert it in the middle to shift the reader's attention.
- Place it at the end to make a comment.

As you work, reduce the wordiness of Writer's Practice 4.3. Focus the work and allow the images to tell the story. Use the cutting skills you learned in Writer's Practice 2.5, in which you created muscular verbs, and Writer's Practice 3.4, in which you cut even those details that you loved in order to create a clear focus. Finally, give your poem a working title. You may change this title later if you wish.

Begin writing if you feel you are ready, or examine our writer's model and explication.

Our Writer

Tapping Feet

Late, I sprint up Pine Trail sure I've missed
Suzanne. I'll never make it to town
in time, turning the corner to accidentally
meet her. I run faster: tap, tap, tap, tap,
5   gold shoes against black asphalt.
Stupid, stupid, stupid, they say.
Why can't you just talk to her? Why
can't you ask: Wanna run together?

As I turn up Snowapple, pain stops me,
10   and I crouch catching my breath and decide
it's hopeless and sit in front of a maple
brilliant red, blazing as if the tree were on fire.
Then I hear a runner's tapping feet behind me,
and Suzanne's voice: "Hey, change your route?"
15   She is panting. Sweat beads on her nose
and mats her blonde bangs brown.
"Look at this tree," I say feeling stupid.
But she says, "Yeah." And we stand wordless.

I'm watching her watch the tree
20   until she says, "Hey, wanna get ice cream?"
My feet tap, stupid, stupid, stupid, but I
say, "Yes." As we walk toward town,
I slip my fingers into hers, and we stroll
past the post office, like we have never seen it
25   before. At Miller's Dairy, we order

double fudge almond and silently lick the cones
smooth as my tapping feet confess
to her. Suzanne, I have run in circles waiting
for your red shorts to turn the corner. Then I sprint
30   to catch you, only to hang back wordless until
your bouncing blonde hair invites me to join you.
Now, it will be easier to speak.

Here, our writer changes the end of his poem and allows his tapping feet to speak for him. This choice highlights the inability of the young speaker to clearly express his attraction to Suzanne, even after she invites him for ice cream. This direct address decision also points out the shyness that our writer discovered about himself as he reviewed his freewrites. In Writer's Practice 4.3, our writer used the auditory detail of the rhythmic tapping of a runner's feet, allowing the tapping feet to speak. He then used the feet again, this time to confess his feelings. His direct address illustrates how difficult honesty is when one is attracted to a person and yet afraid to take a risk. The confession of a feeling is a powerful, rather than a sentimental, image.

Writer Response Groups

At this point, you have at least a two-part poem. The first part is a focused-lens view into a moment that shows an experience and generates feelings in a reader. In the second part, you have inserted direct address somewhere in the poem that connects the focused-lens view to a meaning. In addition, you have shaped the writing with active verbs and stanzas. Now form a response group of four or five members. Examine each other's poems, reading for the following elements:

Essential Elements

- What is the poem about?
- Who is the speaker?
- How is the poem organized?

Craft

- What feelings are created by the details, actions, images, and comparisons in the focused-lens view?
- Who speaks the direct address? Who listens to the direct address?
- How does the direct address connect to the focused-lens view?

Exploring the Free-Verse Poem

Short lines arranged in stanzas or graphic relationships signal poetry to readers. Sometimes the shape of the line arrangement has significance; for example, concrete poetry represents graphically the meaning of a poem. Thus, a
poem titled "Forsythia" is shaped like a wild forsythia bush. More traditional
forms of poetry such as sonnets, sestinas, and villanelles have strict rules
about line length, syllable counts, and words that end or begin lines. In contrast, most contemporary poets choose to write in free verse. In this form, the
poet conceives a pattern that fits the poem and creates meaning. So, within
the world of poetic decisions, you can create even your poem's shape. What
decisions do you have to make?

Look back at Gary Soto's and Mary Oliver's poems to make a brief decision list.

- **Stanzas:** What obvious stanza decision do these poets make? Both
  poets write a single stanza. Soto has twenty-one lines, and Oliver has
  twelve. This compressed single stanza intensifies the moment and its
  meaning.

- **Line Length:** How long are their lines? Soto's lines are four to nine
  words in length. Most lines contain six words. The shortest line,
  "Fingers of blood lengthening," emphasizes the fantasy power of the
  boy. One of the longest lines, "Her hair mussed, and said, 'Let me
  help you,'" sets up the surprise action of the Grandmother. Oliver's
  lines vary more, ranging from three to eleven words in length. The
  shortest line, "frightened; also capable" creates a powerful contrast felt
  by the speaker as she watches the milkweed. The longest lines: "I wish
  you could walk with me out into the world./I wish you could see what
  has to happen, how" shift the poem from the observation to some
  meaning through direct address.

- **Endings and Beginnings of Lines:** What kinds of words end or
  begin lines? Poets pay attention to the first and last word on a line.
  Ending and beginning the line with strong words is important. Notice
  that Oliver ends most of her lines with two-syllable words, while Soto
  uses predominantly one-syllable words. Soto's one-syllable word endings imitate the powerful fame of the boy, while Oliver's two-syllable
  word endings create a conversational tone supported by the beginning
  of line 5 with "moreover," and again at the beginning of lines 9 and
  10 with "I wish you." This creates a pattern, and anytime a poet creates a pattern an opportunity arises to break the pattern to create
  emphasis. Oliver does this with line 6, ending the line with "also," an
  adverb. This decision emphasizes the milkweed's fear.

Revising to Create a Free-Verse Poem

The number of stanzas and the line breaks are the poet's choice in a free-verse poem. Determining a pattern that creates meaning is also the poet's task. Revising your work to create a free-verse poem will reshape both the poem and its meaning. Flexibility is the key to successful revision, so remain open to new ideas as you work in free verse.

A Bit on Forms

The poems you write for the exercises in this book will most likely be in free verse. *Free verse* is without rhyme or pattern and has lines that vary in length. Poems with predefined patterns and line lengths are called *fixed forms*. Some fixed forms also rhyme.

Popular fixed forms include ghazal, haiku, limerick, pantoum, sestina, sonnet, and villanelle. Fixed forms give poets specific requirements to fulfill when writing. The sonnet, for example, is a fourteen-line lyrical poem containing several specific rhyme schemes and a single emotion or theme. There are different types of sonnets, but all sonnets share those basic characteristics.

Some poets find that the constraints associated with writing fixed-form poems are actually freeing—that the forms lead them to new discoveries. Although beyond the scope of this book, fixed forms are an important aspect of poetry.

Writer's Practice 4.5 *Make Stanza and Line Decisions*

Revise your poem from Writer's Practice 4.3 using a maximum of thirty lines. Make stanza and line break decisions to create a pattern. Focus, too, on line length and line breaks. Consider the following options to determine where to break a line:

- Determine a line length, then make one line shorter or longer for emphasis.
- Emphasize a word by placing it at the beginning or end of a line.
- Conclude the lines with single-syllable words, predominantly nouns or verbs.
- Vary the words at the beginning of a line—the first word is as important as the last.

- Create a surprise by breaking a phrase, placing half on one line and half on the next line.
- Create a pattern, then break it to add emphasis.

As you revise using stanza and line decisions, be sure to address the confusions and suggestions revealed in your Writer Response Group. You may find that the line and stanza decisions help you determine what to add and what to cut. The best place to do line and stanza breaks is on a computer. Type the poem, then use the computer to easily work and rework the lines and stanzas. Spend significant time doing this, creating versions until you develop one that satisfies you. Remember, you are creating meaning and emphasis with the decisions you are making. Although not all readers will notice these decisions, you will shape meaning by deciding consciously how and where to create emphasis.

Begin revising if you feel you are ready, or examine our writer's model and explication.

Our Writer

Tapping Feet

I sprint up Pine Trail hoping I'll
see Suzanne. Tap, tap, tap, gold shoes
against black asphalt. Stupid,
stupid, stupid, they say. Why
5   can't you talk to her? Why can't
you ask: Wanna run together?

As I turn up Snowapple, pain stops me.
Catching my breath, I crouch by a maple
brilliant red, blazing as if the tree
10   were on fire. Then I hear a runner behind me,
"Hey, change your route?" Suzanne pants.
Sweat beads on her nose and mats

her blonde bangs brown. Her red shorts
blend with the maple's fire. "Look
15   at this tree," I say feeling stupid.
But she says, "Yeah." And we stand
wordless. I watch her watch the tree
until she says, "Hey, wanna get ice cream?"

My feet say, stupid, stupid, stupid, but I
20   say, "Yes." As we walk toward town,

I slip my fingers into hers, and we stroll
past the post office, like we have never seen it
before. At Miller's Dairy, we order
double fudge almond and silently lick the cones

25   smooth as my tapping feet confess
to her. Suzanne, I have run in circles waiting
for your red shorts to turn the corner. Then I sprint
to catch you, only to hang back wordless until
your bouncing blonde hair invites me to join you.
30   Now, it will be easier to speak.

Our writer's revision focuses on the single meeting and the speaker's feelings. He uses five consistent six-line stanzas. Notice that he ends stanzas one and three with parallel questions spoken first by the feet and then by Suzanne. The placement of the questions and their parallelism emphasize the inability of the speaker to be assertive. Notice that stanzas two and four extend the sentence across the stanza break, as you learned to do in Writer's Practice 3.4. Also notice that most of the lines break on nouns or verbs. The two lines vary this pattern emphasize important words: "Why" and "until." To accomplish this, our writer had to change the pattern of the phrase "a brilliant red maple" to "a maple / brilliant red." It is attention to details such as these that adds subtle but important meaning to a poem.

Examining Student Poems

Life is less dramatic than many young writers wish to portray it. Surprisingly, using small daily events to generate a poem opens a door to a world of poems. The key is in journaling and in reflecting on the daily while looking for small displays of human nature. The student samples that follow illustrate the success that comes from writing simple poems about daily events attached to honest reflection. In addition, these poems illustrate the range of possibilities when students experiment with free verse and craft a poem with careful attention to line and stanza breaks.

Tinting the Rainbow

JILL ORLER

Nat, why am I here
looking into the mall's refracting pool
searching the remote spaces for
our childhood?

5   Sister, remembering is like squinting
    through a tinted rainbow.
    Red paints mix with blue and yellow
    making dingy brown instead of vibrant purple.

    You and I had our own
10   berry baskets to fill.
    "One for the basket
    One for me
    One for the basket
    Two for me."

15   Making it to the end of the row
    was easy.
    I just made sure all the red ones
    disappeared.
    Your four quart basket
20   toppled over
    with succulent berries. You looked at
    my ruby-stained lips
    with disappointment.
    But you didn't see
25   you may have gotten more berries but
    it was obvious who enjoyed
    the morning's chore.

This poem opens with a two-stanza direct address. Jill's speaker addresses Nat, her sister, in an attempt to understand herself. The direct address also accomplishes several things: (1) it sets the poem in a mall by a pool; (2) it tells readers that there are two people, Nat and the speaker; (3) it establishes the purpose of the poem: a speaker questions her need to clarify a childhood memory. Must she search the past to reassure herself?

Stanza two creates a metaphor that suggests the reason for the speaker's confusion. She expects memory to be clear and vibrant, but her memory is confused into a dingy brown. Jill then shifts time in stanzas three and four to recall a memory that illustrates her point. The memory begins with a focus on berry baskets and the speaker's approach to picking berries. The detail of the speaker's ruby-stained lips illustrates her happiness at having finished off the berries. Nat, on the other hand, sees the value in living for the future, and she dutifully picks the succulent berries to eat later. The memory illustrates the difference between the sisters, and possibly their different approaches toward life. It helps the reader understand that the speaker is searching for herself in that pool. The speaker is trying to understand differences and to arrive at the vibrant purple that a rainbow is supposed to offer. Her poem is really an attempt to clarify the past in a hope to clarify the present.

Jill uses four stanzas that grow longer as the return to memory deepens. She alters her line length several times in the poem, shortening her lines to create the singsong of the young girl picking the berries and eating them. Then, in stanza four, Jill varies the length, creating short lines to emphasize the important details of the memory.

A Smaller Man

TODD BAUER

In the mirror,
    A tall brute looks at me
    Slaps a razor against porcelain
    Knocks whiskers into running water
5   Fingers a shark-tooth necklace.

On a bathroom tile,
    A shifting speck—
    A three-sectored body moves on whisker legs.
    The brute thinks, Ah ha! curious ant
10   No match for a man such as I.

He cripples, then grinds the body,
    Leaves it affixed to the tile,
    Half-living.
    That will show you
15   Not to come into a man's house.

The razor scrapes again at
    Dark rigid hairs.
    Each pass, concise and identical
    Clears paths of foam and
20   Uncovers smoothness.

Then, I see a smaller ant.
    It moves quickly to the corpse
    Senses, pauses, lifts,
    Carries him easily, gently over the tile,
25   Says to me,
    Boy, you do not know your strength.

Todd begins the poem with the words, "In the mirror / A tall brute looks at me," which clarifies that the narrator is telling a first-person account of self-observation. The speaker observes himself in a mirror and describes his image as if he is not connected to it, a decision that implies the novelty and pride the boy takes in his masculinity. His details and verbs tell the story of confused power as a brute of a man, who is actually the speaker reflected in the mirror, kills an ant. The brute wears a shark-toothed necklace; he "slaps a razor," "knocks whiskers," then "cripples, grinds" the ant. The brute feels manly doing such ordinary acts. The delicate ant, however, is stronger and speaks openly in the direct address at the end. The shift to first person in the last stanza illustrates the speaker's return to himself and his realization that he is not yet a man. Notice that Todd created the five-line stanza pattern and then altered it in the last stanza as the ant speaks; this interrupts the narrator's fantasy of manhood in the same way it interrupts the pattern of the poem.

Old Stories

RICHARD SWARTOUT

I reject the nit-picking
charges brought on by tossed clothes,
mixed-up piles of wrinkled plaids and
soiled button-downs littering
5   my bedroom floor and closet shelves.
You extinguish my dreams,
smother every instinct for joy
with unwanted advice;
you snivel hurt feelings
10 thinking only of yourself.
Don't tsk, tsk me.
I listened to all your old sad stories
about the unfairness of
motherhood.
15 I have run out of sympathy.
Mothers should sing
hopeful songs about a
child's future, but you have
taken mine away.

Richard's poem has the flavor of a complete direct address, as a pile of dirty shirts triggers memories of a nit-picking mother. He combines images and dialogue to address a mother who is obsessed with cleanliness and who forgets about the other needs of a child. The speaker feels misunderstood, and the poem speaks out for years of being nit-picked and obedient. The poet uses the direct address to create a monologue aimed at his mother, and possibly all mothers, and demands a reprieve from the mother's selfish ways. Writing this poem in first person allowed the anger of the speaker to come through, clear and unfiltered. Richard pays very close attention to his line breaks, placing at the ends of lines words that he wishes to emphasize. He uses predominantly nouns and verbs to end his lines: "clothes/littering/shelves/dreams/joy/advice/feelings/yourself/me/ stories/motherhood/sympathy/sing." He chose to use a single stanza to speed the poem forward and emphasize the anger of the speaker. He consistently places three or more words on a line until line 14. Here Richard places "motherhood" on a line alone, emphasizing that motherhood is at the center of his complaint.

chapter 5

Mining the Memory: Memory and Imagination, Imagery, and Diction

Perception is the first act of the imagination.
-WILLIAM CARLOS WILLIAMS

For me poems usually begin with "true feelings"—people, experiences, quotes—but quickly ride off into that other territory of imagination which lives alongside us as much as we will allow in a world that likes to pay too much attention to "facts" sometimes.

-NAOMI SHIHAB NYE

A poem is words spoken by an imagined or an actual person, prompted by physical, emotional, mental, or imaginative stirrings. From your work in previous chapters, you learned that seemingly insignificant daily life moments can initiate the emotional stirring that leads to a poem. You have had firsthand experience with creating dramatic situation, dialogue, and a first-person narrator.

In this chapter, you will use your understanding of these aspects of poetry as you explore the writer's entry into memory. As a writer, you will return to places, events, and people to recall both indelible and fuzzy perceptions of your past. Memory will be a mine from which you gather the raw material for your poems. In the explorations ahead, you will learn how to use images from the past as a source for poetic images: the sound of a voice raised in anger, the blurred spokes of a whirling bicycle wheel, the scent of freshly sliced lemons, or the pull of a comb dragging through still-wet hair. Using images as raw material for your writing, you will learn to imagine poems that go beyond memory.

Seamus Heaney and Naomi Shihab Nye use images to perpetuate an experience, possibly autobiographical. The speakers unveil each experience through the senses: sight, taste, touch, smell, and hearing. These rich details recall the memory or create the scene in which the poem exists. Meaning is not the center or destination of these poems. The poems' intrigue comes from the tangible details that bring the experiences to life. How many senses are used in each of the following poems?

Blackberry-Picking

SEAMUS HEANEY

For Philip Hobsbaum

Late August, given heavy rain and sun
For a full week, the blackberries would ripen.
At first, just one, a glossy purple clot
Among others, red, green, hard as a knot.
5   You ate that first one and its flesh was sweet
Like thickened wine: summer's blood was in it
Leaving stains upon the tongue and lust for
Picking. Then red ones inked up and that hunger
Sent us out with milk cans, pea tins, jam pots
10   Where briars scratched and wet grass bleached our boots.
Round hayfields, cornfields and potato drills
We trekked and picked until the cans were full,
Until the tinkling bottom had been covered
With green ones, and on top big dark blobs burned
15   Like a plate of eyes. Our hands were peppered
With thorn pricks, our palms sticky as Bluebeard's.

We hoarded the fresh berries in the byre.
But when the bath was filled we found a fur,
A rat grey fungus, glutting on our cache.
20   The juice was stinking too. Once off the bush
The fruit fermented, the sweet flesh would turn sour.
I always felt like crying. It wasn't fair
That all the lovely canfuls smelt of rot.
Each year I hoped they'd keep, knew they would not.

Questions

1. Who is the speaker?
2. How does the speaker feel about blackberry picking?
3. Which sense is used most?
4. Which line makes the experience tangible?

The Trashpickers, Madison Street

NAOMI SHIHAB NYE

On the edge of dawn's pale eye,
the trashpickers are lifting the lid of every can,
poking inside with bent hanger and stick.
They murmur in a language soft as rags.
5   What have we here?
Their colorless overcoats drift and grow wings.

They pull a creaking wagon, tinfoil wads, knotted string,
to the cave where sacraments of usefulness are performed.
Kneel to the triple weddings of an old nail.
10   Rejoice in the rebirth of envelopes.
The crooked skillet finds its first kingdom
on a shelf where nothing is new.

They dream small dreams, furry ones,
a swatch of velvet passed hand-to-hand.
15   Their hearts are compasses fixed to the ground
and their love, more like moss than fire.

Questions

1. Who is the speaker?
2. How does the speaker feel about the trashpickers?
3. Which sense is used most?
4. Which line makes the experience tangible?

Exploring Memory and Imagination

Memories offer opportunities for hundreds of poems. Learn to use memory effectively, and every sound, smell, taste, color, and itch will return exactly as it was experienced: you are back in kindergarten, sheets of heavy orange construction paper on the table and globs of white paste stuck to your fingers. Sometimes, the memories return as empty frames—the emotional experience is powerful, but the facts of the event are fuzzy. But whether vivid or sketchy, memory is deepened when the poet works imagination side by side with fact.

Many practicing writers develop their memory muscles by doing writing that returns memory to them. They keep journals. They write down their dreams every morning. They freewrite and use free association to startle memories from their resting places. If you don't have writing exercises like these in your routine, you may be depriving yourself of an important source of material. The goal of this sort of writing exercise is to gain flexibility and fluency to permit a writer to generate quickly and with ease.

A writer cannot be concerned with the facts—even when the material is autobiographical. Therefore, if you can't remember your childhood friend's name, make it up. If you can't remember what you got from Aunt Gertrude for your tenth birthday, make it up. If you like the imagined detail better than the "truth," go with the imagined detail and adjust your memory. For the creative writer, interesting writing is preferable to allegiance to the "truth."

As you mine your memory, you may find repeating feelings or attitudes. Use these reappearing recollections to explore deeper memories or to study human nature. Ask yourself questions: Why do I always feel cheated when I think about my sister? Why does my dog appear in my memories again and again? Who kept me from taking risks as a kid? Was there a cost for being good? You can use the answers that you find to create a poem.

Seamus Heaney draws the reader into his poem with the memory of a ripened blackberry. He sets the scene—"August," "heavy rain," and "sun"— and then multiplies the power of rain and sun with the words "For a full week." The reader knows that gifts of good weather, berry-making weather, and the expectation of good berries are rewarded with the visual and tactile images in the next two lines:

> At first, just one, a glossy purple clot
> Among others, red, green, hard as a knot.

From this concrete beginning, the memory of blackberry picking unravels, leading to the joy and frenzy of the picking as well as the disappointment when the berries so easily rot. The reader feels, sees, tastes, smells, and hears the experience, understanding the perceptions of the speaker.

Naomi Shihab Nye paints an unlikely canvas: trashpickers. She mixes images and metaphor, piling them up one by one. The metaphoric image of "dawn's pale eye" ushers the reader into the experience. Then visual images and an auditory metaphor establish the scene:

the trashpickers are lifting the lid of every can,
poking inside with bent hanger and stick.
They murmur in a language soft as rags.

The speaker clarifies the picture of people "lifting lids" with a "bent hanger and stick" by asking "What have we here?" The answer captures the experience with a kind of reverence. The speaker's perceptions control the images and thus the feeling of the poem.

Experimenting with Memory and Imagination

Many students claim that they remember very little. Probably that should not be surprising, since most are preoccupied with the present and the future more than with the past. It takes practice to delve into memory, but the rewards for the writer are great.

Writer's Practice 5.1 *Loosen Memory and Imagination*

Freewrite for five to ten minutes every day for the next four days. It is important to write on four separate days in order to accomplish several things. First, you will develop your memory muscles, making recalling memories easier each time you try to do so. Second, you will develop your imagination as you invent details to flesh out memories. Third, you will unwittingly develop a theme in your writings. Although you may not realize it at first, writers who write regularly from memory often find that memories return to them in connected clumps. This can be useful, because writers seek relationships among their memories. Often, a relationship or recurring theme among your memories will point you in the direction of an interesting poem.

Use the starters that follow to nudge your memory and open the door to imagination. When you run out of things to write, simply repeat the starter. In your writing, try to recover the sights, sounds, smells, feelings, and tastes of the past. Try to locate yourself in a singular place and moment in time. This is exploratory, rather than purposeful, writing, so approach it as a form of excavation in which retrieval of one detail leads to another.

- When I was a kid . . .
- One time I went . . .
- I was always afraid of . . .
- A good place to hide was . . .
- A house I loved to visit . . .

- I wasn't supposed to . . .
- I felt free when I . . .
- I felt strange around . . .
- I loved to wear . . .
- I am _____ and _____ . . .

Start by recalling holidays, birthdays, celebrations, and other childhood events. Then work for memories of ordinary days—events that will yield simple moments that lend themselves so well to exploration in a poem.

Begin writing if you feel you are ready, or examine our writer's model and explication.

Our Writer

#1   One time I went to a birthday party that wasn't for one of my cousins. My mom forced me to wear a white shirt. "It's a party," she kept saying as she buttoned the top button. I arrived last. Five other boys were all sitting on a flowered sofa, pressed together like white peas. I squeezed onto one end and Denny's mother took a picture of us before we went outside. We played musical chairs, and I beat Billy to the last chair, squeezing him off the edge. I lost at pin-the-tail-on-the-donkey, poking my tail into the rough bark of Denny's apple tree. I played in the sandbox, pulling my hands clean across the white front of my shirt. I don't remember what I gave Denny. I just remember his cake with blue roses along the edge. I dragged my finger along the back of the cake and let the frosting, sweet and creamy, melt on my tongue. One time I had a birthday party, but nobody came. We invited kids, but they were all gone on vacation. That's the trouble with being born on a holiday. Nobody is ever home. Mom says I shouldn't feel that way since I'm the only kid that has fireworks for his birthday, but they don't do that just for me. My party was all bad; my cousins came. They always came because my cousin Roxie was born the day after me. We shared our birthday parties. Actually, I hated sharing my birthdays with Roxie and I really hated it that day. I got a Superman lunch box from Roxie. I grabbed the box and leaped in a single bound over my cake before Mom yelled at me to stop. I don't remember what I gave Roxie, but I'll bet it was a doll in a pink dress, somethin' girly that mom bought.

#2   I was always afraid of the house next to Wethernon's. An old lady lived there alone. Her gray hair wild as she sang in her yard tending nothing. Her grass was overgrown, weeds sprawling between the cracks in her sidewalk. Her bushes hid the front windows. The interior view blocked by white lace curtains that looked like cobwebs. I raced past the house watching it as if she would leap out of the gray peeling fence. We called her "witch woman." I swear I heard her cackling, rolling her knuckles in her palms. Fat, black bumble bees swarmed on Wethernon's side of the fence, but not one ventured to the witch's bushes. I was always afraid of the Ammenson's dog, a black terrier with a pinched snout and sharp white teeth. I never got close enough to smell its doggy breath, but I heard its snapping as I walked by. The alley, a short-cut to Carl's, took me within chomping distance of that dog. I never passed the house without that black monster charging the fence, throwing his body against the chain link, bouncing off, his toenails raking the metal, angry growls and whining barks. When I got to Carl's we made a castle from kitchen chairs, pulled branches off the willow tree and dueled to the death. His mother canned in the summer and the kitchen always smelled of corn or tomatoes. Rows of mason jars, their blue emptiness waiting, lined the counters. I loved eating lunch there, soft white bread and peanut butter. It stuck to the roof of my mouth and I couldn't talk or laugh without snorting peanut butter. We'd make milk mustaches.

#3   When I was a kid I lived down the street from Denny Leman, a kid with asthma who fell in the river once or twice a week. He was my very best friend of all time. We slept outside together in our tent, we slept on the floor of his basement, we slept in our living rooms. We slept in sleeping bags and he always brought his foam pillow because he had asthma. He had a distinctive smell. He smelled like a laundry room. When I was a kid I walked all over town with Denny Leman, spending the money we earned returning bottles to buy RC colas and Snickers and Twinkies. We sat on the grass in front of the fire station, on a cement pad across the street from Viola Hendrix's spooky white house. When I was a kid they hauled in a water tower in pieces and put it together right there by the fire station, right next to Squeak Nokys's house. The tower was the color of dried blood, until they painted it all assembled, painted it a sick green. I thought it would be silver, like any self-respecting water tower ought to be. With the name of our town written in tall black letters. When I was a kid I wasn't afraid very much. I was confused a lot of the time but not particularly afraid. I had great friends. I don't think I knew it at the time.

#4   I am fifteen, and still learning. No one tells us to do it. Our accomplice, the willow, is just there. One branch at a time is easy. Smooth bark warmed by the sun. Dry leaves are the color of your hair. I go first, find a foothold, then you. Your hand fits in mine. Across the road, over ruined fields, gulls dip to the year-old corn. We still think it's going to be easy, a good story to tell our friends. From the horizon starts a wave of starlings, birds no one has ever thought well of. While we sit together, the flock eventually finds us, creating a tree full of dark confetti. You mock their song. I clap them away. We both climb down laughing, certain those crazy birds know nothing. Later, we sift

through a broken cigar box, one hinge swinging. You lift my grandmother's
pearl necklace in your hands. I barely breathe. You push past a few screws,
three blue buttons, a gold ring, its initials worn away, a leather bracelet with a
silver clasp, photographs and letters, safety pins—in an attempt to discover
who I am as if all my secrets are saved in this box. And I have no answers
when you ask, Why?

Three freewrites repeat the starter to keep themselves going. They use
the senses to recall people, places, and emotions. Freewrite #1 stays close
to the starter, remembering two different parties. Freewrites #2 and #3
leave the starter and allow a new and unrelated memory to surface. This is
free association at work. For example, you may begin writing about frightening moments and end up writing about happy ones. Be open to memories that pop into your writing. In freewrite #3, free association works to
propel the writing: sitting on the grass in front of the fire station causes the
writer to remember the water tower hauled to town in pieces, the color of
dried blood, and assembled on that familiar spot. The writing is a casual
recollection, a searching. Jotting down scraps of memory, the writer
accepts what comes.

Notice that all four freewrites are about friends. In freewrite #3, our
writer states, "I had great friends. I don't think I knew it at the time." This
interesting discovery might never have surfaced if the writer hadn't written repeatedly from memories. Freewrite #4 begins with an age and then
makes a comment on it: the writer is fifteen, and he has a lot to learn. He
intentionally explores the topic of important friendships discovered in
freewrite #3 and then leaps to other childhood relationships.

Telling It Another Way

Your freewrites may lead you to additional poems. Go back to these freewrites
and reread what you wrote. What other images seem strong? What experiences do these objects recall? What dramatic situations come to mind?

As you work through this exercise, and other exercises in this book,
remember that the experiments are intended to be repeated. Your material is
rich enough, and your imagination fertile enough, that you will probably
write enough to get more than one poem from each exercise.

So hang on to those freewrites for another day.

Exploring Imagery

William Carlos Williams wrote at a time when poets were very serious
about the imagery in their poems—so serious, in fact, that they called
themselves "imagists." They tried to squeeze everything out of their

poetry except the powerful image. "No ideas but in things," Williams said. That is, no ideas, no powerful emotions, no meaning existed except as expressed in images or things. Why? Concentration on the image is an attempt to make writing more like other art forms. A painting can't explain itself the way a poem can. The human form in a sculpture can't open its mouth and say, "On my face there is a look of ecstasy, but be sure to look at my hands, which show the human suffering that comes from years of manual labor." Only poems and stories have speakers who can explain themselves. In the case of inexperienced writers, these voices almost always say too much. They sometimes tell the reader what to think and feel. They talk about meaning. Williams liked to let the images speak for him. Here is one of his most famous poems:

The Red Wheelbarrow

William Carlos Williams

so much depends
upon

a red wheel
barrow

5   glazed with rain
water

beside the white
chickens

On the surface it seems as if the poem doesn't say anything. Looking deeper, the reader sees that the poem consists of four two-line stanzas. In each stanza, three words are followed by one word. In three of four stanzas, a concrete image is completed in the one-word lines: "barrow," "water," "chickens." Put together, these three stanzas enable the reader to see and feel one image clearly. The words and images are as primary and direct as perception itself. In contrast to these images, however, is the very insistent first stanza: "so much depends / upon." The first line promises to make a meaningful statement. There is the familiar human voice telling the reader something, but then the message disappears. This speaker doesn't complete the initial thought or explain what the poem means. In fact, the images *are* the point; they are the poem's only meaning.

Prompted to Write

Tangible writing prompts are another way to experiment with memory and imagery. Doing a focused freewrite on an object can generate wonderful material for poems. The object might be something that you own or something with personal significance, or it might be the bird feeder in your neighbor's backyard or a piece of art on display at your local library.

Freewriting on an object can take you to forgotten places. A bowl of strawberries might lead to memories of picking strawberries with your grandmother and falling asleep in the field or having a crush on the boy next door, who had a strawberry patch in his backyard.

The trick is to begin by focusing on the object but then let the freewrite go.

Seamus Heaney uses images to accomplish his poem's meaning, as well. His poem is filled with the pictures of ripening fruit ("Then red ones inked up"); the sights and sounds of berry-picking ("wet grass bleached our boots" and "Until the tinkling bottom had been covered / With green ones, and on top big dark blobs"); and finally the disappointment ("we found a fur, / A rat grey fungus, glutting on our cache"). The description compels the speaker to say:

> I always felt like crying. It wasn't fair
> That all the lovely canfuls smelt of rot.
> Each year I hoped they'd keep, knew they would not.

His emotional comments seem genuinely stimulated by the speaker's memory. The simple perceptions are generated by the inevitable disappointment that follows the ecstasy of the harvest.

Naomi Shihab Nye's speaker asserts her joyous perceptions of trashpickers throughout the poem. She sprinkles the poem with "sacraments," "weddings," "Rejoice," rebirth," and "first kingdom," which transform images of a "crooked skillet," a discarded "envelope," and "a creaking wagon, tinfoil wads, knotted string" into wondrous treasures. Her final stanza comments on the sight and portrays the speaker's awe:

> They dream small dreams, furry ones,
> a swatch of velvet passed hand-to-hand.
> Their hearts are compasses fixed to the ground
> and their love, more like moss than fire.

Again, it is her unexpected word choice that clearly conveys the perceptions of the speaker: "Their hearts are compasses" demonstrates the emotional attachments that urge the trashpickers forward with "bent hanger and stick."

Experimenting with Imagery

You have mined your memory, possibly allowing imagination to flesh out your recollections. The next step is to craft that memory into a poem. The pitfall that novice writers must seek to avoid at this stage is the desire to explain what a remembered experience meant.

Don't explain. Don't tell the reader the meaning of your words. Poems are written to convey actual experience as directly as possible. Although meaning may spring from the perceptions shared by a speaker, that speaker should not be waiting in the wings to tell the reader "and so I realize now what all this meant." Instead, let imagery communicate the meaning. As Williams does, let the images speak for themselves.

Writer's Practice 5.2   *Craft an Imagery Poem*

Take the images that your memory offered you and retell the memory as simply as possible, using as many images as possible. Be open to imagination, allowing new and interesting images to appear in your poem. Remember, do not feel obliged to portray the "truth":

- Pack the poem with images that use multiple senses: sight, hearing, taste, touch, smell.
- Use the images to introduce actions, details, and emotions.
- Repeat or echo an image.

Begin writing if you feel you are ready, or examine our writer's model and explication. The poem that you write should be twenty to fifty lines in length.

Our Writer

I am fifteen and still learning.
One branch at a time is easy.

Smooth bark warmed by the sun.
I go first, find a knobby foothold, then you.
5   Your slim fingers fit in mine.
The dry leaves are the color of your hair.
Across the road, over ruined fields,
gulls dip to year-old corn.
From the horizon a black wave
10   of starlings turns, beating
their wings against the blue sky.
While we press together
the flock finds us, filling the tree with
dark confetti. Certain those crazy birds
15   know nothing, you mock their song,
I clap them away. Later, we sift
through a broken cigar box,
one hinge swinging. You lift
my grandmother's black beads in your hands,
20   starlings roosting on smooth arms.
I barely breathe. You push past
a few silver screws, three blue and gold buttons,
a gold wedding ring, its initials worn away,
a leather identification bracelet with silver clasp,
25   photographs and letters, silver safety pins—
in an attempt to discover who I am as if
all my secrets are saved in this box. And I
have no answers when you ask, "Why?"

How many images retell the memory? The images become the heart of the poem. Notice the repetition: "a black wave / of starlings," "filling the tree with / dark confetti," and, finally, "my grandmother's black beads in your hands, / starlings roosting on smooth arms." The repetition of black images could suggest death. Is their love doomed? Does their story have a bad ending? They know only that they have had a premonition of sorts, "Certain those crazy birds / know nothing," and the speaker claps them away. Following Williams's lead, "No ideas but in things," the writer does not state the poem's meaning. He doesn't say, "That afternoon we were really in love, but it didn't last." Instead, our writer builds impending doom through the images of shared cigar box treasures. Notice that our writer changed the grandmother's necklace from pearl to black beads. This imagined necklace enables him to increase the premonition of a doomed relationship.

Writer Response Groups

At this point you have a poem filled with images that retell a memory. You deliberately avoided explaining the meaning of this collection of images, although you may have inserted imagined details and lines that portray emotions. You have paid close attention to images and inserted multiple senses. Your work has action, detail, and emotion, and you have selected a single image to repeat or echo in the poem. Perhaps you do not know yet what the poem means. Remember, though, that meaning will spring from the images if they become clear. Now form a response group of four or five members. Examine each other's poems, reading for the following elements:

Essential Elements

- What is the poem about?
- Who is the speaker?
- How is the poem organized?

Craft

- Which images instigate feelings? What senses do they use?
- Is an image repeated? What does the repetition suggest?
- What is the speaker's emotional reaction?

Revising with a Careful Eye on Diction

Aiming for the precise image when you write also requires that you think carefully about word choice. There is a difference between a tree and a willow tree, a bird and a starling, a knickknack and a chipped brown coffee mug from Niagara Falls. Similarly, there is a difference between sitting and slouching, between opening a door and flinging a door open. The words we choose can express a vague description of things and actions or a very specific description. Try to fill up a poem with sensory detail, that is, choose words that appeal more directly to the senses. Consider this example from Nye's poem:

> On the edge of dawn's pale eye,
> the trashpickers are lifting the lid of every can,
> poking inside with bent hanger and stick.

They murmur in a language soft as rags.
What have we here?
Their colorless overcoats drift and grow wings.

The first three lines convey a clear image—trashpickers making their rounds. In the course of the poem, these unlikely subjects take on angelic qualities and share in a joyful experience. Nye's word choice conveys not only the direct sensory experience of touching what has been thrown away, but also the larger human experience of ritual and discovery and joy. We see the human characters "poking inside with bent hanger and stick." Thank goodness for "poking," a good active verb, and for "bent hanger." We know how useless a bent hanger is, and how easily it is cast aside, like the "tinfoil wads," "knotted string," and "the crooked skillet." This is the specific diction of trash. These images are connected in stanza three to "small dreams, furry ones, / a swatch of velvet passed hand-to-hand."

The emotional significance of blackberry picking is also conveyed through careful and deliberate diction. Heaney describes the blackberry as "a glossy purple clot," "red ones inked up," and "big dark blobs," which the speaker greedily picked. This description is contrasted by the images of disappointment: "a fur," "A rat grey fungus," and "The juice was stinking too." These images prepare the reader for the speaker's emotional reaction: "I always felt like crying. It wasn't fair."

Writer's Practice 5.3 *Create an Emotional Experience*

You have learned that carefully chosen images can portray emotions. The reader sees the images through the diction that a poet uses to create a world. In choosing the words to craft a poem, a writer must conduct a critical examination: Are my words specific and concrete? Do my words portray an emotion and evoke an emotional response from my reader? This exercise requires you to love your current draft less and to love the possibilities for its improvement more. Be careful, however, that you don't become overzealous in your intent to improve diction. A poem overloaded with "fancy" words is not the way to achieve image clarity. Instead, to express an emotion using images, consider the following suggestions:

• Focus on nouns. If you have to add two or three adjectives to a noun to make it clear and specific, chances are you have chosen a weak noun.

• Make your verbs active. If you must add adverbs to create powerful actions, you probably have selected a weak verb. Try to avoid adverbs. Recall your work on "muscular" verbs in Writer's Practice 2.5.

- Repeat important words. Consider repeating a color or an object.
- Show sound. Consider using *onomatopoeia*—words that imitate a sound. *Buzz* or *whoosh* are examples.

Revise your poem using quality diction as a guide. Be open to adding or cutting whole lines or sentences. You may find that altering diction requires you to move lines around and drop or add details.

Begin revising if you feel you are ready, or examine our writer's model and explication.

Our Writer

What We Save

One branch at a time is easy.
Smooth bark warmed by the sun,
I go first, find a foothold,
then you. Your slender hand
5   fits in mine. Dry leaves
the color of your hair
rustle above us. Across the road,
gulls dip to the corn's brown stubble.
From the horizon a black wave
10   of starlings beats against blue sky.
While we press together, the flock
fills the tree with dark confetti.
Certain those crazy birds know
nothing, you mock their song.
15   I clap them away as we climb
down escaping their chatter.
Later, we sift through a broken cigar box,
one hinge swinging. You push past
a few screws, three blue buttons,
20   a gold ring, its initials worn away,
a leather bracelet with silver clasp,
photographs and letters, safety pins—
in an attempt to discover who I am as if
all my secrets are saved in this box.
25   "Why?" you say, touching a rock
white as bread dough and shaped like a
Russian teacake. Unable to remember
which lake it came from, I think about what we save.
You lift my grandmother's black beads,

30   starlings roosting on your smooth arms.
I barely breathe, sure now what we save
saves us. Careful to avoid my eyes,
you ask, "And this?" But I have no answers.
I am fifteen and still learning.

Attention to diction and the use of precise nouns and minimal adjectives changed our writer's poem considerably. He moved many lines to clarify the story of the budding romance and added dialogue to highlight the young girl's curiosity as well as timidness at wanting to know the speaker's secrets. The speaker shares his understanding that what we save is somehow important: "what we save saves us." The tension of a doomed relationship is removed, leaving only the intimacy of the sharing. What diction changes create the intimate and tender moment? Comparing the poem shown in Writer's Practice 5.2 with this revision, note that "slim fingers" was changed to "slender hand," making the girl seem delicate. The girlfriend's questions also add intimacy, since she wants to understand the speaker through the things he has saved. The timidness of the girlfriend is illustrated with a single phrase: "careful to avoid my eyes." The speaker inherently knows that awkwardness is expected in the young and inexperienced. He has learned how to climb a tree: "One branch at a time is easy." He closes by acknowledging that he has more to learn: "But I have no answers. / I am fifteen and still learning."

Notice the changes that our writer made in revising the poem from Writer's Practice 5.2:

> You push past
> a few screws, three blue buttons,
> a gold ring, its initials worn away,
> a leather bracelet with silver clasp,
> photographs and letters, safety pins

He removed many adjectives, simplifying the image of the items in the cigar box. He also added description, replacing "year-old corn" with "the corn's brown stubble." This change more clearly creates a picture of cornfields in the fall. The word "stubble" suggests that the field has been cut.

Examining Student Poems

This chapter explored strategies to mine memory and techniques to invent images that express ideas. Using the strategies discussed, our writers took images from the past and made them the source for real and imagined poetic images that they used to express emotions. As you read the student poems that follow, pay particular attention to the precise diction the poems contain. Given his statement, "No ideas but in things," how would William Carlos Williams respond to the following poems?

Summer's Call

ASHLEY HALLERAN

On summer's first bright day,
I spread my purple towel
with shining silver stars.
I kick pink jelly shoes into the air,
5   shed a long terry cover-up.
My purple and orange bathing suit
comes alive, ruffled leg holes
waving in sea breeze. I leave
the picnic basket filled with ham
10   sandwiches on Wonder bread, red
Faygo pop, and licorice to melt, and I
stumble through burning sand, to cross
the boundary where liquid meets solid.
When the water is not so cold,
15   I like to run in as fast as I can
like the people in Juicy Fruit commercials,
but today the water is dark blue,
icy cold. I grasp at the wet earth resisting
the tide with my toes. Muddy sand slips
20   through creviced feet. Depth by depth I numb
my ankles, knees, waist. The tide
pulls, but I tiptoe deeper holding my arms
in the air until frigid water invades
my sweaty armpits, slipping over my shoulders,
25   teasing hairs at the nape of my neck.
Pleased with my self-control, I concede
and dunk my head. Swimming alone,
I am free in summer's wild sea.

Ashley describes in specific images the joy of the first swim of the summer. The details in her poem capture her personal relationship with the sea: she likes to run in quickly, having seen this on television; she looks forward to her first daring plunge. The sea calls to her, and she has consistent memories and rituals associated with this first joyful swim. Her specific visual and tactile images of the towel, shoes, cover-up, and lunch create the sense of anticipated

ritual. She continues with controlled and precise nouns and verbs to chronicle her slow walk into the sea. Her self-control contrasts the sea's wildness,
pulling at her as a willing partner in a game anticipated with equal joy.

Perched by Golden Flame

GEOFFREY DENSTAEDT

All that's left is a tattered poncho holder,
blue ink smudged across once readable
lettering. One size fits all, the only words
left. A reminder of past summer
5   camps and fickle weather.

It rained on Thursdays.
The best kept tradition at camp.
Why? No one knew.
I'm sure Spunky ordered the rain
10   so he could sing songs
like "The Star Wars Cantina"
or "They Might Be Giants."
Yawn was how we started each day,
stumbling into the mess hall,
15   clank, clank, dunk, silverware
and cheap plastic pitchers.
Lunch was a humid, cloudy, tired hour.
Rumble, rumble, crash.
Clouds spewed Thursday's addition
20   to our camping experience.
We ran for ponchos,
hoped it wouldn't rain
out the overnighter.
Wilderness survival, the only time
25   like owls we perched by golden flame.
I really didn't mind the rain.
July rain is always warm. Content,
I walked the sandy road to the lake.
My poncho dragged against my heels.

30   This year's different. No more scout
fleur-de-lis, just a regular blue
melt-into-the-crowd poncho. No more
fires at wilderness survival, no more Spunky,
no running back to camp, and no rain on Thursday.

35   When it rains, I sit under the tent fly and talk.
     The weather changes. Everything does.

Geoffrey captures the boy scout camper's experience with his images, alliteration, and precise nouns and verbs. The poem begins with an image of an old poncho-holder, which stirs a memory of a rainy summer at boy scout camp. The poncho appears two more times in the poem, reminding the speaker of familiarity and companionship even when it is replaced in the last stanza by a "regular blue melt-into-the-crowd poncho." Although the poncho initiates and concludes the poem, it is the middle stanza that creates the fond attachment to camp and makes the simple wisdom of the last sentence meaningful. The sense of sound is appealed to here, with the onomatopoeia "clank, clank, dunk," and "rumble, rumble, crash." In the last few lines, the poncho disappears, replaced by a tent fly. The speaker learns from this simple memory that, like the weather, life changes with time.

Yesterday's King Salmon

Susan Golab

Twirling coffee steam forms
water droplets on my cheeks.
Before me a never-ending
cloudless blue frames
5   snow caps. Ankles crossed,
head cradled in his hands,
he chews the meat of white
clover, says, "I could climb it."
I think of yesterday's King Salmon
10   hanging from a hook,
hints of gold and emerald in her scales.
Two scarlet drops traced once-powerful fins,
drizzled to a puddle of darkening red.
Her sliced-open belly revealed ruby
15   marbles of unborn life. He told me:
"The meat is only good
before she lays her eggs." And
today we sit gazing
on muted green carpet
20   a footstep could crush for twenty years.
I crumble brittle blades of tundra,
release the dead particles to the wind.
He will never make it up the mountain,
but I will hold his footprint for a lifetime.

Susan uses color in this visual poem. Descriptions with blue, white, gold, emerald, and scarlet paint a landscape that suggests the vibrant relationship between the man and the woman. Repeated words compare the woman and the tundra: both may appear fragile, but both endure. The speaker deepens the sense that relationships are fragile with the image of the salmon, filled with eggs and hanging from a hook. It is the contrast between the fragile and the enduring that makes the speaker's statement more powerful: "I will hold his footprint for a lifetime."

chapter 6

Creating the Illogical World: Imagination, Third-Person Point of View, and Line Break

When you start to write, you carry to the page one of two
attitudes, though you may not be aware of it.
One is that all music must conform to truth.
The other, that all truth must conform to music.
If you believe the first, you are making your job very difficult.

-RICHARD HUGO

Many writers sit down to write with the intention of telling the truth. They begin with meanings they want to explore: *This is how I felt when my brother ran away from home. This is what it meant when our great oak tree was cut down.* Richard Hugo says that writers who adopt this approach are those who want the music to fit the truth. Thus, these writers are forced to find words that convey their personal truths precisely, or the writers feel disappointed. In fact, frequently they *are* disappointed. Their writing seems to fall short in expressing the actual experience and the associated truth.

Ironically, writers who give up the notion of recapturing deep meaning and concentrate instead on exploring possibilities are better pleased with the results. In the previous chapter, you dabbled in invention, perhaps adding details that were not true in the literal sense. To do so was a bold decision and, most likely, a liberating one. In using imagination to think beyond actual experience, you created *possible* experience.

In this chapter, you will move further into the domain of imagination. In these imaginative, even unreal, worlds, laws of science may be broken in order to magnify the truth of the human heart. In addition, you will experiment with dialogue and third-person point of view. Finally, you will focus on the poetic line.

In the poems that follow, Russell Edson and Charles Baxter use imagination to create the strange worlds in which the poems exist. As you read, notice that meaning is not the center or the destination of these poems; rather, the poems are fascinated with the imagined experience and somehow make sense of the nonsensical.

The Father of Toads

RUSSELL EDSON

A man had just delivered a toad from his wife's armpit. He held it by its legs and spanked it.

Do you love it? said his wife.

It's our child, isn't it?

Does that mean you can't love it? she said.

5   It's hard enough to love a toad, but when it turns out to be your own son then revulsion is without any tender inhibition, he said.

Do you mean you would not like to call it George Jr.? she said.

But we've already called the other toad that, he said.

Well, perhaps we could call the other one George Sr., she said.

But I am George Sr., he said.

10 Well, perhaps if you hid in the attic, so that no one needed to call you anything, there would be no difficulty in calling both of them George, she said.

Yes, if no one talks to me, then what need have I for a name? he said.

No, no one will talk to you for the rest of your life. And when we bury you we shall put *Father of Toads* on your tombstone.

Questions

1. What details situate this poem in a strange world?

2. What details make the world seem logical?

3. How does the dialogue characterize the husband and his wife?

4. Although the poem has no clearly stated meaning, what meaning does it have for you?

Translation from an Unknown Language:
The Man Who Sold His Bed

CHARLES BAXTER

In a single village like this
where ideas run loose, our red-headed man
learned how to skip sleep: he sold his bed
and stood all night counting out stars,
5   beginning his sum in the west
where our mountains leap into darkness,
and ending his count in the east
where the sky falls dead into the roofs.
Every night he planted himself like a statue
10   in another man's yard, raising his head
before his lips began trembling with numbers.
The children called him the star hermit
and knotted his shoelaces together.
At dawn he'd sigh loudly to wake us.
15   When he was old and in bed, and he knew
how hard we would pay attention to him
he said there were over two thousand
thousand stars, and they talked in vibrations.
He said he'd picked up the language,
20   but with all of his listening, no star
would talk sense: most of them
had insane schemes about darkness
and each one thought he was God.
"The stars," he whispered, "are a mistake.
25   *They are such unbelievable criminals."*

Questions

1. What details situate this poem in a strange world?
2. What details make the world seem logical?
3. How does the man who sold his bed become wise for the townspeople?
4. Although the poem has no clearly stated meaning, what meaning does it have for you?

Exploring Imagination

Writers tied to telling the truth set forth with a mistaken idea of what a poet does. Writing a poem gives a poet an opportunity to say something that is not altogether true. Hugo suggests that it is better to make truth fit your music. In other words, you shouldn't worry so much about the truth of what you write. Instead, focus keenly on the words and let the *poem's* meaning come. To make his point, Hugo asks us to think about two towns: the hometown where a poem is generated and the strange town where the poem must find itself. He recommends that we write our poems in the strange town, and that we bring along our loved ones and show them around the town as if it were not strange at all. This allows the poet to be disloyal to truth, while imagining from a base of reality. Freedom comes when the writer takes emotional possession of some other town where anything can happen.

Russell Edson drops the reader into a strange town, yet logical remnants of reality can be found there. Look closely at how Edson entices the reader into the poem with strangeness, then contrasts it with logic:

> A man had just delivered a toad from his wife's armpit. He held it by its legs and spanked it.
> Do you love it? said his wife.

This beginning creates two expectations for the reader. First, the poem will live in an unreal world; second, the poem will be inhabited by people who behave in a logical way, as if the world were not unreal. For the reader to remain engaged, Edson must follow through on these two expectations. In addition, he must deliver one more thing: wisdom. The reader is willing to accept the unreal if there is a payoff—a reason to play along. The reader expects to gain some degree of enlightenment.

Does Edson deliver? Yes, on all three counts. First, the poem lives in an unreal world. The wife expects the husband to give his name to the toad sons. She wants the husband to hide in the attic so this can be accomplished. No one will talk to him. By any standards, this is an unreasonable suggestion, but, true to the unreasonable premise of the poem, the husband agrees.

Second, the inhabitants of this unreal world behave logically. The struggle to name a child, the examination of a husband's place after the birth of sons, the expectation of changing roles, as well as the difficulty of accepting these changes—these are all logical manifestations that could be played out in any hospital nursery anywhere. The poet does not opt for a recognizable hometown. He takes the reader to an unreal world where a man has lost his identity to two sons. His gravestone will read "Father of Toads."

The wisdom in this poem is delivered as the poem dramatizes how couples handle difficult developments in their lives. The uneasy maneuvering and confused expectations between husband and wife after the birth of a child are real. Further, Edson does not solve the frog couple's problem. He only drops the reader into the discussion that possibly is unfinished. This treatment is true to the way such problems play out in reality.

In the same way, Charles Baxter creates a town that seems like something out of a fable:

In a single village like this
where ideas run loose, our red-headed man
learned how to skip sleep: he sold his bed
and stood all night counting out stars,

The opening presents the poem's strange premise. The story that follows maintains the strangeness with the artifacts of a typical village's reactions: a red-headed man skips sleep, attempts the impossible, dares to be ridiculous, suffers the ridicule of children, eventually earns respect, and tells what he has learned about stars and about the cosmos. Though not altogether true, it is somehow believable and seems beautifully made up.

What about the reader's expectations? Does Baxter deliver the contrast of logical behavior in an unreal world to engage the reader and enable wisdom to surface? Certainly, the world is unreal. The red-haired man lives without sleep. He stands in another man's yard like a statue, counting the stars all night, waking people at dawn with his sighs. Despite this futile task he sets for himself, the townspeople accept him.

Second, the inhabitants of this unreal town act logically. Isn't it logical to sell your bed if you plan to give up sleep? Also, like children everywhere, those in this made-up town tease the red-haired man for being odd, calling him "star hermit" as they knot his shoelaces together. Still, when he is old, people pay attention to what he has to say.

How, then, is wisdom revealed? It may be that we all are guilty of acting as if our knowing is deeper and wider than that of others, and that we all make mistakes. The man who gives up sleep learns this wisdom from the stars: "most of them / had insane schemes about darkness / and each one thought he was God."

What do these poems have in common? Using multiple characters and dialogue, both poems tell a story. Both poems have numerous references to the natural world and to the characters who inhabit that world. Finally, both poems deliver wisdom as they contrast the unreal with the logical.

Experimenting with Imagination

It is time, as a poet, to take a risk. Go to a strange town and imagine a dreamlike setting and unreal actions involving characters you may or may not know. In the process, use what you know about concrete images to invoke the dreamlike place and let these images and the language suggest the poem's meaning. Do not plan what the poem means. Instead, allow the action of exploring a strange place to invent meaning. If you do not know what your poem means at the end of the writing, do not worry. Remember, meaning is not the focus of this early experiment in imagination.

Writer's Practice 6.1 *Write a Collaborative Poem*

Do the following exercise with three or four classmates. Write a collaborative poem by passing a piece of paper around the group, moving it on to the next person sentence by sentence. Your group's objective is to create an unreal situation in which the people behave in a logical way. Maybe your poem will arrive at a kind of wisdom—but don't make that the focus. Also, encourage each group member to add a personal twist to the story. This will help you to loosen up and allow your imagination to invent the poem.

In writing, you will use an inventive approach in which you use language threads to propel your sentences. A *language thread* is a word, image, or idea that is repeated, or threaded, through a poem or story. You have already done some writing that involved the language thread concept: in Writer's Practice 5.2, you experimented with echoing an image.

In using this inventive approach, the following rules apply to each group member:

* Add a single sentence.
* Create and follow a language thread through the poem. Use the words made available to you by the previous writer to suggest the next sentence.
* Insert dialogue. Allow your characters to speak. Their speech will create logical reactions to illogical circumstances.

Start a poem by borrowing one of the following first sentences. The first two are by Stephen Dobyns, and the last two are by David James:

1. A child is born with a third eye smack in the middle of his forehead.

2. A man eats a chicken every day for lunch, and each day the ghost of another chicken joins the crowd in the dining room.

3. A woman is hoeing her husband, stooping to pick up a few stubborn weeds by hand and tossing them behind her.

4. Since I was seven, I've had a dream of a man taking off his head and giving it to his girlfriend.

Begin writing if your group feels that it is ready, or examine our writer's model and explication. Although your work will follow from Dobyns's or James's sentences, our writer borrows an opening sentence from a second Russell Edson poem, "Rat":

Our Writer

A rat owns a man, which it operates with apron strings from its rathole in the wall.

The man, Franko, sits silently in the corner counting pennies.

One, two, eight, seven—oh, forget it, rat, pull the string, Franko wants to say, but doesn't.

The rat makes his way deeper into his hole and bakes cookies.

5　"Hmm," Franko says, "smells like peanut butter."

Franko is oblivious to the rat and believes it is his wife who is making the cookies.

"Put some carrots in those cookies," Franko yells at his non-existent wife. "And get me some milk ready, and don't forget to feed the cows and slaughter the pig."

In his mind his invisible wife is beautiful.

The rat hears the yelling and laughs. He readies the milk and laces it with dirt.

10　"Thank you, wife," Franko forces himself to say, as he drinks the milk.

He wants to enjoy the milk, as he does everything his wife makes.

Edson's imaginative opening line puts the poem into an unreal world. Moreover, it leaves the next writer with many language opportunities. In playing with the words used in that first line, what additional language and ideas might be triggered? Whichever word is chosen will determine the new language that is to come.

Our writer recognized that the phrase "apron strings" gave rise to a range of possibilities: pulling the string, baking, being a wife. The word "rat" generated evil actions: the rat laughs at the man's fantasy and laces his milk with dirt. In a sense, this is a game of free association, but it is *focused* free association. In addition, our writer used dialogue to create the character of the man. He says things that might be typical of any man who expects his wife to wait on him. Yet he also considers her feelings, wanting to enjoy the milk—and everything his wife makes—even when the milk tastes dreadful. Thus, in our writer's poem there is both freedom and wackiness in the coherence of characters acting logically in an illogical world.

Writer's Practice 6.2　　*Generate a Dreamlike Freewrite*

So far, the poems examined in this chapter share a dreamlike quality. That is, there are human characters, references to the natural world, images, and dialogue, but everything is upside down. Now, in a solo effort, compose a short passage that tells a story in an unreal, upside-down world. The story will be either a dream you make or a dream you recall having and now want to embellish. Quickly draft the dream, writing in paragraphs. Don't deliberate at length about what to write, and do not revise your work. In addition, follow these guidelines in your writing:

- Write this passage as if you were another person. Do not use "I."
- Place a character in an unreal world in the very first sentence. Then, despite this unreal setting, have your character act in a logical way, abiding by normally accepted rules of social interaction.
- Use dialogue.
- Create language threads by using the opportunities offered in your words.

Remember, don't take your writing too seriously. Look for language opportunities and play at creating.

Begin writing if you feel you are ready, or examine our writer's model and explication.

Our Writer

> A man wakes up in the middle of the ocean. His bed rocks on the waves. Beside him, the woman sleeps quietly, her breath on the back of his neck, or is that salty sea breeze? Overhead, the stars flicker on and off, heedless of their voyage. The woman surfaces from sleep and joins the man. "What?" she says, "The south seas again?" Somehow they get through the night. They fish, they tan themselves, they make a tent of the bed sheets. The days are long. At night they grow bored even with the shooting stars. They decide to name the waves. At first, when the ocean liners loom on the horizon, the man hails them, howling for rescue until there's no voice left in him at all. Those nights, they sink further into their soggy bed, listen to the language of the water. The woman sobs, petting the water. At night, when the man rests his head on what's left of his pillow, the waves tap on the side of the bed and whisper in his ear. They say, "Welcome home." They say, "We know you."

The unreal element introduced early in the writing is the concept of a man and a woman drifting on the sea in their bed. By the sound of it, this isn't the first time they have done so. "What," the wife says, "the south seas again?" Yet, these two people behave in logical ways. They relax and enjoy themselves, they get bored, they call out to ships passing them by, and they resign themselves to their situation.

Exploring Third-Person Point of View

Point of view has to do with a writer's closeness to her material. The narrator's perceptions are a filter through which the poem or story passes. Thus, when you name your main character "the man" and refer to him as "he," you establish some distance from his actions, feelings, and thoughts. You are outside this character. You are observing him the way a bystander—and the reader—might. As his "creator," however, you have access to him that a bystander lacks. You can report the interior events, his feelings and thoughts, with the same precision as the exterior events, his and other characters' actions.

Differences in View

The first-person point of view allows a writer to speak from the *I* perspective. In the first person, the distance between writer and character collapses. The writer is inside the character, impersonating the character's actions, feelings, and thoughts. The result is a poem or a story filtered through a subjective narrator. The Writer's Practice exercises in Chapters 2 through 5 all begin with a first-person speaker, for example.

The second-person point of view provides more distance between the writer and the subject. This more unusual point of view speaks from the *you* perspective: "You size up the dog. He's a mean one all right. You wonder if he means business." This point of view tends to be aggressive, since the writer sounds as if she is commanding her readers to do and think as her character does and thinks.

The third-person point of view allows the most distance from the subject. The writer refers to the main character as *he* or *she* and thus stands outside the character. Within the third-person point of view, the writer may vary the distance from her character: She may choose to relate only a single character's feelings, thoughts, and actions (thus creating a *third-person limited* point of view), or she may detail the main character's thoughts and everything around him—including other character's thoughts—with equal precision (thus creating a *third-person omniscient* point of view). Third-person limited and third-person omniscient are at opposite ends of a gradual scale; many third-person narrators are somewhere in between these two extremes.

Both Edson and Baxter use third-person point of view. However, Edson establishes more distance between the narrator and the characters in his poem. Consider how distance varies in their poems:

> A man had just delivered a toad from his wife's armpit. He held it by its legs and spanked it.
> Do you love it? said his wife.

It's our child, isn't it?
Does that mean you can't love it? she said.
It's hard enough to love a toad, but when it turns out to be your own son
then revulsion is without any tender inhibition, he said.

and

In a single village like this
where ideas run loose, our red-headed man
learned how to skip sleep: he sold his bed
and stood all night counting out stars,
beginning his sum in the west
where our mountains leap into darkness,
and ending his count in the east
where the sky falls dead into the roofs.
Every night he planted himself like a statue
in another man's yard, raising his head
before his lips began trembling with numbers.
The children called him the star hermit

In the first example, the narrator is clearly at some distance from the characters, not connected to their experience or to the events. This effect is created by the reference to "a man," which is even more impersonal and distant than "the man." If you reread the entire poem, you will notice that it consists mostly of dialogue. It is as if the poem is overheard and reported by the narrator, almost with scientific objectivity. Dialogue portrays the husband and wife with initially stereotypical questions. At first, the husband avoids admitting he doesn't love his son. Eventually, he reveals his revulsion and disappointment.

In contrast, the narrator in the second example is clearly much closer to the action. The main character is "our red-headed man." Notice the word choice "our." The narrator is connected to the man's experience and to the events. "In a single village like this" again suggests that the narrator is part of the setting and the story; "this" establishes immediacy. Such closeness is further implied in "where our mountains leap into darkness," a beautiful, even awe-inspiring image that says much about the narrator. Like the red-headed man, this narrator's details illustrate that he is tuned to the mystery of things. However, dialogue does not play a large role in portraying the red-headed man. His words and the words of others are told by the narrator: "his lips began trembling with numbers" and "The children called him the star hermit." This injects a gossipy tone, implying the investment of the narrator in the story. Spoken dialogue is withheld until the red-haired man speaks his wisdom at the end of the poem as if his words must be repeated rather than rephrased by the narrator.

Experimenting with Third-Person Point of View

Creating a third-person narrator requires the writer to be in control of details, actions, and dialogue. The narrator observes and reports what she sees or hears. In Writer's Practice 6.2, you narrated in third-person present tense the story of an unreal world inhabited by characters who acted logically. You used dialogue and word opportunities, or language threads, to invent the poem. Now you will focus on the distance of your narrator from the characters and the effectiveness of your details, action, and dialogue.

Writer's Practice 6.3 *Expand a Narrative with Details, Action, and Dialogue*

Using the freewrite from Writer's Practice 6.2, determine the distance from the story that you want your narrator to have. Will she be personally invested in the story, like Baxter's narrator, or will she be a distant observer who is simply reporting the action? Once you determine your narrator's degree of distance, use details, action, and dialogue to craft the narration. At this point, continue to write in paragraphs; you will shape the poem later.

As before, images created by precise attention to details will play a major role in your work. Use the follow suggestions to sharpen detail:

- Pay close attention to color, texture, and shape.
- Use all the senses: hear, smell, taste, touch, and see the action and the setting.
- Describe the story by picturing the action. For example, if a person pushes through a door with full arms, the narrator might see: *the man pushes the door with his elbow, tipping the box in an attempt to balance the load.* Use the following suggestion to sharpen your skill at picturing action: Close your eyes and watch the character move around in your head. Then, with great attention to detail, describe what you see. Avoid phrases such as "She cleared the table." Instead, say, "She stacked the five plates, then scooped up the forks, centering them on the plates. Like a waitress, she lifted the stack with one hand and palmed the salt and pepper with the other."
- Insert dialogue that makes characters real. Creating authentic dialogue requires you to pay close attention to the character who speaks and the motivation for his words. Use the following suggestions to sharpen your skill at creating dialogue:
  - Use short sentences or phrases.
  - Answer questions with questions.
  - Ignore what is said by another person.

- Change the subject.
- Respond to things that haven't been said.
- Repeat words or expressions.

Keep in mind that it is unlikely that you can use *all* of these suggestions in a single poem.

Begin writing if you feel you are ready, or examine our writer's model and explication.

Our Writer

> The man wakes up in the middle of the ocean, moonlight pooling all around. No walls, no windows, no roof, no carpet, no floor, the bed rising and falling on waves. Beside him, his wife rests, sheathed in her white nightclothes. He props himself on one elbow, rolls away from her, and sits up, his legs dangling in the water. Fish nibble at his ankles. He can dive off and have a swim. Lie back and watch the stars. Overhead, they flicker on and off, heedless of his voyage. Heedless. "Where will we end up?" he says aloud, surprised to hear his voice. His wife surfaces from her sleep, rubbing her eyes with knuckled fists.
>
> "What?" she says. "The south seas, again?" She pulls near him, says, "This time I want to see Tahiti."
>
> "That will take some doing," he says.
>
> She touches the black water. "How deep do you think it is?" she asks.
>
> Somehow they get through the night. They drift for days, straining toward Tahiti. They fish, they tan themselves, they make a tent of the bed sheets. At night they grow bored with the shooting stars. "What will become of our children?" the man says aloud. They name the waves—Crusher, Backhand, Tiff. Days pass into weeks. At first, when the tall ships pass, when the oil tankers loom on the horizon, they hail them, waving pale pillowcase flags, howling for rescue, until their voices fray and the vessels leave them in the night. Such nights they sink to a soggy bed. The wife sobs, petting the waves.
>
> "Please," she says to them, "try to understand."
>
> When the man rests his head on what's left of the pillow, waves tap on the side of the bed and whisper in his ear. They say, "Welcome home." He raises a finger to blue lips. "SShhh, You're supposed to be asleep."

Attention to detail, action, and dialogue enables this writer to make important additions to the dream-vision. For example, there is more exploration of the anxiety of being stranded in the ocean. The narrator reports that the man frets over his children, the wife pets and talks to the waves as if they were her children, and the man quiets the waves in a parental fashion: "You're supposed to be asleep." This statement echoes the fact that he and his wife have now named the waves—named them in aggressive, argumentative terms, such as "Backhand," "Crusher," and "Tiff." Notice that this version of the dream is more visual than the earlier one, establishing a more fully developed language thread. The narrator repeats images of whiteness: "moonlight pooling," "sheathed in her white nightclothes," "a tent of bed sheets," "waving pale pillowcase flags," and "knuckled fists." Also, this version includes more dialogue and pictured action.

Writer Response Groups

Presently, you have a draft in paragraph form in which you have created a strange and imaginary world and inhabited it with characters who act and speak in a logical fashion. You have moved your characters around in this world and perhaps the details, actions, and dialogue of the world have brought you enlightenment, or wisdom. Now form a writer response group. Examine each other's poems, reading for the following elements:

Essential Elements

- What is the poem about?
- Who is the speaker?
- How is the poem organized?

Craft

- How close is the narrator to the action of the poem? What details, actions, or dialogue clarify this?
- Is the poem invented from language opportunities? What language threads are observable?
- Does the poem create a strange world? Do the inhabitants of this world act in a logical way? Is there a wisdom in the unreal?

Revising for the Poetic Line

It is time now to shape your paragraphs into a poem. This will require you to make line-break decisions. Your poem was invented through close attention to words; therefore, emphasizing those words must be the primary concern when determining the poetic line. You will use line breaks to create emphasis utilizing both natural and unnatural language rhythms.

Notice the natural and unnatural line breaks in Russell Edson's poem. Most of the lines end with a speaker tag—"she said" or "he said"—creating a natural break. Lines that end on a natural break are called *end-stopped lines*. A period, semicolon, colon, or comma concludes an end-stopped line. Ending lines on a natural pause adds power to each statement, and in Edson's poem, it emphasizes that the poem is a conversation illuminating the differing perspectives of a husband and wife.

However, several line breaks work against the natural and expected conventions of phrasing. The beginning of Edson's poem does this: "A man had just delivered a toad from his wife's armpit. He held it by its legs and / spanked it." The break at the end of the first line pulls the reader forward into the second line, forcing the reader to ask: What will the man be holding? How will he behave with a toad child? The answer comes quickly and is logical. This type of line break is called a *run-on line*. In line 6, Edson creates another run-on line: "It's hard enough to love a toad, but when it turns out to be your own son then / revulsion is without any tender inhibition, he said." The phrase ends with "son," but Edson continues, ending the line with "then." This hurries the reader to the word "revulsion" on the next line and emphasizes that the man is faced with ownership of the problem of having a son.

Notice the end stops and run-on line break decisions in the beginning of Baxter's poem:

In a single village like this
where ideas run loose, our red-headed man
learned how to skip sleep: he sold his bed
and stood all night counting out stars,
beginning his sum in the west
where our mountains leap into darkness,
and ending his count in the east
where the sky falls dead into the roofs.

Lines 4, 6, and 8 are end-stopped lines. The rest of the line breaks are run-ons. However, each of these run-ons ends with a complete phrase, which minimizes their abruptness. The only startlingly abrupt run-on line in the poem comes later, at line 17: "he said there were over two thousand / thousand stars." On the first reading of the poem, possibly the repetition of "thousand" after the line break surprised you. You expect a noun—two thousand *something*. The repetition works to emphasize the enormity of the heavens and conveys the red-headed man's sense of awe.

Looking further, you might notice that a majority of Baxter's lines end with nouns. In fact, Baxter seems to have made this a rule that he observes almost without exception. Nouns such as "hermit" and "criminals" create concrete images in the mind of the reader. Their placement at the end of the line allows the reader to linger on them momentarily before continuing to the next line.

Writer's Practice 6.4 *Shape Your Poem with Line Breaks*

Because the poem you have drafted for this chapter is written in paragraph form, you are in an ideal position to consider line breaks. Make several drafts of your poem, varying line-break methods. What effect do you get if you break at the natural pauses? What part of speech do you place at the end of the line? Can you use line breaks to create surprise by exploiting the reader's expectations, as Baxter does with "thousand" / "thousand"? As you vary line-break methods, remember that the rewriting process is always an opportunity to add and subtract.

The poem by our writer is a free-verse poem. Free-verse poems do not adhere to the rules of rhyme or meter or even syllable count that other forms of poetry require. You used free verse to revise a poem in Writer's Practice 4.5 when you made stanza and line decisions. As you know, a poet uses a kind of logic in determining when to break the line. The line breaks that you will observe in the following free-verse poem should accomplish these purposes:

- Create a pause.
- Force the reader to keep reading into the next line, which pulls the reader forward.
- Create emphasis by breaking consistently on nouns or other important parts of speech.
- Inject surprise by placing an unexpected word at the beginning of a line. The reader will read the last word on the previous line and imagine the next word. The unexpected word will create a surprise.

Begin shaping your paragraphs into a poem if you feel you are ready, or examine our writer's model and explication.

Our Writer

Sailing to Tahiti

A man wakes up on the ocean,
moonlight pooling on his bed.
Her back to him, his wife rests
sheathed in white light.
5   Fish ram the bedside,
waves lap at their feet

and the man hears faint shrill voices,
sees the flash of impatient eyes.
The children, he remembers aloud,
10   startling the woman from sleep.
She wipes her eyes, grumbling,
What, the south seas, again?
If only we could see Tahiti.
That will take some doing, the man knows.
15   Somehow they get through the night,
They drift all the next day, straining
toward Tahiti. They tan themselves, they make
a tent of the bed sheets. At night
waiting for shooting stars,
20   he names the waves—Crusher, Backhand,
Tiff. It won't be long now, he tells the woman.
Days pass into weeks. She can't wait.
At first, when the tall ships pass,
she hails them, waving pale flags,
25   howling for rescue, until her voice frays.
Such nights they sink to their soggy bed alone
together, and the woman sobs
petting the waves. Please, she says to them,
try to understand. When the man rests
30   his head on what's left of the pillow
waves tap on the side of the bed, a whisper
in his ear. They say, We've forgotten all about you.
They say, No one knows you're gone.
He raises a finger to his lips. SShhh, he says.
35   You're supposed to be asleep.

Our writer made many obvious revision decisions. First, the poem contains no quotation marks. This is not a grammatical error, but a conscious decision. Many contemporary poets do not use quotation marks. Sometimes speech is indicated with italics. In this poem, all speech is tagged with either "he says" or "she says." Using quotation marks in this work would draw attention to the dialogue and make the story more realistic. By excluding quotation marks, the poet makes the story seem more unreal. Second, many of the lines are end-stopped lines. Ending the lines with commas and periods elongates the experience of the couple floating on a bed in the ocean. Several lines are run-on lines, but most end on a natural pause. However, four lines contain strong run-on breaks because they end in the middle of a phrase. For example, lines 17 and 18—"They tan themselves, they make / a tent of the bed sheets"—create a surprise. It is unexpected that the couple would make a tent. By breaking the verb from the direct object, the unrealistic logic of the poem is emphasized. Last, the poem comes to a small wisdom as the true anxiety of the couple's aimless floating becomes clear: they seem not to be noticed at all, for the ships that are supposed to rescue them and the waves that are now their children pay them no mind. The man and the woman hardly seem aware of each other; most of their actions are performed independently. The woman hails ships, sobs, and pets the waves without the man. And, when they go to sleep at night, they are "alone together."

Examining Student Poems

Many dream poems create an unreal landscape in which the characters' logical lives can be closely examined. Both of the following student poems are about people trying to grasp that which is ungraspable: time. Third-person point of view highlights the absurdity, because the emotional distance of the observer allows the reader to study, rather than empathize with, the characters. Concrete details and dialogue make the unreal world seem believable. Line breaks create surprise, tension, and emphasis.

Girl with Book

ELIZABETH MITCHELL

A girl reads books in the shower. This morning
it is the Children's Book of Knowledge. She reads
the rules for the Game of Egg Hat. *Five to ten boys may take*
part in the game. Each must have a cap.
5   Water streams through the girl's dusky hair and onto the page.
Pulling the book to her chest, she looks for a cap.
She had an orange cap once. If only she had kept it.
Her brother yells to her: "Are you clean yet?"
The sun is setting. It is an orange ball. She must
10   read faster. Her brother bangs on the door.
"There is only so much water," he says.
"We are made of water," she says, and raises the book to her lips.
The words are slipping off the page. *Five boys and a cap* are
racing toward the drain. She covers the drain with her heel,
15   but they slip between her toes like eggs.

This is a strange world indeed, where girls read books in the shower and words fall from pages. But the girl's actions are logical: she is reading the book for rules to a game and tries to prevent the words from going down the drain. The dialogue is also realistic, as it reveals the brother's impatience with his sister and a misconception that she is in the shower to get clean. Readers observe this scene through a third-person, distant narrator. We understand the wisdom of the girl's realization: she cannot recapture time or knowledge. Line 9 is broken for surprise. It would seem that the girl must get out of the shower, based on her brother's banging on the door; instead, his insistence and the setting sun cause her to believe "she must / read faster."

Space, Time, and Motion

D'ANNE WITKOWSKI

We eat lightning for breakfast,
Dad eats his sunny-side up. I prefer
a quick bowl of Heaven-O's.
"That's bad for your teeth," Dad says.
5   "Too much sugar."
"It's made by angels," I say.

I ride the community comet
to Angel Training. Today's lesson: Time,
the beginning and the end. We're to choose
10   a subject on earth, apply the quote:
"I was blessed with a birth and a death,
I just want some say in between."

"It's different for angels,"
my Space, Time, and Motion professor
15   explains. "They don't die, they just move
through stages."
I will become an angel
eventually. I will become of myself
and in myself I will find something
20   like gold, but with infinite weight
and measure.

On the way home I think about today's lesson:
how time never stops and I keep moving.
I carve my initials on the comet wall.
25   I look down on earth, wonder what
those little people are doing in such a hurry.
I go down to them, working so hard,
so hard towards death,
whisper, "Slow down,
30   slow down."

Here, a logical child eats breakfast, commutes to school, and thinks about school lessons. The father and teacher, too, are logical, as demonstrated by the lessons they dispense. But all three move in an unreal world of angels and comets. In the final lines, the speaker comes to the wisdom that we all race against time toward death. Lines 2 and 14 are examples of run-on lines; we must read into the next line to see what the speaker prefers and what the professor does. Line 8 is broken for surprise and emphasis: Time is a huge concept, left hanging on the end of the line with a capital *T*. But the next line continues matter-of-factly, as if time were something finite, with a beginning and an end. The absurd notion is explored throughout the poem.

That Way

KAITLIN RUSSELL

A bird watched a fair girl
wait on a shaded street corner.
"What are you waiting for?"
The bird stretched her wings.
5   "My love is coming to take
me far way," the girl said.
"Where will he take you?"
"Wherever he decides to go."
"One time," the bird flew closer,
10   "a man gave me a home.
A small iron cage."
"Oh no." the girl twirled
her hair around her finger. "My
Love will not cage me."
15   "The man said he was afraid
of thieves." The bird ruffled her feathers.
"Why would he fear that?"
"Men think that way," sang the bird.

A man approached and the bird
20   asked, "Is this your love
coming now?" The girl ran
toward him, smiling. "You came!"
"It's all planned," he kissed her.
"I'll buy a house with everything
25   you could want. You'll never
even have to leave." He smiled.
"But what if I want to leave?"
"I'll bring you anything,

cater to your every need."
30 "But I don't want a servant.
I want a husband." She frowned.
"I'll be your husband,
and your servant. You'll be my
little bird with yellow feathers," he said,
35 and touched her blonde head.
The bird whistled, flying into clear sky.
The girl watched and whispered,
"Men think that way."

Kaitlin creates an unreal world immediately. The bird talks to the girl as if it were a girlfriend, a kindred spirit. The bird initiates the conversation that helps the fair girl see her love in a different way. Kaitlin uses dialogue to characterize the bird, the fair girl, and the man and to reveal the conflict between the man and the girl. Using the third-person point of view made this poem almost symbolic, turning the girl and man into stereotypes whose conflict represents a more universal conflict—the wish to control contrasted by the desire to be free. Kaitlin used mostly nouns and verbs at the end of her lines. Her few exceptions emphasize the conflict: "closer," "afraid," "never," and "my." The man sees the girl as a possession, a possession he is willing to serve. He even compares her to a bird.

chapter 7

Creating from Sentences and Words: Sentence Control, Diction, and Cutting

It [the poem] makes both overt and subtle promises in diction, content, structure, rhythm, tone, texture, etc. The subtle promises, when fulfilled, satisfy us most, often long before we know what they are.

-STEPHEN DUNN

Talk with a little luck in it, that's what poetry is—just let the words take you where they want to go. You'll be invited; things will happen; your life will have more in it than other people's lives have.

-WILLIAM STAFFORD

As you have progressed in this book, you have become a decision maker, choosing to use a metaphor and crafting that metaphor here or to make a line break there. You have used your writing to express an observation or to deepen a memory. You have also used images, comparisons, dialogue, and varying points of view to convey your stories and feelings. You have drawn on memory, comparison, close observation, and wild imagination to generate writing. As a decision maker who uses the poet's tools to craft a poem, you are ready for your next challenge: to create the subtle promises that satisfy a reader.

In this chapter, you will focus on the subtleties of the sentence. Controlling the sentence is one strategy for creating the subtle and pleasing promises that satisfy readers. While it may not be the easiest or the most common approach to writing a good poem, it will become a trick in your writer's toolbox that will improve all your future poems. Though readers may not pay particular attention to any single sentence, readers will notice weak sentences. Thus, in crafting a poem, you must know how to write strong sentences to create the almost invisible frame for the work.

Like short stories and essays, poems consist of sentences and sentence fragments. Simplified, the sentence is an arrangement of words whose structure emphasizes some words more than others. As a result, the opportunities found in words continue to be important here, as well. William Stafford gives excellent advice that is often difficult for a novice writer to heed when he urges you to "let the words take you where they want to go." In this chapter, you will experiment with building awareness of sentences and with crafting a poem by closely attending to words. Also, you will focus on cutting and transforming sentences into the poetic line, thus reinventing a poem several times. Each time you rework the poem, you will be sharpening your writer's skills.

In the poems that follow, note how Stephen Dunn and William Stafford control sentences and words. The other craft decisions the poets made in their writing are built upon the powerful frame of controlled sentences. As you read the following poems for the first time, however, do so without concentrating on sentences or words. Simply enjoy the poems. What feelings emerge after reading each poem a single time? Now reread the poems, this time paying attention to the sentences. Which sentences appear controlled? What effect does that control have on you as you read?

The Substitute

STEPHEN DUNN

When the substitute asked my eighth-grade daughter
   to read out loud,
she read in Cockney, an accent she'd mastered

listening to rock music. Her classmates laughed
5   of course, and she kept on,
straightfaced, until the merciful bell.

This began the week my daughter learned
   it takes more than style
to be successfully disobedient.

10   Next day her regular teacher didn't return;
   she had to do it again.
She was from Liverpool, her parents worked

in a mill, had sent her to America to live
   with relatives.
15   At night she read about England, looked at her map

to place and remember exactly where she lived.
   Soon her classmates
became used to it—just a titter from Robert

who'd laugh at anything. Friday morning,
20   exhausted from learning
the manners and industry of modern England,

she had a stomachache, her ears hurt, there were
   pains, she said,
all over. We pointed her toward the door.

25   She left bent over like a charwoman, but near
   the end of the driveway
we saw her right herself, become the girl

who had to be another girl, a substitute
   of sorts,
30   in it now for the duration.

Questions

1. How many long sentences does Dunn use? How many short sentences does he use? Which sentences seem the most powerful to you?

2. Which words emphasize the plight of the daughter?

3. Do you identify with the girl or her parents?

Traveling Through the Dark

WILLIAM STAFFORD

Traveling through the dark I found a deer
dead on the edge of the Wilson River road.
It is usually best to roll them into the canyon:
that road is narrow; to swerve might make more dead.

5   By glow of the tail-light I stumbled back of the car
and stood by the heap, a doe, a recent killing;
she had stiffened already, almost cold.
I dragged her off; she was large in the belly.

My fingers touching her side brought me the reason—
10   her side was warm; her fawn lay there waiting,
alive, still, never to be born.
Beside that mountain road I hesitated.

The car aimed ahead its lowered parking lights;
under the hood purred the steady engine.
15   I stood in the glare of the warm exhaust turning red;
around our group I could hear the wilderness listen.

I thought hard for us all—my only swerving—
then pushed her over the edge into the river.

Questions

1. Stafford uses colons and semicolons frequently. What effect do they have on the poem?
2. Which sentences seem the most powerful to you?
3. Which words emphasize the driver's conflict?
4. What feelings does the speaker reveal toward the deer?

Exploring Sentence Control

Novice writers may spend so much energy concentrating on metaphors and images that they forget to concentrate on their sentences, blithely inserting periods and commas where "it seems right." This seat-of-the-pants approach, however, can create a wordy or choppy effect. Instead, by paying attention to sentence structure, a writer can create a framework for his poem in which punctuation and phrasing will control the pace and the mind of the reader. For example, periods demand a pause, and exclamation points and question marks demand longer pauses. Commas, on the other hand, create a relationship between phrases, and the reader internalizes the relationship either through the accessible first reading or the analytical rereading of the poem. The word choice, punctuation, and structure of the sentence create the texture of the poem. Interestingly, the mechanics that create the poem's texture are often invisible to the reader.

Because this chapter is on sentence control, grammar plays a role. The writer with a strong grammar base will find it easier to write in controlled sentences. However, if basic grammar terms such *subject, verb, preposition, conjunction, phrase,* and *clause* are unfamiliar concepts to you, don't give up. Instead, use this practice as a beginning in learning the following fundamentals:

1. The subject of the sentence does the action.
2. The verb indicates the action of the subject.
3. Phrases, or clauses, introduce or describe the subject's action.

Developing an awareness of subject and verb and their placement in a sentence is the first step toward understanding sentence control.

Look back at Stephen Dunn's and William Stafford's sentences. Dunn uses ten sentences. Nine are long and filled with clauses. They detail the prank turned problem, creating a conversational tone. The poet uses one short sentence to state the parents' powerful and silent reaction to their daughter's self-made dilemma. Dunn places his subject near the beginning of his sentences eight times.

In his poem, Stafford uses nine sentences. Eight are long and filled with phrases. They narrate the predicament caused when someone's car hit a deer on a dark, narrow road, creating an introspective tone. Stafford's only short sentence emphasizes the hesitancy and self-awareness of a man faced with choosing which life to save. In this work he has placed his subjects near the beginning of six of his sentences.

Let's take a closer look at a few of the sentences from Dunn's and Stafford's poems. Note that both poets use long sentences characterized by two qualities: (1) the sentences begin with the subject; (2) the sentences contain lists or a series of actions that cause an emotional reaction for the reader. This type of sentence construction is the most common type found in poems and may be easier to write, because novice writers tend to begin their sentences with the subject. However, it is difficult to control the long sentence while creating an effect.

1. "She was from Liverpool, her parents worked / in a mill, had sent her to America to live / with relatives." This sentence from Dunn's "The Substitute" catalogs the lies the daughter must remember. Grammatically, it has two subjects: "she" and "parents," but it is structured as a list with "she" as the initial subject of the sentence; therefore, "she" becomes the primary focus of the details that follow. The details create a list that makes the lie seem weighty.

2. "My fingers touching her side brought me the reason— / her side was warm; her fawn lay there waiting, / alive, still, never to be born." This sentence from Stafford's "Traveling Through the Dark" reports the condition of the carcass of the dead deer lying at the side of the road. Stafford begins the sentence with a possessive pronoun, "My," and then the subject, "fingers," which personalizes the experience and emphasizes the closeness of the speaker to the deer. The sentence then details the experience, bringing the speaker closer to the deer as the speaker's fingers explore the deer's side. At the end of the sentence, Stafford lists the fingers' findings: "waiting, / alive, still, never

to be born." Each comma adds another detail and emphasizes the speaker's emotional discovery.

In contrast, Dunn and Stafford also use long sentences in which the subject and verb do not appear until later in the sentence. Instead, an introductory phrase or clause begins the sentence. This introductory information emphasizes or describes the subject's actions that follow. Dunn uses this type of sentence construction once in his poem, while Stafford uses it three times. This sentence construction appears less frequently in poetry; however, it can be used very effectively.

1. "When the substitute asked my eighth-grade daughter / to read out loud, / she read in Cockney, an accent she'd mastered / listening to rock music." Dunn begins with a dependent clause, "When the substitute asked my eighth-grade daughter to read out loud," which places the story in time and introduces the daughter. It clarifies the action of the subject: "she read in Cockney." Delaying the subject makes the action seem ordinary and expected, a natural result of being asked to read aloud.

2. "By the glow of the tail-light I stumbled back of the car / and stood by the heap, a doe, a recent killing; / she had stiffened already, almost cold." Stafford introduces the simple sentence with a prepositional phrase, "By the glow." This introductory phrase established the action and emphasizes the danger of the deer's discovery along the edge of the road. The list imitates the discovery process. As the reader continues reading the sentence, more information about the deer—and the driver—is revealed.

Short sentences create emphasis simply due to their brevity. Both Dunn and Stafford use a single short sentence in these poems. Grammatically, the short sentences used in poems are often simple sentences, containing just a single action, but sometimes a sentence fragment is used to create the same emphasis. A short sentence is an immediate contrast to the longer sentences of the poems. Here, each poet uses the short sentence to state an emotional reaction.

1. "We pointed her toward the door." Dunn begins with the subject, "We," followed immediately by the verb, "pointed." The sentence's structure emphasizes the deliberate and clear decision of the parents to make their daughter accountable for her actions.

2. "Beside the mountain road I hesitated." Stafford delays the subject and verb and begins with a prepositional phrase, "Beside the mountain road." The short sentence serves to emphasize the driver's hesitation.

Experimenting with Sentence Control

You should have two goals in mind as you experiment with sentences. First, develop an awareness of sentence structure. Second, do not plan. In the same way you allowed your imagination to propel you forward in Writer's Practice 6.2 and the freewrite of your dream, allow the sentence structure to propel you forward in the following exercise. Writer's Practice 7.1 is a guided freewrite that does not have to make sense, so be open to invention. Focus on letting the sentence structures invent the poem and surprise yourself with each new sentence.

Writer's Practice 7.1 *Surprise Yourself*

As you follow the directions of this guided writing assignment, you will be creating long and short sentences. Don't worry about meaning. Instead, let words from each sentence propel you into the next sentence.

After you write each sentence, ask yourself, What is the obvious next sentence? Then, don't write it. Instead, find a word in the sentence that could take you someplace new. Be led by that word. Remember, don't be afraid to say things that never happened. Notice that Dunn may have used this approach in his first stanza. He begins with the expected: a substitute asks a student to read aloud. However, he does not deliver the expected. Instead, the girl reads in Cockney and the premise of the poem is created.

Each of the following directions is numbered. Write this exercise sentence by sentence, numbering the sentences as you proceed to match the direction number.

1. Write a short, simple sentence.

- Start with *I*, *A*, or *The*.
- Keep it short. Use only four to seven words.

Model: I watch hail streak my window.

2. Write a long sentence. Delay the subject with an introductory clause.

- Pick a word from the first sentence to use as a focus for Sentence 2.
- Start Sentence 2 with one of the following subordinating conjunctions: *after, although, as, as long as, as if, because, before, since, whatever, when, whenever,* or *while.*

- Make this introductory clause long. End the clause or phrase with a comma and take the rest of the sentence in a new direction. Allow a word or detail from Sentence 1 to propel you into a new thought.

Model: Whenever I hear its tinny sound tapping a dangerous hello, glazing the grass, filling the garden with white pebbles, I remember seventh grade.

3. **Write a long sentence. Begin with the subject and include a list.**

- Expand on the direction that appeared in Sentence 2.
- Begin Sentence 3 with the subject and an active verb. (Try to use a different subject than you used in Sentence 1.)
- Add a list of details or actions.
- Save the most important detail for last.

Model: Mrs. Brown tapped her pen on my desk each time she caught me gazing out the window, across the playground, toward Milly's Bake Shop.

4. **Write a long sentence. Delay the subject with a prepositional phrase.**

- Use one of the following prepositions: *after, by, under, between, over, outside,* or *in.*
- Have you surprised yourself yet? If you haven't, use Sentence 4 to go in a new direction. (Tip: use the last detail of Sentence 3 to help you surprise yourself.)

Model: After school I swept Milly's kitchen, carried out the trash, washed piles of pots, and ate warm donuts on the back steps.

5. **Write a long sentence. Begin with the subject and include a list.**

- Begin the sentence with the subject.
- Use a word from Sentence 4 to get you started.

Model: Milly made the lightest glazed donuts, the tenderest chocolate chip cookies, the plumpest honey-raisin oatmeal muffins on earth.

6. **Write a sentence fragment.** Although many English teachers may frown upon sentence fragments, they can be a creative writer's best

friend if they are used sparingly. A fragment will create emphasis because it is short, abrupt, and unexpected. If artfully used, fragments can startle a reader.

• Select a word or words from Sentence 5. Repeat the word or words, thus suggesting increasing importance. Of, if you prefer, use a synonym.

Model: Light and tender.

7. Write another long sentence. Delay the subject with an introductory clause.

• Start Sentence 7 with one of the following subordinating conjunctions: *after, although, as, as long as, as if, because, before, since, whatever, when, whenever,* or *while.*
• Consider using *I* as the subject of the sentence. However, allow the words of the previous sentences to determine your direction if they have begun to suggest ideas to you.

Model: While Mrs. Brown liked fresh air and thought an open window would keep us awake, as soon as that window opened, I couldn't concentrate on math.

8. Write a simple sentence.

• Start with the subject, but do not use *I.* Instead, begin with a different noun. Use a word from one of the previous sentences to get you started. Allow the word you choose to create the sentence.

Model: Honeyed air ruined my grades.

Your work in Writer's Practice 7.1 may have taken you more time and effort than a freewrite because you were focusing on both sentence structure and surprise words. When you trust the words or sentence structures to control the generation of new material, it may seem awkward at first. Yet, this is one approach that can help you start writing by finding something interesting to pursue, even when you control the work as you proceed. The model illustrates the interesting possibilities that emerge if you trust words and sentences to provide opportunities. Of course, it should be noted that if you pursued the writing you have just done as a poem, many of the sentences might be discarded. The goal of this approach to writing, however, is to arrive at a single interesting sentence or identify a topic or event.

Ask yourself the following questions before proceeding to Writer's Practice 7.2. You might discuss these questions with your Writer Response Group:

- Did I follow the directions in an attempt to understand sentence structures?
- Which sentence type is the easiest for me to write? Which one is the hardest?
- Did I use words to propel me into inventing the next sentence or to find a topic?
- Can I identify the subject and the verb of my sentences?
- Can I identify introductory clauses?

Notice the language opportunities used to invent the model sentences. The sentence work begins with a hail storm and ends with poor math grades. Although the poet used "I remember seventh grade" to frame the sense of the work, the sentences that follow are invented from words in previous sentences. For example, Sentence 4 uses the word "Milly"; Sentence 5 uses the baked goods; Sentence 6 returns to the window from Sentence 1; and Sentence 8 uses "honey" from Sentence 5. Returning to earlier sentences for words that help in invention can make generating easier as well as fun.

Writer's Practice 7.2 *Invent from Sentence Frames*

Your work in Writer's Practice 7.1 developed your awareness of subjects and verbs. The next exercise will give you another opportunity to work toward a surprise. Write a second time using varied sentence patterns. Write eight to ten sentences, numbering each as you work. This practice will be the basis for a poem. Be open to surprises by imagining what *might* happen rather than what *did* happen. Write in first-person and use the present tense.

- Use short sentences to emphasize an important moment.
- Use long sentences to add details and information.
- Vary long sentences. Begin with the subject or delay the subject.
- Alternate long and short sentences to slow or speed the pace of the poem.
- Consider using questions.
- Consider using a fragment.

Begin writing if you feel you are ready, or examine our writer's model and explication.

Our Writer

1. I sort my past.

2. As I sift through greeting cards, yellowed news clippings, and recipes saved for someday, I drop the box in the fire.

3. Flames melt through a pink fairy, a white gloved princess, five Christmas trees stacked with presents and pajamaed smiles, seven Easter baskets, two sisters squeezed into an inner tube wearing tinted glasses, thin terry towels, and toothless grins.

4. As if I am under a spell, I hesitate.

5. By the time I recover my senses, it is too late, and I can only watch flames work holes in homemade dresses.

6. Free, I construct youth, touch slimy frogs and baby birds, play baseball in the rain, and climb the tallest tree, yelling I won't fall seven times at the top of my lungs.

7. I see myself tiptoe along train tracks, torn blue jeans, a T-shirt, balancing my arms first one way and then the other, never see a train or a bum.

8. Powerless thieves.

9. How can it be so easy to destroy no, never, and always?

The freewrite surprises itself immediately in Sentence 2. By dropping the box into a fire—certainly an unexpected event—the speaker must deal with the problem. The surprises continue when the speaker does not immediately react to save the box and then becomes overjoyed with her sense of freedom. It offers the writer an interesting poem to craft based on a surprising question. What would happen if you could so easily destroy the powerful thieves of childhood: no, never, and always?

Exploring the Impact of Diction

In Writer's Practice 5.3 you experimented with diction, selecting strong nouns and verbs to create clear images. The importance of strong nouns and verbs was revisited in Writer's Practices 4.5 and 6.4 when you created powerful line breaks. This chapter offers you an invention strategy to improve your poem's diction and deepen its meaning at the same time. Young writers may be too easily satisfied with the familiar words they use. Even attempts to get "bigger" words into poems by using a thesaurus fail since those words stick out and don't really seem to fit. However, gaining a deeper appreciation for words should be the first goal for any writer. A writer must learn to use a word's connotations and denotations. A *denotation* is the literal meaning of the word. A *connotation* is the implied meaning of the word; this meaning suggests a feeling or attitude.

Syntax and Diction

The term *syntax* refers to sentence structure—the arrangement of words into basic sentence patterns. A declarative sentence, for example, has a subject-verb-object pattern: *The cat chased the dog.* Poets manipulate the basic sentence patterns to achieve a poem's content and form.

Diction, on the other hand, refers to the choice of words in a poem or story and their usage. Diction is sometimes classified according to usage, from formal to informal to slang.

The term *poetic diction* is sometimes used to refer to words that are especially appropriate for poetry.

Look closely at William Stafford's diction. He uses words for both their connotation and their denotation. For example, Stafford refers to the dead deer as a "heap." Denotatively, "heap" means a large pile, but the word connotes that the pile is disorderly and possibly unimportant, maybe even a burden. By selecting this word, Stafford creates the actual picture of the deer carcass on the edge of the road and suggests the driver's distance from it. He does not recognize it as a deer; instead, he sees a "heap." Stafford selects words that seem ordinary, yet they create powerful pictures and suggest feelings and attitudes. Consider the words Stafford could have used: "pile," "stack," "mound," or "mass." None of these words would connote the disorderly worthlessness of "heap," however.

Another word with both denotative and connotative usage is "swerve." The word is used twice in Stafford's poem, but the meaning of the word changes in the second usage. At first, the word denotes the driver's decision to stop and roll the dead deer into the canyon. The second usage connotes the driver's momentary deviation from his intent to roll the dead dear into the canyon. The second time "swerve" is used, it changes literal meaning and implies the mental and emotional struggle of the driver to choose people's safety over the life of an unborn fawn. Stafford uses a single word to accomplish a visual picture of an emotional response. Visually, the swerving of a car is presented to the reader; the word is repeated to create an emotional swerving.

Using synonyms is another way to build variety, depth, and clarity into word choice. Stephen Dunn uses two different words to refer to the classmates' reaction. At first, the speaker reports that "her classmates laughed." Later in the poem, the speaker reports, "Soon her classmates / became used to it—just a titter from Robert / who'd laugh at anything." Here, Dunn uses "titter" to denote that Robert's laughter is suppressed, but the word also connotes that Robert's continued amusement is small and possibly annoying.

Experimenting with Diction

The poet's task is larger than getting a story, feeling, or opinion on paper. Many young writers choke a good poem by moving too quickly to finish it and to clean it up. So, no matter how much you love your current draft, expand it. Through this expansion process, the poem may clarify meaning or change direction. Be open to changes and be flexible in your thinking. Allow diction or word choice to invent this expansion. In addition, you can affect the tone of the poem by creating a language thread, a technique that you experimented with in Writer's Practice 6.1. The repetition of a language thread will help the poem to seem more connected, as well.

Writer's Practice 7.3   *Do Diction Research*

Select an important or interesting word from the sentence experiment. Consider one that seems empty and calls for sharpening or one that seems powerful and calls for resonance. Now, go to a dictionary and a thesaurus to complete the following research:

1. List all definitions. List all the definitions that you find for the word. Watch for changes in part of speech (noun, verb, adjective) and for different connotations.

2. List sound relatives. List words from the dictionary that are closely related in spelling, even though they differ in meaning.

3. List synonyms. Watch for words that have different connotations.

You may enjoy this exercise so much that you will want to select several other words to research. Review the following research by our writer to help you create your own research.

Our Writer's Word Research: Tint

Webster's Collegiate Dictionary, Tenth Edition

1. **Definitions:** noun: **1 a:** a usu. slight or pale coloration: HUE **b:** any of various lighter or darker shades of a color: TINGE **2:** a variation of a color produced by adding white to it and characterized by a low saturation with relatively high lightness **3:** a usu. slight modifying quality or characteristic: TOUCH **4:** a shaded effect in engraving produced by fine parallel lines close together **5:** a panel of light color serving as background **6:** dye for the hair *vt:* to impart or apply a tint to: COLOR

2. **Sound relatives:** tinsel, tinstone, tintype, tiny, tinderbox, tingle, tinkle, tine, tin, tin foil, tin plate, tinman, tinker, tintinnabulation, taint

3.   **Synonyms:** hue, tone, shade, tinge, chroma, tinct, undertone, value, irides-
cence, coloration, pigmentation, cast, glow, gush, wash tincture

Writer's Practice 7.4   *Expand Using Diction Research*

Reinvent the freewrite you wrote in Writer's Practice 7.2 by inserting words
found in your diction research in Writer's Practice 7.3. Consider the word's connotation or implied meaning as well as its denotation or literal meaning. Be open
to ways to insert some of the words from your research—even if they do not
seem to fit. You will find this work easier to do if you have not committed yourself to a poem. For now, simply experiment with words to invent a subject. Be
sure to number each sentence and add at least six to ten new sentences. If you
wish, you may drop lines to make way for new ones. Remember to use the words
from your research more than once, varying the connotation or denotation.

Begin writing if you feel you are ready, or examine our writer's model and
explication. Notice the italicized words that were the impetus for changes.
What was dropped? What was added? What was not changed?

Our Writer

1. By the *glow* of blue flames, I shuffle through *tinted variations of* myself.

2. A white gloved princess, a vampire, black hair *tinted* to match her
    Halloween heart, *angular knees and elbows mirrored* in windows.

3. When I uncover two sisters squeezed into an inner tube wearing *tinted*
    glasses, thin terry towels and toothless grins, *I think of the pictures mother
    never took and the time I swam away from shore.*

4. *Mother shouting: "Don't go too deep," and I paddling faster, waves slap-
    ping my face casting my tinted glasses to the bottom.*

5. *The life guard blows his whistle.*

6. *My mother is frantic and I gulp blue air, ride the waves to shore.*

7. *She never took my favorite picture or saw me hike to the top of Smuggler's
    Notch, a mile on a slippery path to see the shale lake shaded by evergreens.*

8. *She waited at the bottom and never saw me struggle to the top, slip and fall.*

9. *She preferred pictures of my sister and me, hands folded, in front of some
    visitor center.*

10. *Her cues: sit up, smile, move closer.*

11. *And we obeyed.*

12. *It is no mistake that I stand, the pictures slipping from my lap into the fire.*

13. I watch flames work holes in *pale hued* dresses, *tinseled* trees stacked with
    presents and pajamaed grins, an *iridescent bike, white training wheels
    caught in silent spin.*

14. Free, I touch slimy frogs and baby birds, play baseball in the rain, climb the tallest tree and yell, I won't fall, seven times at the top of my lungs.

15. I never *consider being a blonde* or wear a dress to play outside.

16. *Sunlight streams through maples freckling my arms as I watch a spider cast itself into midair trusting it will catch the other side.*

17. I tiptoe along train tracks, torn blue jeans, a T-shirt, my arms balancing first one way then the other, never seeing a train or a bum.

18. Powerless thieves.

19. No, never, always gone in gold flames.

What is added? Sentences 4–11 detail the fears of the mother and emphasize the importance of the pictures. This addition offers an opportunity the previous draft did not allow. Now, there is a mother in the poem whose impressions of girlhood contrast with those of the speaker.

Writer Response Groups

At this point, you have a dozen or so sentences of varying lengths that fit loosely together. You have expanded these sentences by creating language threads, inserting details, actions, and descriptions generated from at least one word. Do not cut from what you have written. Rather, take this expansion to your writer response group. Shape this work into a poem by focusing on the speaker. Consider who is speaking and begin the work with that person's voice. Use the response group to help you form a clearer idea about the subject of your poem. Examine each other's work, reading for the following elements:

Essential Elements

- What is the poem about?
- Who is the speaker?
- How is the poem organized?

Craft

- Do the sentences lead to a surprise? What makes it surprising?
- Which sentence is most interesting? Which sentence emphasizes something?
- Is the language thread obvious? What connections or emotions are created by the repeated diction in the poem?

Revising: Cutting for Emphasis and Clarity

So far, you have a dozen or so sentences and some ideas about what works and what doesn't work. Your current writing most likely contains extraneous details, and you need to shape your sentences into a poem. It is time for the finishing activity—cutting. Cutting will reduce unnecessary repetition, make wordy sentences into poetic lines, and emphasize diction and details. Keep in mind that cutting will also create the need to make revisions. Many students confuse "cleaning up" with cutting. Cutting for emphasis and clarity, however, requires the poet to rethink her poem's purpose, speaker, and connections. Sometimes the things we love most just don't help the poem or take it in the wrong direction.

Writer's Practice 7.5   *Cut Extraneous Detail*

In poetry, less is more. Now you must cut words and phrases to make your sentences more poetic and to focus the poem to create emphasis. Use the following tips to cut your current draft:

- Cut extraneous details or dialogue. Weigh the value of things that are repeated and cut repetition unless it is used for emphasis or a shift in thinking. Writer's Practice 7.4 encouraged repetition—especially language threads—but too much repetition can drag down a poem. Look for words, images, or details that might be stronger if they appear only once or twice.

- Cut some unnecessary words such as *often*, *a*, *an*, *the*, and *and*, as well as some adjectives and prepositional phrases. At first, cutting these words may seem awkward. Of course, do not feel obligated to cut all such words.

Begin revising if you feel you are ready, or examine our writer's model and explication.

Our Writer

Caught in Silent Spin

My favorite picture from childhood
was never taken. Instead Mother snapped
my sister and me sitting, hands folded, smiles full,

on a cement bench outside the visitor's center
5   of some national park. Frame by frame she shaped
girlhood's photogenic history on cue. Sit up.

Smile. Move closer. And we obeyed. Tonight,
by the glow of blue flames, I page through shadowed
variations of myself. A white gloved princess, an angular

10   ballerina, all knees and elbows, two sisters squeezed
into an inner tube, tinted glasses, toothless grins.
She did not take my picture swimming. Her

shouting: Don't go too deep. Me paddling
toward open water.
15   The lifeguard's whistle. Her frantic. Me

gulping aqua air, riding lapis waves. Or
me standing atop Smuggler's Notch. A mile hike.
A slippery path. A shale lake mirroring evergreens

twisted with determination. She waited
20   at the bottom never seeing me slip
or right myself, my bloody knee cropped

from her picture. Powerless thieves, I think
and cast chromatic past into the fire. Flames claim
pale hued dresses, tinseled trees stacked with pajamaed

25   smiles, an iridescent bike, white training wheels
caught in silent spin. And I?
I am free to climb the tallest tree, touch baby birds,

play baseball in the rain, tiptoe along train tracks,
torn jeans, red T-shirt, my arms balancing one way
30   and then the other, never seeing a train or a bum.

Our writer began focusing on the pictures: "My favorite picture from childhood / was never taken." She varies her sentence patterns and lengths, using a series of short sentences to imitate the orders of a determined mother: "Sit up. / Smile. Move closer. And we obeyed." She also cut even engaging lines. For example, the spider trusting in the other side was cut because it strayed from the speaker reinventing her childhood. In addition, the female stereotypes—being blonde and wearing dresses—were cut. Instead, the poem is dependent on the contrast between the mother's pictures in the album, which defined her vision of girlhood, and the speaker's childhood pictures, which were never taken. This contrast leads the speaker to free herself and to recreate her childhood. Finally, the use of colors became important after researching the word *tint*. Including color actually tinted the photographs, the memories, and the fantasies of the speaker. The colors move from blues to reds in the revision, suggesting some sense of power is gained by the speaker.

Examining Student Poems

Inventing from a sentence frame and using words to propel the freewrites allows the poet to surprise herself. Further, reinventing the poem requires the poet to trust her generating process. A willingness to invent and to reinvent is essential for a young writer. Too often, a writer holds tightly to a weak draft. This chapter encouraged experimentation with diction to expand a draft and possibly change it radically. Allowing the meaning of a poem to emerge from the opportunities that word research can offer is central to writing creatively.

Fish Out of Water

Sarah Butzine

I peek through the crack
of Todd's bedroom door,
watch him pack a large suitcase,
too small for everything he wants.
5   One nicely sealed package,
containing all he believes is important.
The suitcase looks empty to others.
To me.

Piles of new underwear, a single pair
10   of worn corduroy pants, bubble gum
and a bright orange tackle box.
Where are the things I want
Todd to care about? Like me.
Why am I not neatly folded and packed?
15   I could fit.
I could fit next to the tackle box
brought along on fishing trips.
Barefoot, freckle faced, lugging
a bright orange tackle box under his arm,
20   he went to the lake,
Todd the fisherman.
Searching for fish, but not for me.

I was a four foot bass.
Caught,
25   he tossed me back into the water.
Slimy worms, sharp fish hooks, sun
burn, and a rickety dock
were all more fun than me.

When I ask: "Can I come with you Todd?"
30   he turns around to answer but
forgets and zips it closed,
pushes past me
out the door
with a suitcase under his arm.

Sarah begins with the conflict buried at the end of the first sentence: "a large suitcase, / too small for everything he wants." Her long sentence lists the abundance of things the brother has or is associated with: "Piles of new underwear, a single pair / of worn corduroy pants" and "Barefoot, freckle faced, lugging / a bright orange tackle box under his arm, ..." The fragments reflect the speaker's sense of being deprived by her brother. "The suitcase looks empty to others," she reports, then "To me." This very short fragment also reflects her hesitancy in speaking to her brother. The poem's inventive qualities are based on the repeated use of fishing terms.

Until

Tom Wisniewski

You are unlike the nurses,
mice rushing
from here to there.
And when one finally arrives,
5   she calls me *buddy*,
chit-chats about nothing:
weather,
cough,
crusted tongue.
10   She plops a spoon
in my mouth,
I taste hollowness.
"The doctor will be here soon,"
she says, but it is a lie,
15   office jumbled, bumblebee haste:

prescriptions, patients,
paperwork smothering
everything.

Beyond the window,
20 wind tickles two sisters,
carefree kites. Just there,
unaware.
Fog.
London thick, teases leaves,
25 teases me. A quick lick
tastes it. Rain never
felt this good,
too thin,
like the nurses.

30 Where are you? Come
with your chestnut eyes,
crooked smile,
flowing, midnight hair.
Will you come?
35 Will you come to me?
Let's escape into spring wind,
tease tulips. Let's spoon fog
and tickle our tongues, chase
runaway kites, specs
40 of floating dandelion dust,
until none is left.

Tom creates conflict in his first line by focusing the poem on what the "you" is not. He describes what he wants from the relationship by describing first what he doesn't want and, finally, what he does want. The first stanza's long sentences reflect the fast pace of the hospital. The shorter sentences in the second stanza reflect the speaker's longing for a simple life with a companion outside the hospital. They also slow the pace of the poem, illustrating the speaker's reflective mood. The questions support this reflective and slower pace. Notice, too, the contrast in diction from the first to the third stanzas. The nurse "plops" the spoon in the speaker's mouth, suggesting that the nurse is hurried and busy; the girl he dreams of would "tease" tulips and "spoon" fog, suggesting an interest in him and a willingness to spend time with him. Further, this poet selected an unusual word to research: *fog*. The word's repetition, as well as other weather references, gives the poem a playful quality that emphasizes the wish of the speaker to spend carefree time with the girl.

Oak

NICOLAUS CHAFFIN

I Trilliums

When Mother sawed the legs
off our lion pawed table,
an heirloom from her mother,
we weren't surprised. She'd hated
5   the old, gnarled legs and said
she might take a saw to them.
Trilliums and large glass chips
from the broken vase, we carefully collected
as our bare feet dodged great chunks
10   of Mother's toppled birthday cake.
The smell of familiar burning
lit her face, as the oak claws caught fire.
Paws crackled as flames gnawed
at eighty years of polish.

II Strawberry

15   Chocolate cake mix
and a sculpting saw,
my sister and I
had enough money left to split
a pack of strawberry gum.
20   At the counter, a man,
fat and balding with no eyebrows,
a large fading tattoo
on his shoulder, sold us the gum.
He leaned his arm on the counter,
25   told us where we could pick
Mother pretty flowers.
Rode our bikes the shortest way
to the store. Walked the longest back
enjoying our treat. Grass,
30   long rope-like, pulled at our jeans,
wrapped around the pedals
of our bikes. I heard the snap
of my sister's gum.
Crossed the junkyard
35   climbing tractors rusted.
The flowers had only three pale silk
petals. We picked three

<pre>
      between a mound of tires corroded
      and worn metal. Listened to the mud
40   below us. We counted our footsteps
      of mud from the junkyard and
      stuck our gum
      to the tree before the house.
      My sister made the cake.
</pre>

III   Somersaults

<pre>
45   Father watched as mother wept.
      She slid her chair back and set
      her tissue on her sliced grapefruit.
      Left the house in her red hat
      grabbed the rake from the garage.
50   Father unfolded his arms
      from his sweater and gave us
      fifteen dollars and our coats
      sent us to the store to buy
      stuff for her birthday dinner.
55   It wasn't so cold outside,
      just early. We could see breath
      break and whisper from our lips.
      Mother's face reddened, long
      hair swept through her eyes. Raking
60   clean piles from around the oak
      she sat against the trunk and
      lit a cigarette. We crept
      to the hill before the woods.
      Saw her light fade out of view
65   in smoke, the caboose lights of
      a train. Father taught us how
      to somersault on this hill
      last year. We watched the world spin.
      Sky, ground, Father, Mother, sky.
</pre>

Nicolaus tells the story of the mother's birthday in three parts; each part adds details and repeats words that build the tension that leads the mother to such a desperate act. Nic used long sentences and frequent fragments in the inverted story to produce the spinning confusion of the family's anxiety.

Creating
Fiction

Talking on the Back Porch: Leads, Conflict, First-Person Point of View, Dialogue, and Repetition

A work of art is informed by a vision,
but it's also a matter of structure: chapters, paragraphs,
sentences. On that level the work succeeds or fails.

-JOYCE CAROL OATES

There is a bit of storyteller in all of us. You stop friends to laugh about your latest embarrassment or to describe a recent disappointment. You want to hear the juicy details of the newest gossip. You enjoy these stories told on the back porch, at the drinking fountain, or while you are walking down the hall at school. These stories contain real people.

The writer's job is to create characters as real as those of the back porch storytellers, with voices that speak to a reader as if the characters themselves were sitting on the porch swapping stories. Thinking about storytelling like this, rather than as a momentous literary undertaking, makes writing the short story a less intimidating activity. It then becomes almost as simple as looking closely at your daily life and asking What event seems interesting to me?

This chapter asks you to tell a story from the first-person point of view. In other words, the narrator and main character in your story will be the same person and will be identified by the pronoun *I*. The narrator might be you, or someone like you, or he or she might be someone you invent. Whatever the case, in your story you will present this character's thoughts and actions, letting the reader inside this character. You will report what she said to other characters in the story and what was said to her in response. As you do this, you will be revealing this narrator character's sensibility.

Characterization will be the major focus of your writing in this chapter. You will invent a narrator and reveal in him or her a character flaw that is central to the story's conflict. Building conflict from characterization, and then writing a story based on that conflict, is a basic skill of the storyteller.

Another objective in this chapter will be to examine the uses of dialogue and its stylistic characteristics in a story. Good dialogue will aid you in creating a character with a conflict and will make a story and its characters seem real; similarly, poor dialogue is one of the surest ways of ruining a story, of destroying the illusion that these are real people confronting real situations in life. Once you have drafted a story, you will be asked to revise it, paying special attention to how periodic repetition—returning to particular details every now and then in your narrative—helps create cohesion and enlarges the thematic significance of your story.

In "Choking on Love," Stephen Dunning uses the first-person point of view to heighten the immediacy of the narrative. You will also see that the lead sentence actually frames the plot and conflict of the story. Three times the character chokes. Each time, in one way or another, his friend Feinberg is involved. As you read, look for places where the voice of Brian, the narrator, sounds like an actual human voice—like someone on your back porch telling you this story. How and where are the speaker's thoughts and feelings expressed? How do these thoughts and feelings enhance the story?

Choking on Love

STEPHEN DUNNING

Three times that summer I choke to death, and Feinberg's involved in all three. The first time, Feinberg finds a pack of Chesterfields in his father's bowling bag. "Good," he says, "a few smokes."

Feinberg's in high school. Hang around with him, you pretty much do what he does. We light up without too much trouble. I take a couple of puffs, sucking in hot smoke, squishing it around my mouth, then squeezing it out, trying to look experienced. My eyes water, but I don't choke until Feinberg says, "Inhale," and shows how.

I fall, folding so my arms hug my chest, choking to death. Eventually Feinberg's smile disappears, probably thinking he'll be blamed if I die. He kneels and lands a couple of hard whacks on my back. I'm choking so bad I can't holler Stop!

That was the day after school let out. Two days later Mother drives Feinberg and me to Silver Lake. Feinberg dives off the twelve-foot platform and of course I follow.

My head hits bottom, hard.

Next thing I know I'm on my stomach with some life-guard straddling my back, pumping Silver Lake out of my lungs. I remember gasping, spitting water, trying to get breath, and finally Mother's face, up close, hysterical, choking out my name as if *she'd* almost drowned.

The bump on my head is big as a moose, minus the horns.

My third choking is July fifth. Mary Jo McNulty's been on my mind since Valentine's. Mother found my notebook and saw where I'd written Mary Jo's name a few hundred times. "It looks like Brian is smitten," she says at dinner. Big joke, ha ha, everybody laugh. So I clam up.

After my parents leave on their vacation, I decide to walk to Mary Jo's, two miles each way, to sit on her boulevard.

I wait until my sister Marguerite goes out with her boyfriend Malloy. Supposedly Marguerite's taking care of me, but Wednesday she sneaked out, thinking I'm asleep, and Friday, when the three of us go to watch fireworks, she and Malloy go to buy popsicles. Surprise, surprise! They get lost. I could have found them. Necking in Malloy's Plymouth. Now they're going for a coke. "We'll be back by eleven, Lame Brain," Marguerite says.

My name's Brian, not Brain.

I close my eyes and imagine Mary Jo's house, one block past University, behind Chicken Shack. I'll sit until she notices me. It's the chokings. Already I could have died two times. I think about Life and Death: I shouldn't die without giving Mary Jo some signal. If I see Mary Jo and then die, she'll remember me all her life. Be a nun, probably. Anyway, it's not illegal to sit on a boulevard. "They're the City's," Feinberg says. "You do what you want on boulevards." If Mary Jo's father tries to send me away, I'm supposed to say he doesn't own the boulevard, we pay taxes too.

If Mary Jo comes out I'll tell her I like her, which is why I'm walking two miles.

Malloy works at Texaco until nine, so him and Marguerite leave after that. I hang around until nine thirty, playing with my dog Gus. Then I start walking, cruise past houses, some rooms lighted, some dark. I've never headed out this late before. I'll sit until breakfast, if Mary Jo doesn't come out first.

I pass Emerson Junior High, about half way. Then a few blocks I don't know anyone until Larry Graham's, the high school football star. "Garfield's Galloping Ghost," the paper calls him. Behind Chicken Shack I turn right. Third house on Iglehart. Mary Jo's palace. A street light in front, seven big elms on the boulevard. I head for the middle one, across from the front door, and sit.

Now what? I'm always doing something without thinking first. Ask my father. I sit ten minutes. Fifteen. Last day of school Mary Jo told Connie Kowalski she liked me. Also, in the cloakroom last Valentine's, Mary Jo grabbed my face and kissed me. She's the only girl I've kissed, and on Valentine's I thought Yuck. But here I am, sitting on her boulevard.

The smell from Chicken Shack comes and I wish I had more than forty cents.

The mosquito-control truck's orange lights sweep around University and blink down Iglehart. The driver's face is in shadow, but on my side is Garfield's Galloping Ghost, working his cushy summer job. Feinberg's old man says Coach Riordan goes to the city every spring, getting good jobs for his players. I never found out why the Galloping Ghost wants to kick my butt.

I mention that to Feinberg. He asks, "What did you do, Hackett?"

"Nothing."

"Then he won't do anything. Who's this Galloping Goose think he is?"

"Galloping Goose" makes me laugh. I lean back against my tree. The fogger stops ten feet away. I feel street light on my face. Graham smiles and shoves an overhead lever. A tidal wave of mosquito fog rolls at me. I suck in a good faceful of fog, but like a dope, I stand there. The fog feels greasy and I cough.

"Suck on that, Hackett," Graham yells. I'm flattered he knows my name. I try to yell back, but I choke. My eyes burn like crazy. "How's it taste, Hackett?"

Behind me the fog thins out. Stupidly, I walk toward the truck. "Stop!" I croak.

"Oh ho," Graham says. "Make me."

The fog tastes like spoiled milk. "You—" I start, but break into more coughs. "Jerk," I finish, choking on that word like the time I was drowning.

The Galloping Goose laughs again. "Let's go!" he says to the driver. "Hackett, you twerp," to me. The fogger grinds gears and chugs down Iglehart.

I've been called worse. I hope Feinberg never hears Marguerite calling me Lame Brain.

I stagger back to my tree, making fists of my hands and rubbing them into my eyes. A man's voice asks, "Are you ok?"

I can't see any face, but it's Mary Jo's dad. "Yes, sir," I say. Another coughing fit. "I got the mosquito fog."

"Are you all right? You live around here?"

"Yes, sir," I say, answering his first question. Now I see his dark head outlined in street light. "I'm just going to sit and then go." I give a vague nod. "I live over there."

"Do I know you?" Less friendly. "You from the neighborhood?"

"Jeez!" Choking to death's on my mind. I get up and careen a few steps toward University.

"Listen, you," Mr. McNulty says. I stop dead. "Are you here for Mary Jo?" I'm silent. "I don't want you around here again."

I'm supposed to say that the City owns the boulevards and we pay taxes too, but I haven't the nerve. I clear my throat and walk toward Chicken Shack.

My eyes are on fire and my nose is running like crazy. I stand outside Chicken Shack trying to see the change in my hand. Three coins, forty cents. Enough for a small coke plus the phone. I cough deep, trying to clear my throat.

That dang Feinberg, I think. Him and his boulevards.

Chicken Shack is practically empty. I sit at the counter. A waitress brings me water. "Coke," I say.

"Small or large?"

"Small's good." I'm grateful she asks. I dip a paper napkin into my water and daub at my eyes. I actually dip four and stuff them in my pocket so the waitress won't see what I'm doing. My eyes feel better, but my pants are getting soggy.

The girl brings the coke and I spread my coins on the counter. "How much?"

"Dime."

"Just take it," I say. She points an index finger and pulls a coin toward herself. I pick up the others, grab my coke, and walk to the phone alongside the cigarette machine. Two bleached high school girls sit close by. I pocket the quarter and fumble the nickel into the phone's slot. "Eight eight six six," I say, when the operator comes on. It isn't quite eleven, but I'm hoping Marguerite is home.

Marguerite gets it after the third ring. "Hackett residence," she says, like the maid in some phony movie.

"Can I get a ride?"

Her voice rises two octaves. "Where are you?"

"Chicken Shack."

"Where?"

"The chicken place. Can I get a ride?"

"You're gonna get it, you know. It's eleven."

"Oh jeez." I choke and cough. "You rat, I rat. Do I get a ride?"

"What's wrong with you?"

I choke again, trying to answer. "Wait a minute." I can tell she's put her hand over the phone. Malloy's still there.

"GET ME A RIDE!" I yell. The bleached girls look at each other and smirk.

"Stay there," Marguerite says. "Jimmy'll come. You be outside."

"I've been outside all my life," I say, liking how it sounds.

"What?"

"I'll be outside." The cough comes back hard, almost killing me. I want to yell, Hurry! but the phone's already dead.

I'm leaning against Chicken Shack, waiting for Malloy, blinking my eyes. I think what a jerk Graham is, and for a few seconds imagine it was Coach Riordan driving the fogger. I'll never make Coach Riordan's team. Then I think of our mutt Gus, who hung around Feinberg's poodle until Mr. Feinberg asked Father to keep Gus away.

"He's not much of a neighbor," Father said about Mr. Feinberg. But Father fenced our back yard and we kept Gus there, howling his heart out for love of Fifi Feinberg.

Malloy hardly speaks, driving home. I think about Mary Jo and mosquito fog. I remember Graham's mean smile, taste his oily poison in my throat.

Late that summer Mary Jo calls. My throat tightens. I've been thinking about her. "What teachers do you have?" Mary Jo asks.

"Mrs. Sweet for homeroom," I say. Feinberg says Mrs. Sweet's crazy, but that's because she kicked him out of class every other day.

"Me too," Mary Jo says. "I've got her too."

That's fine with me, but I don't say anything. That starts this long silence. I remember the fog again. I see the Goose's mean face. What would Feinberg say?

Finally I clear my throat. "Gotta go," I say. I touch the quarter in my right pocket. Suddenly I don't need Feinberg. "I might go to Chicken Shack, get a coke." I straighten my shoulders. "That anywhere near you?"

Questions

1. How old is Brian when the chokings occur? How old is Brian when he tells the story of the chokings? How do you know?

2. What character flaw causes Brian conflict? What kind of person is Brian?

3. The story is divided into eight sections. What purpose do these breaks serve?

4. Brian's character is revealed through actions, dialogue, and thoughts. Look carefully at the last section. Which action, line of dialogue, and thought demonstrate that Brian is changing?

5. How often, and in what situations, does the word "choke" or one like it occur in the story?

Exploring the Powerful Lead to Establish Conflict

The first sentence or two of a short story is called the *lead*. A well-crafted lead will grab the reader. Often it establishes a conflict. Stephen Dunning says, "I didn't start off writing 'Choking on Love' knowing exactly where it was going, or even how it would end. I wrote and rewrote the beginning several times, until it seemed right. Like many writers, maybe like most, I begin writing without a sure idea of what comes first, what next. Here, once I got the 'I' character in mind, I began imagining actions Brian might take. First came his choking on cigarette smoke. The story took off once I hit on the idea of Brian's choking."

Look at the first sentence of Dunning's story: "Three times that summer I choke to death, and Feinberg's involved in all three." He introduces a character with a dramatized conflict: "Three times that summer I choke to death." The speaker does not say he almost choked to death, which is the truth. Instead, he says, "I choke to death," which dramatizes the events. Moreover, he adds information that deepens this dramatic conflict: "Feinberg's involved in all three." Now the story is about more than the drama of almost dying three times; it is also about the involvement of another person, the impact of Feinberg on the speaker. The lead sentence grabs the reader. It contains a conflict or problem. Equally important, it introduces the first-person narrator with a clear voice.

Experimenting with the Powerful Lead to Establish Conflict

Many novice writers save their best stuff for the middle of their stories. Doing so is a strategic error, however. These writers may lose their readers early, because their prose is flat and lifeless. Writing and rewriting an opening sentence to find one that seems "right" is excellent practice for the novice writer. What makes an opening sentence seem "right"? Most likely, it hooks readers. They read the sentence and think So what happened? The readers want to continue reading, and the most important goal of an opening sentence has been met.

Writer's Practice 8.1   *Write a Powerful Lead*

Use Dunning's approach. Write and rewrite several opening sentences. Don't worry about the direction in which the writing will take you. Simply write a sentence that shows a character in conflict. Select a small daily conflict from your own life to do this work. Although you may fictionalize it later, it will be easier to begin if you are telling your own story. Avoid dramatic issues or problems, though. Use the lessons that you learned in generating poems in Writer's Practices 2.1, 4.1, 5.1, and 5.2 to help you write.

Begin by thinking about yourself. Maybe you are easily frightened or often intimidated. Maybe you are impulsive and frequently get yourself into trouble, or possibly you are indecisive and wait too long to act. Maybe you wish people would treat you better. Once you have identified a character trait that propels you into experiences, recall a simple and seemingly unimportant moment that happened because you acted frightened, intimidated, impulsive, or indecisive, or because you simply wanted to be appreciated. Rewrite the lead sentence several times until you write one that fits the following criteria. The lead sentence will:

- reveal a first-person voice in which readers sense a speaker behind the words.
- include a small conflict the speaker has faced.
- create a sense that the speaker is being honest.

Do this activity three times, as if you are starting three different stories based on three different events in your life. Each time, revise the lead until you create an authentic first-person voice that reveals a small conflict.

Begin writing if you feel you are ready, or examine our writer's model and explication.

Our Writer

#1

I just wanted someone to say, "Wow, Sally, you really did a great job."
"Give me a break! I'm trying my best."
Looking at his beady brown eyes, I could only lie.

Which sentence creates a clear conflict? It may be different for each reader, but the last sentence seems to create a real character with a real problem. Faced with a person, this character feels compelled to lie. To create a story from this sentence, you must decide who has the beady brown eyes and if the eyes are really beady or just looked beady to Sally, who is telling her story. Of course, you also need to invent a lie. The lie will certainly get Sally into trouble, and so the story begins.

#2

I counted the dishes in the sink: one, two, ten, fifteen.
Billy was waiting for me, I had a big roaster and the gravy was burned to the bottom, and I was going to be late.
I never think I'll get caught.

Again, the last sentence gets right to the conflict. What does the sentence provide for the writer? "I" speaks openly about a misconception that most likely prompts the story. "I" does not expect to get caught, but the story will most likely disprove that theory. Or, possibly, the story proves the theory. Either way, the story begins.

#3

> It never fails, I always seem to get myself in trouble.
> I'm a walking problem.
> Everything people say about Murphy's Law is true.

In this case, each sentence states an honest truth that causes "I" problems. Any of the sentences could propel a character into a story. However, the last sentence adds "Murphy's Law," which leaves the writer an interesting option: the speaker of this sentence knows she gets into trouble, but the speaker prefers to blame the trouble on fate. This addition creates an interesting character with a double conflict. First, she is prone to accidents; second, she does not take responsibility for those accidents.

Exploring First-Person Point of View

Storytelling is one of the first things you learned to do with words. You repeated the stories that were told and read to you, probably fairy tales or children's rhymes. It is likely that you told these stories in the third-person point of view, repeating the story as an outsider who was not necessarily directly involved in the action. Third-person is a common point of view used by writers as well. Essentially, it is a story told by an observer who may or may not be in the action of the story. This third-person narrator tells the story of another character. This is the same point of view that you would use to relate to your mother an argument you overheard between your brother and sister.

Eventually, you learned to tell stories in the first-person, stories in which you were the main character. You may have started: *Do you really want to know why I was late for school? You're never going to believe this. . . .* Perhaps a well-told story in the first-person kept you from an afternoon in detention. At some point, too, your first-person stories may have taken on a psychological dimension. Perhaps your stories explained some change inside you.

Whatever the speaker's motives, the focus of the first-person narrative is the speaker and his fortunes—what happens to him, how he reacts, what he thinks and says. Through the language and voice of the speaker, the reader develops a sense of an actual person telling the story. Part of the pleasure of the first-person narrative is having direct access to the narrator's thoughts and perceptions, his outlook, his idiosyncratic "take" on the world.

Dunning's "Choking on Love" gives us such a character. The story succeeds because the voice is so natural, so compelling. Brian tells his story as if he were sitting on the front porch speaking to a friend. He reveals himself not only through his own actions and words, but also through his comments on the actions and words of other characters in the story. The reader trusts Brian. He is open, even telling us embarrassing things: "I've been called worse. I hope Feinberg never hears Marguerite calling me Lame Brain." Brian's thoughts and the way that they are inserted into the narration make Dunning's story effective. He achieves the sense that a real person is telling a real story in his opening paragraphs:

> Three times that summer I choke to death, and Feinberg's involved in all three. The first time, Feinberg finds a pack of Chesterfields in his father's bowling bag. "Good," he says, "a few smokes."
>
> Feinberg's in high school. Hang around with him, you pretty much do what he does. We light up without too much trouble. I take a couple of puffs, sucking in hot smoke, squishing it around my mouth, then squeezing it out, trying to look experienced. My eyes water, but I don't choke until Feinberg says, "Inhale," and shows how.
>
> I fall, folding so my arms hug my chest, choking to death. Eventually Feinberg's smile disappears, probably thinking he'll be blamed if I die. He kneels and lands a couple of hard whacks on my back. I'm choking so bad I can't holler Stop!

From the first word, it is clear that a kid is talking. We are pulled into the story immediately. We see his weakness and its consequences right away. Part of the trick in this narrative voice is the economy of detail. Brian gets right to the point. "Feinberg's in high school. Hang around with him, you pretty much do what he does." Also, only the essential dialogue is reported. "Good," he says. "A few smokes." And then comes a series of events that are rendered with a string of action verbs, visual and direct as a film clip. "I fall, folding so my arms hug my chest, choking to death. Eventually Feinberg's smile disappears, probably thinking he'll be blamed if I die. He kneels and lands a couple of hard whacks on my back." It is a fast start. In 137 words, the reader is already in the story, inside Brian, and eager for more.

Experimenting with First-Person Point of View

You learned in Writer's Practice 2.1 that an authentic voice is a powerful tool in narrative. You will now create the voice of a first-person narrator. Allow a character to tell his or her own story. The character's version of the story will reveal a personal weakness or a difficulty of which the character is unaware. This weakness or flaw will cause the story's conflict. Explore this character flaw by describing an event that illustrates it. Allow your reader inside your narrator's mind by expressing thoughts that reveal the character's attitude or beliefs.

Writer's Practice 8.2   *Create an Honest or Dishonest Voice*

Write the opening of your story using one of the leads you created in Writer's Practice 8.1. This lead provides you with a character and a conflict to explore while it establishes a character's voice. Your work now will be a two-step process. First you will overwrite; then you will compress what you have written. That is, you will be revising and crafting your story sentence by sentence, paragraph by paragraph, and section by section, rather than rushing to write a complete first draft that gets cut and revised as a whole. Trust that your story will take shape as you write and focus on creating a character with an authentic voice and a character flaw—a habit or weakness that the character is not conscious of—that propels him into the problem of the story.

Step One
Introduce a character with a flaw and explore a dramatic situation in which that flaw is apparent.

- Choose an ordinary and natural situation, close to your experience. This flaw and situation need not be momentous. In fact, it is probably better if they are not.
- Include action, dialogue, and your narrator's thoughts and feelings.
- Write the story in present tense. This is a convention of more contemporary writers who try to capture the voice of the narrator. People tend to tell their stories in present tense, the "This-guy-comes-up-to-me-and-says" approach.

Think of this as a "garbage draft" that you will refine in Step Two. Write as much as you can in ten to fifteen minutes, up to three hundred words or more. Remember to use the first-person point of view and to include the pronoun *I*.

Begin writing if you feel you are ready, or examine our writer's model and explication.

Our Writer

Step One

Everything people say about Murphy's Law is true. I just keep forgetting it. Take the door, my kitchen door, the one I've broken twice. Murphy's Law. It's not really my fault. The door sticks. I've been through the "do-it-this-way" lessons. Mother deliberately turning the knob, placing her left hand firmly on the frame above the knob and shoving one time. "With vigor," she says. I do that and it doesn't work. So I try again, deliberate turn, place hand, shove. It really doesn't work until I place my hip on the side of the door. I find that it works better if you place your hip firmly on the center of the door. The effect of leaning your whole body on the door and applying pressure in one vigorous movement really works. You have to be careful, though, because you will fall into the house on the floor, but the door opens. I've revised her directions to deliberate turn, place hip, shove. It works better until Murphy's Law hits. Then my hip goes through the glass, the door still doesn't open, and I'm in trouble.

Our narrator appears to have an honest voice and is eager to share her perspective. Unlike her mother, this speaker blames her problems on Murphy's Law. Her blindness is interesting: She gets into trouble not because she puts her hip through the door, but because she is experiencing the effects of Murphy's Law. Or so she thinks.

Step Two
Once you have finished the freewrite in Step One, immediately write a compressed revision. In other words, cut the sentences down and combine them. Compression is an important tool for the short story writer. In Writer's Practices 2.5, 5.3, and 7.5, you learned strategies that can help you to compress a draft. Use those strategies, as well as the following tips, to reduce your words and focus your writing. Dunning's sentences, shown below, will serve as models of compression.

- Compress a string of actions into a sentence or two with a series of verbs. (*I remember gasping, spitting water, trying to get breath, and finally Mother's face, up close, hysterical, choking out my name as if she'd almost drowned.*)
- Reduce dialogue to one or two important exchanges. Try to capture the essential words that propel the action. ("*Good,*" he says, "*a few smokes.*")
- Insert commentary, the internal self-talk of your character (what your character thought during his and other characters' actions).

Begin revising if you feel you are ready, or examine our writer's model and explication.

Our Writer

Step Two

Murphy's Law, it's true. Take our French doors, the ones I've broken twice. Mom gives me the sticking-door-do-it-this-way lesson: "Deliberately turn and hold the knob. Place your left hand firmly on the frame. Push once with vigor."

> I do that and it doesn't work. My revision works: Deliberate turn, place hip, shove. Ninety-five percent of the time I'm in without a hitch. The two times I've put my hip through the glass, I chalk it up to Murphy's Law.

Lots of compression was done here. For example, the first sentence—originally eight words—is squeezed to four. Stylistically, this sentence sounds more informal, closer to the way a person might voice an idea in his head. In the compressed version, the writer feels free to attribute much more dialogue to the mother. In the process, she eliminates much of the process detail beginning with "So I try . . ." in Step One. The long experimental process also disappears, a positive result that will help the story get off to a stronger, faster start. In effect, only the essential story is kept: what to do, as instructed by the mother, and the repeated failures, suggested by "The two times I've put my hip through the glass, I chalk it up to Murphy's Law."

Finally, note that our writer chose to write about an event that one might share in a casual conversation with a friend. Though not a life-changing event, it provided all that was needed to introduce a character with a flaw and to explore a dramatic situation.

Exploring Characterization Through Dialogue

Characters reveal themselves to a reader through what they think, say, and do. A writer tries to create the flow of a character's thoughts to make that character real for the reader. To help that happen, the writer must make decisions about how and what a characters says and about what is said about her.

Dialogue is speech reported in a story. Essentially, dialogue is anything said aloud. It is usually marked with quotation marks and followed or preceded by a tag of some sort, such as "he said" or "she asked." A change of speaker is marked by an indent. Further, there are rules of grammar that must be observed, such as placement of commas and use of capitals. In Dunning's example below, note the indent and grammatical rules that were followed:

> "Mrs. Sweet for homeroom," I say. Feinberg says Mrs. Sweet's crazy, but that's because she kicked him out of class every other day.
> "Me too," Mary Jo says. "I've got her too."

Dunning's example illustrates the importance of enclosing spoken dialogue in quotation marks. This helps a reader distinguish between a character's thoughts and her speech. For example, Brian says "Mrs. Sweet for homeroom" to Mary Jo. He thinks about what Feinberg would say, but he does not voice those words aloud in the story.

Dialogue is one of the fastest ways to advance the action of the story, to develop characters, and to show consistencies and inconsistencies. It might seem that dialogue would be easy to write. After all, you spend a good portion of your day in dialogue with others. But writing dialogue is not easy. Many novice writers stumble in their attempts to write dialogue. What they write sounds *written*, when it should sound *spoken*. Writing effective dialogue depends on an ability to listen and to develop an ear for the way people speak, just as a musician develops an ear for melody, harmony, and rhythm. Try to spend a few minutes every day listening carefully to people speaking—at home, in the library, on the street, in stores. No doubt, you will note that speakers often do the following:

- speak in short sentences
- answer questions with questions or simply avoid answering
- ignore what is being said by the other person
- change the subject
- respond to things that haven't been said
- repeat words or expressions

Throughout, Dunning's story illustrates these characteristics of dialogue. He creates dialogue with an ear for the way people speak, at the same time developing his characters as real people with real problems. Consider this exchange between Brian and his sister:

> Marguerite gets it after the third ring. "Hackett residence," she says, like the maid in a phony movie.
> "Can I get a ride?"
> Her voice rises two octaves. "Where are you?"
> "Chicken Shack."
> "Where?"
> "The chicken place. Can I get a ride?"
> "You're gonna get it, you know. It's eleven."
> "Oh jeez." I choke and cough. "You rat, I rat. Do I get a ride?"
> "What's wrong with you?"
> I choke again, trying to answer. "Wait a minute." I can tell she's put her hand over the phone. Malloy's still there. "GET ME A RIDE! " I yell. The bleached girls look at each other and smirk.
> "Stay there," Marguerite says. "Jimmy'll come. You be outside."
> "I've been outside all my life," I say, liking how it sounds.
> "What?"
> "I'll be outside." The cough comes back hard, almost killing me. I want to yell, Hurry! but the phone's already dead.

Perhaps most noticeable in this exchange are short sentences and repetition. The longest sentence of dialogue is six words. Most are five words or less. Note, also, that the dialogue is limited to the essential, with no small talk included. Also noteworthy is the number of questions the characters ask each other. "Can I get a ride?" "Where are you?" The brief verbal exchange between Brian and Marguerite reveals character, shows the tension between one character and another, and moves the story forward. This is an important distinction: Unnecessary dialogue can clutter a story.

We can learn about tagging dialogue from this passage, too. Tags indicate who is the speaker. Somehow, the writer must tag the dialogue so that the reader always knows who is speaking. To maintain the scene, the writer may sometimes add action or characters' thoughts and commentary on what is happening. Dunning accomplishes this in his story. Here are three common ways of tagging dialogue:

1. *Speaker tag.* Indicate the speaker with a simple *says/said.* Avoid adverbs, the *-ly* terms that indicate how something was said. (Marguerite gets it after the third ring. "Hackett residence," she says, like the maid in a phony movie.)

2. *Action tag.* Indicate the speaker with a sentence expressing action before or after the speech. ("Oh jeez." I choke and cough. "You rat, I rat. Do I get a ride?")

3. *Thought tag.* Indicate the speaker with a sentence expressing what your character thinks, feels, knows, or wonders. (Her voice rises two octaves. "Where are you?")

Sometimes writers will not provide a tag at all, when the indentions or the situation make it plain who is speaking. In the following untagged dialogue, for example, the identify of the speaker is perfectly clear:

> Marguerite gets it after the third ring. "Hackett residence," she says, like the maid in a phony movie.
> "Can I get a ride?"
> Her voice rises two octaves. "Where are you?"
> "Chicken Shack."

With these technical elements of dialogue in mind, reread Dunning's story. As you read, pay particular attention to the story's dialogue. Notice how Dunning mixes tags and maintains scene. Consider also how the dialogue reveals character and advances the action of the story. Finally, notice that Dunning avoids elaborate verbs of speech such as "hissed," "whined," or "shrieked." Nor does Dunning use adverbs that express the manner of a character's speech, such as "he blurted awkwardly." It is better for a writer to work on fine-tuning the dialogue rather than writing elaborate tags and adverbial modifiers. Realistic talk and unobtrusive verbs of speech will advance the action.

Experimenting with Characterization Through Dialogue

In Writer's Practice 8.2, you got your story started by experimenting with an authentic voice. From the first word, your narrator began to reveal herself to the reader. In dialogue, she further reveals herself in how she talks and reacts to others in the story. The introduction of additional characters brings new voices into your story. With this interplay of voices comes new opportunities for exploring conflict.

Writer's Practice 8.3   *Tell a Tale of Trouble*

Previously, you created a flawed character. Now, move forward with your story by creating a central event. This section of the story will be the longest and will capture the character most fully. The goal is to narrate the major events that trouble the narrator. Write dialogue tagged with actions and thoughts to tell the story. Proceed using a two-step process, as in Writer's Practice 8.2. This time, however, you will expand your work in Step Two.

Step One
Freewrite to get down the action of the story.

- Begin by setting the story in place and time. Do this quickly with a brief reference to the setting.
- Tell of a single incident or a series of brief incidents, moving the story forward in time.
- Place at least one character in addition to your narrator in the scene. (Suggestion: Minimize the number of characters you write in, because the more characters you put in a scene, the harder you have to work to give each one a reason for being there.)

Begin writing if you feel you are ready, or examine our writer's model and explication.

Our Writer

Step One

The narrator is a Girl Scout who volunteers her time. Helping other people makes her feel good about herself. She especially likes to solve problems—the faster way to mow the lawn or weed the flowers. Unfortunately, these faster, more improved methods sometimes get her into trouble. During this visit to the Senior Center she accidentally mows part of the flower border in an attempt to speed the task. The old ladies at the center seem unconcerned about a few flowers and are grateful for the help and give the narrator and her three friends cookies and punch after the girls finish their work. It is at this point that one of the girls notices that a car parked at the very edge of the road is for sale. It's a small car, old, the paint is peeling, but the For Sale sign says $500 or best offer. The girls walk over and examine the car. It has a tape deck and a CD player installed. That probably ups the value since just the stereo is probably worth $500. Each girl suggests what her best offer would be. Then the narrator notices that the car is sticking out into the road a bit more than it should. She imagines that no one would have purposely put a car so close to the road. The car is parked on an incline and it seems obvious that it must have rolled down the incline. The girls conclude the parking brake isn't so good—which is probably why the car is so cheap. The other girls are no longer interested in the car, but the narrator decides to be a good Samaritan and push the car back into the driveway. She figures it is a small car, and it would be easy for them to do. The girls attempt to push the car, but give up after rolling it two feet back. When they let the car slip back to its original spot, it doesn't stop. Instead it continues rolling across the street, until the curb stops it. It now blocks a full lane of the road, causing a traffic jam.

In the first step, our writer refers to "the narrator" but does not make any attempt to write this step as fiction. The first step is a freewrite that explores a minor event. The writer talks the story out and gets the action down without worrying about the technical elements of fiction.

Step Two
Revise Step One, expanding it with special attention to characters. Insert the characters' dialogue to flesh out the story. As you add dialogue, be careful to do the following:

- Write dialogue that reveals character and is important to action.
- Pay attention to the characteristics of conversation.
- Indent whenever there is a change of speaker.
- Vary tags, using speaker, action, and thought tags, as well as untagged dialogue.
- Maintain the scene by reporting your narrator's commentary and occasional observations of the physical environment.
- Include actions.

Begin writing if you feel you are ready, or examine our writer's model and explication.

Our Writer

Step 2

And it's not just French doors that prove Murphy's Law. Just last week, I was doing my volunteer work at the Senior Center. Phyllis, Jennifer, Carol, and I mow the lawns, weed the garden, paint, or clean. The old ladies at the center are really nice and always give us cookies. Carol's always complaining. I don't think she has a charitable bone in her body. If she weren't getting this service bar for scouts, she'd be long gone.

We get there and I get dibs on the mower. It's really the best job; whoever mows gets done first. Plus, I wanna shave time off Phyllis's personal best of 23 minutes and 35 seconds. I figure if I cut close to the flower border, I won't have to come back with the hand clippers. Of course, I was forgetting about Murphy's Law. Let me tell you, impatiens being sucked up by the mower, the mower swerving into the clump as if it had a mind of its own, and the green stubble left when I finally got control again are not a pretty sight.

How do I hide this? That was my first thought, a stupid one, too.

When Mrs. White appears with a plate of cookies, she looks right at the impatiens and says, "Murphy's Law, huh?"

It's then Carol sees this yellow Fiat parked in the drive across from the center with a red "For Sale" sign on the windshield. We grab another cookie, say, "Next week," to Mrs. White and walk toward the car.

"Hey, it's only 500 bucks."

"Or best offer."

"Char, what's your best offer?"

"For a yellow, peeling, rusted shoe box?" I walk around the car as if I'm a buyer. "Fifty. No, no, thirty."

Carol presses her face against the driver's window, cupping her hands to block the sun. "It's got a CD player and huge speakers. I bet the stereo is worth $500."

Phyllis and Jennifer attach themselves to the passenger window, and I peer through the back window. Sure enough, there are two 12-inch speakers screwed into the back seat.

"I'm in for 125," says Phyllis.

"Cheap! Cheap!" Jennifer shoves the last of her cookie into her mouth, spitting crumbs onto the peeling hood.

A gold Caddy slows down, the driver stares at the Fiat, swerves into the left lane then speeds up. I can't imagine why anyone who could afford a Cadillac would be interested in a junker Fiat. When a Ford truck does the same thing, I realize the Fiat has rolled into the street.

"Hey, this piece of junk is a hazard."

"I wouldn't call peeling paint a hazard." Phyllis runs her hand across the hood.

"The speakers, pea brain. You could go deaf," says Carol.

"No. It's rolled into the street," I say.

"Monster stereo or no monster stereo, if the brake's broke, I wouldn't pay thirty," says Jennifer.

"An accident. It could cause an accident." I flap my arms to get their attention. It doesn't take much to convince them we need to push the car back; it's small, we're strong, just three or four feet would do it. Phyllis finds a rock in the guy's garden, readies herself to slip it under the tire. I call out, "Ready, set, heave." It works. The car moves back. I yell, "The rock," but Phyllis isn't fast enough.

"Be ready," I shout. Then, "Put your hips into it, girls. Ready, set, heave." The car moves.

It's then a convertible full of guys drives past. Carol steps back and waves, and we lose our power. It's just like her, never caring about the other guy. I grit my teeth trying to hold the car, Jennifer's grunting next to me, I can't even say THE ROCK and finally we let go. The car rolls, first to the edge of the street, then into the street, then horns, screeching brakes, and tires bouncing against the opposite curb. We stand and stare as if we never saw a flaking yellow Fiat blocking traffic before.

In the narrative, our writer has adopted the first-person point of view, beginning with the sentence "And it's not just French doors that prove Murphy's Law. Just last week, I was. . . ." The writer presents more illustrations of the effect of Murphy's Law on her. The narrator thinks, calculates, and makes things happen. The more she tries to control the situation, the more surely her acts lead to disaster. She does not see her flaw. She is convinced Murphy's Law is the culprit.

The narrative language in this second step has the informal, easy flow of thought. The narrator responds to and comments on physical setting and events, providing the story with both internal and external action. Finally, the writer inserts realistic dialogue to flesh out the character's thoughts:

It's then Carol sees this yellow Fiat parked in the drive across from the center with a red "For Sale" sign on the windshield. We grab another cookie, say "Next week," to Mrs. White and walk toward the car.

"Hey, it's only 500 bucks."

"Or best offer."

"Char, what's your best offer?"

"For a yellow, peeling, rusted shoe box?" I walk around the car as if I'm a buyer. "Fifty. No, no, thirty."

Still in the draft stage, this material is beginning to look like fiction. The writer is clearly applying what she has learned about voice and dialogue.

Writer's Practice 8.4   *Create a Closing Conversation*

Write a third event for your story in which you end the story and bring your narrator to knowledge. Make this a brief addition of one hundred or two hundred words. In this section, try to do the following:

- Create a shift in time of a day or two, or even a week or a month.
- Use the characters you created previously to close the story. You might use a character who plays a small role in an earlier section, but avoid introducing new characters.
- Have the character you are retrieving from previous sections initiate a conversation with the narrator. Allow the narrator to view the situation in a new way and to respond differently than he or she has before.
- Use dialogue supported with actions and thoughts to illustrate the change in the narrator's character.

Begin writing if you feel you are ready, or examine our writer's model and explication.

Our Writer

> Next week as I mow, Mrs. White stations herself on the steps. Phyllis and Jennifer pull weeds silently. Carol quit two hours short of her service bar. Her words still sting, "I'm done helping others. I'm helping myself from now on."
>
> When the cookie plate gets put in front of me, I don't take one. Penance, I think.
>
> "Take one," says Mrs. White. "They sold the car. Thirty bucks." She smiles and points at the impatiens. "The cropped patch is less noticeable this week."
>
> "Worms?" Jennifer shoves the last of her cookie into her mouth, spitting crumbs onto the sidewalk.
>
> "Good Samaritans," I say and take a cookie.

Our writer closes her story with just 108 words. This tight conclusion is completely dependent on dialogue. Mrs. White is retrieved from the first section. Her knowledge of previous events emphasizes for readers that Char was the cause of the accidents. It would be difficult for her to blame Murphy's Law another time. In this section, Char is no longer blind to her character flaw.

Writer's Practice 8.5   *Assemble the First Draft*

Look back at the passages you wrote for Writer's Practice 8.2 through 8.4 and, without making any changes, put them together. This may require scissors and cellophane tape if you are not working on a word processor. Leave white space between the passages to indicate the breaks in your narrative. A white space break is a simple technique that many contemporary writers use to indicate a shift in time, setting, or even point of view.

Begin assembling the sections if you feel you are ready, or examine our writer's model and explication.

Using White Space

In some short stories, writers use white space to create units of meaning. New writers can often manage a story more easily by creating several well-developed and related units. Each unit serves to move the story forward, and the white space between units allows the writer to make leaps in time and setting.

By using white space and units, the writer doesn't have to include the wordy transitions or dull details that make a story complicated and sometimes confusing. Instead, only the relevant and significant moments of a story are included.

Our Writer

Everything people say about Murphy's Law is true. I just keep forgetting it. Take the door, my kitchen door, the one I've broken twice. Murphy's Law. It's not really my fault. The door sticks. I've been through the "do-it-this-way" lessons. Mother deliberately turning the knob, placing her left hand firmly on the frame above the knob and shoving one time. "With vigor," she says. I do that and it doesn't work. So I try again, deliberate turn, place hand, shove. It really doesn't work until I place my hip on the side of the door. I find that it works better if you place your hip firmly on the center of the door. The effect of leaning your whole body on the door and applying pressure in one vigorous movement really works. You have to be careful, though, because you will fall into the house on the floor, but the door opens. I've revised her directions to deliberate turn, place hip, shove. It works better until Murphy's Law hits. Then my hip goes through the glass, the door still doesn't open, and I'm in trouble.

And it's not just French doors that prove Murphy's Law. Just last week, I was doing my volunteer work at the Senior Center. Phyllis, Jennifer, Carol, and I mow the lawns, weed the garden, paint, or clean. The old ladies at the center are really nice and always give us cookies. Carol's always complaining. I don't think she has a charitable bone in her body. If she weren't getting this service bar for scouts, she'd be long gone.

We get there and I get dibs on the mower. It's really the best job; whoever mows gets done first. Plus, I wanna shave time off Phyllis's personal best of 23 minutes and 35 seconds. I figure if I cut close to the flower border, I won't have to come back with the hand clippers. Of course, I was forgetting about Murphy's Law. Let me tell you, impatiens being sucked up by the mower, the mower swerving into the clump as if it had a mind of its own, and the green stubble left when I finally got control again are not a pretty sight.

How do I hide this? That was my first thought, a stupid one, too.

When Mrs. White appears with a plate of cookies, she looks right at the impatiens and says, "Murphy's Law, huh?"

It's then Carol sees this yellow Fiat parked in the drive across from the center with a red "For Sale" sign on the windshield. We grab another cookie, say, "Next week," to Mrs. White and walk toward the car.

"Hey, it's only 500 bucks."

"Or best offer."

"Char, what's your best offer?"

"For a yellow, peeling, rusted shoe box?" I walk around the car as if I'm a buyer. "Fifty. No, no, thirty."

Carol presses her face against the driver's window, cupping her hands to block the sun. "It's got a CD player and huge speakers. I bet the stereo is worth $500."

Phyllis and Jennifer attach themselves to the passenger window, and I peer through the back window. Sure enough, there are two 12-inch speakers screwed into the back seat.

"I'm in for 125," says Phyllis.

"Cheap! Cheap!" Jennifer shoves the last of her cookie into her mouth, spitting crumbs onto the peeling hood.

A gold Caddy slows down, the driver stares at the Fiat, swerves into the left lane then speeds up. I can't imagine why anyone who could afford a Cadillac would be interested in a junker Fiat. When a Ford truck does the same thing, I realize the Fiat has rolled into the street.

"Hey, this piece of junk is a hazard."

"I wouldn't call peeling paint a hazard." Phyllis runs her hand across the hood.

"The speakers, pea brain. You could go deaf," says Carol.

"No. It's rolled into the street," I say.

"Monster stereo or no monster stereo, if the brake's broke, I wouldn't pay thirty," says Jennifer.

"An accident. It could cause an accident." I flap my arms to get their attention. It doesn't take much to convince them we need to push the car back; it's small, we're strong, just three or four feet would do it. Phyllis finds a rock in the guy's garden, readies herself to slip it under the tire. I call out, "Ready, set, heave." It works. The car moves back. I yell, "The rock," but Phyllis isn't fast enough.

"Be ready," I shout. Then, "Put your hips into it, girls. Ready, set, heave." The car moves.

It's then a convertible full of guys drives past. Carol steps back and waves, and we lose our power. It's just like her, never caring about the other guy. I grit my teeth trying to hold the car, Jennifer's grunting next to me, I can't even say THE ROCK and finally we let go. The car rolls, first to the edge of the street, then into the street, then horns, screeching brakes, and tires bouncing against the opposite curb. We stand and stare as if we never saw a flaking yellow Fiat blocking traffic before.

Next week as I mow, Mrs. White stations herself on the steps. Phyllis and Jennifer pull weeds silently. Carol quit two hours short of her service bar. Her words still sting, "I'm done helping others. I'm helping myself from now on."

When the cookie plate gets put in front of me, I don't take one. Penance, I think.

"Take one," says Mrs. White. "They sold the car. Thirty bucks." She smiles and points at the impatiens. "The cropped patch is less noticeable this week."

"Worms?" Jennifer shoves the last of her cookie into her mouth, spitting crumbs onto the sidewalk.

"Good Samaritans," I say and take a cookie.

Our writer's accident-prone narrator takes us from one mishap to another. In the process, does a change occur in this character? What issues does the story raise? Questions such as these will be explored in a response group.

Writer Response Groups

At this point, you have a story with three sections. Section One reveals a character weakness in a first-person narrator. Section Two relates an event or series of events that tell the story of a problem caused by the character's weakness. Section Three presents a brief event to illustrate how the main character comes to a realization as a result of the problem. Don't cut or clean up your draft, but make it as legible as possible for review by a response group. Examine each other's work, reading for the following elements:

Essential Elements

- Whose story is it?
- What is the conflict?
- How is the action plotted?

Craft

- Can the reader trust the narrator? Is the narrator's voice compelling?
- Are the main character's actions prompted by his or her flaw?
- Where in the narrative are the main character's thoughts expressed?
- What do these thoughts reveal about the main character?
- What does the dialogue reveal about the characters?

Revising with Repetition to Create Meaning

When a writer uses white space in a story, special attention must be paid to connecting the sections. These connections help readers sense that the story sections are related and fit together. While listening to a friend on the back porch, we are willing to let the speaker skip around to explain how the pieces of his story relate, even if he gets off the subject. A fiction writer, however, avoids explanations that get him off the subject; he puts connections in place neatly and economically. A common device for establishing these connections is repetition. In Writer's Practice 3.2, 6.1, 7.3, and 7.5, you learned strategies for creating meaning with metaphorical connections, repeated words and images, and language threads.

Dunning's story provides an illustration. Brian chokes in every section of the story. The word itself occurs repeatedly. Brian's choking is echoed in his inability to get his words out. Also, he chokes in a figurative sense: He cannot be assertive and make things go his way. This echo of the choking image opens the second section of the story:

> My third choking is July fifth. Mary Jo McNulty's been on my mind since Valentine's. Mother found my notebook and saw where I'd written Mary Jo's name a few hundred times. "It looks like Brian is smitten," she says at dinner. Big joke, ha ha, everybody laugh. So I clam up.

Here, Brian clams up and lets himself be bullied. In a sense, his passiveness continues almost to the end of the story. He chokes and coughs with Feinberg, and then again when he is confronted by the Galloping Ghost. When Mary Jo's dad interrogates him, Brian suffers a coughing fit. He never manages to say what he has prepared himself to say. Sitting in the Chicken Shack, he tastes Graham's "oily poison in his throat." The change in Brian, as the story moves to its conclusion, is signaled by the choking image in the last paragraph, "Finally I clear my throat." He finds the assertiveness he needs to speak directly to Mary Jo and make his move. In addition, Dunning replays other details that, though less important, give the story a clear sense of connectedness through the use of repetition.

Writer's Practice 8.6   *Insert Repetition*

Read through your narrative and look for a sensory detail or a phrase that lends itself to repetition. Think in terms of a small detail to be added and echoed in each section. Take this detail from the middle section, but insert it in both the first and last sections.

As you focus on repetition, also consider problems in the narrative. Look closely at the concerns and suggestions pointed out by your Writer Response Group. Be sure that every action and all the dialogue contribute to the story. Removing the nonessential parts of the story may involve making some difficult, but necessary, cuts. It may help to review the compression lessons you learned in Writer's Practice 8.2 as you trim your finished story to six hundred to fifteen hundred words.

Begin revising if you feel you are ready, or examine our writer's model and explication.

Our Writer

The Good Samaritan

Murphy's Law is true, and our French doors, the ones I've broken twice, prove it. Mom's given me the sticking door lesson: "Deliberately turn and hold the knob. Place left hand firmly on the frame. Push once with vigor." But she's stronger than me. I do that and it doesn't work. My revision works: Deliberate turn, place hip, shove. Ninety-five percent of the time I'm in without a hitch. The two times I've put my hip through the glass, I chalk up to Murphy's Law.

And it's not just French doors that prove it. Just last week, I was doing my volunteer work for senior citizens. Jennifer, Carol, and I mow lawns, weed, paint, or clean. Mrs. White is the nicest. She makes the best cookies. Carol's always complaining. I don't think she has a charitable bone in her body. If she weren't getting this service bar for scouts, she'd be long gone.

We get there and I get dibs on the mower. It's the best job. Plus, I wanna shave time off Jen's personal best of 23 minutes and 35 seconds. I figure if I cut close to the flower border, I won't have to come back with the hand clippers. Of course, I was forgetting about the inevitable. Let me tell you, a mower swerving as if it had a mind of its own, sucking up red and pink blossoms and leaving green stubble, is my definition of "wrong."

How do I hide this? That was my first thought, a stupid one, too.

When Mrs. White appears with a plate of cookies, she looks right at the stubble and says, "Murphy's Law, huh?"

It's then Carol sees this yellow Fiat parked in the drive across the street with a red "For Sale" sign on the windshield. We grab another cookie, say, "Next week," to Mrs. White and walk toward the car. I'm glad to have an excuse to leave quick.

"Hey, it's only five hundred bucks."

"Or best offer," Jen corrects. "Char, what's your best offer?"

"For a yellow, peeling, rusted shoe box?" I walk around the car as if I'm a buyer. "Fifty. No, no, thirty."

Carol presses her face against the driver's window, cupping her hands to block the sun. "It's got a CD player and huge speakers. I bet the stereo is worth $500."

Jen and I peer through the passenger window and inspect two 12-inch speakers.

"Monster speakers. I'm in for fifty-five," I say.

"Cheap! Cheap!" Jen shoves the last of her cookie into her mouth, spitting crumbs onto the peeling hood.

A gold Caddy slows down, the driver stares at the Fiat, swerves into the left lane, then speeds up. I can't imagine why anyone who could afford a Cadillac would be interested in a junker Fiat. When a Ford truck does the same thing, I say, "Hey, this piece of junk is a hazard."

"I wouldn't call peeling paint a hazard." Jen runs her hand across the hood.

"The speakers, pea brain. You could go deaf," says Carol.

"No. It's rolled into the street," I say.

"Monster stereo or no monster stereo, if the brake's broke, I wouldn't pay five hundred," says Jen.

"An accident. It could cause an accident." After I flap my arms to get their attention, it doesn't take much to convince them we need to push the car back; it's small, we're strong, just three or four feet would do it. Carol finds a rock and readies herself to slip it under the tire. I call out, "Ready, set, heave." The car moves back. I yell, "The rock," but Carol isn't fast enough, and we can't hold it.

"Be ready," I shout. Then, "Put your hips into it. Ready, set, heave." The car moves.

It's then a convertible full of guys hooting and whistling drives past. Carol looks up and waves. It's just like her, never caring about the other guy. Jen and I are left gritting our teeth trying to hold the car, I can't even grunt THE ROCK, and we let go. The car rolls, first to the edge of the street, then into the street, then horns, screeching brakes, and tires bouncing against the opposite curb. We stand and stare as if we never saw a flaking yellow Fiat blocking traffic before.

All Carol can say is, "This is bad."

The next week Carol tells us from her bedroom window, "I'm done helping others. I'm helping myself from now on." Jen mows, Mrs. White and Mom station themselves on the steps. I pull weeds.

When the cookie plate gets put in front of me, I don't take one. Penance, I think.

"Take one," says Mrs. White. She smiles and points at the stubble in the flower bed. "Not so bad this week."

"Worms?" Mom asks.

Jen shoves me with her hip, "Murphy's Law. Right, Char?"

I shake my head and say, "These hips are retired." Then I take two cookies, hand one to Mom, and smile.

Originally, this story included four girls in the second section. To clarify the speakers and reduce problems in tagging dialogue, our writer cut Phyllis. That character was not essential to the narrative, and eliminating her character solved a technical problem. The Fiat scene illustrates the elements of good dialogue:

A gold Caddy slows down, the driver stares at the Fiat, swerves into the left lane, then speeds up. I can't imagine why anyone who could afford a Cadillac would be interested in a junker Fiat. When a Ford truck does the same thing, I say, "Hey, this piece of junk is a hazard."

"I wouldn't call peeling paint a hazard." Jen runs her hand across the hood.

"The speakers, pea brain. You could go deaf," says Carol.

"No. It's rolled into the street," I say.

"Monster stereo or no monster stereo, if the brake's broke, I wouldn't pay five hundred," says Jen.

"An accident. It could cause an accident."

The girls are so absorbed in their review of the stereo, they appear to be involved in separate conversations, not really paying attention to each other.

Our writer makes repeated references to both Murphy's Law and the hips that get Char into trouble in all three sections. The action of the story issues from a simple character flaw: Char does not want to recognize that she causes the problems.

Examining Student Stories

Masterful handling of technical elements such as character, conflict, and dialogue can draw readers into a fictional world of vivid and interesting characters.

The Boy

KYLE STOUT

We are at the top of the highest roller coaster in the world when I decide I don't want to go. The large chain clinks and I turn around to watch it from the back car. It is black, and greasy.

"That chain won't slip, will it?" I say to Todd's wild blue eyes. He raises his arms to shame me and says, "It's scarier this way!"

"Those churros had better stay down!" I joke to Kim. Todd scares me like he does all the time, so I look away and hold my girlfriend. At the top, we are in space. Weightless for just a moment, the earth finally pulls us down.

I scream like a girl and find my head between my knees. So much for courage. Todd spins around and yells, "Karl, spit for the camera!" We both miss, but the camera gets us puckering, our heads flung back in the air. Now, I look at that picture and smile.

When it came time to leave, I didn't want to go. Sometimes, I don't know why I ever signed up for the Navy. Worse, I haven't heard from anyone since I left last week. I think about them a lot. Nights don't bring me much comfort or sleep now. I miss Tippy curled up at the end of my bed. Too often I lay on my bed in cold sweats shaking, listening to the hum of the propeller, wanting to run, thinking about glorious high school days. It feels like I'm getting larger and the walls are closing in around me. Last night I thought about Homecoming my senior year, I'm waving to Todd in the parade as the Homecoming-King float passes, blue and gold streamers blowing in the wind. Then I thought of Grandpa's funeral, when Todd and I played "Taps" together; our silver trumpets did not waver.

The walls are all gray here. Navy couches and pictures of brave men line the walls. Each picture has a medal above it. I think back to when I was eight and my Grandpa gave me his Silver Star. I lost it. Maybe that's what made me join up. Grandma told me how he stormed a machine-gun nest, how the scar on his head was from a rifle bullet.

Tonight we pull up the couches, turn up the lights, light a few cigarettes, eat some greasy chips, and play euchre. I bring the cards so I deal first. My partner Matt Magar talks about how moving ship crates has increased his muscularity. He always talks about his girlfriend at Bowling Green and about how he thinks she's probably crying every night missing him. "Check these bad boys out," he boasts, pulling back his shirt sleeves and flexing. Both biceps have barbed-wire tattoos around them. I wonder what they will say at the nursing home when he's eighty. "These are what the chicks go for."

"Really?" I reply.

"Sure," he says, "Boy, you hafta work out!"

I think about a Jane Goodall video I saw in high school. He reminds me of one of the apes. "You know, they really aren't that big."

He looks at me quickly, then even more quickly leaps up, grabs my collar, and lifts me out of my seat as I struggle to grab something fixed on the ground. I feel his pimple-covered nose against mine and smell his breath as he presses his face to mine. He makes me stare him in his cold blue eyes. A cocky smile flashes before he drops me.

Now the table breaks up in laughter. Matt sneers, "Kiddies without guts shouldn't talk so much!" I pick up my chair and sit at the table. I'm a chump.

"What's the score?" I ask, a little flustered. Noel, an Indian from Baltimore, has already dealt the next hand during the commotion. We pull our hands close to our chests, assume slight frowns, push our eyebrows together, lean back on our chairs, glance at each other like gangsters in smoke-filled rooms from the movies.

"Ugh, Umm," Matt clears his throat to get my attention and then gives me the secret signal to call hearts if I get the chance. What an idiot. I look at my hand, all black.

"I don't cheat," I say. Matt looks at me cock-eyed and smiles before hitting the table and standing back up. I think of Jane Goodall again.

"Can we go outside for a second?" he asks me, emphasizing each word.

I'm afraid, but pretty sure I can run faster than him if he comes after me. "Yeah," I say and follow him out the large iron door as the other guys smile at each other and peer at us over their shoulders.

"What's wrong with you anyway?" Matt asks.

"Many things," I say.

"That's not cheating. It's part of the game."

"I just don't cheat."

"The only way to win is to cheat."

"I know. I never win."

Matt can see this is going nowhere. "Okay," he says, "I'll cheat so we will win." Before I can grab him, he's back inside. We sit at the table.

I look down and grab an M&M cookie my Mom sent me. It's Matt's deal now. Matt is talking to the other guys about how we should have won that hand, and they smile as he shuffles the maize and blue cards. He tells them he's giving me tips, taking me under his wing, while he stacks the deck. He stacks with the best of them, but I notice and pretend to ignore him as he deals, "One, four, one, four, four, one, four, one."

What am I doing, I think. I don't want to be part of this. "Crap, are we play-ing farmer's hand rules?" I ask trying to keep Matt from calling it up, although I have a great hand. I watch him look at the other guy's hands when they're not looking. He picks it up. I can see there's no way out.

We take every hand despite my efforts and Matt says, "Next time you guys should make it harder for us. You're not that stupid are you?"

Noel laughs and says, "Man, you're such a weaseling cheater!" I smile but stay silent. Our victory makes me sick.

Matt puts his arm around my shoulder, pulls me close, "Hey, you're looking at the picture of a perfect team."

In the morning is Scuba Diving 101. Matt points to me and says, "C'mon, boy." He plans to take me down alone. Looking over the gray water, I don't want to go. I've heard about the nasty currents and am terrified by the height of the waves in the windy conditions. "This is all about courage, not intelli-gence," he says.

"Am I going to die?" I ask him blatantly.

"Boy, face that fear," he jumps into the water and disappears. I put my head between my knees and roll into the water hesitantly behind him.

My mask fills with water because I forget to hold it against my face. The water is so cold that I wonder if ice can form inside of wet suits. Strong currents push me around in the blackness as I desperately try to find Matt, sure I'll see Todd's blue eyes when I look into his face mask. Suddenly I notice bubbles streaming past my face and notice my regulator hose is leaking badly. It's like a dream in slow motion. When Matt reappears, my hands flail signaling that my regulator hose is leaking. He looks down, looks back at me, smiles, puts my thumb over the hole, signals me to descend, and vanishes in the blackness.

For a moment I float in space, my weights pulling me down. My regulator is filling with water. I'm alone. The world is spinning and I kick my fins spasmodically and claw at the blackness, searching for a way out, and I know I am afraid. I think of Todd's wild blue eyes and then it comes to me. I'm a man. And this is not the way to get a silver star. I drop a weight, and slowly but carefully start to ascend.

Kyle creates a character, Karl, who comes to understand what it is to be a man. This rite of passage begins with a moment when Karl was afraid and replays his fear several times in the story. Karl is continually trying to prove himself to others. He tries to hide his fear, and it isn't until the brief but important conversation with Matt in the last section that Karl understands that he is the only person who needs to see himself as a man. This realization helps him to act responsibly. Karl's fear propels the conflicts of the three sections and is central to Karl's rite of passage and eventual self-discovery.

chapter 9

Transforming Memory to Fiction: Setting, Movement, and Theme

I went back to the first paragraph. The character was sitting at the counter of a truck-stop restaurant. A bland third-person narrator—myself, I mean—told the reader this. So in a way I already knew what was uninteresting about the story. I was the wrong person to tell the story, for some reason. So I changed the narration to first person. I didn't know who this new speaker was, but he had to be more interesting than me. He sat at the counter for only a moment before he noticed what I had not. He saw a pie case behind the counter. He looked into the case and saw the pies. He noticed that the meringue was "real dilapidated." Then he noticed the detail that made the story possible, and easy, and fun to write. He saw a couple of flies on the inside of the glass pie case.

-LEWIS NORDAN

In some respects, sitting down to write a story is like sitting down to read one. The same elements urge you forward. In the case of reading, your pleasure is heightened when you are presented with a character speaking to you in a distinct voice. When this character is faced with an interesting conflict, your pleasure is further enhanced. Character and conflict motivate you to read on. In the previous chapter, we established that narrative voice and conflict are important elements to consider when you begin a story. Rather than plotting a story in advance, like you might outline an essay, you are better off beginning with small things: a voice, a person faced with a conflict. Rather than beginning with a point you want your story to make, like the thesis of an essay, you are better off beginning with an interesting situation that draws the reader in. What will happen next?

Another important consideration for early in your writing is setting. This chapter focuses on establishing the place and time of a story, involving characters in an action, and moving the characters and action from one setting to another. You will work at the beginning with a character in a specific place, giving her a problem to solve, and then moving her toward resolution of that problem. Establishing setting is important so that readers don't become confused about time and place as the story develops.

As you read the following story by Michael Martone, notice that the action moves from one setting to another. Pay close attention to the writer's treatment of place and time. At what points in the story does the setting change? What cues does Martone provide to indicate these changes in setting?

On the Planet of the Apes

MICHAEL MARTONE

I was always one of those who hid in the trunk. You paid by the head at the Lincolndale Drive-In off US 30 on the north edge of Fort Wayne. There was an orange A&W shack across the highway from the entrance. We stopped there just as the sun was going down and drank root beers, sitting on the bumpers of somebody's father's car. The parking lot had been oiled and the heat of the day had squeezed out little blobs of tar breaded with dust. You flashed your lights on and off when you were finished, and a car hop who knew we were from the county and ignored us came over to gather up the mugs. Then three or four of us climbed into the trunk, fitting ourselves together like a puzzle. Two others always rode up front, somebody alone would be suspicious. One of them would drop the lid on us, bouncing on it a time or two to make sure it latched.

At first, the dark smelled like rubber, the rubber of the spare tire and someone's sneaker in my face. The car rolled slowly over the packed dirt of the lot, stepped around the ruts, then made a short burst across the highway to join the conga line of cars leading up to the theater gates. It was hot inching our way up to the box office. The trunk was lined with a stadium blanket. Who knows what we were breathing, the mothballs, the exhaust from the idling car. The brakes clinched next to my head. The radio from the cabin was muffled by the seat. I always thought I would almost faint from the lack of oxygen, and then I would. I went light-headed, floating in space, my limbs all pins and needles and the roof of the world pricked by stars.

"Dan O!" They called me Dan O then. They hauled me out of the trunk by the cuffs on my jeans. The car had its nose up, beached on the little hill that aimed it toward the screen. I slumped on the rim of the trunk sniffing the air, looking at the next swell of dirt, a line of cars surfing its crest, moored by the speaker cords to silver posts. It was wrong. I swore I would never do it again. I staggered up out of the trunk, afraid I was turning into some kind of juvenile delinquent. "Book me," I yelled to my friends as they filtered between the cars toward the cinder brick refreshment stand to buy overpriced burgers and fries with the money we saved sneaking in.

I was telling this to Chuck Heston in the green room of the convention. The green room was a trailer with no windows parked beneath the scaffolding of the podium. The crowd on the floor above sounded like the wind, and Chuck looked scoured and bronzed. He listened intently, his smile frozen on his face.

"Do you remember where you were from in *The Planet of the Apes?*" I asked him.

"From Earth?" he asked, without moving his lips.

"That's right," I said, "but where on Earth?" I could see again the inquisitor ape in white robes interrogating the crazed astronaut. This is before we know about the beach with the broken Statue of Liberty buried in the sand. Chuck had been huge on the screen at the drive-in, his head as big and as brilliant as the moon. The screen is now a ruin itself, plywood plates have popped out of its backing exposing the girders rank with pigeons. The box office is abandoned. The neon has been picked over and scavenged. The high fences are sunk in the weeds.

I saw them all, I told him. *The Planet of the Apes. Beneath the Planet of the Apes. Escape from the Planet of the Apes. Conquest of the Planet of the Apes. Battle for the Planet of the Apes.* I saw the first one with my high school friends at the Lincolndale that summer after law school. As a joke they put me in the trunk by myself where I rattled around with the tire iron and the jack.

"I could have been disbarred before I was even barred," I told Chuck. That night at the drive-in, my friends and I sifted through the rows of cars to the playground of swings and seesaws under the screen. I climbed up into the monkey bars and talked with my friends about the future. The huge clock projected above our heads slowly ticked down the time remaining until the movie started.

That night, before I had even seen the movie, I sensed that I was different from the rest, an alien walking among them. I imagined that the amphitheater of parked cars stretching into the dark had come to see me, caught inside a cage. I looked out over the expanse of cars. Clouds of dust floating along the lanes were illuminated by the headlights for a moment before they were extinguished. There was the murmur of the speakers, hundreds of repeating messages reverberating in each car. I thought, I'm your man. I'm the one you're looking for.

Chuck hadn't moved. He had stared at me while I talked, his face sagging some as I went on with my reminiscence. Above us the convention crowd howled, a gale force. We would be on soon.

"You," I said, "were from Fort Wayne in the movie." And he looked a little relieved. "The astronaut you played was from Fort Wayne, and the apes took that as another bit of evidence of your hostile intention."

"Oh," he said, "I had forgotten."

"I'm from near there," I said.

I wanted to tell him that back then it had been important that someone like himself had come from that part of the planet even if it was all made up. And now I was here with him waiting for what would happen next.

His head was huge, I remember. As big as the moon. And when the news of his character's nativity seeped into the cockpit of the car, we pounded fists on the padded dash, hooting and whistling. We flashed the car lights and honked the horn until the steering wheel rang. For several minutes, all the cars rocked and flashed, the blaring horns drowning out what was being said on screen. It seemed at any second these hunks of metal we rode in would rise up and come alive. But they didn't.

Questions

1. How much time passes in this story? How do you know?
2. What are the different settings in the story?
3. What does the narrator want?
4. What recurring images do you notice?

Exploring Setting

Setting is the place and time of a story. Think for a moment about what gives a place its special character, its essential feel. There are sights and sounds and smells. There are objects that loom in your mind when you think of a fairground or beach, a restaurant or church basement. In addition to these concrete details, there are events unfolding in and around the place. A writer learns to look for a dynamic detail to write about. In fact, the detail itself is more important than the style with which it is expressed. Beginning writers frequently try to substitute flowery language and stylistic finesse for simple essential detail.

Martone's story begins with a rich depiction of place and setting: the orange A&W shack; the carhop who ignored the county kids in their cars; the hot road with blobs of tar "breaded with dust." It is a Friday night, anywhere in the United States. Martone also vividly captures the sensation of being closed inside the trunk of a car: the smell of rubber and mothballs and car exhaust, the short burst of the car accelerating across the highway. With a few sentences, Martone draws his reader into a place and an experience. The language in the story is simple and straightforward. The reader has a clear image and sense of place, not because of flowery description, but because of concrete details.

Experimenting with Setting

The approach in this book is to begin small and work toward the interesting possibilities. When writing fiction, you start with a voice and a conflict and a setting. Your reader needs to know where and when the action is happening, including the time of day and, perhaps, the time of year. As a writer, you need to know the details of the setting because they serve to help you establish a foundation for the story. At the outset, this foundation is even more important than the story's theme or meaning.

As you know, writers use their personal experience for raw material in their writing. Fortunately for you, you live in a place where actions occur, so you need not fear a shortage of raw material. Don't make the mistake of believing that your experiences are not interesting or that the only settings that you could describe are too ordinary. What makes a setting an interesting place? The action and the characters make a place unique and real. It is the task of the writer to create a setting that readers can see.

Writer's Practice 9.1   *Describe a Place*

Recall a time and place where you did something prohibited—not necessarily criminal, but perhaps something you were not supposed to do. If you are a paragon of virtue and simply cannot recall breaking a rule, then write about a time and place where someone else did something prohibited and substitute yourself for that person. Use the first-person point of view in your description.

As you write, work in some of the details that help define setting and convey its essential nature to a reader:

- sensory detail (sight, sound, smell, taste, and feel)
- specific objects and living things
- activities and processes typical of the place
- clear reference to time of day and season
- proper names of people, places, and things
- someone's attitude about this particular place

Now reread Martone's story and look for the elements listed above. When you try your hand at establishing setting, remember to use short, direct sentences and simple language.

Begin writing if you feel you are ready, or examine our writer's model and explication.

Show, Don't Tell

Good fiction writers show more than they tell. They use specific words rather than general ones—words that add precision and punch. They use concrete details rather than abstract ones—details based on sight, sound, smell, taste, and touch.

Fiction writers also employ figurative language, using words in an imaginative rather than a literal way. Similes and metaphors are two examples of figurative language.

A *simile* is the comparison of dissimilar things using the words *like* or *as*: *The cookie was as hard as a jaw-breaker.* A *metaphor* is an implied comparison of dissimilar things: *The cookie was a jaw breaker.*

Common similes, such as *The realization hit me like a bucket of cold water*, are *clichés*. Fresh similes and metaphors add freshness to a piece of writing; clichés make writing stale.

Dialogue and action are also useful for showing. Strive for short dialogue exchanges that sound real. Ask yourself how your characters might act while they are interacting and how they might move through the story they are inhabiting.

Our Writer

That summer we went swimming in the pond by the overpass. A few years before, road crews had scraped soil off the field and created a large artificial hole. The hole had filled with spring water. After school was out, we rode bicycles out to the pond. We dumped our bikes at the side of the road and scrambled down through the hot weeds, crossed the railroad tracks, and dropped on the grassy bank above the pond. When you waded into the pond, your feet disappeared in squishy black muck. The muck was colder than the water. You couldn't wait to lean forward and dive in the water, just to get out of the muck. Across the pond was a cornfield. Beyond the field was a barn. Sometimes the smell of manure drifted across the water. Traffic hissed on the highway above us. Every year a reckless kid drowned in a pond like ours. You heard it on the nightly news or read about it in the paper. None of us cared. It was June, and hot, and before long we would have driver's licenses.

I was the first one ever to swim across the pond. I dove in, pulling my body through the water with slow strokes. I wondered how deep it was. Sometimes I'd feel cold currents beneath me. When we were kids we talked about sea monsters. Any pond such as this could be inhabited by beasts. That summer it was simply inhabited by boys with cars and girls on their minds. At the edge of the pond, you'd see dragonflies, a flash of blue in the sun. Down the tracks was the overpass, at the top of which someone had written in red spray paint, I LOVE SHARON!!

Not far from this pond was a restaurant called Lynn's Lunch. It served chili and hamburgers to truckers. It was run by an old guy named Lynn. We could never quite understand that. A guy named Lynn. But none of us questioned it. We would stop in, usually on the way home, grass and dirt stuck to our feet, and have cokes and play electronic bowling. He tolerated us. His business was pretty bad. Before long, a dozer would come and knock his place down. All of the restaurants eventually finished that way. They all went out of business. They couldn't compete with the Chinese place in town, which was so good that whenever celebrities had to lay over at the airport outside of town, they'd take a taxi in and have dinner at the Chinese place. Supposedly Bob Hope had dinner there. Also a weatherman from local TV who cracked jokes.

One time Arnold Stang came to dinner. I saw him get out of a taxi in front of the restaurant and walk inside. He was a skinny guy who did comedy on television. He wore a dark suit and big black-framed glasses. It was hot that night. He seemed angry. When we rode by on bikes and peered at him through the window, sitting at his table, he was holding an eggroll up between thumb and forefinger. It looked like he was snarling at it.

None of us ever ate in that restaurant.

What is your perception of this place? Our writer includes sensory detail: barn smells, hot weeds, and cold squishy muck. There is also action. Local kids who are on the threshold of young adulthood, waiting to drive, are riding their bikes. There is the traffic on the road above the pond. Stepping back, the reader can see the landscape changing from pasture and farmland to terrain crossed by superhighway. And underlying the description of the pond is a threat of danger and possible death. Finally, perhaps most memorable is the tension of *impending* action that our writer has created with this description of place.

Exploring Movement

Many stories take place in just one setting, in one place and time. Often, however, writers construct their stories in scenes. How scenes fit together is a matter of plot. Plot is not a formula. It is not a plan. Plot is a verb. It is something the writer does as he writes. Sometimes a story moves forward in progressive scenes, such as in "Choking on Love" in Chapter 8. Other stories move forward and backward in time. Plotting the story involves choreographing these movements in space and time and the related actions to progress toward a resolution of conflict.

Notice the importance of movement in "On the Planet of the Apes." Michael Martone takes his character from one place and time to another. At each point in time, the narrator quickly establishes the new setting and involves his character in an action. (We might also observe that at each point in time the narrator returns to the same preoccupation: *Who am I?*)

Martone's story focuses on three points in time. At the beginning of the story, most of the action occurs at a drive-in theater. The narrator is a kid, possibly around sixteen. Martone then moves the action forward. Unlike Dunning, who used white space in "Choking on Love" to indicate a move, Martone provides verbal cues to signal the passage of time and the change in setting. Next, the action is at a convention, where the adult narrator meets the actor Charlton Heston. Then Martone moves the action again, backward in time, to return to the drive-in. At this point in time, the narrator has just finished law school and has returned to the Lincolndale Drive-In.

Martone thus moves the action twice—from drive-in to convention, and from convention to drive-in. In both cases, these moves are signaled clearly, and yet with minimal narrative:

> I was telling this to Chuck Heston in the green room of the convention. The green room was a trailer with no windows parked beneath the scaffolding of the podium. The crowd on the floor above sounded like the wind, and Chuck looked scoured and bronzed. He listened intently, his smile frozen on his face.

The move in setting and time is executed in a two-step maneuver. First, in the initial sentence of the paragraph, the phrase "in the green room of the convention" identifies the new setting. Second, in the next two sentences, Martone adds more specific details of place: the trailer with no windows, the podium above, the sound of the crowd, and his companion. The narrator (and thus the reader) is newly situated in a lifelike setting. The action can thus continue.

Experimenting with Movement

You began your draft with a character in a specific place and time and involved him in an action that was prohibited. This first section was based on personal experience. In the next section that you write, you will move this character forward in time. At this point, however, you will fictionalize this character, inventing a life for him that differs from yours.

Martone's story begins with what could be personal experience. Perhaps the author did sneak into drive-in theaters when he was a teenager. The story gets truly interesting, however, when Martone moves his reader to another time and place with the surprising statement, "I was telling this to Chuck Heston in the green room of the convention." "Chuck" is so familiar, it puts the reader off balance. It takes a moment to realize that the narrator is talking about the movie star from *Planet of the Apes*. Did this event actually take place? Did the author of the story really meet Charlton Heston? It is most likely that, while composing the story, Martone made a decision such as Lewis Nordan describes in the headnote of this chapter. Perhaps he invented a character to tell the story who was like him, but was not him. Perhaps Martone simply thought *What if?* and invented a character enthralled by the *Planet of the Apes* movies who actually meets Charlton Heston.

Writer's Practice 9.2 *Move the Action*

Write three scenes that could take place some time after your first scene. Change the setting in each scene. Although you might not actually use these scenes in your story, you will benefit from exploring setting. As you work, try to do the following:

- Use Martone's two-step movement maneuver discussed above.
- Fictionalize your character.
- Involve your character in a simple action at each new place and point in time.

Our writer's three scenes follow. Three times he moves the action from the highway pond to another place in time. In each scene, using Martone's two-step maneuver, he immediately establishes the new place and time. Notice that in each passage, an action is anticipated. Notice, also, that our writer has clearly made an imaginative leap, not once but three times. He has fictionalized his narrator, becoming a physician in the first passage, a father on vacation in the second, and a man about to jump from an airplane in the third. Each of these scenes follows from the first. Each introduces interesting narrative possibilities.

Our Writer

#1

I was thinking of that pond the other night in the hospital. Mrs. Sheehan was in labor. It was her third baby. I expected it to go fast. Not that it mattered. I wasn't going anywhere special. Outside, rain peppered the windows. The willows in the park were all keeled over, branches whipped and flung by the wind. Mrs. Sheehan was dilated to 8 centimeters, but still practically all smiles.

"It shouldn't be long," I said.

The move here is clearly signaled by "the other night in the hospital." The next few sentences add details of place, both inside and outside. The narrator is obviously no longer a boy. The action that is anticipated is the birth of Mrs. Sheehan's baby. There are narrative possibilities here that could take the story in an interesting direction. Could something happen during the birth that requires the narrator to save the baby? How might saving the baby remind him of the kids who drowned in his youth?

#2

"But how could you swim in that water?" my son asked me. He was a boy accustomed to swimming pools. We were eating cereal and fruit for breakfast in the hotel restaurant, on a balcony overlooking the Gulf of Mexico. Eight o'clock, and it was already hot. At nine we would go diving among the coral reefs. I had just seen a pelican drop like a torpedo into the surf, then rise and wing into the sky again. I made a note to remark to Adam how totally prehistoric the bird looked. Totally. It pleased me that I had almost begun to talk like him.

"It was wet," I said. "And we were fifteen."

Moving forward in time, the narrator is now a father. The setting is clear: breakfast table on a hotel terrace, somewhere in the Caribbean. The anticipated action is scuba diving. The narrative possibilities connect directly to the first section, as both sections put people in the water. How will the father's experience in a highway pond differ from a dive with his son among coral reefs? What will happen in the diving scene?

#3

I was telling our jump instructor about those currents. Her name was Sharon. The plane had leveled off at 3500 feet, not long from the appointed time. On the ground beneath us, mottled by the shadows of clouds, was tawny grass I guessed to be wheat. We would jump into that. Sharon chewed a wad of green gum and smiled a lot.

"Tell me again about freefall," I said.

"There's nothing to it." Sharon flung the Cessna door open, letting in a blast of air. "Hold out your arms," she yelled, "arch your back, and dive."

"I don't think I can."

"We've been through this."

"I don't know what possessed me."

"Look," she said, "everyone feels that way. If it helps, close your eyes and think about being something else."

"A bird?"

"All right, a bird." She shook her head. I'd said what everyone said. I was ashamed of my failure of imagination. She grabbed me by my jacket and pulled me over to the door, speaking with her face close to mine. I could feel her minty breath on my cheek. "Don't think. Try to be part of a bird," she said. "A feather, a wing. A bird's breath. You're something so light, so weightless, it's not freefall. It's freeflight."

"I'll try."

"Two minutes to jump." She patted my arm.

Moving forward in time again, the scene change is indicated in the first sentence and developed with detail, including action and dialogue. The narrator, now an adult, is about to take another risk. The next action is clearly anticipated. The question the reader is asking is, Will he do it?

Any of these three scenes could follow our writer's first section. As you write, work on quickly establishing place and time, and be clear about what your character is doing. Notice that in each of the scenes above, there is a reference to the first section, in which the character was swimming in the pond near the highway. Be sure that each of your scenes includes a reference to connect the two experiences.

Writer's Practice 9.3   *Move Back in Time*

After Martone moves his narrator to the convention with Charlton Heston and establishes that scene, he moves back in time. He moves back to the drive-in theater, where he has the narrator once again sneak into the theater and once again confront the question of who he is. At this intermediate point in time, Martone's narrator involves the characters in more action.

Try the same approach. Move your narrator, who is now at least partly a fictional character, back to the familiar setting you began writing about. How will you accomplish this? Think *What if?* and invent a life for this fictional character who is telling the story. In your writing you should do the following:

- Make a clean transition to a new place and time using Martone's two-step movement maneuver.
- Change a few of the details about the place to which you move back to indicate the passage of time.
- Attempt to fictionalize your character.
- Involve your character in a simple action at this new place and point in time. (Think about how this action might relate to prior action in your story.)

Begin writing if you feel you are ready, or examine our writer's model and explication.

Our Writer

I'd gone back to the pond one afternoon a few years ago. It was an overcast day. Where we once gathered was a long white dock. Next to it were orange buoys marking a swimming area. The grass was real green grass, not weeds, and there was a white booth where you could buy soft drinks and ice cream. At the edge of the pond, where we had waded into the muck, I could see three firemen and a sheriff's deputy surrounded by a dozen kids.

I stumbled down through the weeds to the pond, thinking as I ran, Someone has drowned. I felt guilty, like I was fifteen again, or worse, that it was somehow my fault if a kid was lying on the bottom of that pond, getting cold in those currents and muck.

On the water, in a kayak, was a man in a blue shirt and suspenders, another fireman. He was paddling around the middle of the pond. Looking for the body, I guessed. It seemed like a funny way to drag for a body.

On the bank, kids skipped stones in the water and lolled in the grass drinking sodas. The fireman and sheriff's deputy sucked on blades of grass and made jokes.

"What's going on?" I said to the deputy.

"Rescue." He was wearing high black boots. He smiled like he had just heard a good joke, then kicked at the grass and spat.

A blond-haired kid in a swimsuit pointed at the water. "There's a cow in there."

"What?" I said.

The deputy nodded and folded his arms over his chest.

"A cow drowned in our lake," the kid said. "She sunk out in the middle somewhere. We saw her floating around last week." He spread his hands in the air and smiled, his eyes growing large. "Floating like a big brown ball."

"You should've said something." The deputy pointed toward the kayak. "You'd have saved Hinkle a lot of trouble."

"We didn't know what it was," the kid said.

"Whyn't you go look?" the deputy asked.

The kid glanced at me and shook his head at this idiotic question. "Can I try that boat later?" he said to the deputy.

It wasn't going to be much of a rescue. Once they found it and slipped a chain around it, the farmer across the way, whose red barn had begun to lean, would tow the dead animal out of the pond with a tractor, drag it away from the water, and bury it in his field.

"Fertilizer," the deputy said. Then, in an official-sounding voice, "This place will then be off-limits for a while."

"Aw, man!" the blond kid said.

The sheriff said, "There's no telling how bad this water is contaminated. I wouldn't swim in it." He turned to me. "Would you?"

Our writer takes his character back to the pond, which has been dramatically transformed. The weeds have been replaced with real grass, and a dock has been added. No longer a place of forbidden fun, the pond has become a legitimate place to swim. Notice, though, in the first section the boys swam in the pond; now they stand at the edge. In this visit to the pond, our writer retrieves an important feeling from the first section. The narrator's sense of danger is revisited as he watches the authorities drag the pond bottom. Interestingly, the narrator feels responsible for whoever is in the water, as if his illicit swim years ago somehow caused a drowning years later. Our writer also revisits the prohibition theme: as it was before, the pond will now be off limits. Finally, the sheriff's deputy says to the narrator, "I wouldn't swim in it. Would you?" How will the narrator respond? The writer may answer this question in a revision of the story.

Writer's Practice 9.4 *Assemble the First Draft*

At this point, you have three passages that can be drawn together to form a rough draft of a story. You have focused on establishing the setting at each point in time, on moving your characters from place to place, and on inventing possible actions by the characters. You have imagined a fictional world, using an actual place and person you know as a point of departure. Now put the passages you have written together so that the shape and feel of the story can be examined.

Our Writer

Fertilizer

That summer we went swimming in the pond by the overpass. A few years before, road crews had scraped soil off the field and created a large artificial hole. The hole had filled with spring water. After school was out, we rode bicycles out to the pond. We dumped our bikes at the side of the road and scrambled down through the hot weeds, crossed the railroad tracks, and dropped on the grassy bank above the pond. When you waded into the pond, your feet disappeared in squishy black muck. The muck was colder than the water. You couldn't wait to lean forward and dive in the water, just to get out of the muck. Across the pond was a cornfield. Beyond the field was a barn. Sometimes the smell of manure drifted across the water. Traffic hissed on the highway above us. Every year a reckless kid drowned in a pond like ours. You heard it on the nightly news or read about it in the paper. None of us cared. It was June, and hot, and before long we would have driver's licenses.

I was the first one ever to swim across the pond. I dove in, pulling my body through the water with slow strokes. I wondered how deep it was. Sometimes I'd feel cold currents beneath me. When we were kids we talked about sea monsters. Any pond such as this could be inhabited by beasts. That summer it was simply inhabited by boys with cars and girls on their minds. At the edge of the pond, you'd see dragonflies, a flash of blue in the sun. Down the tracks was the overpass, at the top of which someone had written in red spray paint, I LOVE SHARON!!

Not far from this pond was a restaurant called Lynn's Lunch. It served chili and hamburgers to truckers. It was run by an old guy named Lynn. We could never quite understand that. A guy named Lynn. But none of us questioned it. We would stop in, usually on the way home, grass and dirt stuck to our feet, and have cokes and play electronic bowling. He tolerated us. His business was pretty bad. Before long, a dozer would come and knock his place down. All of the restaurants eventually finished that way. They all went out of business. They couldn't compete with the Chinese place in town, which was so good that whenever celebrities had to lay over at the airport outside of town, they'd take a taxi in and have dinner at the Chinese place. Supposedly Bob Hope had dinner there. Also a weatherman from local TV who cracked jokes.

One time Arnold Stang came to dinner. I saw him get out of a taxi in front of the restaurant and walk inside. He was a skinny guy who did comedy on television. He wore a dark suit and big black-framed glasses. It was hot that night. He seemed angry. When we rode by on bikes and peered at him through the window, sitting at his table, he was holding an eggroll up between thumb and forefinger. It looked like he was snarling at it.

None of us ever ate in that restaurant.

I was telling our jump instructor about those currents. Her name was Sharon. The plane had leveled off at 3500 feet, not long from the appointed time. On the ground beneath us, mottled by the shadows of clouds, was tawny grass I guessed to be wheat. We would jump into that. Sharon chewed a wad of green gum and smiled a lot.

"Tell me again about freefall," I said.

"There's nothing to it." Sharon flung the Cessna door open, letting in a blast of air. "Hold out your arms," she yelled, "arch your back, and dive."

"I don't think I can."

"We've been through this."

"I don't know what possessed me."

"Look," she said, "everyone feels that way. If it helps, close your eyes and think about being something else."

"A bird?"

"All right, a bird." She shook her head. I'd said what everyone said. I was ashamed of my failure of imagination. She grabbed me by my jacket and pulled me over to the door, speaking with her face close to mine. I could feel her minty breath on my cheek. "Don't think. Try to be part of a bird," she said. "A feather, a wing. A bird's breath. You're something so light, so weightless, it's not freefall. It's freeflight."

"I'll try."

"Two minutes to jump." She patted my arm.

I'd gone back to the pond one afternoon a few years ago. It was an overcast day. Where we once gathered was a long white dock. Next to it were orange buoys marking a swimming area. The grass was real green grass, not weeds, and there was a white booth where you could buy soft drinks and ice cream. At the edge of the pond, where we had waded into the muck, I could see three firemen and a sheriff's deputy surrounded by a dozen kids.

I stumbled down through the weeds to the pond, thinking as I ran, Someone has drowned. I felt guilty, like I was fifteen again, or worse, that it was somehow my fault if a kid was lying on the bottom of that pond, getting cold in those currents and muck.

On the water, in a kayak, was a man in a blue shirt and suspenders, another fireman. He was paddling around the middle of the pond. Looking for the body, I guessed. It seemed like a funny way to drag for a body.

On the bank, kids skipped stones in the water and lolled in the grass drinking sodas. The fireman and sheriff's deputy sucked on blades of grass and made jokes.

"What's going on?" I said to the deputy.

"Rescue." He was wearing high black boots. He smiled like he had just heard a good joke, then kicked at the grass and spat.

A blond-haired kid in a swimsuit pointed at the water. "There's a cow in there."

"What?" I said.

The deputy nodded and folded his arms over his chest.

"A cow drowned in our lake," the kid said. "She sunk out in the middle somewhere. We saw her floating around last week." He spread his hands in the air and smiled, his eyes growing large. "Floating like a big brown ball."

"You should've said something." The deputy pointed toward the kayak. "You'd have saved Hinkle a lot of trouble."

"We didn't know what it was," the kid said.

"Whyn't you go look?" the deputy asked.

The kid glanced at me and shook his head at this idiotic question. "Can I try that boat later?" he said to the deputy.

It wasn't going to be much of a rescue. Once they found it and slipped a chain around it, the farmer across the way, whose red barn had begun to lean, would tow the dead animal out of the pond with a tractor, drag it away from the water, and bury it in his field.

"Fertilizer," the deputy said. Then, in an official-sounding voice, "This place will then be off-limits for a while."

"Aw, man!" the blond kid said.

The sheriff said, "There's no telling how bad this water is contaminated. I wouldn't swim in it." He turned to me. "Would you?"

These passages fit together, united by the writer's continued references to the pond. The story does not end in a satisfying way, but bear in mind that this is just a draft. The writer's next task is to develop further what seems important in the draft, and to cut what distracts the reader from the important subject. What is this story's subject? This question is best answered in a writer response group.

Writer Response Groups

Working with a group of writers, look now at the three passages you wrote for the exercises in this chapter. Though it is just the skeleton of a story at this point, say five hundred to seven hundred words or more, that is material enough to consider in a response group. Examine each other's work, reading for the following elements:

Essential Elements

- Whose story is it?
- What is the conflict?
- How is the action plotted?

Craft

- How many distinct points in time are there? How many different settings? Are they clearly signaled for the reader?
- What action is the narrator involved in at each point in time? What do these actions have in common?
- How has the writer fictionalized her narrator?
- What changes are apparent in the narrator at each point in time?

As you read and discuss each other's work, stay alert to possibilities for meaning. Watch especially for strong feelings that resonate in the story. Be prepared also to discuss the issues the story addresses. In what way do the changes in time and place indicate changes in character, in nuances of feeling, and in development of theme?

Revising for Meaning and Theme: The Recurring Image

You now have a draft that takes a character from one setting to another, from one action to another. In these movements, there may be something changing inside your character. Your next task is to look to the details in your writing and consider how they relate to meaning and theme.

Theme is the issue or idea or problem that a story dramatizes. "On the Planet of the Apes" is about a young man who sneaks into the movies and then later in life finds himself face-to-face with the star of that movie. In a larger sense, however, the theme of the story is escape. Note that the theme of escape is stated again and again in the details of the story. To do this, Martone uses a recurring image—especially the image of a person in captivity. In the first section, we see the boys hiding in the trunk. The captivity image is then repeated in the captive astronaut on the planet of the apes. It is repeated again when the narrator and Chuck wait in the windowless trailer beneath the podium, in the image of the boys playing on monkey bars at the theater, and finally, at the end of the story, as they wait in the "cockpit of the car." The boys are captives of the small town of Fort Wayne, Indiana. Their cars are "moored by the speaker cords to silver posts." No one is going anywhere. They are captives of Hollywood, which gives them only the illusion of escape. Without using the explicit term *escape*, these repeated images enable Martone to establish it as the theme of his story.

Writer's Practice 9.5   *Repeat an Image*

Read your rough draft and look for opportunities to repeat an image as Martone does. Consider the following suggestions for a revision:

- Look for an action that can be repeated once in your story.
- Look for an image that can be repeated at least twice in your story.

As you revise, think about what is essential to the story. Remember, in a well-plotted story, all the details have a function. They reveal character, relate to conflict, and move both characters and reader toward a resolution or an easing of the conflict. When you revise, you must be critical of each scene. Description, dialogue, action, and even characters without an essential function in the story must be cut. Do save what you cut, however, so that it can be restored if you change your mind.

Begin revising if you feel you are ready, or examine our writer's model and explication.

Our Writer

Floater

Every summer a kid drowned in a pond like ours. You heard the story on the six o'clock news. There were pictures in the next day's paper; stone-faced uniformed people on the bank, a boat pulled up on shore, the body already recovered, swathed in a white sheet.

It could have been one of us.

After school was out, we rode bicycles out to the overpass and dumped them by the side of the road. We scrambled down through the hot weeds, crossed the railroad tracks, and dropped on the grassy bank above the pond. Across the pond was a cornfield, and beyond that, a barn. Sometimes the smell of manure drifted across the water. Above us, from the highway, came the whitewater sound of traffic.

When you waded in, your feet disappeared into squishy black muck, right over your ankles, sometimes up to your shins. It was horrible. The muck was colder than the water. You couldn't wait to lean forward and dive in, just to get out of the muck. Then, to avoid standing, you headed for the deep water. Whenever I dove in and began pulling my body through the water with slow strokes, I thought about those kids. I felt cold currents rising beneath me. Face in the water, eyes closed, I wondered how deep it was, and what made a highway pond more treacherous than, say, a lake or a river. I wondered whether, at that moment, there might be a boy like me floating beneath the surface, facing the mucky bottom, maybe right underneath me.

It was the currents, someone said, that made the pond dangerous.

When we clamored back up the hill to our bikes, our feet shiny black with muck, weeds clinging to our wet legs, we felt lucky. Like we had cheated the odds.

I was telling the jump instructor about those currents. We'd leveled off at 3500 feet, not long from the appointed time. She was thin and aerodynamic, dressed in bright yellow, her brown hair tied back tight. On the ground beneath us, mottled by the shadows of clouds, was tawny grass I guessed to be wheat. We would jump into that. Sharon, the instructor, chewed a small wad of green gum and blew bubbles.

"Tell me again about freefall," I said.

"There's nothing to it." She slid the Cessna door open, letting in a blast of air. "Hold out your arms," she yelled, "arch your back, and dive."

I pictured myself dropping, legs slightly apart, flapping my foolish arms.

"I don't think I can."

"Sure you can."

"I don't know what possessed me."

"Everyone feels that way," she said. "Don't think," she said. "You're going to love it. You're so light, so weightless, it's not even freefall."

"It's landing I'm worried about."

"It's freefloat."

"Will once be enough?" I said.

"For some it is. But usually it isn't." She patted my arm. "Two minutes until."

I'd gone back to the pond one afternoon a few years earlier. I drove out of town, pulled off the road on the overpass, got out of my car, and stood gazing down at the hill.

It was an overcast day. The place where we once gathered now had a dock. Next to it were orange bulbs in the water, marking a swimming area. The grass was real green grass, not weeds, and there was a white booth where you could buy refreshments. At the edge of the pond, where we had waded into the muck, I could see three firemen and a sheriff's deputy surrounded by a dozen kids.

I stumbled down through the weeds to the pond, thinking as I ran that someone had drowned. I felt like I was fifteen again. I felt somehow it was *my fault* if a kid lay on the bottom of that pond, bathed in those cold currents, sinking into the muck.

On the water, in a kayak, was another fireman. He paddled around the middle of the pond. From the bank, kids skipped stones across the water and lolled in the grass drinking sodas. The firemen and deputy sucked on blades of grass. They were laughing.

I nodded at the deputy, pointed at the kayak.

"Cow fishing." He was wearing high black boots.

A blond-haired kid in a swimsuit pointed at the water. "There's a cow in there."

"What?" I said.

The deputy nodded and folded his arms over his chest.

"A cow drowned in our lake," the kid said. "She sunk out in the middle somewhere. We saw her floating around last week." He held his hands in the air, spread them apart and smiled, his eyes growing large. "Floating like a big brown donut."

"You should've said something before that donut sank." The deputy pointed toward the kayak and chuckled. "You'd have saved Hinkle there a lot of trouble."

"We didn't know what it was," the kid said.

"You better hope that donut don't explode," the deputy said.

The kid glanced at me and shrugged. "Can I try that boat later?" he said to the deputy.

It wasn't much of a rescue. They found the cow and slipped a chain around it. The farmer across the way, whose red barn had begun to lean, towed the dead animal out of the pond with a tractor, dragged it across his field, where he had been ordered to bury it in a deep hole.

"Fertilizer," the deputy said to me. Then he added, in an official-sounding voice meant for the boys, "This place will be off-limits for a while."

"Aw, man!" the blond kid said.

"There's no telling how bad this water is contaminated."

"Aw, man!" He puffed up his cheeks and exhaled heavily.

The deputy turned to me. "I wouldn't swim in it anyway." He lowered his voice, "Dead cow or not."

The boy's eyes darted up at me. A light flashed in them. Tomorrow or the next day, he'd be in that water.

"Would you?" the deputy said to me.

Sharon spit her gum out the open door. "Shall we?"

It was almost natural, what we were about to do. Jump out of an airplane 3500 feet up. A few people did it every day, and most of them lived to tell about it. I closed my eyes, visualized my white parachute popping open, like a dialogue

bubble in a comic strip. What if it didn't open? I thought about what the newspapers could not explain, like why we do it. I saw words take shape inside the
comic strip bubble, *He pushed himself.*

"You don't have to," she said.

"I know." I leaned toward the door. I wanted to go, but I couldn't make my
legs work.

"You'll be sorry if you don't."

"I'm trying," I said. "Tell me it's beautiful."

"It's beautiful."

I dragged myself to the door, ready to launch. I hovered in the doorway. I
would just need a little push.

This story is about a man who takes risks. Whether swimming as a boy or
jumping from an airplane as an adult, he is conscious of cheating the odds.
He seems to get no real pleasure from taking these risks, but he can't stop
himself from doing it. It is as if he does these things almost against his will.
The title, "Floater," suggests a passive attitude. A floater isn't really doing
anything, not swimming, not sinking. He's just there. There are multiple
images of floaters in the story: the drowned boy the speaker imagines, the
cow, buoys in the pond, Sharon's bubble gum, the boy's puffed up cheeks in
the second section, the parachute that becomes a comic strip dialogue bubble. The dialogue inside it reports the contradiction inside the narrator.

In revision, our writer both added to and subtracted from his story. The
first section is reorganized and reduced. All references to food and restaurants have been eliminated. Focus is squarely on going to the pond. In the
second section, the dialogue is rewritten to explore the speaker's motives and
fears. Seeing himself in freefall, the narrator sees an image of swimming: "I
pictured myself dropping, legs slightly apart, flapping my foolish arms." In
the third section of the story, the writer blends the two points in time.

"Would you?" the deputy said.

Sharon spit her gum out the open door. "Shall we?"

The writer ends the story in the most recent point in time. Just as the speaker
sees headlines of tragic death in the first section, he imagines them in the final
section. This is another repetition that helps to unify the story.

Examining Student Stories

Review the questions you asked in writer response groups. Next, examine the
story that follows. Look for places where the writer moves character and
action from one location and time to another. Look also for repeated images.

How It Should Really Feel

Kristen Mitchell

It was always on the coldest December nights. I'd stand in front of the living room window and wait for him to signal an "okay" from across the street. We were not allowed to talk. My parents called him "squirrelly." His parents said I was too young. So we lied and sneaked around behind our parents' backs. I'd see him under the streetlight, hands in his pockets. When Ryan saw me, he'd wave okay.

Those nights I told my mom I was going sledding at Hines with friends. I said my brother would drop me off. I even took my red wooden sled. He waited at the bottom of the hill next to the shallow frozen stream. We liked to walk on it, feel the ice crackle under our feet. Whenever he said something funny, I laughed out loud, and sometimes he said my braces caught the light of the moon. Then he kissed me, the kind of kiss you see in the movies when people finally get rid of the bad guys and get to live happily ever after. I'd never kissed a boy before, not like that. It hurt. I knew my braces got in the way of how it should really feel.

I thought of that Ryan now, so many years later. "Ryan," I said, flipping through the chart. "Ryan Morrison."

This Ryan sat with his arms crossed in the chair, his mouth clamped shut. I hate to be dishonest with patients, especially about pain. Pain is honest. It pinches nerves and throbs through the skin.

"So you get your braces today," I said.

"Yeah." He laced his fingers in his lap and pinched his lips back together.

The office was hot. I washed my hands and stared out the window at the fresh morning snow piled on cars.

"Will it hurt?" he said.

I pulled the latex gloves over my hands, snapping them at the wrist. Then I sat down and rolled over to him on the cushioned stool.

"Do you have a girlfriend, Ryan?"

"Yes."

"What's her name?"

"Kelly." He sagged in the chair.

"Is she pretty?"

"I guess." He looked down at his knees. "She's the one . . . ."

"The one for you?"

"She's the one who said braces hurt."

"Does she have braces?"

"Her brother does."

I picked up the molds of his teeth. Crooked incisors. My problem when I was his age. I never smiled in school pictures. When I got braces, Ryan was the only one who could make me smile.

"Well, Ryan," I said. "I'm not going to lie to you. Braces can be a painful annoyance, and yes, they can even get in the way sometimes."

"Like when you eat?"

"Yes." I looked away and smiled. "At various times. You'll see." He drew in a breath and held it. "But it won't last forever, Ryan."

"I know."

"And when it's over, you'll be better off. A little hurt will have been worth it." I touched his chin. He opened his mouth. "Much better off."

We planned it out. The day before spring break. My mother would drop me off early at school and I would meet him in the neighborhood around the corner. After five years of lying and sneaking, and being punished for lying and sneaking, we decided to do it. We had saved a couple grand. California sounded nice. Even though I had a month till graduation, we left. We had a big van and each other. I ran through the dewy grass as fast as possible, my feet slipping in my sandals.

We kissed all the way to Humboldt. For two months, supposedly, we were in love. The sun was constant. Any moment a natural disaster could erupt. I spent money as fast as I could. The third month, all I could think about was getting home. Getting my life straightened out. Going back to school.

"What about how I feel?" Ryan had said.

"I have to go back."

"This was for us."

Tears rushed down his face. I'd never seen a boy cry like that. I wanted to cup my hands and catch the salty drops. I wanted to put them in my pocket as evidence. He really cried.

Then he drove me home. Back to Hines and my future. One bitter kiss and a wave okay. We left each other hurting, both of us wondering how it should really feel.

This is a coming-of-age story. Kristen moves her characters and action twice. At each point, we know where we are, what time of year it is, and what the conflict is. These moves express extremes: east and west, hot and cold, pain and pleasure. The narrator realizes that growing up involves pain, and that pain teaches. If you are lucky, the story seems to say, pain helps you get things straight. The recurring references to braces underscore this theme. Notice in the third section that the episode in California is handled quite swiftly. In a matter of a few sentences, Kristen summarizes events and gets her character back to Hines again, back to where the story originated. Again Kristen uses repetition, retrieving Ryan's "wave okay" from the beginning of the story. At the conclusion, however, the wave is signaling the end of the relationship and the beginning of the narrator's getting straightened out.

chapter 10

Keeping Your Distance: Third-Person Objective Point of View, Suspense, and Tone

Generally speaking, fictional characters have to be on a road that's going to lead toward some kind of interesting trouble.

-CHARLES BAXTER

Most of the writing you have done so far has probably been in the first-person point of view, with yourself as the narrator. Or maybe you took a risk and invented a character who was like you, but different in a way the story required: a little older or younger, with a slightly altered biography. Then again, maybe the character you invented was very different from you in experience, age, and gender. Part of growing as a writer has to do with this controlled invention: You imagine characters, places, and events that the story, even when it is rooted in fact, begins to require. In *fact*, your mother was a tall, thin middle-school biology teacher; in *fiction*, your mother can be short and dark and manage a computerized dating service.

The first-person point of view is close-up and personal, with the writer inside the narrator's head and heart. In contrast, the third-person point of view places distance between the speaker, who is now an unseen character in the story, and the other characters. Sometimes that distance can be extended to a point where the narrator's involvement in her characters is neutral. She maintains equal distance from everyone in the story and merely reports what they do and say.

Your task in this chapter will be to experiment with writing a story in the third-person point of view. As you do so, and as you begin to sketch in the possibilities, you will also experiment with suspense, which is the art of withholding information, and tone, which is the emotional coloring or mood of a story.

In "How Many Boys?" Janet Kauffman uses the third-person objective point of view. On the surface, this is a very simple story. There is little work on character, only a short amount of time passes, and setting does not change. Further, hardly any action takes place. Notice, though, how Kauffman handles thought and feeling in this story.

How Many Boys?

JANET KAUFFMAN

Before they sat down to supper, the phone rang. The father picked up the phone on his way to his chair.

"Is the boy back from the paper?"

It was a woman's voice—nasal, insistent.

"What?" said the father. "One of our boys?"

"Is the boy back from the paper?" the woman asked again. It was the same tone and it made the man think of the phone company's recordings.

"You must have the wrong number," the father said, and hung up.

"Who was that?" asked his son.

"Some woman wanted to know if the boy was back from the paper."

"What boy?"

"Who knows? It didn't make sense. Maybe it was some kind of recording," the father said.

"Recordings don't call, do they?"

"Well, I don't know."

"What paper?" asked the son.

"Maybe she meant the newspaper," the father said.

"What boy went to the newspaper?"

"I don't know! She didn't say. I thought she meant you, or your brother, but you're both here. I don't know what she was talking about," the father said.

"I'm here," the boy said.

"Where's your brother? He's upstairs, isn't he?" The father called to his wife in the kitchen and asked if their other son was upstairs.

"I don't know," his wife said.

"Supper!" the father called. In a minute, when he heard no answer, he walked to the bottom of the stairsteps and called again. "Supper!"

"Did he go to the paper?" the boy asked his mother as she brought in a bowl of yams and set it on the table.

"What paper?" the mother asked.

"A lady that called asked if the boy was back from the paper."

"What paper?"

"We don't know," said the father, joining them. "Son, where's your brother?"

"I thought he was upstairs," the boy said.

"Supper!" the father called once more, loudly. He put his hands on his hips and turned slowly from side to side and looked up at the ceiling, listening.

"I heard something!" said the brother. "I'll get him."

He ran upstairs, two steps at a time.

"He's here!"

"Ah!" the man sighed to his wife. His lips parted and he almost smiled.

"It's a wrong number, for God's sake," she said. "We get them all the time."

"You get called about little boys, out on errands this time of night?"

"No, but it's always something. People just start in. She didn't realize you were a wrong number," she said.

"I don't sound like somebody else. She was upset," he said. "She called whoever she called because she was worried the boy was late."

"Good. Then she'll call the right number and find out."

"He was under the desk," said the boy, coming back into the room.

"I found a millipede," said his brother. "What should I do with it?"

"Out the back door," said the father. "Supper's about set."

The mother brought in a platter with a rolled boneless roast. She set a fat orange yam on each plate, and then she poured tall glasses of milk out of a plastic container.

"Get some napkins," she said to one of the boys.

He went to the cupboard and picked out four paper napkins. As the family sat down at the table, he tossed a napkin, sidearm like a Frisbee, toward each person's plate.

"Stupid," said his brother.

"Boys," said the father. "Just eat."

It was a pleasant meal. The mother and father talked about how many major appliances had failed in the year since they moved into the new house. The father said he knew the statistics for such occurrences.

"This *should* be our last," he said.

The boys shaped large lakes in the center of their mashed yams. They smoothed the rims with their spoons. Then they filled the lakes with the brown gravy, and drank the gravy spoonful by spoonful, out of the middle.

"Well, let's make up our minds about this dishwasher," the man said to his wife.

"Well, *get* it," she said. "I'm using two towels now for the leak. This one's not worth fixing." She wiped her lips and the end of her nose with the paper napkin.

"Maybe the lady said, 'Is the boy back *with* the paper?'" one of the boys said.

"She said it twice. She said *from* the paper," the father said.

"I bet he's a paper boy out on his route," the son said. "The newspaper office wouldn't be open."

"Well, let's hope she found him," said the father.

He crumpled his napkin in his palms, shaped it into a ball, and set it on the table. And since it was no longer dusk, but dark enough for him to see his reflection clearly in the dining-room window, he walked to the living room and turned on two lamps.

The house glowed.

When the father sat down in an easy chair, one of his sons climbed in beside him. The father put his arm around the boy so that the two would fit together just right.

The father kissed the boy's hair.

"So *here* you are," the father whispered.

The mother and the other boy cleared off the table. They rinsed the dishes and loaded the dishwasher. When the table and the counters had been wiped off with a damp rag, the mother set two cloth towels on the floor in front of the dishwasher and pressed the button to make the machine go.

The boy in the kitchen waited in the kitchen doorway until his mother walked by. Then he flicked off the kitchen light. He had taken one step toward the living room when the phone on the wall behind him rang. He jumped to the side and called out, "Telephone!"

The father leaned forward sharply, halfway rising. The boy in the chair beside him slipped backwards and sank against the coarse fabric.

With uninterrupted step, the mother turned and walked back to the phone. "Wrong number," she predicted.

"Just get it," said the father.

"Hello?" said the mother.

"Ma!" It was a child at the other end of the line.

"Hello!" the mother said loudly.

She turned her back to the living room.

"Who are you calling?" she said.

"Ma!" the child cried.

"You have the wrong number," the mother said slowly, clearly. "Hang up and try again. This is not your mother."

"Ma!"

"You must hang up the phone now and dial again. All right?"

The child cried, "Ma!"

"You must hang up the phone. Just dial the telephone again. I'm hanging up now. Good-bye," the mother said.

"The boy! Was it the boy?" the boy in the kitchen asked.

"It sounded like a baby," the mother said. "Some baby dialed a number."

"It was crying?" asked the father.

"It sounded like crying. It just said the same thing," the mother said.

"Call the police!" said the boy in the kitchen.

"What?" said the mother. "What for? They don't trace calls that have already hung up. How could they find the baby? Maybe it just plays with the phone."

"You said it was crying," said the father.

"It said ma," the mother said.

"A child knows how to dial for help," said the father. "Maybe it was hurt. Couldn't it talk?"

"I don't know how to dial for help," said the boy in the chair. He sat up and looked around.

"The kid was trying to call its mother and it got the wrong number. That's all," said the mother. "He'll dial again and get her."

"Maybe he's lost at the paper!" said the boy in the kitchen. He looked off toward the window, out toward the night.

"This was a baby," said the mother.

"It dialed a phone," said the boy. "Maybe he's *at* the paper, and it's closed up."

"Babies don't go on errands to the paper," said the father. "People shouldn't leave a baby alone like that."

"It's probably in its parents' room, thinking it'll call them up on the other phone," said the mother.

"They'd hear it!" one son said.

"Of course," said the father, nodding to his boy. "I think if the baby was crying, it was trying to call its mother."

"That's certainly all that he said," said the mother.

"Was the baby a boy baby?" one son asked.

"I don't know," said the mother. "It sounded like a boy."

"Maybe it couldn't turn on the lights," the other son said.

The family was quiet for a time. One boy went to look out the window. The mother went into the living room. She straightened cushions and sat down in the middle of the red sofa. A hearty smell of beef and gravy lay over the air in the rooms.

The boy at the window rubbed his breath from the pane. He rubbed again. Then he went to the kitchen and switched on the light.

"Well, should I call the police?" he asked. He reached for the phone on the wall.

"No," said his father. "There's nothing they could do."

"Can't we call somebody? There's two boys lost. Isn't that what there is?"

"How many boys?" one boy said.

"Those were wrong numbers!" said his mother firmly. "We get them all the time. They'll dial again and get who they want."

"It's almost time for the news," said the father.

They took their places. They sat together. The family sat together, and listened.

Questions

1. Where does the narrator show or report character emotion in the story? Cite at least two examples.

2. Why do you think Kauffman chose not to name the characters? What difference does that decision make?

3. What importance does time of day have in the story? How many references to time are there?

4. What is the significance of the title?

Exploring Third-Person Objective Point of View

The third-person narrator is sometimes referred to as omniscient. Godlike, he knows everything. He can report what a character does, senses, thinks, knows, remembers, wonders, fears, wants. He is a psychologist, capable of exploring the subtle interplay of desire and motive. He is a philosopher and moralist, ready to comment on the meaning of his characters' achievements or follies. If he attempts to do all of these, the third-person narrator has a very big job—bigger than most contemporary writers care to take on. Very often, novice writers are keenly interested in motives and psychological insights and meaning, and their preoccupation with these things can distract them from the fundamentals of storytelling. Their narratives get cluttered with telling and explanations and the story gets lost.

For that reason, this chapter will explore the third-person *objective* point of view. The point of view is objective because the third-person narrator refrains almost completely from commentary—the psychological and philosophical details mentioned previously. Thus, as you experiment with narrative voice, you regard one character pretty much as equal to another character. You severely limit your report of what anyone thinks, knows, remembers, or believes. Instead, you focus on the storytelling. You move characters, put obstacles in front of them, and report what they say and do. As Baxter says in the headnote of this chapter, you point the characters in the direction of "some kind of interesting trouble."

In Kauffman's story, these qualities of the third-person objective point of view are apparent. There is interesting trouble. There are four characters, none of whom we really get inside or fully get to know. The narrator records their speech, movements, a few gestures, and only *once* describes how a character mentally registers the sound of these disturbing telephone calls. In the story, the directness and austerity of the style, which is a product of the objective point of view, is exaggerated:

> Before they sat down to supper, the phone rang. The father picked up the phone on his way to his chair.
> "Is the boy back from the paper?"
> It was a woman's voice—nasal, insistent.
> "What?" said the father. "One of our boys?"
> "Is the boy back from the paper?" the woman asked again. It was the same tone and it made the man think of the phone company's recordings.
> "You must have the wrong number," the father said, and hung up.

This short sequence, aside from speech, consists of only two actions—the father answers the phone, then hangs up the phone. There is little attempt at setting the scene. For example, we aren't told where the phone is or what the father's chair looks like. The father must look like any other father, and the same for the mother and the boys. The characters and the setting—like everything except the telephone calls on this evening—are neutral. We are told nothing more than that it was "a pleasant meal." This is a narrator maintaining complete objectivity.

Briefly, however, the narrator slips inside a character. He reports that the father hears the caller as "nasal, insistent," and like "the phone company's recordings." Later, when the mother answers the phone, we are told that the child on the line "cries." Other than these minimal emotional cues, the narrator remains outside the story, looking on and recording events. The detail offered in the story is mainly dialogue and visual detail, as these examples illustrate:

> The boys shaped large lakes in the center of their mashed yams. They smoothed the rims with their spoons. Then they filled the lakes with brown gravy, and drank the gravy spoonful by spoonful, out of the middle.

> He crumpled his napkin in his palms, shaped it into a ball, and set it on the table. And since it was no longer dusk, but dark enough for him to see his reflection clearly in the dining-room window, he walked to the living room and turned on two lamps.
> The house glowed.

Why would a writer choose to limit the reader's access to these characters? A plausible answer might well be that it is fun and challenging. Another answer is that the writer develops discipline and control of her writing by being forced to concentrate on storytelling. In Kauffman's story, there is a technical reason for maintaining this distance. This reason will be examined later in this chapter in the discussion on suspense.

Experimenting with Third-Person Objective Point of View

The writer is first and always an observer of people, places, and events. Many writers regard observation and careful listening as a form of research. When they watch and listen, frequently they do so from a distance in order to capture their subjects speaking and acting most naturally. This attitude of detached observation is the active principle in the third-person objective narrative point of view. You begin to tell a story. You do not know your characters' minds. You know only what they say and do, what results, and how their speech and actions take place against the backdrop of a particular setting.

Your task in this experiment is to adopt the third-person objective point of view. As has been the practice in this book, you will begin small, with a situation and a few characters. You will work toward larger issues like theme and meaning in later writings, but for now, try to capture your characters speaking and acting naturally.

Writer's Practice 10.1   *Maintain Your Distance*

For this exercise you will need three or four characters. They must be in a clearly defined place and involved in a definite action. Kauffman's characters are four family members preparing to have dinner. You might choose to have a small group of friends preparing to do something like play a baseball game, for example. You are going to point your characters in the direction of interesting trouble. Kauffman introduces trouble from outside: she makes the phone ring. Our writer below introduces trouble with the arrival of an unfamiliar character. Perhaps in this first step, the nature of the trouble will not quite be apparent to you. You will be writing toward a discovery of it. Note that this trouble does not have to be cataclysmic, life-threatening trouble!

> ### How to Hook a Reader
>
> Many writers begin their stories in midaction, or *in media res* (Latin for "in[to] the middle of things"). Writers use this narrative technique to hook readers, drawing them in and making them want to read more.
>
> *In media res* beginnings typically feature some form of action—although they may contain description, thoughts, and dialogue, as well. For instance, many stories begin with a descriptive action that helps establish setting, situation, and character. Such stories usually show a character performing a specific action or two in response to something that's happening or has already happened. The reader, of course, wants to know what that something is.
>
> In stories that begin *in media res*, flashbacks are often included further along to expand upon or complete the missing action.

Write a scene in which the ordinary routine of your characters is disturbed. As you write, keep in mind the constraints discussed above. Your narrator should do the following:

- Regard all the characters as equal.
- Concentrate only on what the characters do and say, limiting access to their thoughts and feelings.

- Start in the middle (*in medias res*), introducing the potential source of interesting trouble immediately.

Begin your experimentation with the third-person objective point of view by writing up to one hundred fifty words—no more than a page. Place your action in either present or past tense. You may find it difficult putting three or four characters in a scene and distinguishing one from the other. It may be helpful to restrict what you say about them. Treat them equally and keep an equal distance from them.

Begin writing if you feel you are ready, or examine our writer's model and explication.

Our Writer

The three boys took the field, ready for a game of baseball. On the mound, Dan, a lefty, was practicing his windup when a fourth boy, a stranger, came through the hedge and spoke to the center fielder.

"Where do you want me?" the fourth boy said.

"Can you catch?"

"Yes."

The center fielder looked this lanky boy up and down. He wore shorts and a T-shirt that was no longer white. He was barefoot. His blond hair was matted.

"What does he want, Ron?" Dan shouted from the mound.

"He wants to play."

Dan tossed the ball up in the air and caught it. "Can he catch?"

"He says he can," Ron said.

The batter, whose yard they were playing in, tapped home plate impatiently with his bat. He spit on his hands and gripped the bat and dug his feet into the grass.

Dan shrugged his shoulders at the batter, then swung around toward center field and pointed at the dead tree in left center. "Put him up there," he said.

Ron looked at the boy, at the tree, then back at the boy. "You heard him," he said.

The boy ran to the tree, put his long white arms around it, and climbed up. It took only seconds. He stopped at the first branch, scooted out a few feet, and perched himself there, ready.

"What about a glove?" Ron said. "I don't know how you expect to catch anything without a glove."

"Trust me," the boy said.

This story gets started immediately. It is a routine game of baseball. The narrator is merely an observer, recording what happens. The routine is upset by the arrival of a fourth boy, a stranger. But how do three boys expect to play baseball? And when the fourth boy arrives, why don't they make teams of two? The situation is odd. The narrator doesn't explain or answer any questions a reader might have.

Also, this narrator maintains his distance from the characters. The pitcher, it would seem, is in charge. He seems to be a focal character, but the reader is not told what Dan thinks and wants. We see only a lefty standing on the mound, ready to start the game. Now a fourth character enters the scene. In Ron's interaction with this new boy, once again the reader only sees the boys and hears the dialogue. There is no insight into Ron's character that is shared, for example. The narrator doesn't tell us what any of the characters thinks or feels or wants. To handle the difficulty of dealing with many characters at once, our writer uses field position—pitcher, center fielder, batter—to distinguish one boy from the other, and then begins to name them. Otherwise, beyond their speech, there is no attention to their individual characters.

Is there interesting trouble to come? The reader is left wondering at the unexplained oddness of the situation.

Exploring Suspense

Narrative, it has been said, is an art of seduction. The writer arouses the attention of a reader and, through skillful manipulation of the reader's desire, holds that attention for the duration of the story. As you read, the feeling of being in the hands of a skillful writer and surrendering to her maneuvers is very satisfying. That feeling is one of the things that make "a good read."

How do you arouse the reader's attention? An appealing narrative voice and stylistic finesse, compelling characters, and story situations that seem oddly wonderful are all elements that combine to create the seduction of narrative, pulling the reader further into the story. This pleasurable pull of narrative also has to do with suspense. Earlier in this chapter, we observed that suspense is created when a writer withholds information from the reader. Inexperienced writers often tell too much too fast. To produce suspense, you raise questions in the reader's mind and delay providing answers to those questions. Part of the art of storytelling is controlling the flow of information: provide enough to keep the reader happy, and withhold enough to keep the reader hooked.

Kauffman's story illustrates the art of withholding information. There are two telephone calls. We never learn who either caller is or whether the calls are even related. Hence the question stated in the title: how many boys? The fact that Kauffman withholds this information makes the story work. She does not answer the reader's questions, so the reader continues reading. Like the family in the story, the reader becomes involved in the plight of the lost child. While this little mystery propels the reader through the story, it also gives rise to the action in the story. The telephone calls create anxiety. The characters have to deal with this anxiety. In a simple cause-and-effect relationship, each call stimulates talk and action. The structure of the story can be summarized as follows:

   I. Disturbing call #1
       action: discuss its meaning
       action: search for the second son
       action: eat dinner
       action: wash dishes and settle in the living room
  II. Disturbing call #2
       action: discuss its meaning
       action: straighten up the house
       action: turn on lights
       action: settle in the living room

Suspense is bearable so long as the reader lives in hope of discovery. Each action moves the characters (and the reader) in what they *hope* is the direction of discovery. As is the case in Kauffman's story, frequently the characters' discovery is the same as the reader's. Perhaps it will be the case in the story you compose, as well.

Experimenting with Suspense

Often a writer sets to work on a story without knowing exactly how it will turn out. Many writers prefer working that way. They enjoy the process of discovery. They trust their imaginations, control of craft, and good luck to provide them with story development and ideas for their stories' conclusions. Writing these stories, writers live in suspense; writing is a process of discovery. What will happen? What turn will events take? What will characters say and do? What complications will occur? In fact, complication is essential. A writer puts a character on a raft, then leads him into rushing rapids. Further complications ensue: a dropped paddle, boulders breaking the surface of the water. Then the writer gets her characters through these complications. Her suspense in creating the story is the reader's suspense in reading it. It is a movement toward discovery. Will the character get to shore? Will the raft capsize?

Writer's Practice 10.2   *Complicate the Situation*

At this point in your story, you have three or four characters whose routine has been disturbed. You have put these characters in a clearly defined place and have pointed them in the direction of interesting trouble. As you were drafting, perhaps you considered some questions: What happens next? How will the characters react to the trouble? What exactly *is* the trouble?

In this section, you will add substantially to what you have written, doing so with suspense in mind. That is, you will move your story forward as we discussed above. Perhaps the initial source of the disturbance causes your characters to act; the prospect of trouble may be eased or intensified. Your characters speak and act, working toward a discovery. That discovery is either thwarted or achieved. As you work, try to bear these suggestions in mind:

- Maintain your narrator's objective stance (avoid explaining).
- Invent at least two events—like Kauffman's phone calls—that motivate your characters to speak and act purposefully.
- Sustain suspense by controlling the flow of information; don't explain too much.
- Identify the dominant emotion generated in this scene. Show this emotion with specific dialogue and action.

Begin writing if you feel you are ready, or examine our writer's model and explication. In this writing, aim for five hundred to seven hundred words.

Our Writer

"Come on," the batter said. "I don't have all day."

Dan tossed the ball into his glove and licked his fingers. He gripped the ball, reached back with his left arm, and hurled a pitch. The batter swung, and a high fly ball sailed out toward left center. Ron trotted in the direction of the ball, swatting his glove with his fist. "I got it," he yelled. But the ball was too high. It was way over Ron's head. He stopped short and watched it begin its descent to earth. The boy in the tree held out his right hand and the ball dropped into it.

"That was lucky," Ron said.

"I know." The boy held the ball in his hand. He smiled and examined it, as if it were an apple that had just dropped from a branch above his head, then tossed the ball down into Ron's waiting glove.

"What the—," Dan said from the mound.

"He's out," the boy called from his tree.

The batter stood at home plate. The bat rested on his shoulder. "That was just practice," he said.

"This is just warm-up," the pitcher yelled to the boy.

"It didn't count," Ron said. "And that was a lucky catch."

"Let's play." The boy relaxed against the bole of the tree, curled an arm around it affectionately. His legs hung down and his long toes pointed toward the earth.

"Try it again," the pitcher said.

"Play ball," the boy said, swinging his legs.

Dan leaned back and fired another pitch, this one even harder, toward the batter. Once again, the bat cracked and a fly ball rocketed into the air, even higher than the first. Ron scuttled backwards, searching the sky. The ball seemed to go straight up and out of sight, lost in the gray-green light. The boys waited. The silence of the spring day held them. When the ball came down, the boy in the tree had stood up on his limb.

"Me," he said.

The ball dropped into his outstretched hand.

"I don't believe it," Ron said.

"What a pitch!" the batter said.

Dan smiled. "I put some mustard on that one for you."

"So fast, I can't believe I hit it," the batter said. "And so high."

"Out again," the boy in the tree said.

Ron scratched his head. "We told you, it's just practice."

"Show off," Dan said.

"I am not out," the batter, Dean, yelled from home plate.

"Doesn't that hurt your hand?" Ron said.

The boy sat down on his limb again. He peeled bark from the dead tree, crumpled it in his hands, and threw it to the ground.

"Do you want to come down?" Ron said.

"No, tree is a good position," the boy said. "There's a lot of action up here today."

The boys went through a rotation. Dean moved to center, Ron to the mound, Dan to the plate. Before he batted, Dan announced that as a lefty, he always pulled the ball and hit to right field, away from the tree. He said the boy might want to play garden, out in right field, if he was going to show off. The boy said, No, that he really preferred tree. The first ball Ron pitched, Dan hit right to the tree, a line drive the boy snagged with both hands. "Hot," the blond boy said. "But out." Dan said there was junk on the ball, that Ron was juicing it up and making him hit to tree, and to take everything off it on the next one, throw straight and easy. Ron wound up and delivered the ball. Dan drew into himself, gathered all his power like a compressed spring, and then released. Contact, line drive. Again, right to tree. "Out again," the blond boy said. "But a nice try."

"He's doing it," Ron said.

Dan threw the bat into the grass. "It's a coincidence."

They rotated again, the boy still up in the tree. Ron hit every ball into the out-stretched hands of the boy in the tree.

"You're doing it," Dan shouted from center field to Ron, at the plate. "You're hitting to him on purpose!"

"I'm not," Ron answered.

"He isn't," the boy said.

Dan glowered up at the fourth player, who hung upside down from his branch. His shirt fell down over his head. "This is no way to play baseball," Dan said.

"It's practice, remember?" came the boy's muffled voice through his shirt.

"All right," Dan said. "Your turn."

"What?" the boy said.

"Bat," Dan said. "I'll pitch."

"I'll take the tree," Ron said.

"No, you won't," Dan said. "You're left center, Dean's right center."

The boy dropped to the ground and jogged to home plate. He picked up the bat and weighed it in his hands, took a few practice swings, and nodded to Dan that he was ready. Dan watched him.

"Well?" the boy said.

"Who are you?" Dan said.

"I'm the batter."

"No, who are you?" Dan said.

"I'm a home run hitter," the boy said. "So you'd better be good."

Dan ground the ball into his glove. "We'll see about that." He leaned forward, resting his weight on his right foot, closed one eye, rocked back and fired at the batter. The boy swung, and the sound of bat and ball rang like a shot. The ball took flight, over the heads of Ron and Dean, over the dead tree, over the hedge.

"He crushed it," Dean shouted.

"It's outta here!" Ron called.

"All the way to the river," Dean said.

"The river," Dan said.

The four of them stood looking at each other, their arms at their sides. Dan took a step toward center field, then turned around and trudged over to the boy with the bat. "Now what?" he said angrily. "Are you happy?"

"Let's go get it," the boy said.

What information does the writer withhold from the reader? Primarily, the identity of the mystery boy is what is withheld. Whereas Kauffman's story is organized around two phone calls, this story is organized around questions of skill in baseball. Can the boy catch? Can he hit? Once the boy is in the tree, a series of actions follows. The ball is hit; the boy catches it; the boys discuss what happened. Then the process repeats: hit, catch, discussion. These actions create tension in the story, increasing suspense. How does he do it? Why does the ball always go to him? Then, like Kauffman's second phone call, there is a second action. The three boys decide the stranger should go to bat. It is a natural progression. So the boy comes down from the tree. There is discussion, preparation, he hits the ball a mile, and more discussion follows.

In this expansion, tension between Dan and the mystery boy develops, which establishes an emotional dimension of the story. To Dan, this "practice" is clearly becoming a competition. We can infer from the dialogue that Dan doesn't like this boy. Dan doesn't like the fact that someone might usurp his position on the field.

"Who are you?" Dan said.

"I'm the batter."

"No, who are you?" Dan said.

"I'm a home run hitter," the boy said. "So you'd better be good."

Dan ground the ball into his glove. "We'll see about that." He leaned forward, resting his weight on his right foot, closed one eye, rocked back and fired at the batter.

What will happen to Dan, the leader and focal character in this story, if he is outplayed by another character? What will the effect be on the other boys? Perhaps this story will eventually tell the reader not only who the fourth boy is but also who Dan and the other boys are.

Throughout this expansion, narrative distance is maintained. The narrator reports what the characters say and do, but refrains from exploring what they think and feel. Maintaining this distance is part of the exercise. Moreover, you may begin to see that this distance is what makes suspense possible. What if this story were told in first person, from Dan's point of view, or from the point of view of the fourth boy? It would be a completely different story, and the questions asked above would not seem as important.

Finally, the expansion of our writer's story ends on a suspenseful note. Will the boys find the ball? If they do, then what will happen?

Writer's Practice 10.3 *Seek a Resolution*

Reread what you wrote in Writer's Practices 10.1 and 10.2 and write your way to the end of this story. The end of the story might be a definitive action that eases or resolves the conflict. Or, it might be an ending that does not resolve the conflict but signals changes in your characters. In Kauffman's story, the reader is left with an eerie calm. The family is together, but they do not feel completely safe. The episode has come to a close, but the dominant emotion of the story remains: a vague uneasiness, a free-floating fearfulness. Kauffman's ending is true to life. In real life, often we do not resolve our conflicts. Instead, we work on them in episodes. Those episodes come to a close, and we are changed in a small way. We have a new insight. Frequently, however, our conflicts remain.

Write a scene that brings your story to a close. Be sure to do the following:

- Maintain your narrator's objective stance.
- Involve your characters in at least one more action.
- Work with a dominant emotion that is clear when the episode closes.

Begin writing if you feel you are ready, or examine our writer's model and explication.

Our Writer

Dan, Ron, and Dean followed the strange boy through the hedge. They stumbled down the steep hill behind him, stepping over dead trees. They shuffled through wet weeds, glanced about, searching for the ball.

"It's gone," Dan said. "We'll never find it."

"Hopeless," Dean said.

"He couldn't have hit it this far," Dean said.

"Of course not," Dan said.

"He did," Ron said. "You saw it."

The three boys stopped and watched their teammate skip down to the edge of the river. The water was high. In flood, it had risen over the bank. The brown water curled in eddies and whirlpools at his feet. It rushed by the blond boy. He stood in front of it, peering intently into the water.

"He knows where it is," Ron said.

"It's his fault. He wrecked our game," Dan said. "Hey you!"

The boy turned to face them. He held out his hands and motioned them down to the water.

"We just want what belongs to us," Dan said. "We want our ball back."

Ron said, "Wait a minute."

"Let him get it," Dan said.

"We need him," Ron said.

"Go on and get it," Dan yelled down the hill.

The boy stepped backward into the river. The water came up to his knees. A damp breeze swept down the hill over the boys. The boy took another step and fell backward into the water. He spun in the eddy and was quickly pulled into the current and out into the river. His blond head stayed above the surface. From the brown water his arms emerged, swimming strokes, each stroke like a long throw to them from center field. They watched as, overwhelmed by the water, the boy disappeared downstream, his arms bright flashes of white. They watched and waited, listening.

"He's gone," Ron said.

At the top of the hill, they pushed through the hedge again. They stood on the green grass where they had played hours and hours of baseball. Ron went to the tree in center field. He looked up at the branch and said "tree" to himself. The bat lay across home plate where the boy had dropped it.

"We have to get another ball," Dan said.

Ron rested his head against the tree. "He made some great catches."

"That was luck," Dean said. He stood at home plate, bat in hand. "Dumb luck."

"Baseball is a game of skill," Dan said. "He wrecked our game."

"But he sure could hit," Ron said.

"Up in a tree like that." Dan nodded and frowned. He rotated his pitching arm. "It was no way to play baseball. He wrecked our game."

What resolution happened here? The boy is gone, so the source of conflict has disappeared. With him, the ball has also disappeared. Temporarily, at least, the game is over. Yet, our writer has not answered many of the questions raised in the story. We still do not know the identity of the fourth boy. However, it seems clear that a change has occurred in the relationship of the three boys. They seem divided. Dan's remark, "It was no way to play baseball," is certainly true, but something amazing has happened—something Ron seems unwilling to let go of (so he goes to the tree).

Writer's Practice 10.4   *Assemble the First Draft*

Copy the passages you wrote in Writer's Practices 10.1, 10.2, and 10.3, so you have a draft of this story. Do not cut or add or rewrite it. Think about a title for your story. Then read your passages and think about the lessons taught in this chapter. Does your narrator maintain an objective stance? What questions does your story raise? What information do you withhold to create suspense? Once you have put the passages together and reflected on these questions, you will be ready to share your work with other writers in a response group.

Here is our writer's assembled story.

Our Writer

Up a Tree

The three boys took the field, ready for a game of baseball. On the mound, Dan, a lefty, was practicing his windup when a fourth boy, a stranger, came through the hedge and spoke to the center fielder.

"Where do you want me?" the fourth boy said.

"Can you catch?"

"Yes."

The center fielder looked this lanky boy up and down. He wore shorts and a T-shirt that was no longer white. He was barefoot. His blond hair was matted.

"What does he want, Ron?" Dan shouted from the mound.

"He wants to play."

Dan tossed the ball up in the air and caught it. "Can he catch?"

"He says he can," Ron said.

The batter, whose yard they were playing in, tapped home plate impatiently with his bat. He spit on his hands and gripped the bat and dug his feet into the grass.

Dan shrugged his shoulders at the batter, then swung around toward center field and pointed at the dead tree in left center. "Put him up there," he said.

Ron looked at the boy, at the tree, then back at the boy. "You heard him," he said.

The boy ran to the tree, put his long white arms around it, and climbed up. It took only seconds. He stopped at the first branch, scooted out a few feet, and perched himself there, ready.

"What about a glove?" Ron said. "I don't know how you expect to catch anything without a glove."

"Trust me," the boy said.

"Come on," the batter said. "I don't have all day."

Dan tossed the ball into his glove and licked his fingers. He gripped the ball, reached back with his left arm, and hurled a pitch. The batter swung, and a high fly ball sailed out toward left center. Ron trotted in the direction of the ball, swatting his glove with his fist. "I got it," he yelled. But the ball was too high. It was way over Ron's head. He stopped short and watched it begin its descent to earth. The boy in the tree held out his right hand and the ball dropped into it.

"That was lucky," Ron said.

"I know." The boy held the ball in his hand. He smiled and examined it, as if it were an apple that had just dropped from a branch above his head, then tossed the ball down into Ron's waiting glove.

"What the—," Dan said from the mound.

"He's out," the boy called from his tree.

The batter stood at home plate. The bat rested on his shoulder. "That was just practice," he said.

"This is just warm-up," the pitcher yelled to the boy.

"It didn't count," Ron said. "And that was a lucky catch."

"Let's play." The boy relaxed against the bole of the tree, curled an arm around it affectionately. His legs hung down and his long toes pointed toward the earth.

"Try it again," the pitcher said.

"Play ball," the boy said, swinging his legs.

Dan leaned back and fired another pitch, this one even harder, toward the batter. Once again, the bat cracked and a fly ball rocketed into the air, even higher than the first. Ron scuttled backwards, searching the sky. The ball seemed to go straight up and out of sight, lost in the gray-green light. The boys waited. The silence of the spring day held them. When the ball came down, the boy in the tree had stood up on his limb.

"Me," he said. The ball dropped into his outstretched hand.

"I don't believe it," Ron said.

"What a pitch!" the batter said.

Dan smiled. "I put some mustard on that one for you."

"So fast, I can't believe I hit it," the batter said. "And I hit it so high."

"Out again," the boy in the tree said.

Ron scratched his head. "We told you, it's just practice."

"Show off," Dan said.

"I am not out," the batter, Dean, yelled from home plate.

"Doesn't that hurt your hand?" Ron said.

The boy sat down on his limb again. He peeled bark from the dead tree, crumpled it in his hands, and threw it to the ground.

"Do you want to come down?" Ron said.

"No, tree is a good position," the boy said. "There's a lot of action up here today."

The boys went through a rotation. Dean moved to center, Ron to the mound, Dan to the plate. Before he batted, Dan announced that as a lefty, he always pulled the ball and hit to right field, away from the tree. He said the boy might want to play garden, out in right field, if he was going to show off. The boy said, No, that he really preferred tree. The first ball Ron pitched, Dan hit right to tree, a line drive the boy snagged with both hands. "Hot," the blond boy said. "But out." Dan said there was junk on the ball, that Ron was juicing it up and making him hit to tree, and to take everything off it on the next one, throw straight and easy. Ron wound up and delivered the ball. Dan drew into himself, gathered all his power like a compressed spring, and then released. Contact, line drive. Again, right to tree. "Out again," the blond boy said. "But a nice try."

"He's doing it," Ron said.

Dan threw the bat into the grass. "It's a coincidence."

They rotated again, the boy still up in the tree. Ron hit every ball into the out-stretched hands of the boy in the tree.

"You're doing it," Dan shouted from center field to Ron, at the plate. "You're hitting to him on purpose!"

"I'm not," Ron answered.

"He isn't," the boy said.

Dan glowered up at the fourth player, who hung upside down from his branch. His shirt fell down over his head. "This is no way to play baseball," Dan said.

"It's practice, remember?" came the boy's muffled voice through his shirt.

"All right," Dan said. "Your turn."

"What?" the boy said.

"Bat," Dan said. "I'll pitch."

"I'll take the tree," Ron said.

"No, you won't," Dan said. "You're left center, Dean's right center."

The boy dropped to the ground and jogged to home plate. He picked up the bat and weighed it in his hands, took a few practice swings, and nodded to Dan that he was ready. Dan watched him.

"Well?" the boy said.

"Who are you?" Dan said.

"I'm the batter."

"No, who are you?" Dan said.

"I'm a home run hitter," the boy said. "So you'd better be good."

Dan ground the ball into his glove. "We'll see about that." He leaned forward, resting his weight on his right foot, closed one eye, rocked back and fired at the batter. The boy swung, and the sound of bat and ball rang like a shot. The ball took flight, over the heads of Ron and Dean, over the dead tree, over the hedge.

"He crushed it," Dean shouted.

"It's outta here!" Ron called.

"All the way to the river," Dean said.

"The river," Dan said.

The four of them stood looking at each other, their arms at their sides. Dan took a step toward center field, then turned around and trudged over to the boy with the bat. "Now what?" he said angrily. "Are you happy?"

"Let's go get it," the boy said.

Dan, Ron, and Dean followed the strange boy through the hedge. They stumbled down the steep hill behind him, stepping over dead trees. They shuffled through wet weeds, glanced about, searching for the ball.

"It's gone," Dan said. "We'll never find it."

"Hopeless," Dean said.

"He couldn't have hit it this far," Dean said.

"Of course not," Dan said.

"He did," Ron said. "You saw it."

The three boys stopped and watched their teammate skip down to the edge of the river. In flood, it had risen over the bank. The brown water curled in eddies and whirlpools at his feet. It rushed by the blond boy. He stood in front of it, peering intently into the water.

"He knows where it is," Ron said.

"It's his fault. He wrecked our game," Dan said. "Hey you!"

The boy turned to face them. He held out his hands and motioned them down to the water.

"We just want what belongs to us," Dan said. "We want our ball back."

Ron said, "Wait a minute."

"Let him get it," Dan said.

"We need him," Ron said.

"Go on and get it," Dan yelled down the hill.

The boy stepped backward into the river. The water came up to his knees. A breeze swept down the hill over the boys. The boy took another step and fell backward into the water. He was pulled into the current. His blond head stayed above the surface. From the brown water his arms emerged, swimming strokes, each stroke like a throw to them from center field. They watched as, overwhelmed by the water, the boy disappeared downstream, his arms bright flashes of white. They watched and waited until they were sure he was not coming back.

At the top of the hill, they pushed through the hedge again. They stood on the green grass where they had played hours and hours of baseball. Ron went to the tree in center field. He looked up at the branch and said "tree" to himself. The bat lay across home plate where the boy had dropped it.

"We'll have to get another ball," Dan said.

Ron rested his head against the tree. "He made some great catches."

"That was luck," Dean said. He stood at home plate, bat in hand. "Completely."

"Baseball is a game of skill," Dan said. "He wrecked our game."

"But he sure could hit," Ron said.

"Up in a tree like that." Dan nodded and frowned. He rotated his pitching arm. "It was no way to play baseball. He wrecked our game."

Writer Response Groups

At this point, you have a draft of a story. Do not worry if your material is rough. In smoothing and refining, a writer often makes her most important discoveries. Now form response groups. Examine each other's stories, reading for the following elements:

Essential Elements

- Whose story is it?
- What is the conflict?
- How is the action plotted?

Craft

- What routine is disturbed? What is the cause of this disturbance?
- Does the narrator maintain an objective stance in the story?
- What information is withheld in the story?
- What actions do the characters take to work toward a discovery?
- What is the dominant emotion in the story?

Revising Your Story for Tone

Tone refers to the emotional coloring or mood of a story. In very simple terms, you might think of a story as bright or dark. You become aware of a certain feeling as you read. If the writer does his job well, you give yourself emotionally to the story and allow the narrative to do its work. As the story unfolds and you are drawn into it, the tone develops and changes. Bright stories often have a dark side; similarly, dark stories can have subtle humor. Writers who achieve this emotional and tonal complexity are often the most satisfying to read because they succeed at conveying what life is really like.

Kauffman's story is an interesting study in tone. At first, with the nonsensical question "Is the boy back from the paper?" repeated twice without explanation, the story feels like farce. The reader might suppose, at the outset, that this will be a funny story. The goofiness is sustained as the father and boy turn the question inside out, attempting to understand it; indeed, the characters' preoccupation with how the question is stated, and their repeated discussion of it, has an absurd quality. Comedy bits are driven by such misunderstanding and repetition.

Yet Kauffman also provides a darker emotional coloring in the story. A lost child is a serious matter. One of the father's first actions is to determine that his second child is home. After dinner, as they attempt to reestablish the routine of evening at home, the mood of the story takes a darker turn.

> When the father sat down in an easy chair, one of his sons climbed in beside him. The father put his arm around the boy so the two would fit together just right.
> The father kissed the boy's hair.
> "So *here* you are," the father whispered.

It is, of course, the son who was upstairs. (Notice, the narrator does not *tell* the reader that.) The father is eager for the two of them to "fit together just right." The words in the question—"Is the child back from the paper?"—do not fit together just right. He is attempting to assure himself of the order of his home and the safety of his children.

From this point on in the story, however, the darker mood is established. Lights are turned on against this darkness. One character after another goes to the window and peers outside into the dark. The lost child who makes the second call only intensifies the family's feeling of insecurity. The younger of the two boys remarks, "I don't know how to dial for help." How can you live in a world where a child can be inexplicably lost? And what if you cannot respond to a cry for help? "Can't we call somebody?" one character wonders. In the end, the security of this family is terribly undermined. They take their places in the living room, trying to recover their composure. "They sat together," the narrator twice reports at the end of the story. The emotional coloring of the story—the sense of helplessness and fear—is so well established that it lasts beyond the end of the story

Writer's Practice 10.5 *Adjust the Backdrop*

Write a second draft of your story. In this draft, pay closer attention to tone. As we see in Kauffman's story, emotional coloring in the story comes from dialogue and action. Revise your story with an eye on what your characters say and do, attempting to build emotion in your story. Pay attention also to backdrop—details referring to time and place (see also Writer's Practice 9.1). *Backdrop* is a stagecraft term. Behind the players is a screen upon which imagery can be projected, along with a certain quality of light. These atmospheric details help create tone. In like fashion, when you revise your draft, look for at least three changes you can make to further develop the tonal possibilities in your story. In your revision you should do the following:

- Give at least two characters dialogue with emotional coloring; have your characters repeat these words once or twice.
- Give at least two characters actions that express their emotional state (such as Kauffman's characters switching on lights).
- Be sure that time of day and year are clear.
- Report once or twice on atmosphere: qualities in the natural world that correspond to the emotional coloring of your story.
- Speak or act to express the tone qualities of the story.

In his rough draft, our writer did not establish time of day or year; neither did he give the reader a distinct sense of place. As you read his rough draft, you realize that the boys are playing in one boy's backyard, that there is a hedge and, somewhere not far away, a river. In a revision, our writer attempted to provide better spatial orientation for the reader, adjusting a few of these details and, in doing so, preparing to highlight the tone of mystery in the story. What changes in dialogue and action does our writer make?

Our Writer

Spring Training

On the morning the rain stopped, the three boys set up their field in Dean's narrow backyard. They were ready for a game of baseball. Ron took center, standing in front of the thick hedge far back at the end of the yard. On the mound, Dan, the lefty, was practicing his windup when a fourth boy pushed through the hedge and motioned to Ron.

"Hey," the fourth boy said.

Ron said, "Where did you come from, the river?"

The boy looked over his shoulder, back through the hedge, at the flooded river down the hill.

"Where do you want me to play?" he said.

Ron looked this lanky boy up and down. He was barefoot. He wore shorts. His shins were mud-spattered and his T-shirt was no longer white. The boy laced his fingers together and settled his hands on top of his head, waiting. His blond hair was matted.

"Can you catch?"

"Every time," the boy said.

"What does he want, Ron?" Dan shouted from the mound.

"He wants to play."

Dan tossed the ball up in the air and caught it. "Can he catch?"

"He says he can," Ron said.

The batter, whose yard they were playing in, tapped home plate impatiently with his bat. He spit on his hands and gripped the bat and dug his feet into the grass.

Dan shrugged his shoulders at the batter, then swung around toward center field and pointed at the dead tree in left center. "Put him up there," he said.

Ron looked at the boy, at the tree, then back at the boy. "You heard him," he said.

The boy ran to the tree, put his long white arms around it, and climbed up. It took only seconds. He stopped at the first branch, scooted out a few feet, and perched himself there, ready.

"What about a glove?" Ron said. "I don't know how you expect to catch anything without a glove."

"Trust me," the boy said.

"Come on," the batter said. "I don't have all day."

Dan tossed the ball into his glove and licked his fingers. He gripped the ball and wound up, drawing his left arm back and elaborately kicking his right leg, and then hurled his pitch. The batter swung, and a high fly ball sailed out toward left center. Ron flung his hat in the air. "I got it," he yelled. He trotted in the direction of the ball, swatting his glove with his fist. But the ball was too high, disappearing into low misty clouds. Ron stopped short and waited for the ball to begin its descent to earth. The boy in the tree held out his right hand and the ball dropped into it.

"I could have got that," Ron said. "If I dove for it."

"I know." The boy held the ball in his hand. He smiled and examined it, as if a fruit had just dropped into his hand from a branch above his head, then tossed the ball down into Ron's waiting glove.

"You should've had that," Dan said to Ron from the mound.

"Batter's out," the boy called from his tree.

The batter stood at home plate. The bat rested on his shoulder. "That was just practice," he said. He made a few violent swings of the bat.

"This is warm-up," the pitcher yelled to the boy.

"I get the next one," Ron said. "That was a lucky catch."

"You can always use a little luck." The boy relaxed against the bole of the tree, curled an arm around it affectionately. His legs hung down and his long toes pointed toward the earth.

"Try it again," the pitcher said, looking doubtfully at the sky.

"Play ball," the boy said, swinging his legs.

Dan leaned back and fired another pitch, this one even harder, toward the batter. Once again, the bat cracked and a fly ball rocketed into the air, even higher than the first. Ron scuttled backwards, searching the sky. The ball seemed to go straight up and out of sight, lost in the gray-green light. The boys waited. The silence of the spring day held them. When the ball came down, the boy in the tree had stood up on his limb.

"Me," he said. The ball dropped into his outstretched hand.

"I don't believe it," Ron said.

"What a pitch!" the batter said.

Dan smiled. "I put some mustard on that one for you."

"So fast, I can't believe I hit it," the batter said. "And I hit it so high."

"Out again," the boy in the tree said.

Ron scratched his head. "We told you, it's just practice."

"Show off," Dan said.

"I am not out," the batter, Dean, yelled from home plate.

"Doesn't that hurt your hand?" Ron said.

The boy sat down on his limb again. He peeled bark from the dead tree, crumpled it in his hands, and threw it to the ground.

"Do you want to come down?" Ron said.

"No, tree is a good position," the boy said. "There's a lot of action up here today."

The boys went through a rotation. Dean moved to center, Ron to the mound, Dan to the plate. Before he batted, Dan announced that as a lefty, he always pulled the ball and hit to right field, away from the tree. He said the boy might want to play garden, out in right field, if he was going to show off. The boy said, No, that he really preferred tree. The first ball Ron pitched, Dan hit right to tree, a line drive the boy snagged with both hands. "Hot," the blond boy said. "But out." Dan said there was junk on the ball, that Ron was juicing it up and making him hit to tree, and to take everything off it on the next one, throw straight and easy. Ron wound up and delivered the ball. Dan drew into himself, gathered all his power like a compressed spring, and then released. Contact, line drive. Again, right to tree. "Out again," the blond boy said. "But a nice try."

"He's doing it," Ron said.

Dan threw the bat into the grass. "It's a coincidence."

They rotated again, the boy still up in the tree. Ron hit every ball into the outstretched hands of the boy in the tree.

"You're doing it," Dan shouted from center field to Ron, at the plate. "You're hitting to him on purpose!"

"I'm not," Ron answered.

"He isn't," the boy said.

Dan glowered up at the fourth player, who hung upside down from his branch. His shirt fell down over his head. "This is no way to play baseball," Dan said.

"It's practice, remember?" came the boy's muffled voice through his shirt.

"All right," Dan said. "Your turn."

"What?" the boy said.

"Bat," Dan said. "I'll pitch."

"I'll take the tree," Ron said.

"No, you won't," Dan said. "You're left center, Dean's right center."

The boy dropped to the ground and jogged to home plate. He picked up the bat and weighed it in his hands, took a few practice swings, and nodded to Dan that he was ready. Dan watched him.

"Well?" the boy said.

"Who are you?" Dan said.

"I'm the batter."

"No, who are you?" Dan said.

"I'm a home run hitter," the boy said. "So you'd better be good."

Dan ground the ball into his glove. "We'll see about that." He leaned forward, resting his weight on his right foot, closed one eye, rocked back and fired at the batter. The boy swung, and the sound of bat and ball rang like a shot. The ball took flight, over the heads of Ron and Dean, over the dead tree, over the hedge.

"He crushed it," Dean shouted.

"It's outta here!" Ron called.

"All the way to the river," Dean said.

"The river," Dan said.

The four of them stood looking at each other, their arms at their sides. Dan took a step toward center field, then turned around and trudged over to the boy with the bat. "Now what?" he said angrily. "Are you happy?"

"Let's go get it," the boy said.

Dan, Ron, and Dean followed the strange boy through the hedge. They stumbled down the steep hill behind him, stepping over dead trees. They shuffled through wet weeds, glanced about, searching for the ball.

"It's gone," Dan said. "We'll never find it."

"Hopeless," Dean said.

"He couldn't have hit it this far," Dean said.

"Of course not," Dan said.

"He did," Ron said. "You saw it."

The three boys stopped and watched their teammate skip down to the edge of the river. In flood, it had risen over the bank. The brown water curled in eddies and whirlpools at his feet. It rushed by the blond boy. He stood in front of it, peering intently into the water.

"He knows where it is," Ron said.

"It's his fault. He wrecked our game," Dan said. "Hey you!"

The boy turned to face them. He held out his hands and motioned them down to the water.

"We just want what belongs to us," Dan said. "We want our ball back."

Ron said, "Wait a minute."

"Let him get it," Dan said.

"We need him," Ron said.

"Go on and get it," Dan yelled down the hill.

"But we need him!" Ron said.

The boy stepped backward into the river. The water came up to his knees. A breeze swept down the hill over the boys. The boy took another step and fell backward into the water. He was pulled into the current. His blond head stayed above the surface. From the brown water his arms emerged, swimming strokes, each stroke like a long throw to them from center field. They watched as, overwhelmed by the water, the boy disappeared downstream, his throwing arms flashing. They watched and waited until they were sure he was not coming back.

"Now what?" Ron said.

Dan shook his head. "He didn't know how to play."

At the top of the hill, they pushed through the hedge again. They stood on the green grass where they had played hours and hours of baseball. Ron went to the tree in center field. He looked up at the branch and said "tree" to himself. The bat lay across home plate where the boy had dropped it.

"We have to get another ball," Dan said.

Ron rested his head against the tree. He peered up through the dead tree branches and into the swirling clouds, as if he could see beyond them. "He made some great catches."

"That was luck," Dean said. He stood at home plate, bat in hand. "Completely."

"Baseball is a game of skill," Dan said. "He wrecked our game."

"But he sure could hit," Ron said.

"Up in a tree like that." Dan nodded and spat into the grass. He rotated his pitching arm. "It's no way to play baseball. He wrecked our game."

At the end of our writer's revision, the episode is brought to a close. The fourth boy is out of the picture, so his immediate impact on the game is no longer an issue. However, there is a lasting emotional response to the fourth boy's visit. Dan and Dean seem angry, even glad the boy is gone. But Ron goes to the tree. He still seems slightly mesmerized by the boy's play. He does not want to adopt Dan's literal way of looking at baseball, as a game of skill alone. For him, perhaps it is a game of luck and magic, too. The boy's effect on Ron may be long-lasting.

The revised story also features dialogue more clearly focused on the issue of skill and ability, especially at the beginning. In addition, the revision makes time of year much more clear. As a backdrop for the story, the season adds to the tone. The flood suggests a power not easily controlled. The light has a magical quality to it: "The ball seemed to go straight up and out of sight, lost in the gray-green light. The boys waited. The silence of the spring day held them."

The division between the boys is emphasized when the writer has them look in the sky. At one point, Dan looks "doubtfully at the sky." Ron, on the other hand, "peered up through the dead tree branches and into the swirling clouds, as if he could see beyond them." These "echoing" actions show the difference between these two boys—another touch the writer adds to create emotional tone in the story.

Examining Student Stories

The third-person objective point of view allows a writer to focus on the art of storytelling. Concentrating on the unfolding story—rather than what the characters are thinking about—can be freeing for a writer. The story that follows contains a group of characters in a familiar setting and has complications and suspense.

The Nature Area

SHANNON BELL

Three girls sat at the picnic table, finishing their bag lunches.

Carla gazed toward the sugar maple on the edge of the playground. "I love you, Mary Ann," she said, pointing.

That's what someone had scrawled on the paper taped to the maple's trunk, in big block letters: "I love you, Mary Ann." The message was written in magic marker—red, like the tree's October leaves.

Connie giggled. "Wonder who he is."

"I don't care," said Mary Ann.

A boy wearing bright blue pants and carrying a Superman lunchbox sat down by Mary Ann. He handed her his orange. She gave him a yellow apple pale as the noon sun.

"Did you write that?" asked Carla.

"Write what?"

"'I love you, Mary Ann,'" she said, pointing again.

"No." The boy unwrapped his bologna sandwich, peeling away crumpled waxed paper with unsteady fingers.

"Somebody wrote it," said Connie. "Somebody who loves Mary Ann."

"Teddy loves Mary Ann," taunted Carla. "Teddy loves Mary Ann."

Mary Ann pinched Carla's upper arm. "Carla! Leave him alone." She thought about saying so what if Ted wrote it, but she didn't.

Ted rose, shuffled toward the trashcan near the brick schoolhouse, and discarded the waxed paper. On the way back, he tripped over nothing.

"Walk much?" asked Carla.

"No," he answered. "I usually fly."

"That was rude, Carla," said Mary Ann as Ted made his way back to them.

"You're right," said Connie. "We should be nicer." She drew up her knees and rested her chin atop them. "If Ted didn't write 'I Love You, Mary Ann,' who did?"

Carla shrugged.

Ted ate the yellow apple while Carla and Connie worked their fingers through looped blue yarn, making cats-in-the-cradles and Jacob's ladders. A half-dozen girls jump-roped nearby, and a group of boys arm-wrestled at the other table.

"Do you arm-wrestle, Ted?" asked Connie, trying to be nicer.

Ted blinked. "Not like that."

Mary Ann pulled a string of cherry licorice from her skirt pocket and began chewing on it. "There must be lots of Mary Ann's."

Ted spoke. "I only know one."

Carla rolled her eyes, and Connie covered her mouth with her hand.

Mary Ann ignored them. "There must be hundreds of Mary Anns," she said. "In the phone book, for example."

"There must be hundreds of Mary Anns in there," Ted agreed.

Carla smirked. "You don't love people you find in the phone book, Clubfoot."

"Don't call me that."

"Clubfoot. Clubfoot. Clubfoot."

"Stop it," said Mary Ann, standing.

"Stop telling me what to do," Carla told Mary Ann.

Ted stood, too. He pointed at Carla. "You be quiet."

"And if I don't?"

Ted lurched toward her, landing on one knee.

The lunch attendant hurried their way.

Mary Ann threw her licorice onto the ground, marched toward the sugar maple, and sat beneath it, pink-faced.

The lunch attendant helped Ted rise. Nearby where he'd fallen lay a red magic marker.

"Liar, liar, pants on fire," chanted Carla, and soon most of the other kids joined in, despite the lunch attendant's warning.

"I am not," said Ted, searching out Mary Ann.

Mary Ann avoided his eyes, studying the flowers on her skirt.

"Mary Ann?" asked Ted.

She said nothing, pulling out a new piece of licorice and rolling it between her palms.

Ted made for the back of the playground, walking and then trotting, not tripping once. Then he slipped through the metal gate that separated the playground from the nature area beyond and disappeared.

Connie squinted. "Where is he? Where'd he go?" She looked up, following the vapor trail of a jet in the sky.

Carla picked up the magic marker and put it on the table. "Gone." The other children resumed their jump-roping and arm-wrestling. The lunch attendant looked from the nature area to the six-graders she was overseeing. She hurried into the brick schoolhouse, pausing once to look back, as if unsure about what to do.

Mary Ann glanced toward the nature area, too, then at the note on the tree, before rejoining Connie and Carla at the table.

"Have any more licorice?" asked Connie.

Mary Ann gave her a piece.

Carla tapped the table leg with her foot. "Why'd you stick up for him?"

"He's okay. What's wrong with him?"

"Plenty," said Carla.

Mary Ann shook her head. "You don't even know him. He's kinda funny. Really."

Connie looked back up at the sky. "He's different, that's all. You know, spacey."

"I don't like him," said Carla, tearing into the licorice, "and I don't like him at our table."

Mary Ann gave Carla a cool glance, then walked the length of the playground and slipped through the gate. The nature area was overgrown with scrub trees and Scotch pines. There were also a few English hawthorns, and when Mary Ann walked under one of them, a thorn apple bounced off her head.

She picked her way among the trees, looking for Ted. She found him standing beside a pine, arms raised and hands clenched. "What are you doing?" she asked.

"Just being Superman."

"Oh. Are you okay?"

"Sure. Superman's always okay." Ted lowered his arms. "Superman can do anything."

"Not anything."

"Anything."

"Superman knows everything, too," continued Ted, leaning against a lower branch.

"Everything?"

"Everything."

"Does he know who wrote that note?"

"Superman's not saying. But I'll tell you this: Carla is Lex Luther in disguise."

Mary Ann cracked up. "Lex Luther?"

Ted nodded. "When I'm around her, I get weak. Like when Superman gets around Kryptonite."

"That's weird." Mary Ann pulled out her last piece of licorice. "Want it?"

"Yeah," Ted said, but he didn't take it.

"Forget about Carla."

Ted shrugged. "I don't think she likes you, either. She just pretends." He stared up into the sky. "Can you see Krypton?"

"No. The sun's too bright."

"Use your X-ray vision."

"I don't have X-ray vision. Only Superman does."

"Pretend it's night. If you try really hard, you'll see it."

Mary Ann shielded her eyes with both hands and looked up. "I think I see it, Ted. I do. I see it."

"That's the place, Mary Ann. That's where I'm from."

In Shannon's story, the third-person objective narrator tells the story of four classmates on a playground and the conflict that arises from their interaction. The narrator doesn't have to tell us how these characters think or feel; their actions and speech do that. Suspense revolves around Ted, a mysterious boy who doesn't quite fit in. In the end, Mary Ann and Ted return to being friends, although Ted remains a bit of a mystery for the reader.

chapter 11

Moving Inside a Character: Psychological Conflict, Flashback, and Imagery

[Third-person] point of view (style, in a sense) goes for deep consciousness, in the hope that the thoughts and feelings of the character will become the immediate (unmediated) thoughts and feelings of the reader.

-JOHN GARDNER

I n Chapter 10, you were asked to maintain rigorous control of the third-person point of view. You maintained an objective stance, which required you to refrain from slipping inside any particular character to portray his or her inner life. Your narrator was a disinterested observer with a "camera lens" view. Your characters were all equal in the eyes of this narrator as they spoke, acted, and worked their way toward a discovery.

In this chapter, you will move inward, going for what Gardner refers to as "deep consciousness" of one character. Your narrator will become deeply interested in this character. Narrative voice, treated in Writer's Practice 8.2, will become directly identified with your main character's thought. Your purpose in writing will be to explore a psychological conflict in your main character. To this end, your third-person narrator will report only what this particular character sees, thinks, and feels. In other words, your narrator's insight will be limited to this character. Hence, this point of view is called third-person "limited."

Moments of intense inner life are almost always triggered by experiences we have and by our interactions with others. In the story you will write, your main character will be confronted with a disturbing event. As she thinks about it, she will flash back in time, from the present to the past, as she replays the event in her mind and attempts to make sense of what has happened. Your third-person narrator will represent this character's thread of thought as she works toward resolution.

Ursula Hegi's story "Thieves" is written in the third-person limited point of view. Hegi presents a character with a conflict and has a narrator record this character's thoughts and feelings. As you read the story, look for places where the narrator simply replays events in the character's mind. There are disconnections—jumps from one time to another, from one subject to another. Where do these jumps occur?

Thieves

Ursula Hegi

The thieves emptied the refrigerator and freezer. They took the sirloin steak defrosting next to the sink, a nearly empty bottle of Windex, the green potholders, four bottles from the spice rack, three plastic tankards with see-through bottoms, and the pillowcase from Laura's side of the bed. They did not take the silverware, Phil's new fiberglass tennis racket, the film projector, or the TV set. They left a peculiar combination of emptiness and invasion, a feeling of being smothered and abandoned that clung to Laura's pillow although she changed the sheets and pillowcases right away. It was as though their hands were still on the bed, even after Phil turned off the light and his breathing turned into light snoring that rose and fluttered above him like a kite on a fragile string, lifting and falling with the wind.

Quietly she got up. In the dark she carried her pillow into the living room. Against her bare feet the carpet felt matted, unclean. Tomorrow she would rent a Blue Lustre shampooer at the Taylor Rental Center. She sat down in the stuffed chair facing the front door. Phil had secured it with a piece of yellow rope to keep it closed until the locksmith could come. Returning from the airport where Laura had picked him up from his trip to Seattle, he had first seemed angry when they found their front door forced open, but soon he had settled into amused gratefulness.

"It could have been worse," he said.

She hadn't answered.

"You're lucky this didn't happen while I was away," he had said.

His relief that they hadn't taken his tennis racket had been painfully obvious to her. Cautiously, with her fingertips, she had touched the things they hadn't taken: her books, her sunglasses, her violin.

At first she hadn't felt anything but a cold tightness at the bottom of her ribs, a surprised chill that grew into anger and spread until she knew she had to do something before it expanded beyond the limits of her body. How she wished she had come upon them stuffing food and spices into her pillowcase. She would have liked to hurt them. Phil would laugh at her thoughts. How important can those potholders and spices possibly be? he'd ask. For Christ's sake, you're pulling everything out of proportion.

The older of the two policemen had said they were going to check the closed camps by the lake. Most of them wouldn't be opened by their owners until the end of June, almost a month from now. Perhaps someone had broken into one of the cottages and needed food. Their house was the nearest year-round residence to those small A-frames that lay abandoned all winter and bustled into ten weeks of frantic activities and bright bathing suits each summer. But why Windex? she had asked. The other officer, a short man with a mustache of various shades of brown, had shrugged and said it would be worth a try.

Leaving her pillow on the chair, Laura walked back into the bedroom. Falling slanted from the hallway, an oblong block of light covered the foot end of the bed. Phil's snoring, ascending as though he were straining to reach for something above him, dropped and fluttered as he exhaled and then spiraled upward again as if to break the thin kite string. His left arm was flung across the comforter on her side of the bed. She lifted his hand; he flinched but did not wake up. Carefully she set it back down.

For the past eight weeks the bed had been hers. Phil had been away on one of his consulting trips. This afternoon, waiting for him at the airport, she still thought she missed him; but when he walked toward her he wore a beige raincoat she had never seen and looked heavier somehow, paler, as though he had spent most of his time inside offices and restaurants.

She tried to imagine the hands of the thieves, hands that had touched the items she had held so many times, hands that had chosen thyme, garlic powder, dried chives, and paprika. Broad hands with short fingers? Smooth hands with pale skin? Why didn't they select pepper? Cinnamon? Had the thieves been in the middle of preparing a meal and found they were missing several spices? Instead of stopping at the A&P, they had come to her house. Once there, had they emptied her refrigerator and freezer because they decided to finish their shopping trip, much in the manner of someone who stops at the store for a quart of milk and decides, last minute, it might be a good idea to get the weekly shopping over with since the store is so empty? Since there was no bagging service, they must have stuffed everything into her pillowcase: the steak, defrosting for Phil's homecoming dinner, oozing dark blood through the light blue cotton; the open container of cottage cheese, dripping; eggs breaking, running. Why the tankards? Phil had gotten them at a gas station in Holland last fall; they were free with each fill-up. Who would want them? They looked cheap and were uncomfortably light.

She went into the bathroom and took her long robe from the hook on the inside of the door. In the top drawer of Phil's night table she found the flashlight on top of his beige angora socks he kept in there for when his feet got cold at night. It took only seconds to untie the rope that held the front door closed. She left it open and returned into the living room. From the stuffed chair she picked up her pillow and carried it under her left arm, holding the flashlight in her free hand.

Outside, the air was still warm, the humidity lingering from an unreasonably hot May afternoon. Away from her house and the clean scent of freshly cut grass she walked, toward the darkness of the pines that parted to make room for the path she had taken so many times to the lake. The earth felt cool against her bare soles as she stepped into the shadows of the trees. Not once did she stumble. Nearby some small animal scampered into the night.

She could smell the lake, a dank odor of frogskin and milkweed, before she saw its moon-glazed surface. Walking past four of the summer camps, close to each other on quarter acres, she found them looking even more abandoned at night than during the winter.

She turned off the flashlight and pushed it into the right pocket of her robe. Against her bare ankles the damp hem swung heavily. Next to the lake the ground was softer, molding her footsteps and forcing wet particles of soil up between her toes.

She looked at the pillow. Somewhere a bird cried; she didn't recognize its call. Kneeling by the water, she held the pillow in both hands and bent forward. Slowly she lowered it beneath the reflection of the moon until the cold water covered her elbows. Bubbles came up through her fingers. Under her calm hands it moved like a sack of kittens.

Questions

1. In addition to the theft, what conflict preoccupies Laura?
2. What if the thieves had stolen other items, such as the film projector and Phil's tennis racket? What difference would that have made in the story?
3. Each narrative break is indicated with white space. Exactly how many distinct points in time occur in the story?
4. What is the significance of Laura's final act in the story?
5. What might happen if this story continued? Would Laura put her life back together and live it as she had?

Exploring Psychological Conflict

This section explores psychological conflict. You are no stranger to conflict. In the poems you wrote in Chapters 1–7, and in the stories you have drafted in this section, you looked at people in interesting situations and gave them interesting problems to solve. Trouble makes fiction work. In response to trouble, characters speak and act. In response to trouble, they also think, remember, speculate, and analyze. These interior actions are in the realm of psychological conflict.

Hegi's story presents her character with a psychological conflict. There is an external cause and an interior effect. The external cause is a break-in; the internal effect is Laura's feeling of violation. Not only do the thieves make off with an odd assortment of kitchen objects, they leave behind "a peculiar combination of emptiness and invasion, a feeling of being smothered and abandoned that clung to Laura's pillow." A good portion of this story dramatizes Laura's reaction to this inner feeling of violation. How can she get rid of the phantom presence of thieves in the house? She imagines their hands still on her bed. She pictures them touching the kitchen items: "Broad hands with short fingers? Smooth hands with pale skin?" She leaves her bed and sits up at night, facing the door that is now tied shut. The conflict she is experiencing is an inner one, psychological in nature.

While all of this happens, moreover, a second conflict rises to the surface. Her husband has dismissed the incident. On the night of the robbery, he sleeps peacefully. Emotionally, it would seem that he has abandoned her. Thus, the robbery triggers a secondary internal effect. Laura becomes aware that her relationship with Phil is changing. When she recalls picking him up at the airport, she remembers that he looked strange, different, as if he had become someone else. The more she thinks about the relationship, the more these emotional concerns gather weight in the story. The psychological conflict leads to the culminating action at the end of the story. Laura submerges her pillow in the lake. When she does this, she is trying to rid herself of her emotional trauma. She tries to drown the thieves' hands that cover the pillow, as well as smother her doubts about her relationship with her husband.

The external conflict in this story is an unusual event that becomes the occasion for Laura's inner conflicts. Because of the break-in, she realizes something is happening in the settled, ordinary part of her life. This secondary effect becomes the larger subject of the story. Because the story is written in the third-person limited point of view, the reader shares the process of Laura becoming aware of this larger conflict. In places, the reader has direct access to Laura's thoughts (and only hers) as she processes these events.

Experimenting with Psychological Conflict

The third-person limited point of view forces you to be clear about whose story you are telling, whose psychological conflict you are exploring. *Limited* means you choose one character and stay with her. There is a good reason for this restriction. Point of view is an important organizing principle in fiction. Consistent point of view gives a story coherence. Conversely, stories with inconsistent points of view confuse the reader because of their lack of coherence. If you move from one character to another and tell what they all think and feel, it is more difficult for the reader to be sure whose story you are telling. Remember, you can't tell everyone's story. Instead, concentrate on one character and try to make his psychological conflict clear to the reader. Keep in mind that your character may react to what other characters do and say. In fact, their actions and words become external triggers of more internal action in your character.

Frequently, psychological drama begins with an impetus—an event of some kind that brings conflict to the surface. Although the impetus doesn't have to be gut-wrenching, it does have to be bothersome enough to make the character reflect on it and, in a sense, dwell on it. Your first task in this exercise will be to begin with an external conflict from which internal conflict will emerge.

In this exercise, you will focus on a character who has been through a traumatic event or, at the very least, an out-of-the-ordinary experience. For example, a young man drives a car recklessly and has an encounter with the law, an external conflict that causes him to confront a psychological conflict in his life.

Writer's Practice 11.1   *Disturb Your Character's Peace*

Begin with the scene in which the disturbance is occurring and very briefly suggest its aftermath in a second scene shortly after the event. As you write, concentrate on blending both exterior and interior details. In addition, adhere to the following guidelines:

- Begin with your character in a specific place, involved in a definitive action.
- Establish one dominant emotional response to the event—the primary internal reaction that your character has after the event occurs.
- Intertwine description of scene and action with internal commentary, thought, and feeling.
- Keep dialogue to a minimum.

Aim to write two hundred to three hundred words. Compose in either present or past tense, third-person limited.

Begin writing if you feel you are ready, or examine our writer's model and explication.

Differences in Tense

The primary difference between the language in present-tense and past-tense stories is in the verbs within them. Knowing how and when to use these different tenses will give you flexibility with your writing.

Stories written in the present tense have more immediacy because the action is happening now: *Aunt Margie **steals** chocolate chip cookies.* Stories written in the past tense have more distance, reflecting back on an action that happened previously: *Aunt Margie **stole** chocolate chip cookies.*

Flashbacks in present-tense stories are told in the past tense, indicating a jump back in time: *Aunt Margie **steals** chocolate chip cookies. She **stole** $20,000 prior to that.* Similarly, flashbacks in past-tense stories begin in the past-perfect tense: *Aunt Margie **stole** chocolate chip cookies. She **had stolen** $20,000 prior to that.*

Our Writer

He had no idea he would do it. He rounded the curve and the churchyard was there, perfect as a golf course fairway, beyond it the white steeple and empty dark windows. And he thought, *Why not?* He crossed the shoulder and felt the wheels sink into the sod, the old car heavy, churning up the damp ground. Fifty yards and he'd be out. Trouble was a pinpoint of light inside his head, a laser beam cutting through the darkness. He pressed the gas pedal to the floor. Clods of dirt thudded against the floorboards. The car shuddered and Byron's glasses slid off the dashboard onto the floor. When the car finally stopped, the first thing he did was find the glasses and put them on. He was wearing them when the old pastor lumbered across the yard, and when the police arrived.

That night, he could hear them in the next room talking it out, ma crying, his dad's nervous tapping on the table with his pipe, saying Cole'd have to work every Saturday until the Episcopal lawn was perfect again. Cole lay in the dark, on the bed Byron had slept in. Byron had carved a leafy tree on the headboard, his initials on the trunk. On the wall was the Harley poster. Byron rode one like that. He'd taken Cole night riding, slow and easy, just them and the road, a long shaft of light out front.

"Wild," Byron had said.

> The machine lived. Cole had leaned into Byron, smelled the leather on his back. "When you got it, sometimes you have to use it," Byron'd said. Then he gunned it.
>
> Ma had taken the poster down right after. When Cole moved into the room, he put it back up. It was permanent, like the letters carved on that board.

A boy drives his car off the road and tears up a church lawn. He does this without really thinking. On the spur of the moment, he simply acts. "Why not?" he thinks, and away he goes. There are consequences. The police come; his parents are called. He will have to make things right. His father will see to it. Here, then, is the immediate event, like the robbery in Hegi's story. Like the robbery, it has happened, it is over, and now the character's reflection on its meaning begins (or is soon to begin). Other characters are introduced here: the mother, the father, and Byron, whose glasses Cole wears. Byron, it seems, is an older sibling who has had an important effect on Cole and now is out of the picture. Where is he? "Ma had taken the poster down right after." This doesn't sound good. After what? Cole knows. Whatever happened to Byron is part of the problem. Possibly this is the secondary conflict that will come to the surface.

This passage, like Hegi's story, mixes exterior and interior detail. The reader has a view of the churchyard first, and then the bedroom, as seen by Cole. The reader feels the sensation of the car shuddering to a halt on the lawn, as felt by Cole. The concrete detail establishes what's happening and where. Everything is channeled through Cole's sensibility—"Dad's nervous tapping on the table with his pipe." The reader hears what Cole hears. In addition to this exterior concrete detail, the passage also takes the reader inside Cole's character: "Ma had taken the poster down right after." After what? After something happened to Byron. Notice the thought is not finished—"right after the unfortunate incident involving his brother occurred." The thought is not finished because it does not need to be finished. This is Cole thinking. In places, obvious markers of Cole's thought and feeling occur: "He had no idea" and "He thought."

Now Cole has to repair the damaged lawn. But there is deeper damage coming to the surface—damage done in the past—and Cole is going to revisit this past in his thoughts.

Exploring Flashback

Narrative frequently begins with a specific moment in time and simply moves forward. The primary actions in the story occur in chronological order, as you move forward in time. The stories you wrote in Chapters 8 and 10 were probably plotted in strict chronological order. Stories focused on characters' actions frequently are plotted in this manner.

Stories with psychological conflicts, however, often make use of the flash-back, a shift backward in time. The state of mind that a character is in, and her attempt to make sense of it, is explored best by having your character recall an event that came before. In addition to shifting to an earlier point in time, flashback may also involve moving characters and action to a different setting. Sometimes this shift is indicated with white space; other times the move is made more seamlessly, with a minimal verbal cue in a phrase or sentence to indicate the shift (see Writer's Practice 9.2). In a novel, a flashback may be a chapter-length move. In short fiction, the move back in time is frequently an abbreviated, sudden shift. As suggested earlier in this chapter, flashbacks usually are triggered by external causes: an event or a detail in setting, action, or dialogue. Your character thinks about this event or detail, which triggers a move back in time.

Consider Hegi's use of flashback. Less than half of "Thieves" takes place on the night of the robbery. In the story's present, the action can be summarized as follows: Laura and Phil go to bed. She cannot sleep, so she gets up and sits thinking in the living room. She then takes her pillow down to the lake. That is the extent of the action, until the psychological drama is built into the story. The other half of the story takes place in Laura's memory, while she is sitting in the living room. This psychological "action" occurs chiefly in the form of flashback. As Laura thinks, she flashes back to three earlier points in time in the story: picking Phil up at the airport, then their immediate reaction when they discover the break-in, then her conversation with the two police officers. Flashback enables Hegi to present earlier action, as Laura "replays" these events in her memory and considers their meaning. In the passage below, Hegi flashes backward in time and begins moving forward.

> Quietly she got up. In the dark she carried her pillow into the living room. Against her bare feet the carpet felt matted, unclean. Tomorrow she would rent a Blue Lustre shampooer at the Taylor Rental Center. She sat down in the stuffed chair facing the front door. Phil had secured it with a piece of yellow rope to keep it closed until the locksmith could come. Returning from the airport where Laura had picked him up from his trip to Seattle, he had first seemed angry when they found their front door forced open, but soon he had settled into amused gratefulness.
>
> "It could have been worse," he said.
>
> She hadn't answered.
>
> "You're lucky this didn't happen while I was away," he had said.
>
> His relief that they hadn't taken his tennis racket had been painfully obvious to her. Cautiously, with her fingertips, she had touched the things they hadn't taken: her books, her sunglasses, her violin.

We begin at the most recent point in narrative time. Laura gets out of bed. As soon as she sits down, she begins planning what to do, reacting to external detail such as the "matted, unclean" feel of the carpet. "Tomorrow she would rent a Blue Lustre shampooer." Next, looking at the door causes her to flash back to the afternoon. She replays their discovery of the break-in and what happened afterward, with Phil's tying the door shut. Then Laura moves forward in time, when they are inside the house, discovering what has been stolen and verbalizing their reactions. Observe an important technical point here: the flashback is indicated with a shift in tense, from simple past, "She *sat* down," to past perfect, "Phil *had secured* it" and "He *had seemed* angry at first." The earlier scenes are marked with the more complex verb tense.

Also noticeable here is what Hegi does not do. The entire flashback takes place in Laura's memory, but Hegi does not use expressions like "Laura remembered" or "Laura thought." When the narrator observes, "Tomorrow she would rent a Blue Lustre Shampooer," the narrator is giving a direct report of what Laura is thinking. The reader is inside Laura's mind, close to her language of thought. For this reason, such tags as "she remembered" are unnecessary.

Experimenting with Flashback

Frequently, when we replay events in memory, their real or imagined meaning presents itself to us. We think back, recalling conversations in our mind. What happened, what was said or not said, and the smallest gesture that we may have initially overlooked are now important. The event can be examined over and over, and, in the process, the smallest things take on great significance. There may be a breakthrough—*So that's what he meant!* Alternatively, there may be more confusion and the accompanying need for further reflection and additional flashback. As you write and invent a story, using flashback is part of the discovery process. You begin with a character in conflict, and then you examine what happened to him in the immediate past. You explore his interactions with other characters. You work toward understanding with this character. He remembers, reflects, and analyzes prior events, trying to make sense of his present situation.

Writer's Practice 11.2   *Replay a Scene*

In Writer's Practice 11.1, you began a story with a character whose peace has been disturbed by an external conflict of some sort. Sometime after the initial conflict, the character is thinking over what that event means and what she will have to do next. This external conflict causes the character to become aware of an internal conflict. This internal conflict may be connected to a second character. Your main character has a lot to think about: the immediate event, the history she shares with this second character, and how her internal conflict can be resolved or eased.

Reread "Thieves," noticing how Hegi handles flashback and uses it to weave together external action and internal conflict. Then reread the first passage that you wrote. You probably have two distinct points in time: the event and its aftermath. In our writer's story, a boy drives his car across the church lawn; later that night, he lies in bed listening to his parents talk about him. Write at least three more passages of your story. Have your main character recall at least two points in time prior to the story's present. As you write, make a conscious effort to do the following:

- Be clear about where your main character is and what external detail causes her flashbacks; Hegi's character, for example, is sitting in her living room.
- Concentrate one flashback on events immediately following your character's disturbing experience.
- Write at least two flashbacks examining events involving the second character associated with your main character's internal conflict.
- Use a shift in verb tense to indicate the beginning of the flashback.
- Intermingle action and your narrator's thought and commentary on this action.
- Keep dialogue to a minimum.

These additional scenes portray your character's struggle to understand, to take action, or to resolve her psychological conflict. Aim to write up to two hundred words in each scene.

Begin writing if you feel you are ready, or examine our writer's model and explication.

Our Writer

Doors clicked opened and shut. The toilet flushed. He imagined his parents standing outside his door, silent, afraid to knock. Ma's eyes teary and frightened because, for all she knew, it was happening all over; his father's mouth pinched shut tight. Finally the ribbon of light under the bedroom door disappeared. Cole watched the red digits on his clock, waited a full hour, until he was sure. Then he sat up in bed. He pulled on shirt and pants, slipped into his shoes. There was still mud on them from his walk across the yard to the patrol car. He'd held out his hands for cuffs, and the officer had smirked at him, muttering something about no serious threat to life and limb. The day they took Byron, a cop had cuffed him, shoved the top of his head as he bent to climb inside the patrol car, knocking his glasses off. Aviator glasses with mirror lenses. Byron had bought them the same day he drove the Harley home. He pulled in the driveway and the sun splashed off the glasses in blinding spokes of light. Cole saw himself in them. He saw *himself*.

"Keep them for me," Byron had said, when Cole rushed to pick up the glasses. Cole had carefully dusted them off. He held them tight, trying not to let his hands shake.

"Say good-bye, sonny," the cop had said.

Through the window, Cole saw Byron look down at the floor and shake his head. The car sped off. Cole breathed in suddenly, and realized he was crying.

The pastor, an old man with white hair and cloudy eyes, had leaned on the car and said he was just glad no one was hurt. It was only grass. People forgot that. Last week there had been a funeral out of the church. Two young people out for one of their joyrides. A blink of the eye, a misplaced tree, and they were gone. He had officiated plenty of double weddings before, a few double baptisms. A young funeral pierced the heart. A double young one crushed it. Yeah, Cole had said, but I almost made it. The pastor had nudged a clod of dirt with the toe of his long black shoe. Then he looked up, smiled, and asked Cole if he wasn't Byron Burdett's kid brother.

The keys would be in the drawer by the phone. Cole stood in the living room for a moment, the darkness gathered around him. At the end of the hallway, his mother exhaled a long sigh. He opened the drawer, careful to make no noise. His fingers knew where to look, in back, behind the address book, in the corner. There they were, still attached to the penknife. He backed away from the drawer, went to the back door, and let himself out of the house.

You're being just like Byron. In the six years Byron was gone, Cole had heard it every day, with every step. Every misstep. *Don't.* When he looked in the mirror, he wasn't sure who he saw. *Byron.* It was there in the mirror, looking at him, Byron's face in his. And sometimes, stretching and pulling inside him, rising from a dark place he vaguely knew, he felt something. It was like Byron trying to escape.

Lying in his bed the night of the incident, Cole flashes back to a number of prior events. The detail that triggers the first flashback is mud on his shoes, which causes him to replay the events immediately after his car got stuck on the church lawn. How many other points in time do these passages add to the story? Using the shift to the past perfect verb tense, our writer signals each flashback:

1. He'd held out his hands for cuffs. (a scene immediately following the initial incident)
2. The day they took Byron, a cop had cuffed him. (a scene six years before the incident)
3. Byron had bought them (sunglasses) the same day he drove the Harley home. (a scene sometime before Byron's arrest)

4. The pastor, an old man with white hair and cloudy eyes, had leaned on the car. (a scene shortly before Cole drives across the church lawn)

5. Cole had heard it every day. (a reference to the general past, sometime after Byron's departure)

The flashbacks in these passages mainly explore Cole's relationship with his brother, Byron. In this added writing, we learn that Byron has been an important figure in Cole's life and that Byron has been in a lot of trouble. We also learn of Cole's identity crisis. Notice that along with these flashbacks, there are also references to action in the story's present. Cole thinks back to these times while lying in his room. The writer reminds us of this when Cole gets up from bed in the night, dresses, and goes to a drawer for keys. He is preparing to do something.

Much of this passage is written as Cole might think it. He has decided to do something. He needs keys. "The keys would be in the drawer by the phone." This is how the thought might occur to him. So he looks for the keys. "There they were, still attached to the penknife." Again, just what he might think when he puts his hands on them. But whose penknife? What keys? The narrator doesn't explain. The naturalness of the language, which is a report of Cole's thought, gives the reader the illusion of thinking Cole's thoughts. By suppressing explanations and connections between thoughts, the narrator withholds information, which creates suspense (see Writer's Practice 10.2). Cole knows what he is going to do, but the reader doesn't. The reader has to continue reading.

Writer's Practice 11.3 *Assemble the First Draft*

At this point, you should have a number of passages that fit together to tell most of a short story. While writing these passages, you began with an event the disturbs your main character's peace. You used the third-person limited point of view to show a character's psychological conflict arising in response to this event. Then you moved that character back in time, showing the basis of the conflict with flashback. Possibly this conflict is connected to another character, and your character's flashbacks have involved scenes with this second character.

Now put these pieces together so they form a good portion of a story. Use white space between passages to show transitions. Perhaps you have an ending in mind for your story already. On the other hand, possibly you are waiting for the resolution to suggest itself in your reading and rereading of your material. You may also find this resolution and some useful suggestions for how to end your story by discussing your passages with other writers in your response group. Assemble what you have produced up to now, as our writer has below.

Our Writer

He had no idea he would do it. He rounded the curve and the churchyard was there, perfect as a golf course fairway, beyond it the white steeple and empty dark windows. And he thought, Why not? He crossed the shoulder and felt the wheels sink into the sod, the old car heavy, churning up the damp ground. Fifty yards and he'd be out. Trouble was a pinpoint of light inside his head, a laser beam cutting through the darkness. He pressed the gas pedal to the floor. Clods of dirt thudded against the floorboards. The car shuddered and Byron's glasses slid off the dashboard onto the floor. When the car finally stopped, the first thing he did was find the glasses and put them on. He was wearing them when the old pastor lumbered across the yard, and when the police arrived.

That night, he could hear them in the next room talking it out, ma crying, his dad's nervous tapping on the table with his pipe, saying Cole'd have to work every Saturday until the Episcopal lawn was perfect again. Cole lay in the dark, on the bed Byron had slept in. Byron had carved a leafy tree on the headboard, his initials on the trunk. On the wall was the Harley poster. Byron rode one like that. He'd taken Cole night riding, slow and easy, just them and the road, a long shaft of light out front.

"Wild," Byron had said.

The machine lived. Cole had leaned into Byron, smelled the leather on his back.

"When you got it, sometimes you have to use it," Byron'd said. Then he gunned it.

Ma had taken the poster down right after. When Cole moved into the room, he put it back up. It was permanent, like the letters carved on that board.

Doors clicked opened and shut. The toilet flushed. He imagined his parents standing outside his door, silent, afraid to knock. Ma's eyes teary and frightened because, for all she knew, it was happening all over; his father's mouth pinched shut tight. Finally the ribbon of light under the bedroom door disappeared. Cole watched the red digits on his clock, waited a full hour, until he was sure. Then he sat up in bed. He pulled on shirt and pants, slipped into his shoes. There was still mud on them from his walk across the yard to the patrol car. He'd held out his hands for cuffs, and the officer had smirked at him, muttering something about no serious threat to life and limb. The day they took Byron, a cop had cuffed him, shoved the top of his head as he bent to climb inside the patrol car, knocking his glasses off. Aviator glasses with mirror lenses. Byron had bought them the same day he drove the Harley home. He pulled in the driveway and the sun splashed off the glasses in blinding spokes of light. Cole saw himself in them. He saw himself.

"Keep them for me," Byron had said, when Cole rushed to pick up the glasses.

Cole had carefully dusted them off. He held them tight, trying not to let his hands shake.

"Say good-bye, sonny," the cop had said.

Through the window, Cole saw Byron look down at the floor and shake his head. The car sped off. Cole breathed in suddenly, and realized he was crying.

The pastor, an old man with white hair and cloudy eyes, had leaned on the car and said he was just glad no one was hurt. It was only grass. People forgot that. Last week there had been a funeral out of the church. Two young people out for one of their joyrides. A blink of the eye, a misplaced tree, and they were gone. He had officiated plenty of double weddings before, a few double baptisms. A young funeral pierced the heart. A double young one crushed it. Yeah, Cole had said, but I almost made it. The pastor had nudged a clod of dirt with the toe of his long black shoe. Then he looked up, smiled, and asked Cole if he wasn't Byron Burdett's kid brother.

The keys would be in the drawer by the phone. Cole stood in the living room for a moment, the darkness gathered around him. At the end of the hallway, his mother exhaled a long sigh. He opened the drawer, careful to make no noise. His fingers knew where to look, in back, behind the address book, in the corner. There they were, still attached to the penknife. He backed away from the drawer, went to the back door, and let himself out of the house.

You're being just like Byron. In the six years Byron was gone, Cole had heard it every day, with every step. Every misstep. *Don't.* When he looked in the mirror, he wasn't sure who he saw. *Byron.* It was there in the mirror, looking at him, Byron's face in his. And sometimes, stretching and pulling inside him, rising from a dark place he vaguely knew, he felt something. It was like Byron trying to escape.

 Writer Response Groups

Form a response group with three or four other writers and examine your stories for the following elements:

Essential Elements

- Whose story is it?
- What is the conflict?
- How is the action plotted?

Craft

- How many points in time are established in the story? Where do the shifts occur?
- Does the narrative language sound like the language of thought?
- Is point of view limited to one character? Does your narrator ever slip into the mind of another character or report what another character feels, thinks, knows, and sees?

Revising for Imagery

Often, an image in a story will become invested with meaning. This meaning exceeds the image's actual meaning, just as words in poems can take on significance that goes beyond their usual denotative and connotative meaning (see Writer's Practice 7.3). A rose is not just a rose. A bridge is not just a bridge. The image takes on greater meaning because of repeated references to it in the story. In addition to its actual meaning, the image suggests meaning related to character, plot, and theme.

In the story you are building, your main character has become aware of an inner conflict. In the process of becoming aware, she has flashed back to a number of events and experiences, replaying them in her mind. In this flashback process, you have the opportunity to select an image and insert it into your character's thoughts repeatedly. In Hegi's story, for example, references to the pillow and hand imagery recur. A pillow is an object ordinarily associated with rest, comfort, and security. In the story's dramatic situation, however, through repeated references Laura's pillow loses all those associations. It comes to stand for invasion and violation. This meaning is accentuated by hand imagery. Laura imagines thieves' hands in her home, touching her possessions, including her pillow. Increasingly, she associates these hands with her husband's hands. His hands and the thieves' are joined in her mind and in her imagination.

In practical terms, Laura's submerging her pillow in the lake may not mean very much. In symbolic terms, however, it is a startling and satisfying expression of emotional truth. The pillow that she takes down to the lake and holds under the water is a receptacle. It contains her fear aroused by the break-in. It contains her feelings of invasion and abandonment. It also contains her disturbing realization that her husband is not the person she thought he was and that, in all likelihood, she no longer loves him.

Writer's Practice 11.4   *Invest an Image*

Revise your story from the beginning with imagery in mind. When you began this section of the chapter, you may have associated an object or image with your main character. Perhaps that object or image can be invested with meaning. Look for opportunities to insert this object into the narrative. As you revise, try do the following:

- Mention this object at least three or four times.

- Look for related images; for example, our writer's main character is obsessed with his brother's sunglasses—throughout the story, there are many related references to sight imagery, mirror images, and night and day images relating to sight.

- Maintain the narrative point of view, especially the intertwining of thought and commentary on external detail.

- Work to a conclusion that involves a definitive action in which this image or object is involved.

Symbols and Meaning

Such fictional details as objects, actions, people, animals, or even settings often have more than one meaning in a story—the literal meaning found on the surface and the figurative meaning found beneath it. Details such as these are called *symbols*.

Metaphors and similes give meaning *to* their contexts: *the sun* (context) *is a red ball* (metaphor) or *the sun* (context) *is like a red ball* (simile). In contrast, symbols get meaning *from* their contexts. A black cat in a story often represents bad luck, for example.

Symbols infuse meaning into a story. Thus, be careful about the symbols you use in your writing. Select those that define the characters or advance the plot and thus have a reason for being.

An old axiom in creative writing is Show, don't tell. You might be tempted to explain the meaning of images to your reader, but be careful. In explaining, you may lose the tone and style of third-person limited, the language of thought. As your main character thinks, he will not explain images to himself. That is, your narrator will not say, "He wanted to put on the glasses, *which would finally transform him into a new person*." Your narrator will simply say, "He needed the glasses." Keep in mind that, in creative writing, understatement gives better results.

Begin writing if you feel you are ready, or examine our writer's model and explication.

Our Writer

Heading Home

He had no idea he would do it. He rounded the curve and the churchyard was there, perfect as a golf course fairway, beyond it the white steeple and empty dark windows. And he thought, *Why not?* He crossed the shoulder and felt the wheels sink into the sod, the old car heavy, churning up the damp ground. Fifty yards and he'd be out. Trouble was a pinpoint of light inside his head, a laser beam cutting through the darkness. He pressed the gas pedal to the floor. Clods of dirt thudded against the floorboards. The car shuddered and Byron's glasses slid off the dashboard onto the floor. When the car finally stopped, the first thing he did was find the glasses and put them on. He was wearing them when the old pastor lumbered across the yard, and when the police arrived.

That night, he could hear them in the next room talking it out, ma crying, his dad's nervous tapping on the table with his pipe, saying Cole'd have to work every Saturday until the Episcopal lawn was perfect again. Cole lay in the dark, on the bed Byron had slept in. Byron had carved a leafy tree on the headboard, his initials on the trunk. On the wall was the Harley poster. Byron rode one like that. He'd taken Cole night riding, slow and easy, just them and the road, a long shaft of light out front.

"It's a wild animal," Byron had said.

The machine lived. Cole had leaned into Byron, smelled the leather on his back.

"When you got it in you, sometimes you have to let it out," Byron had said. Then he gunned it.

Ma had taken the poster down right after. When Cole moved into the room, he put it back up. It was permanent, like the letters carved on that board.

Doors clicked opened and shut. The toilet flushed. He imagined his parents standing outside his door, silent, afraid to knock. Ma's eyes teary and frightened because, for all she knew, it was happening all over; his father's mouth pinched shut tight. Finally the ribbon of light under the bedroom door disappeared. Cole watched the red digits on his clock, waited a full hour, until he was sure. Then he sat up in bed. He pulled on shirt and pants, slipped into his shoes. There was still mud on them from his walk across the yard to the patrol car. He'd held out his hands for cuffs, and the officer had smirked at him, muttering something about no serious threat to life and limb. The day they took Byron, a cop had cuffed him, shoved the top of his head as he bent to climb inside the patrol car, knocking his glasses off. Aviator glasses with mirror lenses. Byron had bought them the same day he drove the Harley home. He pulled in the driveway and the sun splashed off the glasses in blinding spokes of light. Cole saw himself in them. He saw *himself*.

"Keep them for me," Byron had said, when Cole rushed to pick up the glasses.

Cole had carefully dusted them off. He held them tight, trying not to let his hands shake.

"Say good-bye, sonny," the cop had said.

Through the window, Cole saw Byron look down at the floor and shake his head. The car sped off. Cole breathed in suddenly, and realized he was crying.

The pastor, an old man with white hair and cloudy eyes, had leaned on the car and said he was just glad no one was hurt. It was only grass. People forgot that. Last week there had been a funeral out of the church. Two young people out for one of their joyrides. A blink of the eye, a misplaced tree, and they were gone. He had officiated plenty of double weddings before, a few double baptisms. A young funeral pierced the heart. A double young one crushed it. Yeah, Cole had said, but I almost made it. The pastor had nudged a clod of dirt with the toe of his long black shoe. Then he looked up, smiled, and asked Cole if he wasn't Byron Burdett's kid brother.

The keys would be in the drawer by the phone. Cole stood in the living room for a moment, the darkness gathered around him. At the end of the hallway, his mother exhaled a long sigh. He opened the drawer, careful to make no noise. His fingers knew where to look, in back, behind the address book, in the corner. There they were, still attached to the penknife. He backed away from the drawer, went to the back door, and let himself out of the house.

You're being just like Byron. In the six years Byron was gone, Cole had heard it every day, with every step. Every misstep. *Don't*. When he looked in the mirror, he wasn't sure who he saw. *Byron*. It was there in the mirror, looking at him, Byron's face in his. And sometimes, stretching and pulling inside him, rising from a dark place he vaguely knew, he felt something. It was like Byron trying to escape.

Cole shivered on the back porch, opening and closing the penknife. He'd have to work tomorrow. The ruts were deep. All by himself, it would take forever. He jumped off the porch and ran to the garage. Inside, he pulled the tarp off Byron's bike. Oil and gas smell rose from the Harley. He inhaled deeply, felt himself shudder, then inhaled again. I'm letting you out, he said to himself. On the night rides, trees along the road pressed their black shapes in on them. They roared through the dark. It was all speed and sound and darkness, like shooting through a tunnel. Once in a while, rounding a curve, they would surprise an animal on the road. A raccoon, a possum. It would look up, its startled yellow eyes shining in the Harley's light. Cole reached down and fitted a key into the ignition, flicked the light switch with his thumb. He flicked it on and off. Nothing.

The bike was so heavy, it was hard to believe it had once flown down the road with Byron and him on its back. In the back of the garage, pointed at the west wall, he leaned over the handle bars, growling, pretending to ride. He reached in his pocket, took out the glasses, and put them on. It was as if he had closed his eyes. Once more, he leaned forward, gunning the engine in his mind, and hurled forward through silence and darkness.

From the beginning of this story, Cole is moving toward a defining moment. Who is he? When he gets into trouble, his parents see the older sibling. They are afraid Cole is going to be just like Byron. When Cole looks in the mirror, he sees both himself and Byron. He wears the sunglasses, just as Byron did. There are times when Cole thinks he even feels Byron inside him. How will he "get rid of" Byron? Does he want to get rid of the Byron in him? As the story moves toward its conclusion, it is about the kind of person Cole may now will himself to be.

The problem of will—of choosing the kind of person he wants to be—is stated in the very first sentence. "He had no idea he would do it." He acts without thinking, seemingly without even choosing. In a flashback, Cole remembers what Byron had said of the motorcycle:

> "Wild," Byron had said.
> The machine lived. Cole had leaned into Byron, smelled the leather on his back.
> "When you got it, sometimes you have to use it," Byron'd said. Then he gunned it.

In a revision, our writer changes this to:

> "It's a wild animal," Byron had said.
> The machine lived. Cole had leaned into Byron, smelled the leather on his back.
> "When you got it in you, sometimes you have to let it out," Byron had said. Then he gunned it.

The language in the passage above echoes Cole's feeling later in the story: "And sometimes, stretching and pulling inside him, rising from a dark place he vaguely knew, he felt something. It was like Byron trying to escape."

Taken together, these images of something strong and violent inside Cole prepare the writer for the final scene, where Cole lets the animal out—or is it Byron he finally ejects from within? Cole puts on the glasses, a symbol for the Byron inside him. Entirely in the dark, he hurls himself toward the future, toward silence and darkness. It sounds frightening. Yet, elsewhere in the draft, multiple images of light are symbolic of trouble, such as "spokes of light" reflected in Byron's glasses and "Trouble was a pinpoint of light inside his head, a laser beam cutting through the darkness." That light is now completely gone. Cole is in the dark, "heading home," the title tells us. As in the Hegi story, it is not clear exactly what practical results the end of the story has. Cole's act of climbing on the motorcycle and steering it himself, however, has an emotional truth that the images and symbols carry.

Examining Student Stories

The third-person limited point of view allows a writer to follow a character's inner thoughts and speak in a character's inner voice. Because of this, writers working in third-person limited can examine characters' inner psychological conflicts. Writers may draw on such elements as flashback and symbol to do this, connecting and associating events, feelings, and objects. The story that follows illustrates how psychological conflict, flashback, and symbol can be combined in stories told in the third-person limited point of view.

Paralyzed

Dana Baker

Bailey hears the clip of the mare's hooves; sees Shorty's head and neck disappear; feels the reins rip through her fingers and the cow path roll up to meet her. She lies there. She bends her right arm, leans on her elbow, and watches Shorty rise. Front legs splayed, neck bowed, the mare tilts her head from side to side. She looks embarrassed, as if she knows falling on her head is a stupid thing for a horse to do.

The mare begins to graze. Bailey sits up, wondering if she's broken anything. Then she stands. She balances on her right foot, left ankle, knee, and elbow shrieking. Pain. Pain is good. She thinks about trying to get back on but hops Shorty to the barn instead.

Listening to "Ghost" on her Indigo Girls CD that night, ace-bandaged leg propped on a pillow, Bailey feels the cow path roll back up to meet her. She overhears her mom on the phone in the kitchen, voice low: No concussion; nothing broken; ligaments. Lig-a-ments. Her mom's voice rises. "No, I don't know if she got back on." It's her dad's guiding principle: If you fall, get right back up. She can't hear her mom. Then, "I don't care if she ever gets back on! I hope she doesn't!"

Ten P.M.—seven West Coast time. Last fall, when Bailey visited her dad in Ventura, she could tell he loved California. Paragliding and surfing were a rush, he said, and the dry heat was good for his old back. Her dad loves rushes. Bailey knows why: It's galloping Shorty down a tree-lined trail, hair combed by the wind, eyes streaming. Lost. Found. Lost and found. Bailey rubs her neck. Whiplash? She fingers the silver horseshoe pendant dangling from her neck.

In the emergency waiting room, her mom kept asking what caused the mare to fall. Was the path slippery from the spring rain? Did she trip on something? Did she need new shoes? A sick feeling coated Bailey's stomach. The more her mom questioned her, the stronger it became. She tried to remember. They were cantering. On their right, a black cat crouched in a windrow of the cornfield, tail low. When it pounced, the corn husks crackled. Shorty tensed, but she didn't spook: Her hooves clipped. We almost somersaulted, Bailey said, starting to cry. She could have rolled on me. When her mom, pale as bone, patted her hand, she snatched it away.

The sack-eyed resident who finally checked her out insisted that torn ligaments could be as bad as breaks. "How can that be?" Bailey's mom asked. Instead of answering, he told them to keep her leg up and wrapped, marveled at the healing properties of the young, and promised she'd be back in the saddle soon. Bailey didn't think so. "We get more people in here from horseback riding accidents than auto accidents," he said, helping her into a wheelchair. Near the front desk, they passed a dark-haired guy in a wheelchair. Only his eyes moved. Bailey looked away, right hand reaching for her silver horseshoe.

Bailey hobbles to the kitchen. "Mom?" She finds a notepad instead: Her mom's gone to the drugstore to get her pain med. Waste of time. When Shorty pulled up lame last winter, Bailey used her allowance to buy Absorbine to rub her down with. It smelled up her jeans and the laundry room, but Shorty got better. Bailey rubs her neck and sits at the kitchen table.

She decides to write her dad and ask how his paragliding business is going. He moved to California the summer before, saying it was a good place to start over. Paradise. Her mom thought he was crazy. She just couldn't understand why people would pay to jump off cliffs in flimsy paragliders. Until this afternoon, Bailey wanted to try it. A bona fide rush, her dad called it. The best ever.

She picks up the pen and pad her mom left. "There was this black cat," she begins. She knows what her dad will say: Stop blaming the cat. They used to have one, Calico Cally. Whenever a piece of glassware or a knickknack broke, it was Cally's fault. Whenever they ran out of milk, tuna fish, or goldfish crackers, it was her fault, too. And when Freddy Finch had a stroke, Cally was definitely to blame.

Bailey crumples the paper in a ball. She tries again. "I couldn't stop it," she writes. "I've never been so scared." This isn't true: She was more scared when her mom and dad split and kept saying "custody battle" when they thought she wasn't listening. "It wasn't Shorty's fault," she continues, chewing the end of the pen. "And it wasn't mine, either. It was a fluke."

Her mom enters through the side door. "You're still up?"

"It's not me, it's my ghost."

"Not funny," her mom says, handing her a small paper bag. "Go to bed."

Bailey nods, shooing her mom away.

She reads what she's written. "Just ligament damage," she adds. "Lucky me."

Lucky him. What would it take for her dad to give up paragliding? Once, when a strap broke as he soared kitelike groundward, he broke three ribs. The worse thing about it, he said, was not being able to deep-breathe. The worse thing about it, Bailey thinks, is not being able to breathe at all.

But she can't stop the mantra. Deep-breathing will get you through. Deep-breathing and visualization. Deep-breathing. Visualization. Bailey closes her eyes and breathes deep, imagining she's paragliding atop Shorty, sailing over the cow path, cornfields, and a big black cat. They glide clear across the United States, landing near Ventura. Glad you came to visit, her dad says. But where'd you get that cat?

She holds her breath. When you were little, her father chides, you'd do that until you turned blue. You looked putrid in blue. And you'd pass out, too. Deep breathing! Visualization!

Bailey takes a deeper breath. She's jumping Shorty at the hunt club, the mare's newly shod hooves barely touching down between the white fences. Rounding the back corner of the arena, she sees it: A black cat sitting on the top pole of the final fence. She drives Shorty at it. As the mare's head and neck begin to rise, Bailey winks. Out of the corner of her eye, the black cat hisses, then darts away.

The extraordinary event the writer chose for this story—the fall of a rider, Bailey, and her horse, Shorty—sets up a psychological conflict for the main character that revolves around fear. Will Bailey ride Shorty again after taking what could have been a life-threatening, or at least paralyzing, fall? This is the initial fear that plagues Bailey. The writer then creates a related inner conflict for the character: Bailey fears for the life of her father, who loves paragliding the way she loves horseback riding. These fears connect throughout the story.

Flashbacks of the hospital where she was examined and treated after the accident and of the cat her family used to have echo the symbols in the story: a recurring black cat that brings bad luck and a silver horseshoe pendant that Bailey wears for good luck. The writer returns to these symbols in the story's final scene, where Bailey imagines her sport and her father's sport combining in such a way that the black cat is banished as her mare's newly shod hooves clear the fences.

chapter 12

Revisiting Your Craft, Repeating Your Story: Conflict, Repetition, and Theme

I was determined to write short stories about people who,
in no way, could seem to be me, and also, perhaps,
to broaden my stories in both the amount of time
they take and the amount of space they take.

-JOHN UPDIKE

This chapter gives you the opportunity to revisit and use the basic storytelling devices that you were introduced to in previous chapters. So far, your experience with narrative structure has consisted of introducing conflict to disturb your character's peace and then working toward resolving your character's conflict. In this chapter, you will learn a somewhat more complex method of structuring your narrative—the frame-tale.

A frame-tale is a popular story-telling device. It is a story within a story. The frame-tale structure dates back to much earlier times. In the fourteenth century, for example, Chaucer wrote *The Canterbury Tales*, a long narrative poem about a group of travelers making a pilgrimage to Canterbury. There are a number of stories within the story of this pilgrimage, as the pilgrims pass the time by telling stories to amuse each other. Mary Shelley's *Frankenstein* also is a frame-tale. In that book, Robert Walton writes letters to his sister, telling her the story of Victor Frankenstein and his monster. A more recent and excellent example of a frame-tale is *The Princess Bride*. In this tale, Billy is sick with pneumonia. His grandfather settles down on the foot of Billy's bed and announces he's going to read a story. From time to time, Billy interrupts the tale, which alerts the reader to the fact that there are two stories in progress: a grandfather is trying to connect with his grandson (the frame), and a princess is trying to reunite with her first true love (the tale).

A Never-Ending Tale

The Arabian Nights, a collection of tales in Arabic, began as early as the tenth century with stories transmitted orally by storytellers. Today, the collection consists of 264 tales. The framework relates how the Sultan Shahriar, convinced that women were unfaithful, married a new wife each evening and had her put to death the following morning. A new bride, Scheherazade, won a temporary suspension by starting a story on her wedding night and artfully maintaining his curiosity about its outcome.

The sultan finally gave up his original plan after "The Thousand and One Nights" (part of the collection). Numerous characters from the tales have become familiar to people all over the world, including Ali Baba, Aladdin and his Magic Lamp, and Sinbad the Sailor.

One of the most inventive recent frame-tales is Stephen Dixon's "A Sloppy Story," involving a writer trying to sell a "story project." It is a complex frame-tale, involving multiple tellings of a tale. As you read, watch for the differences between the story and the story within the story, the frame and the tale.

A Sloppy Story

STEPHEN DIXON

"Listen to this," I say. "This guy comes in and says to me and I say to him and he says and I say and the next thing I know he does this to me and I do that to him and he this and I that and a woman comes in and sees us and says and I say to her and he says to me and she to him and he says and does this to her and I say and do that to him and she doesn't say anything but does this and that to us both and then a second time and he says and she says and I say and we all do and say and that's it, the end, what happened, now what do you think?"

"It won't work," a man says. His partner says "It will work, I know it will," and I say "Please, gentlemen, make up your minds. Do you think it will work or not?" The first man says no and his partner yes and I clasp my hands in front of my chest hoping they'll agree it will work and give me money for it so I won't have to be broke anymore or at least not for the next year, when the phone rings and the first man picks up the receiver and says "Yuh?" The person on the other end says something and the man says "You're kidding me now, aren't you?" His partner says "Who is it, something important?" and the man says and his partner says "Just tell him to go fly away with his project, now and forever," and I just sit there and the man hangs up the phone and says to us "Now where were we?"

"I was," I say. "He was," his partner says. "Okay," he says, "let's continue where we left off from, though quickly, as I got a long day," and we talk and he says "I still don't go for it," and his partner says "I'm starting to agree with you, now and forever," and I say "Please, gentlemen, let me tell the story over. Maybe it will be more convincing the second time around and I promise to be quicker about it," and I start the story from the beginning: guy coming in, says to me, me to him, does this, I do, woman, what we all said and did and then the partner, not agreeing, phone ringing, call ending, my retelling the story. After I finish I say "So what do you think? Will it work?"

"No," they both say and I say "Well, no harm in my having tried, I guess," and the first man says "No harm is right except for our precious lost time," and sticks out his hand and I shake it and shake his partner's hand and say "Can I use your men's room before I go? It might be my last chance for a while." His partner says "Second door to the right on your way out to the elevator," and I say "Which way is the elevator again, left or right when I get out of your office?" and he says and I say "Thanks," and they say and I leave, wave good-bye to the receptionist, go to the men's room on their floor, take the elevator down, go through the building's lobby to the street. It's a nice day, finally. It was raining heavily when I came in. My umbrella! Damn, left it upstairs, should I go back for it? No. Yes. What the hell, why not, it's not an old umbrella, it's still a good serviceable umbrella. And if I don't get it I'll have to buy a new umbrella at probably twice what the one upstairs cost me three years ago the way inflation's going crazy today.

I go back through the lobby, elevator, get on it, upstairs, their floor, past the men's room, into their office and the receptionist says and I say "I know, but I," and point to it and the partners come out of the room we were talking in before just as I grab my umbrella and look at me but don't say anything when I say hello but just walk into another room and I say good-bye to the receptionist and she nods at me and starts typing rapidly and I leave the office, elevator, lobby and see it's raining heavily again. Rain coming down like, streets filled with water like, people running out of the rain like, sky like, traffic like, I open the umbrella and walk in the rain totally protected because of my umbrella, long raincoat and boots and think "Well, I at least did one thing right today and that's going back for the umbrella, and maybe one other thing and that's wearing the right rain clothes," when someone ducks under my umbrella, a woman, hair soaked by the rain, and says "Mind if I walk with you as far as the bank on the corner? It closes in a few minutes and I have to put in some money by today."

"Sure," I say and we walk, I hold the umbrella, she her coat together at the collar, and talk, she "Can we walk faster?" I say sure, she asks where am I going, I say to an office building a block past her bank, she asks, I tell her, she says "Well what do you know," because it seems she's a good friend of the very man I want to see most about the same story project I spoke to those partners about, but whom I haven't been able to get an appointment with for more than a month. So I suggest, she says "Yes, but let me get done with my bank first," goes in, comes out, we have coffee at a coffee shop across the street, she asks, I tell, starting with the guy who comes in and says and I say and we do and the woman and all we said and did and then the partners, men's room, lobby, sunshine, umbrella, should I? shouldn't I? upstairs, receptionist and partners again, I retrieve, I leave, typing rapidly, raining heavily, everything looking like something else, open the umbrella, woman ducks under, though at first I didn't think it was a woman, I thought it was a mugger, walk, talk, faster, she asks, I say, well what do you know, she knows so and so, I suggest, she says yes, bank, coffee shop and coffees. "So what do you think?" I say. "Your friend will like it or am I fooling myself?"

"If he doesn't like it he ought to change professions," she says and borrows a coin from me, makes a phone call, comes back, "He says to hustle right over," we do, elevator, office, receptionist, secretary, big how do you do from her friend who I tell the whole story to from the beginning, he says "Better than I expected even from what Pam told me it would be over the phone. I'll take it," and we shake hands, sign a contract, he writes out a check, we drink champagne to our future success, Pam and I leave, downstairs, lobby, sunny outside. Oh my God, I think, I forgot my umbrella again. "Oh my God," I say, "I left my umbrella upstairs."

"Leave it," she says, "since you now have enough money to buy ten umbrellas. Twenty if you want, though I don't know why you would." "True," I say. "Want to go for another coffee?" "Coffee?" she says. "I think a drink's more what we deserve. I know I sure do after what I just did for you." "True," I say, "and we'll go to the best place possible," and we start walking. Sun goes, clouds come, we walk faster, looking for a classier bar than the three we pass, but not fast enough, as the rain suddenly comes, drenching us before we can find protection from it.

"I knew I should have gone up for my umbrella," I say. "So we're wet," she says. "So what? It'll make the day more memorable for you. In fact, what I'd do if I were you, just to make the day one of the most memorable of your life, is—" but I cut her off and say "I know, I might," and she says "Not you might, you should," and I say "I know, I will," and she smiles, I smile, we take each other's hands, put our arms around each other's waists, "Let's," she says, "Let's," I say, and run out from under the awning into the rain. "Dad, look at those crazy people getting wet," a boy says, protected by his father's umbrella.

"You know what I want most of all now that I've sold my story project?" I say to her, standing in the pouring rain and holding and hugging her and looking over her shoulder at the boy being pulled along by his father because he wants to stay and watch us and she says "What?" and I tell her and she says and I say "And also to eventually walk in the pouring rain with an umbrella over my future wife and me and future daughter or son, but with the child being around that boy's age." "Why an umbrella?" she says and I say and she says "Silly, you don't get colds that way," and I say and she says "No," and I say "Oh." Just then a cab drives by too close to the curb and splashes us up to our waists and I start

254 Chapter 12 Revisiting Your Craft, Repeating Your Story

cursing and shaking my fist at it and she says and I say "You're right, raincoats and all, we're already slopping wet," and we laugh and go into a bar a half-block away and order a glass of wine each.

"What are you two so happy about," the bartender says, "besides getting yourselves dripping wet and probably catching your death?" and I say "Really interested?" and he says "Interested," and I say "Then I'll tell you," and do, starting from the time the man came in, woman, partners, office, men's room, lobby, sunny again, umbrella and rain, woman and bank, coffees, what do you know, so and so, deal, champagne, check, no umbrella, mixing the story up a little here and there, sun goes, rain falls, running through it, father and son, my thoughts and wants, bar, drinks, bartender and he says "That story rates a drink on the house if I ever heard one," and pours some more wine into our glasses, we toast and drink, he holds up his glass of soda water, people coming in ask what the celebration's about, I tell them, from beginning to end, leaving a little out now and then. "Very interesting," one of them says and buys us another wine each. By that time the rain's stopped but we're not dry yet and I say to Pam "Let's make it a perfect end to a great day," and she says "No, really, I've had a change of mind, besides my boyfriend waiting at home," and: goes.

Just then a man comes in and I say "You wouldn't believe—" and he says "Wouldn't believe what? Because if you think you've something to say, listen to my story first," and he tells me about his wife who suddenly left him last week same day his dad got a coronary and his dog ran away and I say "Excuse me, you're right, and I think I better get home before it rains again," and I get off the stool. "Wait," he says, "you haven't heard the worst of it yet," but I'm out the door, rain's started again, I hail a cab, feel in my pockets, no wallet, wave the cab away and walk the two miles to my home. Phone's ringing when I enter the apartment. It's the man who bought my story project. He says "Tear up that check and contract as I just received a cable from overseas that says our company's gone bankrupt." I shout "Liar." He says "Not so." I slam down the receiver, am shivering, sneezing, want to get into a hot tub, but for some reason the water only runs cold.

Questions

1. What is the frame? What problems and conflicts does the narrator face?
2. What is the tale?
3. How many times does the narrator tell the tale?
4. What is the relationship of the frame (the narrator's immediate situation and events occurring) to the tale?
5. How many references to weather occur? What is the function of this weather detail?

Exploring Conflict and Character

We all have stories we tell repeatedly. There was the time Uncle Herbert's ice cream cone broke and leaked all over the car; the day you jumped off the high dive platform for the first time at the civic center pool; the night the telephone rang and it was your sister Evelyn calling with such bad news. Some of our stories are funny, some painful. In a very real sense, who we are depends on the fact that we remember these stories and tell them over and over. Telling the story is an act of recovery, an assertion of your identity. "I'll never forget the time. . . ." You are channeling back to a scene earlier in time, and the person to whom you are talking knows a story is coming. She prepares to listen and to enter that remembered scene with you.

Stephen Dixon's story, bizarre and "sloppy" as it is, illustrates this process of telling and retelling a story. It also emphasizes the importance of conflict in a story. Dixon's story is about a man with a story. Perhaps he is a writer, or maybe he works in the television or film industry. Whatever the case, the man would like to sell his story to someone. He needs the money. He has one encounter after another—in an office, on the street, in another office, in a bar. During each encounter with each new character, the man tells this story he would like to sell. There is a frame—will he make the sale and get the money he wants?—and a tale—the story he would like to sell. Here Dixon's narrator launches into the tale, the story within the story:

> Listen to this I say. "This guy comes in and says to me and I say to him and he says and I say and the next thing I know he does this to me. . . ."

> I start the story from the beginning: guy coming in, says to me, me to him, does this, I do. . . .

> I tell, starting with the guy who comes in and says and I say and we do. . . .

In each instance, the narrator takes the listener to the *scene* of this tale, such as it is. Scene consists of characters in a specific place, speaking and taking action (Writer's Practice 9.1). In Dixon's story, we cannot tell who the characters are or what exactly is happening or even what they say and do, but it is clear that the narrator is telling someone this very sketchy story and that the story is expanding and contracting. He adapts the story to each new character he encounters.

Experimenting with Conflict and Character

A story often has very humble origins. In Writer's Practice 9.1 you remembered an experience, wrote a brief narrative describing what happened, and then let your imagination take over. Sometimes, though, stories are "found." Perhaps you are in a public place and witness an interaction among people. Observing this event, you find the germ of a story; in thinking and writing about it, you take imaginative possession of it. At the heart of these recollections or observations is an interesting character, situation, and conflict. These elements induce you to develop a story. You fictionalize and adapt as needed as you experiment with conflict and character.

Writer's Practice 12.1 *Tell the Tale*

In this exercise, you will begin with a tale—an incident—and have a character tell this story again and again, adapting it to each new audience. First, be clear about the story or incident. Know where it occurs, who is involved, and the conflict that is at issue. These are essential elements of narrative writing. The tale in Dixon's story is reduced to absolute minimum: "I start the story from the beginning: guy coming in, says to me, me to him, does this, I do. . . ." For the story you will write, however, we suggest that you develop this scene in further detail.

Draft a short narrative (one to two pages) showing two or more characters involved in a conflict. The incident should last no more than five to ten minutes in real time. The narrative can be made up, loosely based on an actual experience you witnessed or were involved in, or, better yet, a combination of imagination and experience. Include some dialogue and describe the action in as much detail as possible. Make at least two references to the environment or atmosphere of the place.

For this story, use either the first-person point of view, as in Dixon's "A Sloppy Story," or the third-person limited point of view, as our writer does below (for more on point of view, see Writer's Practices 8.2 and 11.1). Consider these elements as you tell the tale:

- Keep your characters to a minimum—two will suffice. Consider naming these characters.
- Provide a few details of place so the reader knows exactly where the action occurs.
- Introduce the conflict or problem in your lead (see Writer's Practice 8.1).
- Show your characters in action.
- Include dialogue immediately connected to the conflict only (avoid small talk).

Begin writing if you feel you are ready, or examine our writer's model and explication.

Our Writer

> Archer, a field representative, stalks into the payroll department all hot and angry with a complaint. Claims the payroll clerk, Annie, shorted him on his payroll check. "You shorted me," he tells her. He throws down his check stub and a scrap of paper on her desk. "Look at that," he says. "Doesn't take a genius to see you've shorted me."
>
> Annie looks at the stub, but everything's in order. She looks at the scrap paper. Can't read it. She tightens up, turns red. She doesn't make mistakes. Never. She sees the other clerks staring. Miss Filmore, Marlowe's secretary, looks from across the room. Annie tugs her skirt.
>
> "Well?" he says. "Don't you understand?"
>
> She feels like scolding him, but holds back. *Try to be nice.* "Are you aware of the increase in Social Security this year?"
>
> "You shorted me! Can't you hear?"
>
> "Did you count up your overtime accurately?"
>
> "You shorted me!"
>
> "You got a complaint, you go talk to Mr. Marlowe. I don't make mistakes. Door's right over there. Name's on it. If you can read." She hands back his check stub and the scrap paper.
>
> "Incompetent cow," he says and makes his way to Marlowe's office, behind Miss Filmore's desk.
>
> "You!" Annie calls out. "I don't make mistakes!"
>
> He doesn't stop, goes into Mr. M's office without knocking.
>
> The other clerks keep looking at her, so she pretends like nothing happened.
>
> Then Marlowe's door flies open and Marlowe himself comes marching over with Archer in tow.
>
> "Annie," Marlowe says. "You've made an error on Mr. Archer's paycheck."
>
> "I don't make errors," she says.
>
> "But you have, Annie. A twelve dollar error."
>
> Annie tugs at her skirt. All the young gals keep staring at her. And this Archer man standing there smirking. Name should be Mr. Obnoxious. First name Rude. "I've been doing the payroll for twenty-five years, Mr. Marlowe, long before you got here, and I've never made a mistake. Can you show me where I've made a mistake?"

The tale, then, is that an angry employee claims his check is short and blames the payroll secretary. *This guy comes in, he says and the woman answers back, he does and she won't, him, her.* It is Dixon's model, only the details are filled in, giving this passage the feel of a more fully realized story.

The writer doesn't waste any time getting into the story. The first five lines establish who and where the characters are and what the conflict is. The scene can develop quickly because the writer uses proper names and gives the characters specific jobs. Having established these characters and given them roles to play, he can immediately go to work on the exchanges between them. The writer uses definitive action to develop character. In addition, the dialogue is terse and directly related to the conflict:

> "You shorted me! Can't you hear?"
> "Did you count up your overtime accurately?"
> "You shorted me!"
> "You got a complaint, you go talk to Mr. Marlowe. I don't make mistakes. Door's right over there. Name's on it. If you can read." She hands back his check stub and the scrap paper.

Archer, the field rep, repeats his accusation four times; Annie either thinks or asserts "I don't make mistakes" five times. The simplicity and concentration of this scene are also its strengths. The writer provides just enough detail of place to show the reader the office: the clerks, Marlowe's secretary, the young gals. It all feels quite real through the third-person limited point of view, in which the reader sees what Annie sees and hears what she hears and thinks: *Try to be nice*.

Exploring Repetition

The stories we tell repeatedly undergo subtle changes as we modify them for each audience. We emphasize one detail or omit another to make the story appropriate to the current situation. The story itself is flexible. How we tell the tale and what it means depends on our audience, however.

In this section, we turn our attention to the frame—outer story. This is the series of scenes, or dramatic situations, in which your character tells her tale. A story may consist of a number of dramatic situations. In Dixon's "A Sloppy Story," for example, the narrator has multiple occasions to tell his story. He tells it to the two men twice in their office. He goes outside, gives a woman the shelter of his umbrella, and, over coffee, tells the story again. They go to meet her friend, where once again he tells the story and sells it. This series of scenes and these new characters are the frame of the frame-tale.

Experimenting with Repetition

A writer cannot expect a story to spring fully formed from his forehead. Usually, stories are written scene by scene, sentence by sentence. Each step lays a little more of the foundation for the fictional world you create.

It is this incremental quality of the composing process that gives the writer pleasure. You answer questions with each sentence you write. By now, perhaps you are beginning to trust your imagination and to have faith in your capacity to create a realistic narrative scene. Your task in the following exercise is to have your main character repeat his tale to each new individual he encounters. In each repetition, you will be discovering new possibilities in your story.

Writer's Practice 12.2 *Tell the Tale a Second Time*

For now, don't worry about how your character gets from the end of the previous scene to the beginning of this one. Instead, put your character in a situation in which she will tell someone her story. Of course, your character will need an audience. To help you choose an appropriate one, think about your character's purpose for telling her audience what happened. For example, perhaps your character gets called to the school principal's office to explain her actions. Or, perhaps a younger sister must confess to her older sister that she borrowed and lost her favorite sweater. Consider the following guidelines as you write your repetitive tale:

- Use fewer than half the number of words you used to create your original scene; you can easily accomplish this by having your narrator summarize or paraphrase parts or most of the scene.
- Consider the word choices your narrator makes in the telling; vary the vocabulary and emphasize different details according to the audience.
- Include a few reactions of the listener to your narrator's tale, either as it unfolds or after it is finished.
- Make clear the outcome, or consequences, of the telling.
- Be open to changes or additions to the original scene that occur to you while drafting this freewrite.

Begin writing if you feel you are ready, or examine our writer's model and explication. Here, Annie, the character introduced previously, tells her story to another woman in the office:

Our Writer

Annie joins Marietta, her best friend, for lunch.

"You'll never believe what happened to me," Annie says as she walks into Marietta's office.

Marietta smiles. "Tell me everything!"

Annie does. Tells her everything. How Mr. Rude Obnoxious came into Payroll yelling and causing such a commotion. How he kept yelling that she, Annie

Johnson, faithful employee for twenty-five years without a mistake, shorted him on his stupid paycheck. "It was terrible, Marietta. Everyone kept looking at me, and he kept shouting, 'You shorted me! You shorted me!' And then—you won't believe this, Marietta—he called me a cow. 'Incompetent cow,' was the term he used."

She tells her about Marlowe's role in the incident. How he automatically assumed she was at fault in the calculation of Mr. Rude's paycheck. How he demanded she apologize to that terrible man. "'You've made an error on Mr. Archer's paycheck,'" Annie says, mimicking the nasal quality of Marlowe's voice. "'Mr. Archer works hard for us.'"

"Annie!" Marietta says. "That's terrible! You should complain to Mr. Benson, director of accounting!"

"Yes!" Annie says, standing up. "Yes!"

The scene has shifted. Annie is now in Marietta's office and tells Marietta the story. It is the same story, except this version is told in about half as many words as the initial scene used. Through paraphrase, the writer is able to condense. "Tells her everything. How Mr. Rude Obnoxious came into Payroll yelling and causing such a commotion." Here, the writer has Annie use direct address, and she emphasizes the wrong that has been done to her: "It was terrible, Marietta. Everyone kept looking at me, and he kept shouting, 'You shorted me! You shorted me!' And then—you won't believe this, Marietta— he called me a cow." Most of Annie's reported speech in this scene concentrates on other people. This version of the story emphasizes Annie's impression of what Mr. Archer and Mr. Marlowe did wrong.

With Marietta, Annie obviously feels that she has a sympathetic audience. Marietta is on Annie's side, or, at the very least, she is an office gossip who loves a juicy story. "Marietta smiles. 'Tell me everything!'" The fact that Marietta is so interested affects how Annie tells the story. Archer has become "Mr. Rude Obnoxious." Annie makes fun of Mr. Marlowe's nasal voice. Only once does she mention that she has never made a mistake (down from five such statements in the original scene). By the end of this telling, Annie has what she wants. She has a friend in Marietta, who assures her that she, Annie, faithful employee for twenty-five years, has been wronged and should take her problem to the director of accounting.

The basic ingredients for the plot of this story are now in place. The main character sees herself as competent and faithful, while another employee has a different view. Armed with this story to tell, Annie is ready to arrange one meeting after another in which to seek justice. With each telling of the story, she will adjust it slightly to fit her audience.

Writer's Practice 12.3 *Tell the Tale a Third Time*

Draft a scene in which you move your character from his first listener to the next one. This may involve shifting your character to a different place and time. Dixon's narrator moves from indoors to outdoors; Annie will move down the hall to the office of Mr. Benson. Wherever your character goes next, make sure that the reaction of the new listener will be *opposite* that of the first listener. That is, if the first listener reacted negatively, the second should respond positively. If the first audience was a suspicious one, the second is to be gullible. Further, as you draft your work, consider these guidelines, as well:

- Include a few more details on setting, so the reader's sense of physical place is maintained.
- Go deeper inside your main character, recording her internal commentary on setting, as well as her impression of the character to whom she will next tell her story (see Writer's Practices 8.2, 11.1, and 11.2).
- Give this new character a prop of some kind—a newspaper, a hat, a portable CD player, a string of pearls—that can become an "indicator" of his or her character.
- Include more dialogue in this scene—more give and take—and more analyzing of the main character's story.

Begin writing if you feel you are ready, or examine our writer's model and explication. In our writer's story, Marietta helped us to decide with whom Annie's next encounter should be: "You should complain to Mr. Benson, director of accounting!"

Our Writer

Annie can't eat her lunch. She leaves Marietta and marches down the hall to Mr. Benson's office. Angela, Mr. B's secretary, is not at her desk, but his door is open and she sees him sitting at his desk talking on the phone.

He waves her in and she sits in the secretary's chair next to his desk, waiting for him to finish his phone conversation. He's looking at Annie, smiling, and saying things like "Sure, sure," "Yes," and "Sounds good" into the phone. On the wall behind his desk is a shelf supporting three bowling trophies. Under that is a framed, oversized enlargement of a color photograph: Mr. B shaking Mr. Quinlan's hand on the occasion of Mr. B's promotion to vice president. Mr. Quinlan, president and chairman of the board. Mr. B is wearing his well-known light blue suit and red bow tie. The same suit and tie that he's wearing at the moment, sitting there talking on the phone. "Yes, yes. Sounds good."

Annie imagines occupying Mr. Marlowe's office. She'd keep a vase of fresh cut flowers on her desk. She'd get rid of those junky calendars Marlowe has thumbtacked to the wall. One of them features a scantily clad woman named Miss Universal Tools. And she'd get rid of those horrid snapshots of dead deer, bucks with magnificent racks, tied to the tops of cars or strung from trees, with the men who'd killed them, Marlowe included, posing next to them.

She'd put up her cat posters instead—kittens hiding in boxes and shoes, and a close-up of a white Persian.

"A terrible thing has occurred, Mr. Benson," Annie says when Mr. B concludes his phone conversation.

He looks at his watch. "Will this take long, Annie? Haven't had my lunch."

"It's important, Mr. Benson."

Mr. B smiles. "Well, Annie, okay. But let me tell you, based on my experience, things that seem terrible at the moment rarely turn out to be so bad in the end. But don't let me stop you. Go ahead. Tell me about this terrible thing of yours." He smiles some more.

Annie clutches her lunch bag in her lap. She tells him what Mr. A—Mr. Rude Obnoxious—accused her of less than one hour ago. How she'd tried telling him it was he who'd made the mistake, because in her twenty-five years as a dedicated and valued employee, she'd never made one. Not one. "He kept shouting, 'You shorted me! You shorted me!'" Annie tells him.

"That doesn't sound like the Bob Archer I know, Annie."

"He treated me terribly, Mr. Benson."

"Bob's usually a pretty mild fellow."

"He called me incompetent, Mr. Benson."

"Don't you think that if you take time out and really think about it, you'll have an entirely different perspective about what you think he said?"

"He called me a cow, Mr. Benson."

"I can't remember Bobby ever saying mean things."

"And that's not the half of it, Mr. Benson." Annie squeezed her lunch bag.

Mr. B toys with the letter opener on his desk. He flicks its blade, making it spin. It's a tiny version of a pirate's sword.

Annie tells him about Mr. M's grievous behavior. Him taking Mr. Rude Obnoxious's word. Demanding that she, Ann H. Johnson, employee without a mistake, apologize in front of the entire clerk pool and that snotty Miss Filmore.

Mr. B leans back in his chair and starts cleaning his fingernails with his letter opener. "So. What do you expect me to do, Annie?"

"Marietta told me if anybody can do something about the injury done to me by this terrible man who does who-knows-what behind closed doors, it's you, Mr. Benson. It's you." Annie squeezes the apple inside her lunch bag.

Mr. B looks up from his work on his fingernails. "Injury? Injury, Annie?"

"You're not going to do anything, are you, Mr. Benson?"

"Do? What do you expect me to do, Annie?"

"You're going to let Mr. Marlowe keep his job, aren't you?"

"Keep his job? Of course, Annie. Why shouldn't I?"

"I taught him everything he knows!" Annie says, almost yelling.

"Now Annie, calm down."

"You're not even going to make him apologize, are you?"

"Annie!" Mr. B stands up. "It's *you* I'm asking to do the apologizing!"

The details of place are especially important in this scene. The trophies and photographs are all images of male power: male executives shaking hands with each other; men with animals they have killed; the calendar. Annie has stepped into a man's world. She thinks about redecorating Mr. Marlowe's office as her own. "She'd put up her cat posters instead—kittens hiding in boxes and shoes, and a close-up of a white Persian." But Annie is not in a position of power. For a prop, the writer gives Mr. B. a swordlike letter opener, a visual image of his power, which he flourishes casually. When Mr. B. exercises his power as a director of accounting, he slices up Annie's story.

This slicing is skillfully executed in dialogue. Twice, Mr. Benson expresses support of Archer, saying, in so many words, that he doesn't believe Annie's story: "That doesn't sound like the Bob Archer I know, Annie." Worse, he talks down to her, treating her like a child: "Don't you think that if you take time out and really think about it, you'll have an entirely different perspective about what you think he said?" Three times he tells her to *think*. It is clear that Annie has no chance with Mr. Benson, but she keeps talking. Her story is all she has. In this retelling, she adds to it, incorporating Marietta's remark, "if anybody can do something about the injury done to me by this terrible man who does who-knows-what behind closed doors, it's you, Mr. Benson. It's you."

Where should Annie go from here? Our writer, plotting the story as he writes, has already thought of that. At the beginning of this scene, Annie notices the photograph of Mr. Benson shaking hands with Mr. Quinlan, the company president. Mr. Quinlan's office will be Annie's next opportunity to retell her story. At this point, our writer might be unsure of what will happen in the next scene, but he has chosen a direction in which to move.

Writer's Practice 12.4   *Tell the Tale a Fourth Time*

Now, write one more scene with one more character who will listen to your main character's tale. This final scene will provide a resolution to the conflict. Look at how Dixon's story ends. Each time his narrator tells the tale, he enjoys or suffers a reversal in fortune. The first time, the partners reject his story. The second time, he wins the girl of his dreams and sells his story. The third, he loses the girl and the sale of his story. What if Dixon had changed the order of reversals? Indeed, it would be a different story.

We suggest experimenting with the ending. In one version, give your narrator some kind of significant reward, victory, or success. Then, like Dixon does, find a good way to take away the reward. Next, try rewarding your character to compensate for an earlier loss. As you write this final scene, follow these guidelines:

- Provide some details of place, as you have in prior scenes.
- Include in this telling anything new that happened since the previous telling.
- Experiment with reversing the fortune of your central character once again.

This is what happens to Annie when she takes her complaint to the president of the company:

Our Writer

Mr. Q's office. Furnished with a heavy, mahogany desk. The wall behind Mr. Q's swivel chair is decorated with framed, eight-by-ten photographs—a tinted Mr. Q in his World War I army uniform, standing in front of a huge cannon; several color photos of Mr. Q's three children along with their own families and children; one of Mr. Q hugging his third wife, less than half Annie's age, blonde hair styled in a pageboy.

Annie sits in front of the desk, her knees pressed together. She squeezes her apple to keep her hands from shaking.

"Say what, Annie? You have a problem? Hazel tells me you have a complaint about Benson?"

"Yes I do, Mr. Quinlan," Annie says, voice husky. She tells him everything from the beginning: Mr. A coming in, check stub and scrap paper, the hateful things he called her, what she said, other clerks watching, Miss Filmore staring, Mr. M coming over and taking Mr. A's side without listening to hers, what she said, what he said, her never making a mistake in twenty-five years, and him putting his hand on Mr. A's shoulder.

"Good grief, Annie," Mr. Q says. "What does this have to do with Benson?"

"That's only the half of it, Mr. Quinlan." She tells him about carrying her calculator to Records, rechecking the figures, her visit with Marietta, what Marietta said, what happened in Mr. B's office, her telling him what Mr. A said and then what Mr. M said. "He demanded that I do all the apologizing, Mr. Quinlan. And it wasn't me made the mistake!"

"Say what, Annie? Speak up. You have a complaint about Benson? Our Larry Benson?"

"Yes I do, Mr. Quinlan," Annie says, speaking up.

Annie pulled her chair closer to the desk and leaned toward him. "A terrible thing has happened to me, Mr. Quinlan!"

"A terrible thing? To you? An accident? Were you injured?"

Annie told him about Mr. A, paycheck, names, Filmore gawking, Mr. M hugging Mr. A, no mistakes, Marietta, Mr. B's reaction.

"Of course!" Mr. Q said. "I agree!"

Annie looked at him, puzzled. "Agree? With what?"

"With you, Annie. Yes! I agree with you totally!"

"I'm glad you feel that way, Mr. Quinlan. That's the best thing I've heard all day!"

"Our company is a family, Annie. I always say that! We take care of our own here, just like you said."

Annie paused for a moment, a little uncertain. Were those her words? She leaned even closer, her shoulders touching the desk.

Mr. Q leaned closer to her, too.

"Do you think a brother has the right to blame his sister for a mistake she didn't make?" Annie asked him.

"No! Doesn't have that right!"

"Is it okay for this brother to call his sister bad names?"

Mr. Q slapped his hand on his desk. "No! Of course not!"

Annie looked at the pictures of his children behind him. "Would you take your son's word over your daughter's without checking the facts?"

"Absolutely not!"

"I'm so happy to hear you say that, Mr. Quinlan!" Annie said, feeling both a little stunned and remarkably exhilarated. "I hope you'll tell Mr. Benson and Mr. Marlowe that!"

"You bet I will, Annie. Next chance I get. You can count on it!"

Annie felt the apple inside her lunch bag. Hard and cool.

Mr. Q beamed.

For a moment, Annie thought he was going to reach out and touch her.

In our writer's example, the end is ambiguous. Has Mr. Q. really taken Annie's side? Will he speak to Mr. Benson and Mr. Marlowe? Can Annie count on Mr. Q. to do the right thing? Is Mr. Q's view of the right thing the same as Annie's? The feeling of victory Annie feels in Quinlan's office may be short-lived. The writer has written toward a resolution, but is it satisfying? Is it realistic? Or is it a basis upon which to build? Having drafted the story, our writer, like you, will want to hear other writers respond to it, to consider how he can develop this raw material into a carefully crafted story.

Writer's Practice 12.5 *Assemble the First Draft*

Connect the pieces to see how your story reads. Your story should move from scene to scene, as your main character repeats her story. Think about the connections between these scenes. To signal the scene shifts, you might use white space, as discussed in Writer's Practice 8.5, or the two-step maneuver, as discussed in Writer's Practice 9.2.

Our Writer

Archer, a field representative, stalks into the payroll department all hot and angry with a complaint. Claims the payroll clerk, Annie, shorted him on his payroll check. "You shorted me," he tells her. He throws down his check stub and a scrap of paper on her desk. "Look at that," he says. "Doesn't take a genius to see you've shorted me."

Annie looks at the stub, but everything's in order. She looks at the scrap paper. Can't read it. She tightens up, turns red. She doesn't make mistakes. Never. She sees the other clerks staring. Miss Filmore, Marlowe's secretary, looks from across the room. Annie tugs her skirt.

"Well?" he says. "Don't you understand?"

She feels like scolding him, but holds back. *Try to be nice.* "Are you aware of the increase in Social Security this year?"

"You shorted me! Can't you hear?"

"Did you count up your overtime accurately?"

"You shorted me!"

"You got a complaint, you go talk to Mr. Marlowe. I don't make mistakes. Door's right over there. Name's on it. If you can read." She hands back his check stub and the scrap paper.

"Incompetent cow," he says and makes his way to Marlowe's office, behind Miss Filmore's desk.

"You!" Annie calls out. "I don't make mistakes!"

He doesn't stop, goes into Mr. M's office without knocking.

The other clerks keep looking at her, so she pretends like nothing happened.

Then Marlowe's door flies open and Marlowe himself comes marching over with Archer in tow.

"Annie," Marlowe says. "You've made an error on Mr. Archer's paycheck."

"I don't make errors," she says.

"But you have, Annie. A twelve-dollar error."

Annie tugs at her skirt. All the young gals keep staring at her. And this Archer man standing there smirking. Name should be Mr. Obnoxious. First name Rude. "I've been doing the payroll for twenty-five years, Mr. Marlowe, long before you got here, and I've never made a mistake. Can you show me where I've made a mistake?"

Annie joins Marietta, her best friend, for lunch.

"You'll never believe what happened to me," Annie says as she walks into Marietta's office.

Marietta smiles. "Tell me everything!"

Annie does. Tells her everything. How Mr. Rude Obnoxious came into Payroll yelling and causing such a commotion. How he kept yelling that she, Annie Johnson, faithful employee for twenty-five years without a mistake, shorted him on his stupid paycheck. "It was terrible, Marietta. Everyone kept looking at me, and he kept shouting, 'You shorted me! You shorted me!' And then—you won't believe this, Marietta—he called me a cow. 'Incompetent cow,' was the term he used."

She tells her about Marlowe's role in the incident. How he automatically assumed she was at fault in the calculation of Mr. Rude's paycheck. How he demanded she apologize to that terrible man. "'You've made an error on Mr. Archer's paycheck,'" Annie says, mimicking the nasal quality of Marlowe's voice. "'Mr. Archer works hard for us.'"

"Annie!" Marietta says. "That's terrible! You should complain to Mr. Benson, director of accounting!"

"Yes!" Annie says, standing up. "Yes!"

Annie can't eat her lunch. She leaves Marietta and marches down the hall to Mr. Benson's office. Angela, Mr. B's secretary, is not at her desk, but his door is open and she sees him sitting at his desk talking on the phone.

He waves her in and she sits in the secretary's chair next to his desk, waiting for him to finish his phone conversation. He's looking at Annie, smiling, and saying things like "Sure, sure," "Yes," and "Sounds good" into the phone. On the wall behind his desk is a shelf supporting three bowling trophies. Under that is a framed, oversized enlargement of a color photograph: Mr. B shaking Mr. Quinlan's hand on the occasion of Mr. B's promotion to vice president. Mr. Quinlan, president and chairman of the board. Mr. B is wearing his well-known light blue suit and red bow tie. The same suit and tie that he's wearing at the moment, sitting there talking on the phone. "Yes, yes. Sounds good."

Annie imagines occupying Mr. Marlowe's office. She'd keep a vase of fresh cut flowers on her desk. She'd get rid of those junky calendars Marlowe has thumbtacked to the wall. One of them features a scantily clad woman named Miss Universal Tools. And she'd get rid of those horrid snapshots of dead deer, bucks with magnificent racks, tied to the tops of cars or strung from trees, with the men who'd killed them, Marlowe included, posing next to them. She'd put up her cat posters instead—kittens hiding in boxes and shoes, and a close-up of a white Persian.

"A terrible thing has occurred, Mr. Benson," Annie says when Mr. B concludes his phone conversation.

He looks at his watch. "Will this take long, Annie? Haven't had my lunch."

"It's important, Mr. Benson."

Mr. B smiles. "Well, Annie, okay. But let me tell you, based on my experience, things that seem terrible at the moment rarely turn out to be so bad in the end. But don't let me stop you. Go ahead. Tell me about this terrible thing of yours." He smiles some more.

Annie clutches her lunch bag in her lap. She tells him what Mr. A, Mr. Rude Obnoxious, accused her of less than one hour ago. How she'd tried telling him it was he who'd made the mistake, because in her twenty-five years as a dedicated and valued employee, she'd never made one. Not one. "He kept shouting, 'You shorted me! You shorted me!'" Annie tells him.

"That doesn't sound like the Bob Archer I know, Annie."

"He treated me terribly, Mr. Benson."

"Bob's usually a pretty mild fellow."

"He called me incompetent, Mr. Benson."

"Don't you think that if you take time out and really think about it, you'll have an entirely different perspective about what you think he said?"

"He called me a cow, Mr. Benson."

"I can't remember Bobby ever saying mean things."

"And that's not the half of it, Mr. Benson." Annie squeezed her lunch bag.

Mr. B toys with the letter opener on his desk. He flicks its blade, making it spin. It's a tiny version of a pirate's sword.

Annie tells him about Mr. M's grievous behavior. Him taking Mr. Rude Obnoxious's word. Demanding that she, Ann H. Johnson, employee without a mistake, apologize in front of the entire clerk pool and that snotty Miss Filmore.

Mr. B leans back in his chair and starts cleaning his fingernails with his letter opener. "So. What do you expect me to do, Annie?"

"Marietta told me if anybody can do something about the injury done to me by this terrible man who does who-knows-what behind closed doors, it's you, Mr. Benson. It's you." Annie squeezes the apple inside her lunch bag.

Mr. B looks up from his work on his fingernails. "Injury? Injury, Annie?"

"You're not going to do anything, are you, Mr. Benson?"

"Do? What do you expect me to do, Annie?"

"You're going to let Mr. Marlowe keep his job, aren't you?"

"Keep his job? Of course, Annie. Why shouldn't I?"

"I taught him everything he knows!" Annie says, almost yelling.

"Now Annie, calm down."

"You're not even going to make him apologize, are you?"

"Annie!" Mr. B stands up. "It's *you* I'm asking to do the apologizing!"

Mr. Q's office. Furnished with a heavy, mahogany desk. The wall behind Mr. Q's swivel chair is decorated with framed, eight-by-ten photographs—a tinted Mr. Q in his World War I army uniform, standing in front of a huge cannon; several color photos of Mr. Q's three children along with their own families and children; one of Mr. Q hugging his third wife, less than half Annie's age, blonde hair styled in a pageboy.

Annie sits in front of the desk, her knees pressed together. She squeezes her apple to keep her hands from shaking.

"Say what, Annie? You have a problem? Hazel tells me you have a complaint about Benson?"

"Yes I do, Mr. Quinlan," Annie says, voice husky. She tells him everything from the beginning: Mr. A coming in, check stub and scrap paper, the hateful things he called her, what she said, other clerks watching, Miss Filmore staring, Mr. M coming over and taking Mr. A's side without listening to hers, what she said, what he said, her never making a mistake in twenty-five years, and him putting his hand on Mr. A's shoulder.

"Good grief, Annie," Mr. Q says. "What does this have to do with Benson?"

"That's only the half of it, Mr. Quinlan." She tells him about carrying her calculator to Records, rechecking the figures, her visit with Marietta, what Marietta said, what happened in Mr. B's office, her telling him what Mr. A said and then what Mr. M said. "He demanded that I do all the apologizing, Mr. Quinlan. And it wasn't me made the mistake!"

"Say what, Annie? Speak up. You have a complaint about Benson? Our Larry Benson?"

"Yes I do, Mr. Quinlan," Annie says, speaking up.

Annie pulled her chair closer to the desk and leaned toward him. "A terrible thing has happened to me, Mr. Quinlan!"

"A terrible thing? To you? An accident? Were you injured?"

Annie told him about Mr. A, paycheck, names, Filmore gawking, Mr. M hugging Mr. A, no mistakes, Marietta, Mr. B's reaction.

"Of course!" Mr. Q said. "I agree!"

Annie looked at him, puzzled. "Agree? With what?"

"With you, Annie. Yes! I agree with you totally!"

"I'm glad you feel that way, Mr. Quinlan. That's the best thing I've heard all day!"

"Our company is a family, Annie. I always say that! We take care of our own here, just like you said."

Annie paused for a moment, a little uncertain. Were those her words? She leaned even closer, her shoulders touching the desk.

Mr. Q leaned closer to her, too.

"Do you think a brother has the right to blame his sister for a mistake she didn't make?" Annie asked him.

"No! Doesn't have that right!"

"Is it okay for this brother to call his sister bad names?"

Mr. Q slapped his hand on his desk. "No! Of course not!"

Annie looked at the pictures of his children behind him. "Would you take your son's word over your daughter's without checking the facts?"

"Absolutely not!"

"I'm so happy to hear you say that, Mr. Quinlan!" Annie said, feeling both a little stunned and remarkably exhilarated. "I hope you'll tell Mr. Benson and Mr. Marlowe that!"

"You bet I will, Annie. Next chance I get. You can count on it!"

Annie felt the apple inside her lunch bag. Hard and cool.

Mr. Q beamed.

For a moment, Annie thought he was going to reach out and touch her.

Writer Response Groups

At this point, you have developed material for a complex narrative. You have a story within a story. Your narrator has told this story at least three times—each time for a different audience and with a slightly different effect. In weaving together these consecutive versions of the story within the story, you have likely become increasingly familiar with the goals of your main character. In a sense, the story is an assertion of your main character's identity.

As you gather in response groups to review your drafts, consider these questions:

Essential Elements

- Whose story is it?
- What is the conflict?
- How is the action plotted?

Craft

- How does one version of the story differ from another in length? in emphasis? in the audience's response?
- Has the writer paid adequate attention to word choice and detail in each successive telling?
- Does description of place relate to the character's conflict?
- What images and actions reverberate and seem especially meaningful?

Revising for Theme

Having written quite a lengthy story, you are learning about the difficulty of maintaining coherence and connection throughout a long piece. Thus, our revision strategy is designed to help you rewrite for theme and meaning, to establish connections to link the parts of your story into a coherent whole. The fact that your character repeats her story helps create coherence, but repetition alone may not be sufficient to establish connections.

In the response group, your readers were asked to look for images and actions that seemed meaningful. In the case of Dixon's story, weather imagery and the continuing drama of the umbrella have a kind of thematic resonance. Dixon's story is about a writer's life. It is a life that is precarious—subject to sudden changes of fortune and considerable risk. This theme is carried out through references to weather and the umbrella. Look for opportunities to accentuate meaning through imagery in your draft, as well.

Our writer's draft illustrates possibilities that can be highlighted in a revision. In the last scene, Mr. Q. makes a conciliatory remark to Annie about family. "Our company is a family, Annie. I always say that! We take care of our own here, just like you said." Annie's reaction is guarded. Did she hear that right? she wonders. Mr. Q's support for her seems almost too good to be true, especially after she has been cut to pieces in Mr. B's office, and before that by Mr. Marlowe. Is Mr. Quinlan just managing her anger? Is he really going to support her, a payroll clerk, rather than side with his vice president?

What if this "our company is a family" line is not only empty talk? On the other hand, what if *more* images of family were insinuated into the story, through photographs and other characters' words? These additions would enable our writer to extend his subject and, in the process, to clarify the meaning of the story.

Writer's Practice 12.6 *Connect Your Imagery and Theme*

Write a second draft of your story. As you write, think about the comments of your response group concerning important images and passages. Think about theme—the controlling idea or significant insight in your story. You might consider adding a character who can respond to the repeated story by telling a story of his own—another story within the story. In our example, the writer gives this role to Benson, who tells a story about neighborhood harmony as a way to minimize Annie's personal concerns. The family story Mr. Benson tells forms a thematic connection with the family reference Mr. Quinlan makes near the end of the story. In so doing, the writer links the parts of the story. In your revision, try to do the following:

- Identify an image that can be insinuated into the story on at least three occasions.
- Give a secondary character a story to tell.
- Make the moral of the second character's story connect, either as support or opposition, to your main character's story.

Revision offers you an opportunity to take your story in a different direction. In this case, as you add your secondary character's story, you have a chance to venture into this secondary character's neighborhood or family or circle of friends. How will this new setting mirror the setting in your story? Stay alert to opportunities. Even in revision, you are still discovering your story.

Begin writing if you feel you are ready, or examine our writer's model and explication.

Our Writer

Payroll Annie

If looks could kill, Mr. M, Annie's boss, shouldn't have reached his office door. From her desk Annie could see everyone who entered or left Payroll, so when she saw him return and, without looking at her, make a beeline for his office door, she glared at him. She imagined Mr. M suddenly clutching at his chest and keeling over. Serve him right.

Fifteen minutes earlier, at eleven-twenty A.M., Mr. A, a field representative, had come in all hot and angry with a complaint. Claimed she shorted him twelve dollars and eighty-five cents on his payroll check. He put his check stub on her desk. "You shorted me," Mr. A said. Then he threw down a scrap of paper with figures scrawled all over it. "Look at that," he said. "Doesn't take a genius to see you've shorted me."

Annie looked at his check stub, but everything looked in order. She looked at his piece of scrap paper. A jumble of numbers.

"Well?" he said.

She felt herself tighten up, turn red. She'd been on payroll for twenty-five years and never made a mistake. She could see the other clerks at their desks—all younger than herself—twist around in their chairs and stare. Miss Filmore, Mr. M's secretary, was watching from across the room. Annie tugged at her skirt.

"Well?" he said again. "Don't you understand? You shorted my paycheck! Right there. Twelve dollars and eighty-five cents."

She felt like scolding him, telling him she didn't make mistakes, but held back. Said to herself, Try to be nice. "Are you aware of the increase in Social Security this year?" she asked.

"What I'm aware of is that I'm talking to a clerk who's shorted me."

"Did you count up your overtime accurately?"

"You owe me twelve dollars and eighty-five cents!"

"You got a complaint," she said, "you go talk to Mr. Marlowe. I don't make mistakes. Door's right over there. His name's on it." If you can read, she wanted to say. She picked up his check stub and the scrap paper and held them out to him.

He took them and stared at her for a moment, mouth open. "Incompetent cow," he said. He whirled around and headed for Mr. M's office.

"You!" Annie called out to his back. "Mr. Archer! I don't make mistakes!" He didn't stop, kept right on going, right past Miss Filmore, right into Mr. M's office, without knocking. Annie heard him start yelling, then saw Mr. M close his door.

The other clerks were still staring at her, so she had to sit there pretending like nothing happened. Who did that man think he was, talking to her in such a way? Twenty-five years without a mistake. Not one. And what did he call her? A cow? Incompetent? She tried getting back to work—she had been calculating the wages of two new employees when this Mr. Obnoxious came in—but her hands were shaking so much she couldn't press the buttons.

Then Mr. M's door flew open and Mr. M himself came marching over with Mr. A following along, smirk on his face.

"Annie," Mr. M said. "It seems you've made an error on Mr. Archer's paycheck."

"I don't make errors," she said, trying to control her voice.

"But it seems you have this time, Annie," Mr. M said. "A twelve-dollar error."

Annie kept her head down, tugged at her skirt. She could see all the young gals still staring at her. And this Archer man standing there smirking. Name should be Mr. Obnoxious. First name Rude.

"Annie," Mr. M said. "Can't you say anything? Don't you think you owe this man an apology?"

"I've been doing the payroll for twenty-five years, Mr. Marlowe, long before you got here, and I've never made a mistake. Can you show me where I've made a mistake?"

"Annie, Mr. Archer works hard for us. Maybe after lunch you'll have thought this over and apologize."

Then Mr. M told Mr. Rude Obnoxious not to worry, that he'd personally make sure Mr. A would be reimbursed for everything he had coming. They left, Mr. M walking along with his hand on Mr. A's shoulder.

Annie glared at the other clerks, who all turned back to their desks, acting like they hadn't heard.

After Mr. M returned and didn't drop dead, Annie unplugged her adding machine and carried it to Records. She checked numbers. She refigured totals. She'd made no mistake.

Annie carried her lunch—she always packed an egg salad sandwich and an apple—to eat with Marietta in Marietta's office in Purchasing.

"You won't believe what just happened to me, Marietta," Annie said when she walked in. "I feel like I've been dragged through the dirt."

Marietta's face brightened. She opened a desk drawer and pulled out her lunch bag. "Tell me," she said. "Tell me everything."

Annie did. Told her everything. How Mr. Rude Obnoxious came in forty minutes before lunch yelling and causing such a commotion. How he kept yelling that she, Annie Johnson, faithful employee for twenty-five years without a mistake, shorted him on his stupid paycheck. "It was terrible, Marietta. Everyone kept looking at me, and he kept shouting, 'You shorted me! You shorted me!' And then—you won't believe this, Marietta—he called me a cow. 'Incompetent cow,' was the term he used."

"Annie, that's horrible!"

"And that's not the half of it."

"I don't know what I'd do if a man called me a cow," Marietta said, taking a bite of her ham sandwich.

Annie couldn't eat. She told Marietta about Mr. M's role in the incident. How he automatically assumed she was at fault in the calculation of Mr. Rude's paycheck. How he suggested (or was it a demand?) that she, Annie H. Johnson, faithful employee for twenty-five years without a mistake, apologize to that terrible man. "'It seems you've made an error on Mr. Archer's paycheck,'" Annie said, mimicking the nasal quality of Mr. M's voice. "'Mr. Archer works hard for us.' And I don't? I work harder than anybody. In accounting, I mean, Marietta. What does Mr. M do all day? Closes his door and does who-knows-what. Calls his mistresses for all I know. Looks at pictures from those awful men's magazines for all I know."

"Annie," Marietta said, "you have been slandered. Your reputation is at stake. Do something! Go talk to Mr. B!"

"Mr. B! Of course. I'll demand *he* make Mr. M do the apologizing."

"Demand more," Marietta said. "Demand that he fire Mr. M! You deserve that job, Annie. You taught Mr. M everything he knows about the payroll, and he still doesn't know a fraction of what he should. Demand his removal from Director of Payroll."

Mr. B's office was a large one. Carpeted. Annie sat in the secretary's chair next to Mr. B's desk, waiting for him to finish a phone conversation. He was looking at Annie, smiling, and saying things like "Sure, sure," "Yes," and "Sounds good" into the phone. On the wall behind his desk was a shelf supporting three bowl-ing trophies. Under that was a framed, oversized enlargement of a color photo-graph: Mr. B shaking Mr. Q's hand on the occasion of Mr. B's promotion to vice president. Mr. Q, president and chairman of the board. In the photo his hearing-aid showed, its twisted wire going down from his left ear to his shirt pocket. Mr. B was wearing his well-known light blue suit and red bow tie. The same suit and tie that he was wearing at the moment, sitting there talking on the phone. "Yes, yes. Sounds good."

Annie imagined herself occupying Mr. M's office. She'd keep a vase of fresh cut flowers on her desk. She'd get rid of those junky calendars Mr. M had thumb-tacked to the wall. One of them featured a scantily clad woman named Miss Universal Tools. And she'd get rid of those horrid snapshots of dead deer—bucks with magnificent racks, tied to the tops of cars or strung from trees, with the men who'd killed them, Mr. M included, posing next to them. She'd put up her cat posters instead—kittens hiding in boxes and shoes, a close-up of a white Persian, and the Chessie calendar Marietta gave her for Christmas. And she'd treat the girls in the clerk pool really nice. But she'd make sure Miss Filmore had plenty to do, so she wouldn't have time to sit there and polish her fingernails all day long.

"A terrible thing has occurred, Mr. Benson," Annie said when Mr. B finally concluded his phone conversation.

Mr. B looked at his watch. "Will this take long, Annie? Haven't had my lunch."

"It's important, Mr. Benson."

Mr. B smiled. "Well, Annie, okay. But let me tell you, based on my experi-ence, things that seem terrible at the moment rarely turn out to be so bad in the end. But don't let me stop you. Go ahead. Tell me about this terrible thing of yours." He smiled some more.

Annie clutched her lunch bag in her lap. She told him what Mr. A, Mr. Rude Obnoxious, accused her of less than one hour ago. How she'd tried telling him it was he who'd made the mistake, because in her twenty-five years as a dedicated and valued employee, she'd never made one. Not one. "He kept shouting, 'You shorted me! You shorted me!'" Annie told him.

"That doesn't sound like the Bob Archer I know, Annie."

"He treated me terribly, Mr. Benson."

"Bob's usually a pretty mild fellow."

"He called me incompetent, Mr. Benson."

"Don't you think that if you take time out and really think about it, you'll have an entirely different perspective about what you think he said?"

"He called me a cow, Mr. Benson."

"I can't remember Bobby ever saying mean things."

"And that's not the half of it, Mr. Benson." Annie squeezed her lunch bag.

Mr. B started toying with the letter opener on his desk. He'd flick its blade, making it spin. It was a tiny version of a pirate's sword.

Annie told him about Mr. M's grievous behavior. Him taking Mr. Rude Obnoxious's word. Demanding that she, Ann H. Johnson, employee without a mistake, apologize in front of the entire clerk pool and that snotty Miss Filmore.

Mr. B leaned back in his chair and smiled. He started cleaning his fingernails with his letter opener.

Annie told him that Marietta suggested she come and explain everything to him, Mr. Benson, vice president. "She said if anybody can do something about the injury done to me by this terrible man who does who-knows-what behind closed doors, it's you, Mr. Benson. It's you." Annie squeezed the apple inside her lunch bag.

Mr. B looked up from his work on his fingernails. "There is one other important thing to consider, Annie," he said. "Besides your own feelings, that is."

"What?"

"Harmony, Annie. Harmony."

"Harmony?"

"Harmony," Mr. B said. "My mother taught me that."

The apple felt hard and cool in the sack.

"Once, back when I was growing up, Annie, the neighborhood bully—his name was Charles—well, this Charles gave me a terrible beating. Right in front of all my friends. I begged him to stop, but he just kept punching me and punching me."

"Why Mr. Benson, that's awful."

"Awful? Yes, yes it was. I felt so humiliated."

"I know the feeling, Mr. Benson."

"Oh, Annie, I wanted so badly to get even. I wanted Mom to march right over to Charlie's and demand his parents give him a whipping. But she wouldn't do that, Annie." Mr. B. tapped the edge of his desk with the blade of his tiny sword. "Do you know why she wouldn't do that for me, Annie?"

"Why?"

"Harmony, Annie. Mom sat me down at the kitchen table and got me a glass of milk. And as she wiped the blood off my face, she explained to me, now listen to this, she explained how harmful it could be for me, for her, and gosh, for our whole family, if Charles got punished because of me. She explained the importance of harmony, Annie. 'Harmony of the Neighborhood,' she called it."

"Mr. Marlowe said I'd made an error, Mr. Benson. But I didn't. I checked."

"So. From then on I avoided Charles, and there was harmony in the neighborhood."

"It wasn't me who made an error, Mr. Benson."

"Annie, you are a member of our family."

"It was Mr. Archer made the error, and it was Mr. Marlowe took his side," Annie said.

"A very important member, I might add."

"Mr. Marlowe embarrassed me in front of all those people!"

"And as a member, I'm asking you to achieve harmony in our neighborhood."

"Me? You're going to let Mr. Marlowe keep his job, aren't you?"

"Keep his job? Of course, Annie. Why shouldn't I?"

"I taught him everything he knows!" Annie yelled.

"Now Annie, calm down."

"You're not even going to make him apologize, are you?" she yelled.

"Annie!" Mr. B stood up. "It's *you* I'm asking to do the apologizing!"

Mr. Q's office, last one in the main hallway. Furnished with a heavy, mahogany desk. A matching side table along the window wall serving as a bar. The wall behind Mr. Q's swivel chair was decorated with framed, eight-by-ten photographs—a tinted Mr. Q in his World War I army uniform, standing in front of a huge cannon; a black-and-white of Mr. Q shaking hands with vice president Richard Nixon, taken not long ago when Mr. N stopped in town on a fund-raiser for his and Ike's second term. Several color photos of Mr. Q's three children along with their own families and children. One of Mr. Q hugging his third wife, less than half Annie's age, blonde hair styled in a pageboy. On the wall to the right, next to the window, was Mr. Q's collection of famous World War II photos—marines coming ashore at Normandy, soldiers raising the flag on Iwo Jima, MacArthur's return to the Philippines, De Gaulle's return to Paris, the mushroom over Nagasaki, and the last one, the terrible one on the lower right, Mussolini and his girl friend, Clara, both dead, hanging upside down from the rafters. Clara's skirt looked indecently short, as short as Miss Filmore's when she sits at her desk. Annie pictured Mr. B hanging there, surrounded by Mr. A, Mr. M, and Miss Filmore, their tongues all hanging out.

Annie sat in front of the desk, her knees pressed together. She squeezed her apple to keep her hands from shaking.

"Say what, Annie? You have a problem? Hazel tells me you have a complaint about Benson?"

"Yes I do, Mr. Quinlan," Annie said. She told him everything from the beginning: Mr. A coming in, check stub and scrap paper, the hateful things he called her, what she said, other clerks watching, Miss Filmore staring, Mr. M coming over and taking Mr. A's side without listening to hers, what she said, what he said, her never making a mistake in twenty-five years, and him putting his hand on Mr. A's shoulder.

"Good grief, Annie," Mr. Q said. "What does this have to do with Benson?"

"That's only the half of it, Mr. Quinlan." She told him about carrying her calculator to Records, rechecking the figures, her visit with Marietta, what Marietta said, what happened in Mr. B's office, her telling him what Mr. A said and then what Mr. M said, and Mr. B telling her about Charles, Mr. B's mother, family, and neighborhood harmony. "He demanded that I do all the apologizing, Mr. Quinlan," Annie said. "And it wasn't me made the mistake!"

"Say what, Annie? Speak up. You have a complaint about Benson? Our Larry Benson?"

"Yes I do, Mr. Quinlan," Annie said, speaking up. She pulled her chair closer to the desk and leaned toward him. "A terrible thing has happened to me, Mr. Quinlan!"

"A terrible thing? To you? An accident? Were you injured?"

Annie told him about Mr. A, paycheck, names, Filmore gawking, Mr. M hugging Mr. A, no mistakes, Marietta, Mr. B's Charles, his ma, family, harmony.

"Of course!" Mr. Q said. "I agree!"

Annie looked at him, puzzled. "Agree? With what?"

"With you, Annie. Yes! I agree with you totally!"

"I'm glad you feel that way, Mr. Quinlan. That's the best thing I've heard all day!"

"Our company *is* a family, Annie. I always say that! We take care of our own here, just like you said."

Annie paused for a moment, a little uncertain. She leaned even closer, her shoulders touching the desk.

Mr. Q leaned closer to her, too.

"Do you think a brother has the right to blame his sister for a mistake she didn't make?" Annie asked him.

"No! Doesn't have that right!"

"Is it okay for this brother to call his sister bad names?"

Mr. Q slapped his hand on his desk. "No! Of course not!"

Annie looked at the pictures of his children behind him. "Would you take your son's word over your daughter's without checking the facts?"

"Absolutely not!"

"I'm so happy to hear you say that, Mr. Quinlan!" Annie said, feeling both a little stunned and remarkably exhilarated. "I hope you'll tell Mr. Benson and Mr. Marlowe that!"

"You bet I will, Annie. Next chance I get. You can count on it!"

Annie felt the apple inside her lunch bag. Hard and cool.

Mr. Q beamed.

Annie hadn't felt so good in years. She felt just like she did on that marvelous Saturday afternoon when her papa took her to the soda fountain in Farley's Drugstore to celebrate her tenth birthday. The place was packed. Her papa found her an empty stool and stood behind her. She leaned against the edge of the countertop, intently watching Old Man Farley frantically scooping out ice cream sundaes, floats, malts, and banana splits, lining them up along the counter right in front of her face, too busy to take her order.

Her papa finally shouted out, "You! Mr. Ice Man! Give my Annie anything she wants! It's her birthday today!"

Everyone around them stopped talking and looked.

Mr. Farley dropped his scoop, clicked his heels, and snapped to attention.

"Yes, Miss Annie," he said, smiling. "On the house!"

Everyone was watching.

Her papa squeezed her shoulders.

She would never again feel so wonderful, she was sure. What could be better than this?

Annie just doesn't stand a chance with Mr. Benson. The story he tells is about *not* getting satisfaction, about *not* getting family support. Harmony has its cost, and if Mr. Benson has anything to say about it, Annie will have to pay. In this revised draft of the story, notice also how images of family recur in the story, even in Annie's reminiscence, in the last scene.

Examining Student Stories

In our writer's frame tale, the main character ruminates on an event. Telling it repeatedly, she reveals who she is and discovers the significance of the story and her position in the workplace. The essential challenge in the frame tale is in the retelling. In the story below, Lisa's character tells her story only twice. How she tells the story has subtle differences. In the case of this story, too, self-discovery seems to be the outcome of the story.

Oracle

Lisa Davis

The third night Jen saw him, she decided to stop. He was on Halsted, in front of the market, leaning against the wet brick wall like he was waiting for her. He wore a dirty beige overcoat, and as she approached, he held his cracked hands toward her. She had promised Robert she would meet him no later than 8:30, but there was a light in the old man's eyes, a look in his face. Like he recognized her. She decided to take a chance.

"Hey," she said.

"It's your night," he said.

She pointed at the market. "You want something warm? You want some coffee?"

"You want your fortune told, don't you."

"What?"

"You don't believe," he said. "But what don't you believe?" He shook his head and laughed.

"I don't believe in fortunes," she said.

"What I'm going to tell you is cheap. Just $3.23."

The price of a pint? she thought. Then felt ashamed. That's what Robert would say.

"You're gonna see."

Why not, she thought. She opened her wallet and pulled out four dollars. "Just the $3.23."

"And I'm gonna see," she said.

It was a misty October night. The dampness and just standing still made her chilled. "For starts," he said, "you ain't gonna die anytime soon. So don't worry 'bout that. Gonna be around a long time." He pocketed the money and stared off at the fuzzy night sky. "Gonna live a good long life, maybe even be happy. Once you accept it."

"What?"

"You fight it, but it ain't no use."

"What?"

"That you gotta be free!" His watery eyes were wide and unblinking.

"From what?"

"You know."

"No, I don't know."

He nodded his head, clenched his fist, and struck his chest rhythmically. "To be what's inside of you."

"That doesn't tell me anything."

"Sure it does," he said. "You best run on."

"Free," she said.

"There's a shadow stretching out in front of you, my baby. It's yours."

"What does that mean?"

"Get along now." He pointed toward the corner. "You don't want to keep your boyfriend waiting."

She ran the two blocks to the theater. It was 8:40. Ten minutes late. Robert was waiting inside the doorway, tapping tickets across the palm of his hand. When he looked up as she pushed through the door, the harsh indoor light glared on his forehead.

"It's a good thing I lied," he said.

"What?"

"I knew you'd be late. The film starts at nine."

Nasty when he has to wait, Jen thought. "Aren't you clever," she said.

"Careful." He shook his head, looked at her with scolding eyes.

"You won't believe this. This guy stopped me on Halsted." The words came tumbling out of her. She told him about his cracked hands, how she thought he looked so familiar. There were people like that. You just instantly had rapport with them.

"Rapport with a bum?"

"He wasn't a bum," she said. He had asked her for a few dollars to tell her fortune, and then said she needed to be free, striking his chest with his fist like that. She needed to be what was inside of her. She raised her hand, opened it, and laid it across her chest.

Robert crossed his arms and frowned. "Rule numero uno: don't feed the bears."

"Very funny."

"A fortune-telling bum?"

"I told you. He wasn't a bum. My shadow stretching. . . ." She glanced into his face. He tried to smile, but she could see he was angry, the way his mouth worked. Angry that he had to wait. Angry that she was late. Angry at who she was, that she would stop and talk to a stranger standing on the rainy street.

He waved two tickets at her. "Well?"

"Well?" she said. "What do we do now? We *are* a half hour early."

"Twenty minutes. You were late."

She turned her head and looked outside, at the shadows slanting along the sidewalk. "I'm not late," she said. "I'm gone."

She put her shoulder to the glass door, rolled as it opened, and spun outside. The cold hit her. It had started to rain gently. She was glad for it. She heard Robert calling after her, saw him standing in the theater foyer, tickets in hand, his image blurred in the rain-spattered window. She could call him tomorrow, if she wanted to.

Jen looked for her shadow stretching away from her. She went with it. At the crosswalk, a woman with an umbrella stepped up beside her.

"Care to share?" the woman said.

"Love to," Jen said.

"What a perfect night."

"You said it." Jen strained to make out the woman's pale features in the dark under the umbrella. When the light changed, they moved across the street together.

"Student?" the woman said.

Jen said she was, dreading the question that always came next. In what? Robert was pre-law, had been since he was born. Jen wasn't anything for certain. She'd dabbled in art a little, in water colors. She told the woman she might have been an art student at one time.

"At one time?"

"I don't want to starve."

"You don't have to. I'm in art down at the university, and I'm not starving."

A taxi streaked by, a blur of yellow. The woman glanced over at Jen and smiled an amused smile. Her face was thin, her mouth small. *Not that much older than me,* Jen thought. "What year?" she said.

"I teach there."

Jen drew into herself, felt herself tighten. "I just doodle, mostly."

They came into a pool of light in front of a coffee shop. Jen's shadow played out in front off her on the wet sidewalk. They stood together. The woman held out her free hand and introduced herself as Carolyn Dennis. Her eyes deep and quiet. Jen found herself talking, telling the story, about the old man and her fortune, and then Robert calling him a bum and ridiculing her for listening, chastising her for being late.

"If you asked me," the woman said, "he gave you good advice."

"Robert?"

"Your oracle. He said to look inside yourself. Accept what you see there."

"And be free." The movie would have started by now. Jen wondered if Robert had gone in by himself. Probably not. He wasn't that happy by himself. "It was just a guy," she said. "A guy standing there."

"My father used to tell me to do a kindness every so often. The more random the better. He taught me what *you* need to learn: accept your gifts from wherever they come. And give some gifts back."

"I was so mad at Robert."

"You're free of him, for now. And I'm soaking wet. Let's have some coffee. You can tell me about your doodling."

"All right."

They stepped inside the coffee shop. Outside the rain continued. Jen sat facing the street. She watched the raindrops trail down the windows and felt grateful for the rain and the night and her oracle. The coffee warmed her. She leaned forward, ready to listen.

Lisa's main character, Jen, has a curious experience. She does the most natural thing. She tells someone about it. Robert's reaction to the story helps to reveal both his character and Jen's. It also deepens Jen's curiosity about what she has been told—to free herself and to become herself. Then she moves on and tells another person what happened. In the second telling, Jen begins to grasp what being free and being herself might mean.

Early in the story, Lisa prepares the reader for the conflict with Robert, *"The price of a pint?* she thought. Then felt ashamed. That's what Robert would say."* Jen and Robert do not share the same values. When she tells him the story, Jen becomes more fully aware of this conflict. Lisa builds on this conflict and uses it to move Jen to her next encounter in the story, with the professor. In this telling of her story, Jen finds a more sympathetic listener. The story's recurring image, the shadowing stretching out in front of Jen, conveys the sense of Jen pursuing herself, following her own lead, an intuition of which way to go in life. Recurring images of rain and the suggested pleasure Jen takes in it also point to something important in her temperament. There is an artist inside trying to get out. There is a sensibility that is waiting to be expressed. The story dramatizes Jen's growing perception of who she is.

Creating
Drama

chapter 13

Exploring the Elements of Plays: Dramatic Characters, Dialogue, Structure, Conflict, and Action

All the world's a stage.
-WILLIAM SHAKESPEARE

The essential difference between short stories and plays is obvious, at least from the audience's point of view: One we read, the other we watch. But from the viewpoint of the writer, similarities abound. Plays, like short stories, consist of characters, dialogue, settings, action, conflicts, and ideas. In fact, the skills you developed in writing both short stories and poetry will go a long way toward helping you create successful plays.

This chapter will teach the basic elements of the one-act play. The subject matter and styles of one-acts are quite varied, but most depend on realistic dialogue and strong characters in conflict, caught up in extreme situations and confronting their greatest fears. This chapter will teach those elements, with a special focus on two-character conflict. Manuscript form, an important consideration for the performance of a play, is also taught in this chapter.

An excellent example of a modern one-act play is Tina Howe's *Teeth*. Tina Howe is a prize-winning playwright whose works have premiered at such places as the Los Angeles Actors Theatre, the Kennedy Center, and The Second Stage. As you read her play, consider to what extent her characters are caught up in extreme situations, confronting their greatest fears.

A Brief History of Short Drama

In ancient times, drama arose from religious rituals and enactments of tribal history. Witch doctors and high priests conducted rites, ceremonies, and dances. Tribe members acted out the roles that the gods, enemies, animals, and the elements (wind, rain, and fire) played in their lives. Tribal historians spun tales of tribal origins, great victories, and catastrophic events, often mimicking tribal heroes' actions.

In medieval times, short dramas depicting Christ's life became part of religious services. These popular plays were taken over by acting guilds and performed on pageant wagons during summer festivals. Later, longer plays depicted the lives of ordinary people, legendary heroes, and historical figures.

Longer plays flourished during the Renaissance and Elizabethan times, but short plays and skits maintained their popularity, performed by bands of wandering actors and musicians in village markets or town squares.

Traveling entertainers brought short drama into the eighteenth century when a variety show—vaudeville—was developed. Vaudeville was popular in England during the eighteenth and nineteenth centuries and in America in the early years of the twentieth century. During the 1950s and 1960s, vaudevillian skits on television shows such as *Milton Berle's Texaco Star Theater* and *The Jackie Gleason Show* helped keep short drama alive.

The one-act play—a thirty- to forty-minute drama developed around the turn of the century—was adopted by many serious playwrights. Such plays were often grouped and staged as an evening's entertainment. Recently, a shorter version of the one-act play has evolved: the ten-minute play. Featured in drama festivals across the country, ten-minute plays, despite their name, sometimes run less than ten minutes.

Teeth

TINA HOWE

CHARACTERS

Dr. Rose, dentist.

Amy, his patient.

SCENE: *A modest one-man dentist's office in midtown Manhattan. An FM radio is tuned to a classical music station. It's March 21st, Bach's birthday, and Glenn Gould is playing the rollicking Presto from his Toccata in C minor. The whine of a high-powered dentist's drill slowly asserts itself. In blackout . . .*

DR ROSE: Still with me . . . ?

AMY: [*Garbled because his hands are in her mouth.*] Aargh . . .

DR ROSE: [*Hums along as the drilling gets louder.*] You've heard his Goldberg re-issue, haven't you?

AMY: Aargh. . . .

DR ROSE: [*Groans with pleasure.*] . . . Unbelievable!

[*The drilling gets ferocious.*]

AMY: OW . . . OW!

DR ROSE: Woops, sorry about that. O.K., you can rinse.

[*Lights up on* AMY *lying prone in a dentist's chair with a bib around her neck. She raises up, takes a swig of water, sloshes it around in her mouth and spits it emphatically into the little bowl next to her. She flops back down, wiping her mouth. She's in her forties.* DR ROSE *is several years older and on the disheveled side.*]

DR ROSE: Glenn Gould. Glenn Gould is the penultimate Bach keyboard artist of this century, period! Open please. [*He resumes drilling.*] No one else can touch him!

AMY: Aarg. . . .

DR ROSE: Wanda Landowska, Roselyn Turek, Trevor Pinnock . . . forget it!

AMY: Aarg. . . .

DR ROSE: [*Drilling with rising intensity.*] Andras Schiff, Igor Kipness, Anthony Newman . . . no contest!

AMY: Aarg. . . .

DR ROSE: Listen to the man . . . ! The elegance of his phrasing, the clarity of his touch . . . The joy! The joy! [*He roars.*]

AMY: [*Practically jumping out of her seat.*] OOOOOWWWWWWW!

DR ROSE: Sorry, sorry—afraid I slipped. [*His drilling returns to normal.*] Hear how he hums along in a different key? The man can't contain himself . . . [*He roars again, then calms down for a spate of drilling. He idly starts humming along with Gould.*] You know, you're my third patient . . . no, make that fourth . . . that's pulled out a filling with candy this week. What was the culprit again?

AMY: [*Garbled.*] Bit O'Honey.

DR ROSE: Almond Roca?

AMY: [*Garbled.*] Bit O'Honey.

DR ROSE: Ju Jubes?

AMY: [*Less garbled.*] Bit O'Honey, Bit O'Honey!

DR ROSE: Yup, saltwater taffy will do it every time! O.K., Amy, the worst is over. You can rinse. [*He hangs up the drill.*]

[AMY *rinses and spits with even more fury.*]

DR ROSE: Hey, hey, don't break my bowl on me! [*Fussing with his tools.*] Now, where did I put that probe? . . . I can't seem to hold on to anything these days . . .

[AMY *flops back down with a sigh.*]

DR ROSE: [*In a little sing-song.*] Where are you? . . . Where are you? . . . Ahhhhh, here it is! O.K. . . . let's just take one more last look before we fill you up. Open. [*He disappears into her mouth with the probe.*] Amy, Amy, you're still grinding your teeth at night, aren't you?

AMY: [*Anguished.*] Aaaaarrrrrrrhhh!

DR ROSE: You've got to wear that rubber guard I gave you!

AMY: [*Completely garbled.*] But I can't breathe when it's on!

AMY: [*Incomprehensible.*] I feel like I'm choking! I've tried to wear it, I really have, I just always wake up gasping for air. See, I can't breathe through my nose. If I could breathe through my nose, it wouldn't be a problem . . .

DR ROSE: I know they take getting used to, but you're doing irreparable damage to your supporting bone layer, and once that goes . . . [*He whistles her fate.*]

[*A radio announcer has come on in the background during this.*]

RADIO ANNOUNCER: That was Glenn Gould playing Bach's Toccata in C minor, BWV listing 911. And to continue with our birthday tribute to J. S. Bach, we now turn to his Cantata BWV 80, "Ein Feste Burg," as performed by the English Chamber Orchestra under the direction of Raymond Leppard. [*It begins.*]

DR ROSE: [*Comes out of her mouth.*] Well, let's whip up a temporary filling and get you out of here. [*He rummages through his tray of tools.*]

AMY: Dr. Rose, could I ask you something?

DR ROSE: Of course, today's March 21st, Bach's birthday! [*Some instruments fall, he quickly recovers them.*] Woops . . .

AMY: I keep having this recurring nightmare.

DR ROSE: Oh, I love this piece. I used to sing it in college. Mind if I turn it up?

AMY: I just wonder if you've heard it before.

DR ROSE: [*Turns up the volume, singing along. He returns to his tray and starts sorting out his things which keep dropping. He quickly retrieves them, never stopping his singing.*]
Ein feste Burg ist unser Gott,
Ein gute Wehr und Waffen . . . woops.
Er hilft uns frei aus aller, Not,
Die uns itzt hat . . . woops . . . betroffen.

AMY: I have it at least three times a week now.

DR ROSE: I came this close to being a music major. *This* close!

AMY: I wake up exhausted with my whole jaw throbbing. Waa . . . waa . . . waa!

DR ROSE: O.K. let's just open this little bottle of cement here. [*He starts struggling with the lid.*]

AMY: You know, the old . . . TEETH-GRANULATING-ON-YOU-DREAM! [*She stifles a sob.*] You're at a party flashing a perfect smile when suddenly you hear this splintering sound like someone smashing teacups in the next room . . . . . . ping . . . . . . tock . . . . . . crackkkkkkkkkk . . . tinkle, tinkle . . . "Well, someone's having a good time!" you say to yourself expecting to see some maniac swinging a sledgehammer . . .

[*Having a worse and worse time with the bottle,* DR. ROSE *moves behind her chair so she can't see him.*]

DR ROSE: Ugh . . . . . . ugh . . . . . . ugh . . . . . . ugh . . . . . . ugh!

AMY: So you casually look around, and of course there *is* no maniac! . . . Then you feel these prickly shards clinging to your lips. . . . You try and brush them away, but suddenly your mouth is filled with them. You can't spit them out fast enough! [*She tries.*]

DR ROSE: DAMNIT! [*He goes through a series of silent contortions trying to open it—behind his back, up over this head, down between his legs, etc. etc.*]

AMY: [*Still spitting and wiping.*] People are starting to stare. . . . You try to save face. [*To the imagined partygoers.*] "Well, what do you know . . . I seem to have taken a bite out of my coffee cup! Silly me!" [*She laughs, frantically wiping.*]

DR ROSE: DAMN. WHAT'S GOING ON HERE!

AMY: That's just what *I* want to know!

DR ROSE: IS THIS SOME KIND OF CONSPIRACY OR WHAT?

AMY: Why me? What did I do?

DR ROSE: They must weld these tops on.

AMY: Then I catch a glimpse of myself in the mirror . . .

DR ROSE: [*Starting to cackle.*] Think you can outsmart me? [*He starts whacking a heavy tool down on the lid.*]

AMY: You got it! My teeth are spilling out of my mouth in little pieces. I frantically try and moosh them back in, but there's nothing to hold on to. Then they start granulating on me . . . fsssssssssssssss . . . it's like trying to build a sand castle inside an hour glass!

[DR ROSE *is having a worse and worse time. He finally just sits on the floor and bangs the bottle down as hard as he can, again and again.*]

AMY: My mouth is a blaze of gums. We are talking pink for *miles* . . . ! Magellan staring out over the Pacific Ocean during a sunset in 1520 —[*As Magellan.*] "Pink . . . pink . . . pink . . . pink!"

[DR ROSE *starts to whimper as he pounds.*]

AMY: What does it *mean*, is what I'd like to know! I mean, teeth are supposed to last forever, right? They hold up through floods, fires, earthquakes and wars . . . the one part of us that endures.

DR ROSE: Open, damnit. Open, damnit. Open, damnit. . . .

AMY: So if they granulate on you, where does that leave you? *Nowhere!*

DR ROSE: [*Curls into the fetal position and focuses on smaller moves in a tiny voice.*] Come on . . . come on . . . Please? Pretty please? Pretty, lovely, ravishing please?

AMY: You could have been rain or wind for all anybody knows. That's pretty scary. . . . [*Starting to get weepy.*] One minute you're laughing at a party and the next you've evaporated into thin air. . . . [*Putting on a voice.*] "Remember Amy? Gee, I wonder whatever happened to her?" [*In another voice.*] "Gosh, it's suddenly gotten awfully chilly in here. Where's that *wind* coming from?" [*Teary again.*] I mean, we're not around for that long as it is, so then to suddenly. . . . I'm sorry, I'm sorry. It's just that I have this um . . . long-standing . . . Oh God, here we go . . . [*Starting to break down.*] Control yourself! Control . . . control!

[*DR ROSE is now rolled up in a ball beyond speech. He clutches the bottle whimpering and emitting strange little sobs.*]

AMY: See, I have this long-standing um . . . fear of death? It's something you're born with. I used to sob in my father's arms when I was only . . . Oh boy! See, once you start thinking about it, I mean . . . *really* thinking about it . . . You know, time going on for ever and ever and ever and ever and you're not there . . . it can get pretty scary! . . . We're not talking missing out on a few measly centuries here, but boom! And back to dinosaurs again? . . . [*More and more weepy.*] Eternity . . . Camel trains, cities, holy wars, boom! Dinosaurs, camel trains, cities, holy wars, boom!. . . . Dinosaurs, camel trains, cities, holy wars. . . . Stop it Amy . . . just . . . *stop it!*

DR ROSE: [*Broken.*] I can't open this bottle.

AMY: [*Wiping away her tears.*] Dr. Rose! What are you doing down there?

DR ROSE: I've tried everything.

AMY: What's wrong?

DR ROSE: [*Reaching the bottle up to her.*] I can't open it.

AMY: [*Taking it.*] Oh here, let me try.

DR ROSE: I'm afraid I'm having a breakdown.

AMY: I'm good at this kind of thing.

DR ROSE: I don't know, for some time now I just haven't . . .

AMY: [*Puts the bottle in her mouth, clamps down on it with her back teeth and unscrews the lid with one turn. She hands it back to him.*] Here you go.

DR ROSE: [*Rises and advances towards her menacingly.*] You should never . . . NEVER DO THAT!

AMY: [*Drawing back.*] What?

DR ROSE: Open a bottle with your teeth.

AMY: I do it all the time.

DR ROSE: Teeth are very fragile. They're not meant to be used as tools!

AMY: Sorry, sorry.

DR ROSE: I just don't believe the way people mistreat them. We're only given one set of permanent teeth in a lifetime. ONE SET, AND THAT'S IT!

AMY: I won't do it again. I promise.

DR ROSE: Species flourish and disappear, only our teeth remain. Open please. [*He puts cotton wadding in her mouth.*] You must respect them, take care of them. . . . Oh, why even bother talking about it, no one ever listens to me anyway. Wider, please. [*He puts in more cotton and a bubbling saliva drain.*] O.K., let's fill this baby and get you on your way. [*He dabs in bits of compound.*] So, how's work these days?

AMY: Aarg . . .

DR ROSE: Same old rat race, huh?

AMY: Aarg. . . .

    [*During this, the final chorus, "Das Wort sie sollen lassen stahn" has started to play.*]

AMY: [*Slightly garbled.*] What is that tune? It's so familiar.

DR ROSE: "A Mighty Fortress is Our God"

AMY: Right, right! I used to sing it in Sunday school 100 years ago.

DR ROSE: Actually, Bach stole the melody from Martin Luther.

AMY: [*Bursts into song, garbled, the saliva drain bubbling.*] "A mighty fortress is Our God . . ."

AMY:	**DR ROSE:** [*Joining her.*]
. . . a bulwark never failing	. . . Und kein' Dank dazu haben
Our helper he amid the flood	Er ist bei uns wohl auf dem Plan
Of mortal ills prevailing.	Mit seinem Geist und Gaben.
For still our ancient foe,	Nehmen sie uns den Leib,
Doth seek to work us woe . . .	Gut, Ehr, Kind und Weib. . . .

[*Their voices swell louder and louder.*]

[*BLACKOUT.*]

Questions

1. Are the characters caught up in extreme situations?
2. Do any of them confront their greatest fears?
3. What are the important conflicts in the play?
4. What role does dialogue play in the plot and action of the play?

Exploring Strong Characters and Dramatic Dialogue

A secret to writing successful plays is to create strong characters who try to take control of their lives, who make decisions, and who act on those decisions. You want to create characters who are interesting and entertaining and unusual. The characters who tend to work best on the stage have an air of "theatricality"—the ability to stand up and pursue resolutions to their problems. Most exhibit one or more of the following traits:

- a tendency to be verbal
- the ability to stand up for themselves and others
- a readiness to be confrontational
- the passion to support what they perceive is truth or right

How, then, can such characters be identified? Mainly by the way they talk. They communicate their ideas, stories, and concerns enthusiastically. They use dramatic verbal devices. You can hear drama in their words.

As you might expect, writing such dialogue is not an easy task. First attempts may sound wordy and unnatural and not at all spontaneous. Further, novice writers tend to give the audience unnecessary information by making their characters say too much, say things that are obvious, or use long sentences. Consider the following example: A mother requires her twelve-year-old son to help with the dishes before he can go out to play. He says, "I hope the guys don't show up and catch me washing these dishes. They'll probably think I'm some sort of sissy or something." Yet, all the son really needs to say is, "Hope the guys don't see me doing this." He doesn't need to say "washing the dishes" because it is already clear that that is what he is doing. He probably doesn't have to express his fears about what the guys will think because that is clear through implication. That he doesn't want to be seen by his friends is all the audience needs to know.

Like conversational, spontaneous talk, dramatic dialogue tends to be economical. You explored uses of dialogue in Chapter 8, and you experimented at creating it in Writing Practice 8.3. You noticed that people use shortcuts when they speak. On the stage, characters tend to use similar techniques to maintain interest, to manipulate conversation, and to draw out another character. Here is a summary of the shortcuts and techniques addressed in the discussion of dialogue:

- Speak in short sentences.
- Answer questions with questions, or simply avoid answering.
- Ignore what is being said by the other person.

- Change the subject.
- Respond to things that haven't been said.
- Repeat words or expressions.

The dialogue in Tina Howe's *Teeth* utilizes several of these devices. Many of the verbal exchanges between Dr. Rose and Amy are short, often consisting of two- and three-word fragments. Consider this exchange early in the play:

> **DR. ROSE:** You know, you're my third patient . . . no, make that fourth . . . that's pulled out a filling with candy this week. What was the culprit again?
>
> **AMY:** [*Garbled.*] Bit O'Honey.
>
> **DR ROSE:** Almond Roca?
>
> **AMY:** [*Garbled.*] Bit O'Honey.
>
> **DR ROSE:** Ju Jubes?
>
> **AMY:** [*Less garbled.*] Bit O'Honey, Bit O'Honey!
>
> **DR ROSE:** Yup, saltwater taffy will do it every time! O.K., Amy, the worst is over. You can rinse.

Both characters in *Teeth* ask rhetorical questions and, not expecting a reply, at times answer their own questions. For example, early in the play Dr. Rose asks, "Hear how he [Glenn Gould, who is the pianist playing Bach's music on the radio] hums along in a different key?" He immediately provides the response: "The man can't contain himself. . . ." A moment later, he responds to another of his own questions: "Now, where did I put that probe? . . . I can't seem to hold on to anything these days. . . ." Later, when Amy is trying to tell Dr. Rose about her terrible nightmare of her teeth shattering and granulating, she uses this same pattern: "So if they granulate on you, where does that leave you? *Nowhere!*"

Both characters are guilty of ignoring each other during the course of the play. When Amy tries to describe her terrible nightmares, Dr. Rose is either talking about his interest in classical music or is struggling with the lid of the cement bottle. At one moment he asks a rhetorical question (actually yells it) concerning that struggle: "IS THIS SOME KIND OF CONSPIRACY OR WHAT?" Amy, ignoring him, asks a rhetorical question concerning her nightmares: "Why me? What did I do?"

Experimenting with Strong Characters and Dramatic Dialogue

Writing convincing dialogue for the stage requires recording actual, spontaneous conversations, either as they occur or from memory. Both approaches are also excellent methods for discovering subject matter, characters, conflicts, and dialogue for plays. The conversations to pay attention to—those most fruitful for drama—center on some kind of direct conflict involving argumentation, confrontation, anger, or strife.

Complete Writer's Practices 13.1 and 13.2 on writing dialogue. Use the simple script illustrated in our writer's examples. We suggest that you repeat this practice even if you are pleased with the results of your first attempt. Listening to and transcribing dialogue is to drama what playing scales is to music: the best way to develop your ear for rhythm and sound. In a later section of this chapter, you will use one of your practice scripts as the basis for a one-act play of your own.

Writer's Practice 13.1 *Record a Conversation from Memory*

Memory can provide you with an endless source of dramatic conversations. Although it is perfectly permissible to record conversations in which you participated, it may be easier to focus on those you overheard. If possible, write down the actual words, those that you can hear spoken in your head. If at times you don't remember everything, write what was probably said, but avoid writing made-up passages that are lengthy. Again, focus on the words and voices you can hear. If you can't remember or do not know the names of the speakers, invent suitable designations: Woman #1/Woman #2; Tall Man/Thin Man; Redhead/Mr. Ugly.

Start with conversations between two speakers. Try to capture the confrontational or argumentative words. These words tend to be the most dramatic, as well as the most memorable, anyway. Also, don't be concerned if the conversations you remember seem short. You will have the opportunity to expand promising ones in the Writer's Practices that follow. To help you get started, read the following list of situations to stir your memories:

- a couple having a lively conversation in a nearby booth at a restaurant
- members of your family sniping at each other during breakfast
- two guys in the seat behind yours on the bus arguing about something
- a mother disciplining her child in the checkout line at the supermarket
- an irate customer and an uncaring waiter exchanging words at a restaurant
- you and one of your parents discussing the way you cleaned your room (or performed some other tedious task)
- a parent or other adult trying to teach you to do something you find disagreeable—how to clean a fish, change a baby's diaper, or wash and wax the car

Begin recording if you feel you are ready, or examine our writer's model and explication.

Our Writer

The following script is based on a conversation overheard in a supermarket (the fourth suggestion listed above). Our writer recorded it four or five hours after she witnessed it. A little boy, sitting in the child's seat of a grocery cart, kept reaching for a candy bar:

LITTLE BOY: I want this one!

MOTHER: No, not until you learn to eat your vegetables.

LITTLE BOY: I want this one!

MOTHER: No vegetables, no candy.

LITTLE BOY: I want this one!

MOTHER: No!

OLD WOMAN BEHIND THEM: Listen to your mother.

How many characteristics of spontaneous, argumentative talk can you find in this script? Several. With the exception of one nine-word sentence, the sentences are short, ranging from one to four words. The little boy ignores his mother's comments about eating vegetables, and he repeats his demand for a candy bar three times. She repeats the word "No" three times in her responses.

Writer's Practice 13.2 *Record a Conversation from Direct Observation*

Write down a conversation in progress. Although it is possible to capture some excellent examples from people close to you—class members, friends, and family members—often well-populated public places such as libraries, restaurants, buses, grandstands of athletic events, parks, and beaches can provide comfortable situations where you can write and remain invisible. As you begin listening to people closely and writing down their words, you will notice similar characteristics of conversation that will be useful in creating realistic dialogue for a play.

Probably you will find this activity more difficult than writing down remembered conversations. When writing from memory, you can take as much time as you need to get down all the words. When writing while the talk is under way, however, it can be a challenge to keep up. You should be aware, too, that you can't be a participant in the talk and also do the writing; there isn't enough time. And if, at times, you don't catch some of the words used, leave blank spaces that you can fill in later. Then, if still you can't remember the exact words used, write down what was probably said.

Begin writing if you feel you are ready, or examine our writer's model and explication.

Our Writer

The following conversation was recorded in the seating area of a food court in a mall. A teenage girl and her father were sitting at a nearby table. The father was clearly agitated. He kept glaring at his daughter, who appeared to be sulking. They didn't talk at first, and then the daughter broke the ice:

> **GIRL:** Well? Aren't you going to say anything?
>
> **FATHER:** Say? You tell me what to say. I have nothing to say.
>
> **GIRL:** Aren't you going to yell at me?
>
> **FATHER:** Yell? Why should I yell? You tell me.
>
> **GIRL:** Because they caught me shoplifting, that's why.
>
> **FATHER:** You think me yelling will change that?
>
> **GIRL:** I feel so rotten!
>
> **FATHER:** Your poor mother. What will this do to her?

How many characteristics of spontaneous talk can you find in this script? You should notice several characteristics. For example, the utterances and sentences are short, ranging from one to seven words. Also, the father answers his daughter's questions with questions. Finally, the father ignores his daughter's apparent shame by directing his focus to the girl's mother's reaction to the news.

Exploring the Actions of a Play

So far, we have been focusing on dialogue but have said little about *action*—what characters *do* as the dialogue unfolds. A play is meant to be seen, after all. As members of the audience, we see the characters walk in and out of rooms, slouch in chairs, fuss with neckties, sweep the floor—the same actions we see people do in real-life situations. Even when seated at a dining table, characters can be quite animated, reaching to pass a bowl, cutting food, and fiddling with the silverware. A script contains all of the dialogue, of course, but includes only those actions essential to the emotional portrayal of the characters or to the ideas of the play.

Actors like to determine the smaller, unessential actions of the characters they play. Their interpretations of characters are imitations of the actions and speech of people they have encountered in their own lives. This is the actor's contribution to the theatrical composition of a play. Thus, only the essential or basic action suggested by the playwright is included in the parenthetical or bracketed stage directions of a script. If you study the stage directions of *Teeth*, you will find plenty of action. Here's a brief example:

The Elements of Drama

Contemporary playwrights use a variety of tools when writing plays. These include the following:

Character. Who the play is about. The most interesting characters have strong desires, needs, and problems.

Action and conflict. Action hinges on conflict, usually expressed as a person opposing another person, opposing society, opposing nature, or opposing herself. Playwrights usually explore the lives of people in the midst of conflict.

Language. The dialogue or words the actors speak contribute to character and plot development.

Theme. The ideas of the play and what the play illustrates or reveals about people or life. Theme is typically the last thing a playwright discovers in the process of writing a play.

DR ROSE: Sorry, sorry—afraid I slipped. [*His drilling returns to normal.*] Hear how he hums along in a different key? The man can't contain himself . . . [*He roars again, then calms down for a spate of drilling. He idly starts humming along with Gould.*] You know, you're my third patient . . . no, make that fourth . . . that's pulled out a filling with candy this week. What was the culprit again?

AMY: [*Garbled.*] Bit O'Honey.

DR ROSE: Almond Roca?

AMY: [*Garbled.*] Bit O'Honey.

DR ROSE: Ju Jubes?

AMY: [*Less garbled.*] Bit O'Honey, Bit O'Honey!

DR ROSE: Yup, saltwater taffy will do it every time! O.K., Amy, the worst is over. You can rinse. [*He hangs up the drill.*]

   [AMY *rinses and spits with even more fury.*]

DR ROSE: Hey, hey, don't break my bowl on me! [*Fussing with his tools.*] Now, where did I put that probe? . . . I can't seem to hold on to anything these days . . .

   [AMY *flops back down with a sigh.*]

Although Amy is confined to the dentist's chair for the entire play, it should be apparent that the actor who plays her part still will have plenty of opportunity for action. Dr. Rose, too, is very animated. Initially he is somewhat stationary, busily working on Amy's teeth, but in the middle of the play he starts bending over to pick up the tools he's dropped, struggles with the cement bottle lid, and "goes through a series of silent contortions trying to open it—behind his back, up over his head, down between his legs, etc. etc." He sits on the floor banging the bottle, rolls up in a ball, whimpering, and then stands up again to finish Amy's filling.

Some of the bracketed actions are cues for the way the playwright envisions delivery of the line. For example, some of Amy's lines are "garbled" because Dr. Rose's fingers are in her mouth. Like character actions, cues for delivery should also be limited to essential situations, such as Amy's lines above.

Experimenting with the Actions of a Play

When describing the parenthetical action in a script, inexperienced writers may include descriptions that are overly specific and detailed or actions that are not suitable for the stage, such as those that can't be seen by an audience. As a writer, you should focus on actions that are essential or basic. Give the actors room to interpret your scripts.

Writer's Practice 13.3 *Compose Parenthetical Actions*

Rewrite some of your most promising scripts from Writer's Practices 13.1 and 13.2 and include actions to accompany the dialogue. Choose scripts that have the most potential to be the seeds of a play. Of the two models written by our writer, the one written for Writer's Practice 13.2 provides the best staging possibilities. The other one, involving the mother and child in the checkout line at the grocery store, would be more difficult to stage because the set would require a counter, cash register, and shopping cart. The script involving the girl and her father in the seating area of a shopping mall food court, however, would require only a table and two chairs. Here are some guidelines for writing parenthetical action:

- Enclose the directions for actions in parentheses or brackets immediately following the character's name.
- Include only those actions that are basic or essential for the performance of the play.
- Include cues for line delivery only when necessary.
- Avoid including actions that cannot be seen by an audience.

Begin writing if you feel you are ready, or examine our writer's model and explication.

Our Writer

[*Both characters sit in silence initially. The father glares at the girl a few times, then stares at his hands.*]

GIRL: [*Glancing anxiously at her father.*] Well? Aren't you going to say anything?

FATHER: Say? You tell me what to say. I have nothing to say.

[*Both sit in silence for a few more moments, staring straight ahead.*]

GIRL: Aren't you going to yell at me?

FATHER: Yell? Why should I yell? You tell me.

GIRL: [*She clutches her stomach.*] Because they caught me shoplifting, that's why.

FATHER: You think me yelling will change that?

GIRL: I feel so rotten!

FATHER: [*Looks off in the distance and shakes his head.*] Your poor mother. What will this do to her?

The parenthetical directions in this model provide a good illustration of the type of actions playwrights use in their scripts. The brackets clearly separate the actions from the dialogue. Notice that the actions are selective and simply stated. In addition, all of them could be visible to an audience.

Exploring Dramatic Structure and Two-Character Conflict

The dramatic structure of a play is determined by the evolution of the conflict that exists between its characters. When a play features two characters, the conflict tends to be direct and confrontational. This structure can be illustrated in rafting terms with the three-act plot line of a full-length play:

Act I: Push your character into the river without a paddle.
Act II: Send the character into white water.
Act III: Get the character to shore.

Although one-act plays don't pause for intermissions, most are based on this same structure, with the acts simply blending into one another. "Act I" starts the action by showing the situation that initiates the conflict—the situation that pushes the central character into white water. For example, if the main character has a fear of flying, a playwright will find a way to get him on a plane. Perhaps the character's rich uncle—on his deathbed and desperate for visitors—tells his nephew on the phone that he doesn't have anyone to whom he can leave his money. The nephew, greedy for his uncle's inheritance, is forced to fly across the country to reach his uncle's bedside in time. The play opens as the greedy nephew boards the plane. The audience learns about the nephew's fear of flying and the rich uncle's inheritance in the context of the dialogue and action of the play. Now, something happens to intensify the conflict: The plane takes off and encounters bad weather.

What other fears might prove useful for a playwright? Almost any phobia has dramatic possibilities. We have all heard of claustrophobia, the fear of closed spaces. As a writer, consider afflicting your character with a more unusual fear, however, such as xenophobia, the fear of strangers; acrophobia, the fear of heights; ailurophobia, the fear of cats, ergophobia, the fear of work; trichophobia, the fear of hair; or ochlophobia, the fear of crowds. One of these phobias might present an unusual situation suitable for drama. Of course, ordinary fears will also prove useful to the playwright, including the fear of being found out, the fear of being caught, and the fear of failure.

In "Act II" the conflict develops and becomes so intense that something has to break. And it does. Your character's worst nightmare comes true, sending him into white water and possibly over a waterfall. Consider, for example, the nephew who is afraid of flying. The conflict intensifies dramatically if the pilot of the plane he is a passenger on has a flashback to his barnstorming years and starts flying erratically. Our character is pushed over the waterfall if the pilot, reliving his youth, puts the plane into a plunging nosedive. Maybe the plane really isn't in danger, but the character must think that a crash is imminent.

"Act III" resolves the conflict and gets the character back to shore. How he gets back to shore, and the shape he's in when he reaches it, help to determine the play's meaning, or the theme. If the plane crashes into a mountain, killing everyone aboard, the play is a tragedy. A man's life ends before he has a chance to do something meaningful with it. Perhaps, though, the man's fear forces him to make his way to the cockpit to confront the stuntman pilot and save the day, suggesting that human beings have a terrific capacity to endure.

Although *Teeth* is a one-act play, it still contains this dramatic structure. Amy's greatest fear has to do with losing her teeth—she grinds them at night and has nightmares about them granulating and splintering into prickly shards. She's lost a filling and must visit a dentist—a dentist, we realize, who should be gentle, caring, understanding, and reassuring. Dr. Rose, unfortunately, is not. Considering her nightmares and fears, the situation Amy is in when the play opens *is* extreme. In terms of the rafter, she's in the river without a paddle.

> **DR ROSE:** [*Groans with pleasure.*] . . . Unbelievable!
>
> [*The drilling gets ferocious.*]
>
> **AMY:** OW . . . OW!
>
> **DR ROSE:** Woops, sorry about that. O.K., you can rinse.

When the lights come up, the same pattern of grinding, ignoring, and talking about something else is repeated.

> **DR ROSE:** Glenn Gould. Glenn Gould is the penultimate Bach keyboard artist of this century, period! Open please. [*He resumes drilling.*] No one else can touch him!
>
> **AMY:** Aarg. . . .

DR ROSE: Wanda Landowska, Roselyn Turek, Trevor Pinnock . . . forget it!

AMY: Aarg. . . .

DR ROSE: [*Drilling with rising intensity.*] Andras Schiff, Igor Kipness, Anthony Newman . . . no contest!

AMY: Aarg. . . .

DR ROSE: Listen to the man . . . ! The elegance of his phrasing, the clarity of his touch . . . The joy! The joy! [*He roars.*]

AMY: [*Practically jumping out of her seat.*] OOOOOWWWWWWW!

DR ROSE: Sorry, sorry—afraid I slipped.

In what would comprise Act II of *Teeth*, a series of incidents intensify Amy's conflict. Dr. Rose asks her questions, but leaves his fingers in her mouth so she can't answer clearly enough for him to understand her answers. He drops his instruments on the floor and doesn't bother to sterilize them. He chastises her for grinding her teeth but ignores her explanation. The situation becomes almost unbearable for Amy when she tells Dr. Rose about her nightmares, but because he's wrapped up in his own world—first raving about his interest in music and then struggling to remove the lid of the cement bottle—he does not listen to her. Both characters talk *at* each other, which intensifies their problems to the extent that they both are brought to the verge of breakdowns. Amy's fear of her teeth granulating, allowed to grow unchecked, becomes a symbol of death: "One minute you're laughing at a party and the next you've evaporated into thin air," and concludes with a fearful, nihilistic view of life: "Eternity . . . Camel trains, cities, holy wars, boom! Dinosaurs, camel trains, cities, holy wars, boom!" Dr. Rose, no longer capable of managing even simple tasks related to his job, eventually rolls up into a ball and whimpers. Both characters are pushed over the brink.

What constitutes the play's Act III? How do Amy and Dr. Rose get back to shore? Miraculously, they become aware of each other and unwittingly help resolve each other's dilemmas. Amy removes the bottle cap with her teeth, and Dr. Rose, while admonishing her not to mistreat her teeth that way, makes it clear that teeth are extremely hardy and will never granulate: "Species flourish and disappear, only our teeth remain."

Their conflicts resolved, the play ends with the two characters on the same wavelength—literally, on the same note—singing Bach's "A Mighty Fortress Is Our God."

Experimenting with Dramatic Structure and Two-Character Conflict

In the introduction of this chapter, it was noted that successful one-act plays depend on realistic dialogue and strong characters in conflict, caught up in extreme situations and confronting their greatest fears. An excellent source for such dialogue and characters can be found in overheard or remembered conversations like those you recorded for Writer's Practices 13.1, 13.2, and 13.3. Read through your collection now and select one conversation that features two characters involved in an argument. Look for a conflict that is direct—one that pits two characters with opposing wills, desires, or beliefs.

The recorded conversation fragment you choose will provide the seeds for a play of your own. Three writing practices will guide you in roughing out the three-act structure of a typical one-act play.

Writer's Practice 13.4   *Create the Beginning of a Play*

When we overhear the conversations of strangers, we have to listen for a few minutes before we can understand exactly what it is they are discussing. Plays begin in the same way, with the story already under way (see Writer's Practice 10.1). The characters say and do things, and, after a few minutes, the audience becomes aware of the identity of the characters and the nature of their conflict.

Using characters from the recorded conversation you have chosen as the basis of your play, write some possible opening dialogue. Use the "playscript" format, explained below, and adhere to the following guidelines:

- Set the scene for the play.
- Begin the dialogue in the middle of the action.
- Intensify your character's conflict with the beginning action.
- Avoid revealing past history or important facts too quickly.
- Include in parentheses any important action that accompanies the dialogue.

The preferred format for writing staged plays, sometimes called "playscript," is illustrated in our writer's sample below. With the characters' names centered, this format differs from the condensed format typically used for published plays, where characters' names are capitalized and positioned on the left margin, followed by dialogue. *Teeth* is written in condensed format. In contrast, in the playscript format characters' names are capitalized and centered above the dialogue. The stage directions are indented halfway between the left margin and center page, and, unlike the condensed format, are not italicized and are surrounded with parentheses rather than brackets. The dialogue starts on the left margin. Characters' names also are capitalized in the stage directions, as are their entrances and exits. This is done so actors and the director can clearly see who is to speak and who is to move. Scripts prepared in the playscript format are easy to read and are a familiar format in theater. Since you are encouraged to write plays that are worthy of production, you should practice writing plays using the playscript format. Finally, to estimate the duration of your play when performed, assume approximately one minute per script page.

Begin writing if you feel you are ready, or examine our writer's model and explication.

Our Writer

The overheard conversation that our writer chose to use for the seeds of a play was the one involving the girl and her father at the mall (Writer's Practice 13.2). Notice the changes that our writer made to the original to create a good beginning.

Scene: Lights up on a girl and her father sitting at a table in a food court in a shopping mall.

GIRL

Well? Aren't you going to say anything?

FATHER

Say? You tell me what to say. I have nothing to say.

GIRL

Aren't you going to yell at me?

FATHER

Yell? Why should I yell? You tell me.

GIRL

Why shouldn't you?

FATHER

Your poor mother. What will this do to her?

GIRL

But what about me? What will this do to me?

FATHER

She'll probably throw up . . .

GIRL

It was so terrible!

FATHER

. . . and spend a week in bed.

GIRL

Dad! Listen to me!

FATHER

You want to be yelled at?

GIRL

I didn't want to do it.

FATHER

Just wait till we get home!

GIRL

It was Lisa's idea.

FATHER

There'll be no end to your mother's yelling, thanks to you!

GIRL

It was so awful! That mean-eyed bag watching me the whole time!

This dialogue does begin in the middle of the action. Something has happened previously, and the girl expects her father to react by yelling at her. Although the father refuses to do that, he is clearly upset about the girl's behavior. Also, his responses seems to make matters worse for his daughter.

Notice the important information that our writer withheld in this script. An audience will initially wonder why the girl wants her father to yell at her. They will wonder what it was that was so terrible—and who Lisa is. As you learned in Writer's Practice 10.2, however, this is an excellent way to draw the audience in, involving them as they look for answers. Those answers are just beginning to come at the end of the exchange. Whatever the girl did, she was observed or caught by "a mean-eyed bag."

Writer's Practice 13.5 *Intensify the Conflict*

The action that would comprise "Act II" of your one-act play should intensify the conflict and bring your character to the brink, caught up in white water and about to go over the falls. Think of a series of two or three events to accomplish this. Review your two characters' opposing wills, desires, or beliefs. Then consider your main character's greatest fears or needs. Use these ideas to do the following:

- Expand your script by introducing a new situation or subject that increases your character's conflict.
- Find ways to include past history or important information that you withheld from the audience in the opening of your play.
- Include important actions of the characters in parentheses.
- Add one or two more situations to heighten your character's conflict.

Begin writing if you feel your are ready, or examine our writer's model and explication. How does she manage to intensify the conflict?

Our Writer

FATHER
"Thief!" she'll yell. "Thief!"

GIRL
Oh yes! Yes! Oh Daddy—I feel so terrible!

FATHER
There'll be no end to her yelling, thanks to you! "Robber!"

GIRL
Oh yes! It was so awful! That awful woman watching us the whole time!

FATHER
"Obnoxious juvenile!"

GIRL
Obnoxious *what?*

FATHER
Adolescent.

GIRL
So, as I'm trying to tell you, this Mrs. Mean Eyes stopped us when we left the changing room. She made us go back and change, give the jeans back.

FATHER
"Insolent scamp!"

GIRL
Okay! Okay! Please listen! I was trying to tell you that Mean Eyes took us to her office and called the cops. Made us sit there in silence and wait for them.

FATHER
Actually, I stole some records once.

GIRL
(Rolls her eyes.)

Dad! Won't you listen?

FATHER
I was just about your age.

GIRL
They finally came to get us, a big goon named Officer Strickland and a skinny woman cop—Officer Flint, her name tag said.

FATHER
But I never got caught. How could you be so stupid?

GIRL
They treated us like dirt!

FATHER

My college buddy—Ross and I—we waited for a rainy day and walked in the Log Cabin Record Shop wearing trench coats.

GIRL

They handcuffed us and marched us through the mall.

FATHER

That was before the days of electronic warning systems, of course.

GIRL

Everybody was looking at us. Then they stuck us in the back room of the security office. It was so creepy—like being in a prison cell.

FATHER

We slipped the albums inside our coats.

GIRL

Strickland kept saying parents couldn't control their kids anymore, and Flint said she was glad she didn't have daughters like us.

FATHER

We were smart. Sometimes we'd buy an album on the way out, just to keep them from getting suspicious.

GIRL

At the station they made us wait for two hours before they called you and Lisa's mom. (She wraps her arms around her stomach and bends forward.) I feel like I'm going to be sick!

Notice the information that is revealed in this expansion. We learn why the girl feels she should be yelled at—she has been caught trying to shoplift a pair of jeans. How does this new scene intensify the conflict? The father continues to ignore his daughter's apparent need to be censured. Oblivious to his daughter's state of mind, he switches the topic of conversation, like Dr. Rose did in *Teeth*. In response, she becomes more on edge and more despondent.

Writer's Practice 13.6 *Find a Resolution and End Your Play*

Many inexperienced playwrights are tempted to go for one of two extremes: a sad ending that tries to elicit sympathetic feeling for the main character, or a happy ending that gives the character a soft landing. Although either type of ending might be effective for your play, consider something in between, like Howe's ending of *Teeth*. As mentioned previously, the conflict of that play is resolved when Amy notices Dr. Rose on the floor and opens his bottle with her teeth. He admonishes her, but at the same time he reduces her concern about her teeth disintegrating. Miles apart during the beginning and middle of the play, Amy and Dr. Rose inadvertently end up on the same wavelength, singing the same song. As you consider the resolution that you will write for your play, consider the following specific suggestions:

- Find a way to make the condition that caused the conflict to change or disappear.
- Have one character make a discovery about the other character that brings about a resolution.
- Have both characters stumble upon a conflict resolution—something causes them to unwittingly respond to each other's needs; try Howe's trick of having the characters speak at the same time and end on the same note.

Begin writing if you feel you are ready, or examine our writer's model and explication.

Our Writer

FATHER: We'd carry out eight to ten albums at a time. Sold 'em for half price! Never got caught, not once. Were they ever stupid! Man, those were the days!

GIRL: I wish I were still eight and taking dance lessons, roller skating, going to Girl Scouts, birthday parties, and stuff like that. Boy, those were the days!

BOTH

Yeah! Those were the days!

This satisfies the requirement for an ending similar to the ending for *Teeth*. At least momentarily, the characters' conflicts have evaporated because they are both in tune, both saying at the same time, "Those were the days." Both characters are remembering happier times. Both seem to be taking comfort in the discovery that they are more alike than they had realized. A theme that seems to be emerging here is similar to a biblical theme: the sins of the father are visited upon his children.

Exploring Stage Directions

The stage directions are the parenthetical suggestions and directions the playwright includes in a script for the actors. Besides the action, these directions also include other information important to the performance of a play: the list of characters, a description of the scene (or set), scene changes during the course of the play, exits and entrances by the actors, descriptions of sound effects, curtain openings and closings, and blackouts or lights-up commands. If any characters are to be on the stage when the curtain opens or the lights come up, their activities are included in the scene description that precedes the dialogue.

The description of the scene or set includes only basic or essential items important to the performance of a play. These include any items that the actors use or refer to while on stage. Placement of the items may also be indicated. Beyond these references, however, the playwright is not responsible for designing the set.

Various words and commands are conventionally capitalized to make a script easier to use by the actors and the director: actor's names, all exits and entrances, and cues for the stage and lighting managers. For example, when characters enter or exit during the course of a play (unlike Amy and Dr. Rose, who are on stage for the duration of *Teeth*), any directions concerning movement are capitalized, as are the names of the characters who are to move: "KATHY WALKS IN" or "TOM opens the door abruptly and EXITS" or "BOTH EXIT."

Following are the stage directions for the beginning of *Teeth*. The characters begin talking even before the lights come up. Unlike many playwrights, Howe does not capitalize the terms "lights up" and "in blackout" in this beginning.

> **SCENE:** *A modest one-man dentist's office in midtown Manhattan. An FM radio is tuned to a classical music station. It's March 21st, Bach's birthday, and Glenn Gould is playing the rollicking Presto from his Toccata in C minor. The whine of a high-powered dentist's drill slowly asserts itself. In blackout . . .*

DR ROSE: Still with me . . . ?

AMY: [*Garbled because his hands are in her mouth.*] Aargh . . .

DR ROSE: [*Hums along as the drilling gets louder.*] You've heard his Goldberg re-issue, haven't you?

AMY: Aargh. . . .

DR ROSE: [*Groans with pleasure.*] . . . Unbelievable!

[*The drilling gets ferocious.*]

AMY: OW . . . OW!

DR ROSE: Woops, sorry about that. O.K., you can rinse.

[*Lights up on AMY lying prone in a dentist's chair with a bib around her neck. She raises up, takes a swig of water, sloshes it around in her mouth and spits it emphatically into the little bowl next to her. She flops back down, wiping her mouth. She's in her forties. DR ROSE is several years older and on the disheveled side.*]

Notice the description of the set: "A modest one-man dentist's office in midtown Manhattan." No other description is provided. We all have an idea what this set looks like, and Howe leaves the exact details up to a set designer. Howe does include sound effects, however. We can hear the dentist's drill and the radio program playing Glenn Gould. Included in this portion of the script are cues for how some of the lines are spoken ("Garbled because his hands are in her mouth") as well as actions of the characters ("She raises up, takes a swig of water, sloshes it around in her mouth and spits it emphatically into the little bowl next to her"). Lastly, notice that the character's names are capitalized in stage directions for ease in following the script.

Experimenting with Stage Directions

Start by describing the scene for your play, as Howe does at the beginning of *Teeth*. Then rewrite your entire play, assembling the three "acts" and adding the actions of your characters in bracketed stage directions. Use the playscript format illustrated in the previous Writer's Practices. Remember to include only the important or essential actions. After completing your work, make copies of your play to share in a response group. The following guidelines may prove helpful:

- Keep your set simple.
- Include the initial actions of your characters in the scene description.
- Capitalize important terms for the actors, including character names, entrance/exit cues, and lighting/curtain cues.

Also include the actions of the characters, as you did for Writer's Practice 13.3. Here are the guidelines we suggested for inserting actions into your script:

- Enclose the directions for actions in parentheses or brackets immediately following the characters' names.
- Include only those actions that are basic or essential for the performance of the play.
- Include cues for line delivery only when necessary.
- Avoid including actions that cannot be seen by an audience.

Writer's Practice 13.7 *Add Stage Directions*

Begin rewriting if you feel you are ready, or examine our writer's model and explication.

Our Writer

The characters in our writer's model now have names: The father is DAD, and the girl is DEBBIE. Note that only the first few lines of the play are included here—just enough to illustrate stage directions. To read our writer's stage directions for the entire play, refer to the final draft at the end of this chapter.

> **SCENE:** Two chairs and a small table (representing a food court in a mall) placed stage center, facing the audience. It's late afternoon, on a Saturday. LIGHTS UP on DAD ENTERING from stage right. He sits next to DEBBIE. They don't talk at first. DAD is obviously angry with DEBBIE, glares at her when he first sits down, then stares at his hands. DEBBIE sits stiffly, taking furtive, anxious glances at her father before she finally starts to talk.

> **DEBBIE**
>
Well? Aren't you going to say anything?

> **DAD**
>
Say? I have nothing to say. You tell me what to say!

> (BOTH sit in silence for a few more moments, staring straight ahead.)

> **DEBBIE**
>
Why aren't you yelling at me? Aren't you going to yell?

> **DAD**
>
Yell? What would that accomplish? You tell me!

> **DEBBIE**
>
Why shouldn't you?

> (She clutches her stomach.)
>
I wish you'd yell at me!

> **DAD**
>
> (Still looking at his hands.)
>
Your mother. What will this do to her?

Notice that the description of the set in the scene paragraph is simple enough to create anywhere, including in the classroom, and that the initial actions of the characters are indicated. The character names, entrances, and lighting cues are capitalized. Actions accompanying the dialogue are specified, separated from the speaking parts with parentheses.

Writer Response Groups

At this point, you have a short one-act play, structured according to the three-act format, that features two characters. You have created dialogue, included accompanying actions, and added stage directions. Now, working with a response group, volunteer to read the character parts of each other's plays. Hearing your play read by others will give you a sense of its pacing and flow. Examine each other's work for the following elements:

Essential Elements

- To what extent does the dialogue reveal characteristics of real talk—short sentences, repetitive expressions, answering questions with questions, ignoring, changing the subject, and so on?
- What does the dialogue reveal about the personalities of the speakers?
- How closely does the play follow the three-act structure?

Craft

- How consistent are the characterizations?
- Are the action and stage directions clear?
- Does the resolution work to create meaning?

Revising for Consistency in Characterization

The extent to which characters seem realistic depends on the consistency of their dialogue and actions. This means that the dialogue and actions of a character in the beginning of the play should be harmonious with those in the middle or at the end of the play. Unless an author intends to show at the end of the play that a character has changed, inconsistencies can be disconcerting. For example, it may be confusing if a character who demonstrates determination at the beginning of a play gives up too quickly when presented with an obstacle in the middle of play. It may also seem puzzling if a character exhibits a repetitive speech expression in half of the play, but does not do so in the other half.

If your characters are based on real-life people—ones you know well—chances are inconsistencies are bound to occur. Even experienced playwrights must pay attention to consistency. Real people tend to be filled with inconsistencies that are difficult to translate in a convincing manner on the stage.

For example, just because your father—normally a careful, conservative person—drives like a demon, it doesn't mean you should give that demonic trait to a character you are basing on him.

Writer's Practice 13.8 *Revise for Character Consistency*

Possibly, the feedback you received in your response group gave you just the information you need for the process of making characters consistent. If not, read through your play, looking for discrepancies in each character's dialogue and actions. Look for the following problems in your portrayal of a character:

- performs an action differently from one part of the play to the next
- uses verbal expressions inconsistently
- expresses emotions that are inappropriate to the character's personality
- makes conflicting assertions or claims

Begin revising if you feel you are ready, or examine our writer's model and explication.

Our Writer

THE SHOPLIFTING GENE REARS ITS UGLY HEAD

CHARACTERS
Debbie, 16, a cheerleader type.
Dad, Debbie's father.

> **SCENE:** Two chairs and a small table (representing a food court in a mall) placed stage center, facing the audience. It's late afternoon, on a Saturday. LIGHTS UP on DAD ENTERING from stage right. He sits next to DEBBIE. They don't talk at first. DAD is obviously angry with DEBBIE, glares at her when he first sits down, then stares at his hands. DEBBIE sits stiffly, taking furtive, anxious glances at her father before she finally starts to talk.

DEBBIE
(Loudly.)
Well? Aren't you going to say anything?

DAD

Say? I have nothing to say. You tell me what to say!

> (They sit in silence for a few more moments, BOTH staring straight ahead.)

DEBBIE

Why aren't you yelling at me? Aren't you going to yell?

DAD

Yell? What would that accomplish? You tell me!

DEBBIE

Why shouldn't you?

> (She clutches her stomach.)

I wish you'd yell at me!

DAD

> (Looking straight ahead.)

Your mother. What will this do to her?

DEBBIE

They said I have to be evaluated by a social worker!

DAD

> (Bitterly.)

She'll make life miserable for the both of us!

DEBBIE

I didn't even want those stupid jeans! It was Lisa—she talked me into stealing them! She said we could get away with it!

DAD

Talk about yelling . . .

DEBBIE

We put them on under our clothes in the dressing room.

DAD

. . . there'll be no end to her yelling! She'll yell for days!

DEBBIE

Lisa said they really don't have people behind those mirrors.

DAD

You want to be yelled at?

DEBBIE

But they did. A short fat woman with mean little eyes.

DAD

Just wait till we get home!

DEBBIE

She was waiting for us when we came out of the dressing room.

DAD

"Thief!" she'll yell.

> (He tries imitating his wife's voice, creating a high-pitched, nasal shrill.)

"Ingrate!" "Spoiled child!"

> (Pauses.)

"Ungrateful brat!"

DEBBIE

Oh yes! Yes!

> (She clutches her stomach again and rocks back and forth.)

Oh Daddy—I feel so terrible!

DAD

There'll be no end to her yelling, thanks to you! "Robber!"

DEBBIE

Oh yes! It was so awful!

> (Covers her face with her hands, remembering.)

That mean-eyed bag watching us the whole time!

DAD

"Obnoxious juvenile!"

DEBBIE

> (Startled.)

Obnoxious what?

DAD

> (Thinks for a moment, shrugs his shoulders.)

Adolescent.

DEBBIE

> (Her voice taking on a peevish tone.)

Okay, okay. So, as I was saying, Mrs. Mean Eyes made us go back and change, give the jeans back.

DAD

> (Again in a shrill voice.)

"Insolent scamp!"

DEBBIE

> (Becoming angry.)

Okay! Okay! That's enough, all right? I was trying to tell you that Mean Eyes took us to her office and called the cops. Made us sit there in silence and wait for them.

DAD

> (Shifts in his seat, his voice taking on a secretive tone.)

Actually, I stole some records once.

DEBBIE

For crying out loud, Dad! I've heard that story before! Can't you listen to mine?

DAD

I was just about your age.

DEBBIE

So, as I was saying, they finally came to get us, a big goon named Officer Strickland and a skinny woman cop—Officer Flint, her name tag said.

DAD

But I never got caught.

DEBBIE

They treated us like dirt!

DAD

(Enthusiastically.)

My college buddy—Ross and I—we waited for a rainy day and walked in the Log Cabin Record Shop wearing trench coats.

(Chuckles.)

DEBBIE

(Somberly now, giving up and looking away from DAD.)

They marched us through the mall.

DAD

That was before the days of electronic warning systems, of course.

DEBBIE

Everybody was looking at us. Then they stuck us in the back seat of the squad car. It was so creepy . . .

(Shudders.)

 . . . like being in a cage.

DAD

We slipped the albums inside our coats and walked around with our hands in our pockets.

DEBBIE

Strickland the Goon kept saying parents couldn't control their kids anymore, and Skinny Flint said she was glad she didn't have daughters like us.

DAD

Sometimes we'd buy an album on the way out, just to keep them from getting suspicious.

DEBBIE

At the station they made us wait for two hours before they called you and Lisa's mom.

DAD: We'd carry out eight to ten albums at a time. Sold 'em for half price! Never got caught, not once. Were they ever stupid! Man, those were the days!

DEBBIE: I wish I were still eight and taking dance lessons, roller skating, going to Girl Scouts, birthday parties, and stuff like that. Boy, those were the days!

BOTH

Yeah!

(They turn and look at each other, surprised they're on the same note.)

Those were the days!

(BLACKOUT.)

Although our writer made numerous small changes and improvements in the final version of the play, perhaps the most significant change concerns the father's talk about his wife near the beginning of the play. Was it consistent that the mother would react to her daughter's crime by getting sick and spending a week in bed, while at the same time showing strength by yelling? Our writer eliminated the inconsistency by changing the father's lines regarding his wife's reaction to Debbie's shoplifting.

In a response group, a reader indicated that the premise of the play could be related to the idea that *both* the characters are thieves—something similar to "Like father, like daughter," or the biblical quotation, "The sins of the fathers are visited on their children." The writer liked that idea, and decided to name the play "The Shoplifting Gene Rears Its Ugly Head," which suggests the possibility of a biological or genetic heredity that the ending seems to echo. Besides stealing, Debbie and her father share other behavior patterns. For example, each is so concerned with personal issues that neither listens to the other. Also, although the father doesn't acknowledge it, he may have the same need for punishment for his crime that his daughter seems to be seeking. Is that why he married a presumably controlling wife who yells?

Examining Student Plays

Though only one act, the following play illustrates the three-act plot structure discussed in this chapter. As you read the play, pay attention to the stage directions and shifts in scene.

At Least It's Something

MARTY TOOHEY

CHARACTERS

DAD, 50, a widowed father and factory worker.
EMILY, 15, his daughter, a high school sophomore.
DIANE'S VOICE, heard on an answering machine

SETTING: The living area of a small home. Drab living room furniture including a thread-bare couch and easy chair are arranged stage center and stage left; a small dining room table with three chairs are stage right. A doorway upstage right opens into the kitchen. A small table holding the phone and answering machine is centered on the up stage wall. LIGHTS UP on EMILY draped over a sewing machine, feverishly working on a pink formal gown. DAD ENTERS stage left through living room entryway, home from another day at the factory.

DAD
(Sounding weary.)

Well, at least it's something.

EMILY
(Frazzled. Doesn't look up.)

Oh no! Dad! You're not supposed to be home! You said you were going to work overtime! I don't have time for you. I must get this dress finished tonight!

DAD

Doesn't matter, Emily. Listen. I was walking Maude this morning.

EMILY
(Talking rapidly.)

I'm afraid you're on your own tonight. There's no dinner. Cold cuts in the fridge. Just made another pot of coffee. Your mug's still on the kitchen counter. Breakfast dishes still in the sink. I'm sewing all night.

DAD
(Dad walks into the kitchen and returns with a mug filled with coffee.)

And I met someone.

(He stops by the table across from where EMILY is working. He sips from the mug.)

EMILY

Another start-up? I can't listen to this one, Dad. Not now.

(Spreads material across table.)

DAD

She was walking her retriever.

EMILY

This is crazy! I've been on this thing all afternoon.

DAD

She's a little overweight.

EMILY

I'll never finish in time!

DAD

I told her I don't want to walk this way again.

EMILY

You're not helping.

DAD

I told her I'm tired of drifting through life.

EMILY

Hand me those scissors.

> (Points to the other side of the table, next to where DAD is standing.)

DAD

She's a school teacher.

EMILY

> (Stands up and retrieves the scissors herself.)

Why don't you take your coffee inside and watch the six o'clock news? I hear El Nino's tearing up the west coast again.

DAD

Her name's Diane.

EMILY

My name will be mud if I don't finish this gown!

DAD

School teachers don't make it with me.

EMILY

I wish I could listen to you, but not now! PLEASE!

DAD

They're always going to bed early.

EMILY

Dad. Please listen. I've got a lot to do.

DAD

She called me this morning after I got back with Maude. You'd left for school.

EMILY

I know what you're about to say, Dad. I've listened to these stories before and I'll listen again, but not tonight. Try to understand my problems for a change. We can talk tomorrow! If I don't finish this gown there won't be a tomorrow!

DAD

She must've looked my number up.

EMILY

Dad, did you hear what I just said?

DAD

Listen to the tape.

> (Places his coffee mug next to the material spread out over the table and then moves the answering machine from its stand to the dining table and turns it on.)

DIANE'S VOICE

Hi. This is Diane, the one with the dog. Let's get together before you end your mid-life crisis . . ."

EMILY

> (Exasperated, reaches over and turns off answering machine in mid-message.)

Get that answering machine off my gown. And please move your coffee mug before it spills. That's all I need right now!

DAD

She wants to get together with me.

EMILY

> (Begging.)

And I want to finish this gown. Please? I have no time!

DAD

You didn't hear all of the tape.

> (Turns answering machine back on.)

DIANE'S VOICE

. . . or if you're going somewhere, I'll be happy to mind Maude.

EMILY

> (Out of patience, attempts to move the answering machine from the dining table and knocks over the coffee mug, spilling coffee all over the gown. Horrified, she drops the answering machine to the floor.)

Oh my God! Now look what you've done! My gown is ruined. My life is ruined! I asked you to go inside! I don't care about this lady you keep droning on about. I don't care about any of the women you go on and on about! The only thing I cared about in this whole entire world was this gown! And now it's gone! My gown is gone, the dance is gone, my life is over!

(The crash to the floor causes the tape in the answering machine to rewind and replay Diane's message.)

DIANE'S VOICE

Hi. This is Diane, the one with the dog. Let's get together before you end your mid-life crisis, or if you're going somewhere, I'll be happy to mind Maude.

DAD

Think I oughta call her back?

EMILY

(Throws her hands up in disgust.)

Leave me alone! I can't live like this! You have no feeling for my needs. You're like that dumb answering machine. You're a living one-way conversation. Never mind feelings! Do you have ears? Can you listen? You never listen to me! Has it ever occurred to you that since Mom died I've had no one to listen to *my* problems?

DAD

Problems?

EMILY

See? That's exactly what I mean. I'm fifteen years old going on forty-five putting up with you. Never mind that I can't date because I have to fix your dinner seven nights a week. Will it be dinner at six or dinner at ten? Like tonight. Doesn't matter to you!

(Mimics her father's voice.)

Doesn't matter, Emily.

(Back to her own voice.)

You're here anyway, Emily! Just do it! Just do the laundry, do the housework, do the shopping! Just do it! I don't need a gown. All I need is a Nike T-shirt!

DAD

Gee, Emily, I never asked you to clean the house or do the shopping.

EMILY

Isn't it clear that I'm having trouble with this stupid dress? I wish I could buy one like everyone else!

DAD

But Emily . . .

EMILY

Didn't you hear me ask you at least nineteen times to PLEASE wait until tomorrow to tell me your story? No! You just droned on and on about this stupid women.

(Kicks the answering machine.)

Any woman would be nuts to put up with you! Now there's something for you to think about! Shouldn't be too difficult for you. Because all you have to think about is YOURSELF!

(Breaks down and storms off stage, EXITING stage right into the kitchen.)

(DAD approaches the table, examines the coffee stain on the pink gown, and tries to wipe some off. Coffee drips onto the floor. He wipes his wet hands on his trousers. EMILY is heard sobbing in the kitchen as he picks up the answering machine and places it back on its own table.)

DAD

Emily, I'm real sorry about your gown.

(Attempts to enter kitchen.)

EMILY

(Sobbing.)

Please don't come in, Dad.

DAD

(Distressed over his daughter's reaction, he slowly trudges away from the kitchen door and starts pacing along the front of the stage. He doesn't seem to know what to do with hands.)

Gee! I've never seen her like this. Sounded just like her mother, God rest her soul. "You don't do this, you don't do that." I can hear her now. In fact, I think I just heard her.

(Looks over his shoulder at the kitchen door for a moment.)

Boy, the arguments we had when we were first married were really something. She got over 'em, though. She realized after a while that husbands don't do things like housework and shopping and laundry and that kind of stuff. I was a provider. And a good one. I mean, I worked at the factory. That's what I did. Just like I do now. Wives did all that other stuff.

(He stops pacing and looks up abruptly: a revelation. He gives himself a mock punch to the head and makes his way back to the open kitchen door, stopping next to it so EMILY can't see him. He takes a big breath and then starts speaking, perhaps a little too loudly.)

Sorry about what happened, honey.

(He puts his hands in his pockets.)

EMILY

(Her sobbing subsides.)

It's okay, Dad. I just need some time alone. I'll come out in a few minutes. Go watch the news. I'll come in later.

DAD

> (Pulls his hands out of his pockets and folds them under his arms.)

It's okay, honey. I'll give you all the time you need. Guess I've been taking you for granted. You're so much like your mom.

> (He starts walking in circles, gesturing with his hands.)

Heck, I didn't know we had that much laundry. I can do the laundry. I'll do all the laundry.

> (Pauses.)

Well, most of it anyway.

> (Pauses.)

Maybe not my sweaters. And don't worry about my dinner. I can eat out with the guys from the factory. You don't have to make dinner for me every night.

> (Pauses.)

I mean not every night. Maybe just a few nights. But only if you don't have a date. I mean, if you have a date, that's it! I'll eat out that night! That takes care of that!

> (Pauses.)

And no more having to listen to my long-winded stories about those women I meet when I walk Maude. I can tell my stories to the guys while I'm eating out.

EMILY

> (Emotions now under control, she smiles lovingly as she walks into the dining room, wiping her tears.)

Don't you dare tell those guys about your romantic escapades unless you tell me first!

> (She throws her arms around him.)

I love you, Daddy. I'm so sorry for what I said. Please forgive me.

DAD

I'm the one you should forgive. Just look at your gown. Ruined. All because of me.

EMILY

No, it's my fault, Dad. I should have listened to you. Your wonderful stories are all you have at the end of the day. I was thinking of myself. And here I am accusing you.

DAD

Now, now, now. This kind of talk isn't getting us anywhere. What's important is a new gown for you. When is this dance, anyway?

EMILY

Tomorrow night. That's what I've been trying to tell you.

DAD

So what's the problem? Tomorrow's Saturday. We got all day to get you a gown! You pick out a gown store and we'll go together. I'm gonna buy you the best gown in town. Hey! That rhymes!

EMILY

Buy a gown? We can't afford . . .

DAD

Can't afford a gown for you? What makes you think that?

EMILY

But you're always complaining about money, about the cost of things!

DAD

Nonsense!

(Starts singing.)

"I'm gonna buy you the best gown in town, the best gown in town, the best gown in town! I'm gonna buy you the best gown in town, so you can dance by the light of the moon." Hey, not bad, eh?

EMILY

(Laughs.)

But I'll probably need new shoes, too. They're supposed to match.

DAD

New shoes? Of course. Now what rhymes with shoes?

EMILY

Dues, Daddy. Dues! It's time you paid your dues!

(Laughs.)

DAD

About time I did, Emily. I'll start tomorrow. I'll get my own dinner. You go and have a good time.

EMILY

(Gives DAD a big hug.)

Oh, thank you Daddy!

DAD

At least it's something.

✦

CURTAIN

The relationship between the father and daughter in Marty's play provides a good example of a two-character conflict. During the course of the play, it becomes clear that Emily has been trying to fulfill two roles—one as a typical high school girl getting ready for a big dance and the other as a companion and confidant to her father. The latter is a role that Emily resents. Dad has unwittingly cast Emily in the role that his deceased wife used to play, that of a wife who takes care of his every need. Similar to Dr. Rose's insensitive behavior toward his patient Amy in Tina Howe's *Teeth*, Dad is oblivious to his daughter's needs and babbles on and on about the new woman he has met, an action that intensifies the resentment that Emily feels.

The structure of Marty's play follows the format of the compressed three-act plot line that is discussed in this chapter. The play begins with Emily already under pressure. She is struggling to complete her gown for what is probably her first big dance, but the project isn't going smoothly, and she fears she won't be able to finish on time. This conflict is intensified when Dad arrives home and interrupts with his own concerns. The fact that he won't listen to Emily only makes matters worse. When his coffee spills on her dress, she explodes, a reaction that reminds him of his deceased wife and that leads to the play's resolution. Dad apparently realizes that he has unfairly expected his fifteen-year-old daughter to fulfill the role of a wife, and the play ends with him beginning to rectify his parental errors.

It should be noted that the plays presented in this chapter all end happily. All three get their characters "back to shore" in good shape. You should not feel that your play must end in the same way. When you begin to explore the world of modern play writing, you will discover that some characters are badly bruised at play's end, and some may not make it back to shore at all.

Expanding Dramatic Possibilities: Three-Character Conflict, Twists and Turns, and Discovery or Reversal

The most unlikely tale can make a play, if it has
magnetism, forward motion, and something at stake;
we want to see how it comes out.

-DAVID COPELIN

I n Chapter 13, you learned to create lively characters through the use of dialogue and action, to establish conflict between two characters, and to use that conflict as the basis for a play. Building on this understanding, now we will examine slightly more complex dramatic situations.

The play you wrote in the previous chapter probably contains two characters and a two-character conflict—a direct confrontation that pits the goals or desires of one character against those of another. Plays that contain more than two characters often have three-character conflicts, allowing for a wider variety of dramatic possibilities. Knowing how to use this type of expanded conflict will give you increased flexibility and depth as a playwright.

In addition, the manner in which a play twists, turns, and is resolved merits study. In this chapter, we will return to the three-act structure presented in Chapter 13: Push your character into the river without a paddle, send him into the white water, and get him to shore. And when the curtain drops, some sort of discovery and/or reversal involving the main character—also called the protagonist—should have occurred.

In this chapter, you will write a play with three-character conflict, a twist and turn of some sort, and an ending with a discovery and/or reversal. First, however, read one such play. In *The Pitch*, by Norm Foster, two characters begin as allies with a common goal, but then they do an about-face concerning a third character. By the end of the play, a new alliance has been formed.

The Pitch

Norm Foster

CHARACTERS

GORDON: Gordon Blaine, a film producer.
FRANCINE: Francine Majors, Gordon's co-producer.
BOBBY: Bobby Holland, a successful Hollywood director.

SETTING

GORDON's office. The present.

> [GORDON *and* FRANCINE *are in his office.* GORDON *paces.* FRANCINE *sits on the couch.*]

GORDON: It's three forty-five. Who does he think he is, keeping us waiting like this?

FRANCINE: Now, Gordon, he's only fifteen minutes late.

GORDON: Who the hell does he think he is?

FRANCINE: He's new to the city. Maybe he got lost. We should've sent a car for him.

GORDON: No. No, that would make us look too anxious. Too accommodating.

FRANCINE: I think it would have been the courteous thing to do.

GORDON: No. He would've mistaken it for sucking up. I mean, he's probably got producers groveling at his feet constantly. I want us to be different. I want him to notice us.

FRANCINE: By being rude? I don't think we have to be rude.

GORDON: We're not being rude. We're just laying the ground rules. We're letting him know there's going to be no sucking up here.

> [*There is a knock on the office door.*]

Well, it's about bloody time. Are you ready?

> [FRANCINE *stands and moves to the center of the office.*]

FRANCINE: Yes. All set.

GORDON: Remember. No sucking up.

> [GORDON *opens the door.* BOBBY *stands there.*]

GORDON: Bobby Holland! Bobby! Bobby! Come in, please, come in.

BOBBY: Thank you.

[BOBBY *enters.*]

GORDON: So good to see you. So very nice. I'm Gordon Blaine, and this is my co-producer, Francine Majors.

[*They all shake hands.*]

FRANCINE: Hello.

BOBBY: Hi. Sorry I'm late. I got lost.

GORDON: You what?

BOBBY: I got lost.

GORDON: Oh, no.

FRANCINE: Ohhh.

GORDON: Are you serious?

BOBBY: Well, the cabbie wasn't sure where the place was, and then traffic was tied up because of a guy on a ledge down the street.

GORDON: A what?

BOBBY: Yeah, there's some nut on a ledge threatening to jump.

GORDON: This close to rush hour? Some people have no consideration.

BOBBY: Well, I'm here now anyway.

GORDON: I can't believe this. [*To* FRANCINE.] I knew we should've sent a car.

BOBBY: No, that's okay.

GORDON: No, you're new in town. [*To* FRANCINE.] We should've sent a car for the man.

FRANCINE: Well, we will know better next time.

GORDON: That's right. Live and learn. We're very sorry, Bobby. This is extremely embarrassing.

BOBBY: It's nothing, really.

GORDON: Can you forgive us?

BOBBY: It's nothing.

GORDON: I can't believe that.

BOBBY: Forget it.

GORDON: Well, have a seat, please. Make yourself comfortable.

BOBBY: Thank you.

[*He sits.*]

GORDON: [*To* FRANCINE.] Next time, we send a car. [*To* BOBBY.] Well, this is really a treat. I'm a very big fan. Very big. We both are, isn't that right, Frannie?

FRANCINE: Very big.

GORDON: Huge.

BOBBY: Well, thank you. You're very kind.

GORDON: Yes, what an honor. You know, I can't tell you how surprised I was when you called me last week and said you wanted to come up here and pitch a movie idea to us.

FRANCINE: He was beside himself.

GORDON: I was more than beside myself. I was *encircling* myself. I mean, Bobby Holland, the most successful director in Hollywood over the past fifteen years. The Wunderkind! Well, your very first movie, *Cold Steel,* grossed over twenty million, right?

BOBBY: Right.

GORDON: And then there was *Footsteps in the Alley,* about organized crime infiltrating professional bowling. God, I loved that one. And the casting was inspired. I mean, who knew that Sean Connery could bowl? And that one pulled in over, what, thirty million?

BOBBY: About that.

GORDON: And then *Cold Steel Two,* my God, that one did fifty mil', right?

BOBBY: I'm not sure really . . .

GORDON: Fifty mil'. And that was just the beginning. I haven't even mentioned your *Lambada* trilogy. That has to total over a hundred million by now, what with the video sales and all.

BOBBY: Well, I've been pretty lucky.

GORDON: Lucky, hell! You haven't had one flop. That's a remarkable record. That's why I couldn't believe it when you called. Not that we're not capable of producing good work, Frannie and me. We have produced some films we're very proud of, haven't we Frannie?

FRANCINE: Extremely proud.

GORDON: Extremely. And you know, right now we're very close to securing the movie rights to Margaux Kenyon's new book. Isn't that right, Fran?

FRANCINE: Very close.

BOBBY: [*Impressed.*] Margaux Kenyon?

GORDON: That's right. Got a big meeting with her agent on Monday. Disney's after it too, but I don't think it's Disney's style. Disney doesn't do sex very well. Dogs and cats traversing continents, they do great. Sex, I don't think so.

BOBBY: Well, I hope it works out for you.

GORDON: Thank you. So, we are making a name for ourselves. In fact, one of the local TV stations did a feature on us last month. What did they call us, Frannie?

FRANCINE: A couple of plucky producers.

GORDON: Plucky producers. It was a shlocky piece but it gets our name out there, right?

BOBBY: That's right. That's very important.

GORDON: So, tell me, Bobby, why come to Canada?

BOBBY: Well . . .

GORDON: I mean, a man of your immense talent must have producers in the States just begging to produce one of your movies?

BOBBY: Well, Gordon . . . Can I call you Gordon?

GORDON: Hey, call me whatever you like. Call me Ishmael, for godsake.

BOBBY: Well, the truth is, Gordon, I don't like what's happening down there right now. It seems that all they're worried about these days is how much money the film will make.

GORDON: The bastards. I hate that.

FRANCINE: That's such a shame.

BOBBY: You see, the problem is, they lack vision.

GORDON: Hey, we have got vision. Hell, Superman doesn't have as much vision.

BOBBY: Well, that's what I was hoping.

FRANCINE: Excuse me. I know this may be inappropriate to bring up at this point, Bobby, but the buzz around the industry is that . . . well, that you have run out of ideas.

GORDON: You're right. That's very inappropriate.

BOBBY: No, let her talk. Please. Go on, Francine.

FRANCINE: Well, I mean, you haven't made a movie in almost four years now, and I've asked around and, well, the talk is that the idea well has dried up. I'm sorry, but that's what I hear.

BOBBY: No, don't be sorry. I've heard the talk too. But no, that's not why I haven't made a movie in so long.

GORDON: Of course it's not.

BOBBY: I just haven't been able to find a producer that I have faith in.

GORDON: That's all it is.

BOBBY: It seems like nobody cares about the quality of the product anymore.

GORDON: It sickens me to hear that, Bobby. Sickens me. Why, you're a giant in the industry. You should be given *carte blanche* to make whatever kind of movie you want. Quality or not.

BOBBY: Well, I appreciate that, Gordon.

GORDON: Well, it's true.

FRANCINE: So, the idea well isn't dry?

GORDON: Francine, please . . .

BOBBY: It's okay, Gordon. Francine has every right to ask these questions. I mean, if all goes well, you two are going to be sinking a lot of money into this project. And I won't lie to you. I don't make cheap movies.

GORDON: And we don't want you to.

FRANCINE: Well, we do have budgets we have to adhere to, Gordon. We don't want to start throwing money into a bottomless pit.

[*Beat, as* GORDON *stares at* FRANCINE.]

GORDON: Uh, excuse us, Bobby.

[*He stands and moves away.*]

Francine? [*Motioning for her to join him.*] A moment? Thank you.

[FRANCINE *moves to* GORDON.]

What are you doing?

FRANCINE: What?

GORDON: What are you doing?

FRANCINE: Nothing.

GORDON: Are you trying to blow this for us?

FRANCINE: I'm voicing legitimate concerns.

GORDON: Legitimate concerns?

FRANCINE: Well, we don't want to lose money do we?

GORDON: This is Bobby Holland for godsake! He could make *Hamlet* starring Don Knotts and we'd make money. Now please?! Let's try and be a little less strident, shall we, and a little more accommodating.

FRANCINE: What happened to not sucking up?

GORDON: What happened to not being rude?

FRANCINE: What happened to being different?

GORDON: What happened to being courteous?

FRANCINE: Fine.

GORDON: Are we on the same page now?

FRANCINE: Whatever you say.

GORDON: We're on the same page?

FRANCINE: Same page.

GORDON: Thank you. Bottomless pit.

[*They move back to* BOBBY *and sit.*]

Sorry, Bobby. A little producers' *tête-à-tête,* that's all. Now, tell us about this movie you want to make.

BOBBY: Well, Gordon, Francine, it's something I'm very excited about. Very excited. Mind you, it's not *Death of a Salesman*.

GORDON: What is?

BOBBY: But it has substance, and it has meaning, and I think I can get Charlie Sheen.

GORDON: Charlie Sheen?

BOBBY: Charlie Sheen.

GORDON: Get out of here.

BOBBY: He owes me one.

GORDON: Charlie Sheen? Did you hear that, Frannie?

BOBBY: And if not Charlie then one of the Baldwins for sure.

GORDON: The Baldwins. Oh, they're very hot. Very hot. Which one?

BOBBY: Alec, maybe.

GORDON: Oooh, Alec.

BOBBY: Maybe Billy.

GORDON: Billy is good.

BOBBY: Daniel for sure.

GORDON: Who cares? They all look the same anyway. We will get Daniel. We will bill him as Alec.

BOBBY: All right, here it is. Let's start from the opening shot.

GORDON: Opening shot.

BOBBY: It's an aerial view of nothing but trees.

GORDON: Trees. Environment. Good.

BOBBY: Now, as we fly over these trees we see smoke coming from what appears to be wreckage down below.

GORDON: Oh-oh.

BOBBY: So, we move in closer, zooming in through the billowing smoke, zooming, zooming, smoke flying past, wondering what we're going to find, wondering, zooming, wondering, zooming, and then suddenly we see it! It's the wreckage of a small plane. Bang! Opening credits.

GORDON: Whew! I might need a minute to catch my breath.

BOBBY: Now, there is only one survivor of the plane crash, and it's a small boy, about one-, maybe two-years-old. His parents both have perished, we find out, when we see their wedding picture smoldering in the ruins.

GORDON: How do we know they're dead from the picture?

BOBBY: Through symbolism. The picture bursts into flames.

GORDON: Oh, like that map at the beginning of "Bonanza."

BOBBY: Right. Now, the child is all alone, and as it turns out, the plane has crashed on an escarpment in the jungles of Africa.

GORDON: Oh, my god.

FRANCINE: An escarpment?

BOBBY: That's right.

FRANCINE: In Africa?

BOBBY: Yes. And there isn't a human being within a hundred-mile radius.

GORDON: Well, how does the kid survive?

BOBBY: Well, now, this is where it takes a crazy kind of a turn.

GORDON: A twist. I like it. Twists are very big these days.

BOBBY: Now, you're going to have to be very open-minded here. Can you do that?

GORDON: I'm open.

BOBBY: You're open?

GORDON: Twenty-four hours. I never close.

BOBBY: All right. Here it is. [*Beat.*] The boy is raised by apes.

GORDON: Apes?

BOBBY: Apes.

GORDON: Apes. Okay, okay, I can see that. The apes treat him like one of their own.

BOBBY: Exactly.

GORDON: I can see that.

FRANCINE: Excuse me, but isn't that like—

GORDON: Francine, please. Let him finish. Go on, Bobby. Go on.

BOBBY: Okay, so this boy is raised by this colony of apes and he grows up there in the jungle not even knowing that an outside world exists.

GORDON: Does he have a name? What do we call this kid?

BOBBY: Oh, he's got a name, sure. Trevor.

FRANCINE: Trevor?

BOBBY: Trevor.

GORDON: Well, how does he get Trevor? Is that his real name?

BOBBY: No, of course not. How would the apes know his real name? He was too young to tell them, right?

GORDON: Oh, right. So, how does he get Trevor?

BOBBY: Well, that's the irony, you see. Trevor is actually his father's name, and the apes find his father's passport in the wreckage and they think it's the kid's.

GORDON: [*Beat.*] So they get the name Trevor off the father's passport?

BOBBY: Right.

GORDON: Oh.

FRANCINE: Now, wait a minute—

BOBBY: No, please, I don't want to lose my train of thought.

GORDON: Please, Francine, let the man talk.

BOBBY: So, Trevor grows up among the apes and pretty soon because of his ability to reason, he becomes kind of the lord of the jungle. The master, if you will, of all of the animals. And he communicates to them through a series of sounds. Not words really, but just sounds that he makes up.

GORDON: Okay, okay, now here's where I start to get worried because—and I don't want to be a naysayer, Bobby, believe me. That's the last thing I wanna be, but this is starting to sound a little derivative in parts.

BOBBY: Derivative how?

GORDON: Well, it's starting to sound a little bit like that Rex Harrison *Doctor Dolittle* thing. You know, talking to the animals.

BOBBY: No, not at all.

GORDON: You don't think so?

BOBBY: No, those animals weren't real animals. Dolittle was talking to two-headed llamas. Trevor talks to real animals. Lions, elephants.

GORDON: Okay.

BOBBY: This is real. Very real.

GORDON: Absolutely. Just playing devil's advocate. Please, go on.

FRANCINE: Gordon? Doesn't this sound like—

GORDON: Francine, the man is speaking. Please.

BOBBY: Okay. Now, Trevor becomes a true friend to these jungle animals, you know, helping them out of quicksand, giving them a boost up to eat from the higher branches, but he develops a closer, more special relationship with one animal in particular.

FRANCINE: Let me guess. A chimpanzee.

BOBBY: No, it's not a chimpanzee.

GORDON: Of course, it's not a chimpanzee. What kind of an idea is that? It's been done to death. Don't you remember Zippy? Huh? Zippy the chimp? It's old.

FRANCINE: Gordon, can't you see—

GORDON: Francine, would you let the man get a word in edgewise? I want to hear who this animal friend is. Bobby, who is it?

BOBBY: It's an orangutan.

GORDON: You're kidding me?

BOBBY: No, it's an orangutan.

GORDON: Of course. Why didn't I think of that? It's brilliant.

BOBBY: Okay, now we come to the love interest.

GORDON: That's not an orangutan, too, I hope?

BOBBY: No.

GORDON: Good, because Canadian film-goers are cool to that sort of thing. I don't know what it is. Maybe we're not worldly, I don't know.

BOBBY: Well, no, it's not an orangutan.

GORDON: Good.

BOBBY: It's an anthropologist named Jean who crash lands on the escarpment.

FRANCINE: Okay, that's it.

BOBBY: What?

FRANCINE: That's it.

BOBBY: Is there a problem, Francine?

FRANCINE: I'll say there's a problem. There's a big problem.

GORDON: Actually, Bobby, I'm afraid I have to side with Francine on this one.

FRANCINE: Well, it's about time.

GORDON: I mean, two plane crashes on the same escarpment? That's just too much of a coincidence for me.

BOBBY: Well, Gordon, we are talking about a twenty-year gap between the first one and the second one.

GORDON: A twenty-year gap?

BOBBY: Twenty years.

GORDON: Oh!

BOBBY: You didn't think they happened one after the other?

GORDON: [*Laughing.*] I don't know what I was thinking. So, there's a gap then?

BOBBY: Twenty years.

GORDON: Oh, well, that's fine. No, that's fine.

BOBBY: Good.

GORDON: I didn't know there was a gap.

BOBBY: Well, there is.

GORDON: Well, that's fine then. Yes.

FRANCINE: Gordon?

GORDON: What?

FRANCINE: Is that your only complaint?

GORDON: Uh . . . well, I am wondering where we will film it, with all those trees, but maybe the interior of B.C. . . . . [*To* BOBBY.] Does Charlie Sheen travel well?

FRANCINE: Gordon?

GORDON: What?

FRANCINE: Haven't you noticed?

GORDON: Noticed what?

FRANCINE: The story. It's *Tarzan*.

GORDON: It's what?

FRANCINE: It's *Tarzan*. The Ape Man.

GORDON: *Tarzan?*

FRANCINE: Yes, the escarpment. The jungle. The apes. It's *Tarzan*.

GORDON: Frannie, his name is Trevor. How can it be *Tarzan* when his name is Trevor?

FRANCINE: It's the same story! It's *Tarzan!*

BOBBY: Actually, Francine, this story has nothing to do with the jungle.

FRANCINE: But, you just said it was set in the jungle.

BOBBY: Yes, but you see, the jungle is merely a metaphor for North America's decaying inner cities, and the young boy represents inner city youth and the insurmountable odds they face as they struggle to survive in a modern cesspool.

GORDON: And the orangutan?

BOBBY: Is hope.

GORDON: [*To* FRANCINE.]: There, you see? Now, does that sound like *Tarzan* to you?

FRANCINE: But, it is *Tarzan*.

GORDON: Francine?

FRANCINE: It is!

GORDON: Francine, please! This is Bobby Holland. Bobby Holland does not steal other people's ideas. He's an American film-making genius. He's gifted. I'm sorry you have to hear this, Bobby.

BOBBY: Quite all right, Gordon.

GORDON: [*To* FRANCINE.] And to imply even for a moment that he would rip off somebody else's story, especially something as timeworn as *Tarzan*, well, that's more than I can abide.

FRANCINE: But it is *Tarzan*. Tarzan and Jane? Trevor and Jean?

GORDON: Bobby, I'm sorry, but would you give us a moment please?

BOBBY: Hmmm?

GORDON: Could you step out of the office for just a moment?

BOBBY: Oh, certainly. Yes.

[*He stands and moves to the office door.*]

GORDON: I'm really sorry, but I think Francine and I should talk.

BOBBY: No problem.

GORDON: Please forgive us.

BOBBY: I understand completely. Take all the time you need.

GORDON: Thank you. Thank you very much. Help yourself to some coffee out there. It's Amaretto Almond.

   [BOBBY *exits and closes the door*.]

FRANCINE: Gordon, what is wrong with you? You know bloody well that story is *Tarzan*.

GORDON: I don't know anything of the sort.

FRANCINE: Gordon . . .

GORDON: Look Francine, I don't have many shots left, all right?

FRANCINE: But, come on, you can't . . .

GORDON: No. Now, I've always wanted to be a success in this industry. Always wanted to have my name attached to a hit movie. Just one. From the first time I saw Gary Cooper up on that screen, that's all I've wanted to do: make movies. Movies that millions of people would come to see. Well, Bobby Holland may be the only chance I have to see that dream come true.

FRANCINE: But, Gordon, it's *Tarzan*.

GORDON: No. No, I don't wanna hear that it's *Tarzan* or anything else. I don't wanna hear that. All I care about is that it's Bobby Holland. That's all I need to know.

FRANCINE: Well, fine, but I can't go along with you on this one.

GORDON: I'd like to have you there, Francine. I mean, we're partners. Are we still partners?

FRANCINE: Not on this project, Gordon. I'm afraid I can't.

GORDON: What about our meeting with that agent on Monday?

FRANCINE: I'll be there for that, but, I wish you'd reconsider about this one.

GORDON: I'm sorry, Francine. I can't. [*He opens the door and calls*.] Bobby? Please?

   [BOBBY *enters the room again*.]

Bobby, I'm afraid Francine's decided not to join us on this particular project.

BOBBY: Oh, I'm sorry to hear that.

GORDON: Well, she has other things that are going to be occupying her time—the Margaux Kenyon project, in particular—and we don't want her attentions divided, as it were.

BOBBY: Completely understandable.

FRANCINE: Before I leave though, I do have one question, Bobby. How do the apes get the name Trevor from the passport?

BOBBY: Well, that's obvious, isn't it?

FRANCINE: How?

BOBBY: Do you have a passport?

FRANCINE: Yes.

BOBBY: Does it have your name on it?

FRANCINE: Yes.

BOBBY: Well?

    [FRANCINE *looks at* GORDON.]

GORDON: Makes sense to me.

    [FRANCINE *exits.*]

I'm very sorry, Bobby.

BOBBY: No problem.

GORDON: She's usually so open to new ideas.

BOBBY: People change, Gordon. It's the business.

GORDON: It's a damn shame.

BOBBY: It's sad.

GORDON: Now, please go on with the story.

BOBBY: All right. Did I mention the swinging on the vines?

GORDON: I don't think so.

BOBBY: Well, Trevor swings on these jungle vines.

GORDON: Oh, that's marvelous. That is marvelous. Of course we'd use a stunt double for Charlie.

BOBBY: I think we might have to, yes.

GORDON: Marvelous. Tell me more.

    [*They fade out. Lights down. The end.*]

Questions

1. What do Gordon and Francine initially agree to do but quickly part ways on when Bobby Holland arrives? How does this introduce three-party conflict into the play?

2. What does the play's title suggest about its meaning? Which characters are giving a pitch? How does this affect the conflict?

3. What twists and turns does this play take? How do these twists and turns correspond to the three-act structure discussed in Chapter 13?

4. What makes the play's ending a reversal? Is a discovery also involved?

Exploring Three-Character Conflict

As noted in Chapter 13, the action or plot of a play hinges on conflict, expressed as a person opposing another person or persons, opposing nature, opposing society, or even opposing herself. Although drama uses all four types of conflict, and sometimes combinations of several, the first type—conflict between people—is the most common. As long as a play has two or more characters, conflict between or among characters can occur.

Conflict between or among characters is typically two-character or three-character in nature. If one character is pitted against another, there's a direct, one-on-one interaction between the two of them. One character wants something; the other character opposes it—who's going to prevail? It's that simple. Three-character-conflict is more complicated, however, offering opportunities for shifting interactions and realignments among characters that two-character conflict cannot provide.

Drama mirrors life and mimics the patterns of interaction and communication that occur in real-life conflicts and confrontations. Real-life two-character conflicts occur daily. Little Sister wants to borrow Big Sister's sweater and Big Sister says no; a fight erupts. Husband wants to relocate to another state and Wife doesn't want to go; a great debate begins. Unless Little Sister and Big Sister or Husband and Wife bring another person or people into the fray, the conflict in such situations is limited to two characters. But sometimes other people get caught in the crossfire of such situations, and three-character conflict occurs. Little Sister brings Mom into the picture. Mom disciplines both girls for fighting. Big Sister and Little Sister side together against Mom. A new fight erupts. Wife asks Husband's Mother to talk him into staying. He says no; Husband's Mother sides with Wife. Wife moves in with Husband's Mother! Such real-life situations—simple situations with dramatic possibilities—give playwrights ideas to build on. As with the writing of poetry and fiction, many of the best ideas for plays come from real life.

In both real-life and dramatic three-character conflicts, relationships change as conflicts play themselves out. Suppose that two characters differ in their opinions of a third character, or that two characters compete for the attentions of a third character. In both scenarios, the relationship between the first two characters will change. Maybe Mom disapproves of Son's Girlfriend, but she doesn't want to drive him away. Or, perhaps Manager is upset with Lazy Clerk, but Lazy Clerk is friends with Company President. What might happen to these characters, and what would be the effect on their relationships in a play? It's the playwright's job to explore these questions. Of course, the examples given here are just a few scenarios that yield third-party conflict; many other possibilities exist. Inherent in all of them are opportunities for escalating conflict and for realigned relationships among characters.

In *The Pitch*, three-character conflict results in a humorous interchange between a film producer, his co-producer, and the Hollywood director who is pitching a "new" script to them. Remember how conflict can be illustrated with the three-act structure? Let's apply it to *The Pitch* to see how the three-character conflict plays out.

- *Push your character into the river without a paddle.* During the opening lines of the play, while Gordon and Francine are waiting for Bobby to arrive, Francine suggests that they should have sent a car for him. Gordon strongly opposes her on this because he wants no groveling, and Francine seems willing to support him on this. "Are you ready?" Gordon asks her before letting Bobby in. "Yes. All set," Francine replies. They are united to begin with; they are of one mind. But as soon as Bobby enters their office, Gordon begins doing exactly what he admonished Francine not to do—groveling at Bobby's feet. And when Francine voices some "legitimate concerns," like why Bobby hasn't done a movie in almost four years, Gordon objects, beginning to side with Bobby rather than his partner. A change in alliances has begun.

- *Send him into the white water.* Gordon continues to grovel, and Francine continues to be skeptical—especially when Bobby pitches a movie about a plane crash on an escarpment in the jungle that leaves one survivor, a small boy. The boy, Trevor, is raised by apes, later befriends an orangutan, and falls in love with Jean, an anthropologist whose plane also crashes on the escarpment. Francine sees the distinct similarities between Bobby's pitch and the movie *Tarzan;* Gordon doesn't. The two argue, with Gordon incensed that Francine would accuse Bobby of stealing someone else's story. There is a definite division between Gordon and Francine—and it's about to get even more definitive.

- *Get him to shore.* When Francine calls Gordon on the *Tarzan* issue, he admits that he wants his name associated with Bobby Holland and that he doesn't care what the movie is about. "All I care about is that it's Bobby Holland," he says. "That's all I need to know." That's his discovery. And that's all Francine needs to hear: She tells Gordon that she won't be his partner on this project. By the play's end, Francine has departed and Gordon has bought Bobby's pitch. The change in alliances is complete; a reversal has occurred.

This play is an example of a three-character conflict that has two characters with different opinions of a third character. By the end of the play, the relationships of the three characters have been realigned, a clue that this play contains three-character conflict.

Experimenting with Three-Character Conflict

Not surprisingly, the first requirement for a play with three-character conflict is to have at least three characters. Although you could have three-character conflict with more than three characters in the script, we will be focusing here on three-character conflict plays with three characters. To begin with, it is easier to write. The more characters you put on the stage, the harder is your work as a playwright. Further, these characters should have something in common and be in a specific place related to that commonality. They could work together or in conjunction with each other, like the characters in *The Pitch*, and thus occupy the same work environment. Or, they could play on the same team, like our writer's example, and thus share a sports environment.

Building Character

Novice playwrights should avoid "cloning"—creating characters who sound and act alike. Instead, they should develop characters with definite differences—characters who think, talk, and act from distinctive viewpoints and backgrounds.

Some playwrights do character sketches on new characters before writing, describing their family background, personal appearance, personal characteristics, psychological makeup, and motivation. Other playwrights use body-type or personality-type profiles to help develop their characters.

Here's a fun way to create characters with different personality traits, moods, and motives. From the following chart, choose two types from each of the four groups:

Type 1
Follows the rules
Follows others
Self-conscious
Reserved
Tries not to attract attention

Type 2
Argumentative
Opinionated
Extroverted
Feisty
Selective about his/her friends
Dislikes schedules

continued on page 340

---

continued from page 339

Type 3
Peacemaker
Even-keeled
Likable
Reliable
Generous to a fault
Dislikes changes

Type 4
Creative
High-energy
Craves attention
Helpful to others
Thrives on change

Now create character sketches for both a protagonist (main character) and an antagonist (opposing character), giving one of the traits from each category to each character. Try to make these characters different in nature but equal in strength. This will make the conflict between them more interesting. Or try the opposite: Create two characters who have similar natures but differing strengths and see what happens.

Playwrights look to everyday circumstances such as these for inspiration when writing plays with three-character conflict. Remembering that drama mirrors life, ask yourself what types of three-character conflicts might be good material for a short play. In what type of situation might you move two characters away from each other in some way while moving one of them toward a third character?

Begin by recording a conversation between two characters. Later, you will be asked to add a third character.

Writer's Practice 14.1   *Record a Conversation*

In Chapter 13, you recorded conversations between two people as an early step in writing a scene. You will be doing the same thing here; however, in this short conversation, your first character and second character will be discussing a third character to whom something has happened or will happen. The conversation doesn't need to be long. In fact, the only requirement is that you stop recording when you arrive at a line that really interests you.

The recording should take you no more than ten minutes. If you have trouble getting started, think back to a real-life conversation you overheard that resulted in a three-character conflict. At this point, however, write dialogue for only two of the three characters.

Begin recording if you feel you are ready, or examine our writer's model and explication.

Our Writer

TOM: What happened? What's wrong with Coach Gerke?

BRANDON: The football hit him in the head.

TOM: Is he okay?

BRANDON: I don't know. Help me help him sit down. Are you okay, Coach?

TOM: I don't think he's okay. Coach Gerke? Can you hear me?

BRANDON: Maybe he's got a head injury. Maybe he can't understand you.

TOM: He's always had a head injury. And he's never understood me.

The dialogue here is merely a start that our writer can work from. Your recorded conversation may be shorter, or it may be longer. Our writer stopped when she arrived at something that interested her: Tom's comment that Coach Gerke never understood him. Even if this line never makes it into the play, our writer now has an idea from which to begin.

Writer's Practice 14.2   *Construct a Scene*

Sometimes the dialogue that a playwright writes first serves to "inform" his play; it may provide background information or a line to jump-start the play. In Chapter 10, you learned that short stories sometimes begin *in media res*, or in the midst of things. Plays almost always begin this way. So feel free to begin your play before or after the conversation that you recorded in Writer's Practice 14.1 occurred. Think about the interesting comment or statement that caused you to stop your recording where you did. This idea may be what your play will be about. In this assignment, you will write a scene prompted by the conversation you began recording in Writer's Practice 14.1. Note that the term *scene* is used informally here. Short plays such as the one you're writing don't have the multiple scenes found within acts in full-length plays. However, the term is useful for describing a section in a short play.

You may decide to include most of the conversation from Writer's Practice 14.1, or you may choose to include very little or even none of it. To begin, list your three characters: the two who were having the conversation in Writer's Practice 14.1 and the one about whom they were talking. Then, create a scene in which the conversation is happening: a work, school, or sports environment, perhaps. Begin by describing what's happening at rise—when the curtain comes up. As you write the scene, add stage directions, showing the three characters in action. While writing, keep the following guidelines in mind:

- In the opening lines, two characters should be working together or have a common problem or goal.
- A third character should enter shortly thereafter amidst some confusion.
- Following the third character's entrance, the first two characters should begin to disagree about something that concerns the third character.
- All three characters should have clearly defined personalities, indicated by their dialogue, actions, and interactions.

Write at least two pages of dialogue and corresponding stage directions involving these three characters. As you did in Writer's Practice 13.4, write your draft using the preferred format for playscripts.

Begin writing if you feel you are ready, or examine our writer's model and explication. The situation in this scene involves a football coach and two of his players. The coach just got hit in the head with the football and is dazed.

Our Writer

CHARACTERS

Tom, second-string quarterback, a junior
Brandon, All-State quarterback, a senior
Coach Gerke, Lancaster High's football coach
Voice of audience

SETTING: *A bench beside the Lancaster High football field, homecoming game. The Lancaster Lancers are behind at the end of the second quarter. On the last play, Coach Gerke gets hit in the head by the football.*

AT RISE: *Two young men and an older man ENTER from stage left and walk toward the bench. A water jug and a stack of towels sit at the end of it.*

COACH GERKE

(Sits.)

Sacked again!

BRANDON
(Removes his helmet.)

Sacked? I wasn't sacked.

COACH GERKE

Who am I?

BRANDON

Maybe he's got a head injury.

TOM

He's always had a head injury.

BRANDON

Think he's gonna be all right?

TOM

Ten minutes and some water, he'll be fine.

COACH GERKE
(Rubs his head.)

Who am I?

TOM

Joe Montana.

(BRANDON pours COACH GERKE a glass of water and hands it to him.)

COACH GERKE
(Sips the water.)

Joe who?

BRANDON

Think we should call EMS?

TOM

Give him nine more minutes. And more water.

(BRANDON refills COACH GERKE'S glass.)

COACH GERKE
(Points at BRANDON.)

Who's he?

TOM

Number one on every Big Ten coach's wish list; Lancaster High's ticket to the state championships. The Big Cheese.

BRANDON

Knock it off, Tom. I'm Brandon. Your quarterback.

COACH GERKE
(To Tom.)

Who are you?

> **TOM**
>
> Terry Bradshaw.
>
> **BRANDON**
>
> It's not funny. Something's wrong with his head.
>
> **TOM**
> (Watches the game going on at stage left.)
>
> No kidding.
>
> **COACH GERKE**
> (To TOM)
>
> Who'd you say he was?
>
> **TOM**
> (Whispers.)
>
> A cheerleader.
>
> **BRANDON**
> (Wets a towel and wipes COACH GERKE'S brow with it.)
>
> I said knock it off. Do you know where you are? What day it is?
>
> **COACH GERKE**
>
> Halftime?
>
> **BRANDON**
>
> That's it. I'm calling EMS.
>
> (BRANDON EXITS stage right.)

Although Tom and Brandon seem to be working together at the beginning of the play, the dialogue illustrates the competitive tension between them. It is clear that Brandon is the starting quarterback and Tom is the substitute. But, because of Coach Gerke's head injury, the "playing field" between the boys has suddenly been leveled. In other words, after his head injury, Coach Gerke regards Tom and Brandon as equally capable. The relationship between Tom and Brandon soon breaks down, however, as evidenced by their dialogue. This change in relationship among the characters is a central ingredient in the play's three-character conflict.

Exploring Twists and Turns

After you push your character into the river without a paddle (introduction of conflict), you send her into the white water, where the going gets even more treacherous (turning point and rising action). To do this, you need some type of twist that propels her forward, right toward the white water. Note that the character may or may not know that she has experienced this twist.

In *The Pitch*, for instance, it's not the fact that Gordon tells Francine not to grovel and then instantly begins groveling himself that causes the conflict to intensify between them. Rather, it's Gordon's obsession with being associated with Bobby, with being rich and famous. In his own words, it's that, in Gordon's opinion, Bobby "could make *Hamlet* starring Don Knotts and we'd make money." Gordon's folly is that he is dazzled by Bobby's reputation.

Near the end of the three-act structure's "second act," after a playwright sends the character into the white water, a change of some kind often occurs. This rising action—where the conflict is intensified—sets up the action that is to come. What will happen next? Will Gordon succumb to his folly? Will Francine be able to save him? Such twists and turns make plays interesting because the twists and turns prompt the action. Surprisingly, plays that don't have twists and turns of some kind can be harder to write. In making the twists happen, the writer explores a development as he works his way toward discovery. Twists and turns intensify the conflict, and conflict is the essence of drama.

Experimenting with Twists and Turns

By now, you should have three characters, two of whom are beginning to differ in their assessment of a third character. Unless there's a specific reason to make them similar, the dialogue and actions of the character should mark each as unique. Although you can't show your characters' thoughts in a play, you can reveal a great deal about their thinking through what they say and do. Knowing what you know about your characters thus far, how might they respond to a twist or turn? What might they say or do to each other?

In Writer's Practice 14.2, you wrote an introductory "scene" that introduced the conflict through confusion or a disagreement. Now you will add to the conflict. Throw your character into the white water and see how he reacts. You may prefer to first record the conversation, as you did in Writer's Practice 14.1, and then expand it into a scene with stage directions. On the other hand, you may want to simply incorporate the stage directions as you write.

Writer's Practice 14.3   *Change a Character's Behavior Using a Twist or Turn*

Write a scene in which something a bit bizarre happens that intensifies the conflict between at least two of your characters. As you write, keep the following guidelines in mind:

- One of your characters may have a limited role in this scene, or even be offstage, but the relationship previously established between this character and the others should continue to be influential.

- As the scene progresses, the behavior of one of the characters should change in some way.
- The dialogue and action between the characters should support this change.

Keep in mind that when one character's back is turned, one or both of your other characters may act differently. Again, drama mirrors life: think about how Little Sister and Big Sister act differently when Mother is absent.

Begin writing if you feel you are ready, or examine our writer's model and explication. Aim to write two to three more pages of dialogue.

Our Writer

COACH GERKE

What am I doing here?

TOM

Waiting.

COACH GERKE

For what?

TOM

To get in the game.

COACH GERKE
(Stands up and fakes a throw.)

Come on, coach. Let me at 'em.

TOM

Sit down. You're not going anywhere.

COACH GERKE

Why?

(The audience boos.)
TOM

Because I don't like you.

COACH GERKE
(Watches the game.)

You don't like me?

TOM

I don't like your attitude.

COACH GERKE

My attitude? What's wrong with my attitude?

TOM

You're pushy. And you talk back.

> **COACH GERKE**
> (Shakes his head, as if to clear it.)

What did you say? Stop rambling—I'm confused. Which team's ours?

> **TOM**

The Lancers. Gold and black.

> **COACH GERKE**

The Lancers? That's a stupid name.

> (The audience boos again.)

> **TOM**

Touchdown! We're getting slaughtered.

> **COACH GERKE**
> (Looks closer.)

Those uniforms make me want to puke.

> **TOM**

This game makes me want to puke.

> (BRANDON ENTERS from stage right.)

> **BRANDON**

EMS is on the way.

> (Scans stage left.)

I gotta get out there.

> (BRANDON EXITS stage left, helmet in hand.)

> **COACH GERKE**
> (Rises and turns toward TOM.)

What about me? Come on. Give me a chance. One chance.

> (TOM ignores him. The audience boos.)

> **TOM**

He got sacked. Brandon got sacked.

> **COACH GERKE**
> (Grabs TOM'S helmet and holds it under his arm.)

The quarterback's not getting up. The quarterback's hurt!

Here, the focus moves from the two quarterbacks, Brandon and Tom, to Tom and Coach Gerke. Having been hit in the head with the football, the coach thinks that he is the second-string quarterback and that Tom is the Lancers' coach. Tom exploits this twist, taking out his frustrations on Coach Gerke, whose confusion continues. He's definitely in the white water! After the opposing team gets a touchdown, Brandon returns and re-enters the game. Almost immediately, however, Brandon gets injured—a turn that neither Tom nor Coach Gerke expected. Where will the action take us next?

Exploring a Discovery or Reversal

Let's briefly return to the three-act structure discussed earlier. The playwright has left a character in the white water without a paddle. The audience is wondering what will be the outcome. Given this, it's now time for the playwright to resolve the conflict by writing the resolution and the final action.

In most plays, the resolution brings change. Audiences expect some type of change at the end of a play, preceding the fall of the curtain. Plays typically end with a discovery and/or a reversal. Either one causes a character to change, and the state of things to change as a result. In plays with three-character conflict, this state of things that undergoes a change usually concerns the balance of relationships. For example, in *The Pitch*, the relationships between Gordon and Francine and Gordon and Bobby change.

In *The Pitch*, Gordon discovers that he cares about the chance to work with Bobby Holland more than he cares about working with Francine. This is a direct reversal from the beginning of the play, where Gordon and Francine were partners. By the play's end, Bobby is in and Francine is out.

Notice how the dialogue exchanges in the following excerpt from the end of *The Pitch* support this discovery and reversal:

FRANCINE: Gordon, what is wrong with you? You know bloody well that story is *Tarzan*.

GORDON: I don't know anything of the sort.

> [Gordon denies Francine's allegations.]

FRANCINE: Gordon . . .

GORDON: Look Francine, I don't have many shots left, all right?

> [Gordon addresses his own concerns.]

FRANCINE: But, come on, you can't . . .

GORDON: No. Now, I've always wanted to be a success in this industry. Always wanted to have my name attached to a hit movie. Just one. From the first time I saw Gary Cooper up on that screen, that's all I've wanted to do: make movies. Movies that millions of people would come to see. Well, Bobby Holland may be the only chance I have to see that dream come true.

> [Gordon hits upon what he really wants: To have his name attached to a hit movie, something he associates with Bobby Holland.]

FRANCINE: But, Gordon, it's *Tarzan*.

GORDON: No. No, I don't wanna hear that it's *Tarzan* or anything else. I don't wanna hear that. All I care about is that it's Bobby Holland. That's all I need to know.

> [Gordon shuts Francine out again. Bobby is all that matters.]

FRANCINE: Well, fine, but I can't go along with you on this one.

GORDON: I'd like to have you there, Francine. I mean, we're partners. Are we still partners?

FRANCINE: Not on this project, Gordon. I'm afraid I can't.

GORDON: What about our meeting with that agent on Monday?

FRANCINE: I'll be there for that, but, I wish you'd reconsider about this one.

GORDON: I'm sorry, Francine. I can't. (*He opens the door and calls.*) Bobby? Please?

(BOBBY *enters the room again.*)

Bobby, I'm afraid Francine's decided not to join us on this particular project.

> [When asked to reconsider working with Bobby on the *Tarzan* derivative, Gordon refuses. He opens the door and calls for Bobby, knowing that Francine will soon be gone.]

As the bracketed comments show, the dialogue moves Gordon and Francine forward, toward their inevitable parting of ways. In effect, the play has come full circle, with Gordon waiting for Bobby to re-enter the room.

Experimenting with a Discovery or Reversal

To conclude your short play with three-character conflict, you will want to have your main character reach some sort of discovery concerning one of the other characters. This discovery may surprise the main character as much as it surprises the other character; although the main character may have felt this way all along, he may not have been able or ready to admit it, however. It may also lead to a reversal—a drastic change from the beginning of the play.

Writer's Practice 14.4 *End Your Play Using a Discovery or Reversal*

As you write a final scene in which some type of discovery or reversal occurs, consider the following:

- Your main character should make a revelation suggestive of the final action.
- The dialogue between characters should be suggestive of the final action.
- If your play has a reversal, it may do a loop at the end—almost as if a new play is about to begin.

As with fiction, most contemporary plays don't end too neatly. Real life isn't like that, and remember, drama mimics life. Endings that are too pat or too unbelievable typically are not satisfying. Endings that make the audience think, question, and wonder are stronger and more enduring. Perhaps you can recall a play or screenplay that you saw and couldn't stop thinking about afterward. Indeed, such memorable endings are rare.

Bring your play to a close now by writing two to three pages of dialogue and action. You may already have a discovery and/or a reversal in mind.

Begin writing if you feel you are ready, or examine our writer's model and explication.

Our Writer

(BRANDON ENTERS from stage left, limps back toward the bench, and removes his helmet.)

BRANDON
(Holds his head.)

Go on. Get out there, Tom.

TOM
(Grabs BRANDON'S helmet, puts it on, and EXITS stage left.)

What luck! Man.

BRANDON

Shut up!

COACH GERKE
(Follows after TOM.)

Why him? What about me?

BRANDON
(Goes after him.)

Sit down! You're injured! And so am I.

COACH GERKE
(Paces.)

I'm sick of sitting.

BRANDON
(Leads him back to the bench and makes him sit.)

Sit still!

(COACH GERKE and BRANDON look to stage left. When
the audience cheers, COACH GERKE stands again.)

COACH GERKE

First down!

BRANDON
(Head in his hands.)

I don't believe it.

COACH GERKE

That guy wearing 12—Bradshaw's number—who's he? Where'd he come from?

BRANDON

Tom Banks. Junior Varsity.

(The audience cheers again.)

COACH GERKE

Another first down! Yes!

BRANDON

I don't believe it.

COACH GERKE
(Moves toward stage left.)

Throw the ball . . . throw the ball. Touchdown! Halftime!

(Returns to the bench, pours two glasses of water, and
grabs a towel.)

Where'd all the water go? Brandon, why are you just sitting there?

(TOM ENTERS from stage left and removes BRANDON'S
helmet.)

COACH GERKE

Way to go, Tom! I knew you could do it.

BRANDON

EMS is here. Do what you want to do. I'm getting my head checked.

(As BRANDON exits stage right, COACH GERKE hands
TOM a glass of water.)

TOM
(Sips the water.)

You knew I could do it?

COACH GERKE
(Pats TOM on the back.)

Sure, Tom. I was just like you as a kid. Just like you.

TOM

But you were the starting quarterback.

COACH GERKE

Not at the start. I had to work my behind off for that. Come on, let me tell you about it. . . .

(COACH GERKE and TOM EXIT stage right together.)

(CURTAIN.)

By the end of the play, the relationship between Coach Gerke and his two quarterbacks has shifted. Brandon exits to get his head checked, and Tom's relationship with the coach has improved dramatically.

 ## Writer Response Groups

At this point, you should have three parts of a play that form a rough draft, perhaps six or seven pages long. Don't worry if your play isn't as smooth yet as you would like it to be. After discussion in your response group, you may even decide to write a new beginning or a new ending for your draft.

As you did in Chapter 13, assign parts for the various characters, and have one response group member read the stage directions. Read and discuss each group member's play for the following elements:

Essential Elements

- Who are the characters in the play?
- What is the conflict?
- What is the play about?

Craft

- How do the dialogue and action dramatize the three-character conflict?
- What twists and turns does the play take?
- What is the discovery and/or reversal at the play's end?

Revising Stage Directions

A playwright's placement of stage directions in the script affects how her play will be performed. Stage directions describe the action that will precede and follow the dialogue. You wrote stage directions in Writer's Practices 14.2, 14.3, and 14.4, but now it's time to check their placement, quality, and quantity.

"Hearing" stage directions takes a well-trained ear. That's one of the reasons it is so important that a play be reviewed in a response group, just like a poem or a short story. Further, you should read your play aloud to yourself. Read both the dialogue and the stage directions, trying to hear what the characters are saying and to imagine them performing the corresponding actions. Consider how you talk and act; gestures often accompany speech, but sometimes actions precede it. A character may take a sip of coffee or cola before speaking, for example, or pace in the midst of an outburst. Actions define character just as much as dialogue does, so try to vary the actions of your characters. After all, in life people don't all move and perform tasks in the same way, and neither should your characters.

Additionally, a playwright should check her stage directions to ensure that there's an appropriate amount of activity on stage. She may find that she needs some added action—or even less action. Though a play should not be presented as an adventure movie, neither should its staging resemble a still-life painting. Indeed, a play lacking in action is as difficult to perform as it is to watch. On the other hand, playwrights should allow directors and actors a certain amount of control when it comes to performance. That is, include enough stage directions to shape the play, but don't make the directions long and cumbersome. When in doubt, err on the side of minimal, flexible stage directions.

Writer's Practice 14.5   *Reconsider Stage Directions*

Read your play twice over, reviewing it for misplaced stage directions and for lines that could benefit from additional action. Begin by highlighting all the stage directions in your play. Read the dialogue that precedes and follows these stage directions. Better yet, recruit a friend or two to do an informal staged reading and actually act the stage directions as you have written them. Does the action happen where it should? Are there enough stage directions? Are the stage directions too wordy and overly specific?

Begin reviewing if you feel you are ready, or examine our writer's model and explication.

Our Writer

HALFTIME

CHARACTERS
Tom, second-string quarterback, a junior
Brandon, All-State quarterback, a senior
Coach Gerke, Lancaster High's football coach
Voice of audience

SETTING: A bench beside the Lancaster High football field, homecoming game. The Lancaster Lancers are well behind near the end of the second quarter. On the last play, Coach Gerke gets hit in the head by the football. The Walkertown Whalers have the ball.

AT RISE: Two young men, one wearing a football helmet and one carrying one, ENTER from stage left, guiding an older man toward the bench. A water jug and a stack of towels sit at the end of it.

TOM

The ball took a bad bounce.

BRANDON

Yeah, right off Coach Gerke's head.

COACH GERKE

(Sits down.)

Sacked on the fourth down!

BRANDON

(Removes his helmet.)

Sacked? I wasn't sacked.

COACH GERKE

(Rubs his head.)

Who am I?

BRANDON

Maybe he's got a head injury.

TOM

He's always had a head injury.

BRANDON

Think he's gonna be all right?

TOM
Ten minutes and some water, he'll be fine.

COACH GERKE
Who am I?

TOM
Number 19, Joe Montana.

> (BRANDON pours COACH GERKE a glass of water and hands it to him.)

COACH GERKE
> (Sips the water.)

Joe who?

BRANDON
Think we should call EMS?

TOM
Give him nine more minutes. And more water.

> (BRANDON refills COACH GERKE'S glass.)

COACH GERKE
> (Points at BRANDON.)

Who's he?

TOM
> (Takes the glass from COACH GERKE, sips from it, and hands it back.)

The coach's favorite.

BRANDON
Knock it off, Tom. It's me, Coach. Your quarterback.

COACH GERKE
> (To TOM.)

And who are you?

TOM
Terry Bradshaw.

BRANDON
It's not funny. Something's wrong with his head.

TOM
> (Watches the game going on at stage left.)

No kidding.

COACH GERKE
> (To TOM, again pointing at BRANDON.)

Who'd you say he was?

TOM

(Whispers.)

A cheerleader.

BRANDON

(Wets a towel and wipes COACH GERKE'S brow with it.)

I said knock it off. Do you know where you are? What day it is?

COACH GERKE

Halftime?

BRANDON

That's it. I'm calling EMS.

(BRANDON EXITS stage right.)

COACH GERKE

What am I doing here?

TOM

(Takes the glass of water from COACH GERKE and drains it.)

Waiting.

COACH GERKE

For what?

TOM

For the coach to put you in the game.

COACH GERKE

(Stands up and fakes a throw.)

Come on, coach. Let me at 'em.

TOM

Sit down, Gerke. You're not going anywhere.

COACH GERKE

Why?

TOM

Because I don't like you.

(The audience boos.)

COACH GERKE

(Watches the game.)

You don't like me? Why?

TOM

I don't like your attitude.

COACH GERKE

My attitude? What's wrong with my attitude?

TOM

You're pushy. And you talk back.

COACH GERKE

(Shakes his head, as if to clear it.)

What did you say? Stop rambling—I'm confused. Which team's ours?

TOM

The Lancers. Gold and black.

COACH GERKE

The Lancers? What a stupid name.

(The audience boos again.)

TOM

Touchdown! The Whalers are slaughtering us.

COACH GERKE

(Looks closer.)

Those uniforms make me want to puke.

TOM

This game makes me want to puke.

(BRANDON ENTERS from stage right.)

BRANDON

EMS is on the way.

(Scans stage left.)

I gotta get out there.

(BRANDON EXITS stage left, helmet in hand.)

COACH GERKE

(Rises and turns toward TOM.)

What about me? Come on. Give me a chance. One chance.

(TOM ignores him. The audience boos.)

TOM

He got sacked. Brandon got sacked.

COACH GERKE

(Grabs TOM'S helmet and holds it under his arm.)

The quarterback's not getting up. The quarterback's hurt!

(BRANDON ENTERS from stage left, limps back toward the bench, and removes his helmet.)

BRANDON

(Holds his head.)

Go on. Get out there, Tom.

TOM

(Grabs BRANDON'S helmet, puts it on, and EXITS stage left.)

What luck! Man.

BRANDON

Shut up!

COACH GERKE

(Follows after TOM.)

Why him? What about me?

BRANDON

(Goes after him.)

Sit down! You're injured! And so am I.

COACH GERKE

(Paces.)

I'm sick of sitting.

BRANDON

(Leads him back to the bench and makes him sit.)

Sit still!

(COACH GERKE and BRANDON look to stage left. When the audience cheers, COACH GERKE stands.)

COACH GERKE

First down!

BRANDON

(Head in his hands.)

I don't believe it.

COACH GERKE

That guy wearing 12—Bradshaw's number—where'd he come from?

BRANDON

Junior Varsity.

(The audience cheers again.)

COACH GERKE

Another first down! Yes!

BRANDON

I do not believe it.

COACH GERKE

(Moves toward stage left.)

Throw the ball . . . throw the ball. Touchdown! Halftime!

(Returns to the bench, pours two glasses of water, and grabs a towel.)

Where'd all the water go? Brandon, why are you just sitting there?

(TOM ENTERS from stage left and removes BRANDON'S helmet.)

COACH GERKE

Way to go, Tom! I knew you could do it.

BRANDON

EMS is here. Do what you want to do. I'm getting my head checked.

> (As BRANDON EXITS stage right, COACH GERKE hands TOM a glass of water.)

TOM

> (Sips the water.)

You knew I could do it?

COACH GERKE

> (Pats TOM on the back.)

Sure, Tom. I was just like you when I was a kid. Just like you.

TOM

But you were the starting quarterback, right?

COACH GERKE

Not at the start. I had to work my behind off for that. Come on, I'll tell you about it. . . .

> (COACH GERKE and TOM EXIT stage right together.
>
> CURTAIN.)

During the revision, the initial "setting" and "at rise" directions were made a bit more specific: The Walkertown Whalers have the ball—it's not yet half-time—and Brandon and Tom are guiding Coach Gerke toward the bench, an immediate indicator that something's wrong. In addition, the stage directions that describe the interaction between Tom and Coach Gerke over the glass of water were modified to help show Tom's cavalier attitude toward the coach. With the revised stage direction, Tom takes Coach Gerke's glass and drains it as soon as Brandon is out of sight.

The placement of the stage direction in the following example was also revised when *Halftime* was read aloud. Can you tell why? Additionally, some stage directions were added and some were cut in an effort to clarify the action without assuming directorial control:

TOM

Sit down. You're not going anywhere.

COACH GERKE

Why?

> (The audience boos.)

TOM

Because I don't like you.

In an earlier draft, the first time the audience gives its first boo follows Coach Gerke asking "Why?" Although the audience could be booing in response to the action on the field, using the voice to enhance the dialogue would be more effective. In the revision below, the audience gives its first boo after Tom says "Because I don't like you"; it's an agreement of sorts. See the difference?

Examining Student Plays

When writing a play with three-character conflict, twists and turns, and a discovery/reversal, the playwright needs to carefully consider the characters' interactions and reactions. These interactions and reactions can intensify the conflict or lessen it. In addition, the manner in which the characters respond to each other and to the twists and turns in the play will affect the discovery/reversal effect at the end of the play, as the student who wrote the following play learned.

Emerald's Wake

NANCY ALBORELL

CHARACTERS

Martha Jane, Emerald's widow, age 67. Southern (Louisiana) accent.
Lainie, Emerald's sister, age 56. Southern (Louisiana) accent.
Patty, Lainie's daughter, age 16.

SETTING: The screened porch of Martha Jane's house, the present. The porch is furnished with a glider, a side table, a lawn chair, and a small cupboard topped with a TV.

AT RISE: LAINIE and PATTY ENTER stage right, pausing just outside the porch.

PATTY
When can we go home, Ma? I'm so bummed.

LAINIE
(Reaches into her purse for a tissue.)

Really, Patty! We have to at least offer comfort to Martha Jane.

PATTY
I don't know why I had to come in the first place. I hardly remember Uncle Emerald.

LAINIE

(Daubs her nose.)

Well, that's just the point, isn't it? Now try to behave a little longer.

(LAINIE and PATTY enter the screened porch. They find MARTHA JANE sitting on the glider, smiling. She's reading a tabloid paper and listening to music on her Walkman.)

LAINIE

Martha Jane, what on earth?

MARTHA JANE

(Cheerfully.)

Lainie! Oh, and you brought Patty along! Come here and sit by me, Patty darling!

(Removes the Walkman and puts it and the tabloid on the side table.)

Look at you! How many years has it been?

PATTY

(Crosses and sits next to MARTHA JANE.)

I remember coming to a high-school graduation. I can't remember which one.

LAINIE

Martha Jane, everybody inside thinks you're out here crying your eyes out, which would be more appropriate, I might add.

MARTHA JANE

(With a dismissive wave.)

Oh, I told them all to leave me alone so I could come out here and listen to Johnny Cash.

(Turns to PATTY.)

Patty, honey, you turned out prettier than your momma ever was.

PATTY

(Sits by MARTHA JANE, casts an apprehensive glance at LAINIE.)

Thank you, I think.

LAINIE

(Sits in a lawn chair.)

I might have known you wouldn't give a hoot what people think.

MARTHA JANE

Lainie, I've reached a point in my life where people ought to worry about what *I* think. That means you.

(To PATTY.)

That's the good part about getting old.

LAINIE

And that trashy tabloid, *really* Martha Jane!

MARTHA JANE

Lainie, it's a wake. You can't tell me they aren't in there laughing it up and stuffing their faces. You know, you've gotten mighty stiff ever since you moved to Bloomfield Hills. You spend so much time with those Garden Club biddies, I think you've forgot where you came from.

(To PATTY.)

Think how rattled she'd be if I'd gave Emerald a *real* New Orleans funeral! He'd have loved that.

(Disdainfully.)

No proper jazz bands this far north.

LAINIE

(Flustered.)

Well, it's a fine example you're setting for a young girl like Patty!

MARTHA JANE

Young girl! Why, Patty's all grown up!

(To PATTY.)

How old are you now?

PATTY

I'll be seventeen in August.

MARTHA JANE

Seventeen? Why, that's older than I was when I married Emerald. Bet you didn't know that, did you?

PATTY

No, I didn't.

LAINIE

Martha Jane, don't fill her head!

MARTHA JANE

Met him down in New Orleans. He was working the shrimp boats, and I was working at the cannery. First time I saw him he was just coming into port. I watched him throwing those dock lines, with no shirt on. He was brown as a coffee bean and all shiny with sweat, and I thought, "Gotta get me one of those!"

(MARTHA JANE laughs and slaps her thigh.)

LAINIE

Martha Jane!

MARTHA JANE

Oh, simmer down, Lainie.

(To PATTY.)

Until the day he died, I swear, he still had a whiff of the gulf waters on him, but I didn't mind. Just took me back to when we were courting.

LAINIE

(To PATTY.)

Don't listen to her nonsense. She's always had too much imagination.

MARTHA JANE

Well, maybe I am imagining that part. Could be he just always had a bit of a scent on him from all the fishing he did. Hell, he was out on Maceday Lake with our boy Bobby the day before he died! Anybody tell you that, Lainie?

LAINIE

No, but I'm not surprised. Emerald always liked to fish. Said Jesus loved the fishermen. He didn't care how many times Daddy whipped him; he'd still cut school to go fishing.

(MARTHA JANE and PATTY both laugh.)

MARTHA JANE

That's my Emerald, all right. Every summer he'd take all three of our boys and off they'd go to fish up in Algonquin. They'd come back all bit up from black flies and mosquitoes, grinning like cats, coolers full of fish. Had to buy a doublewide freezer for the fish they caught.

LAINIE

He used to take me fishing some when I was little.

(To PATTY.)

He was thirteen years older than me, you know.

(Reflectively.)

I didn't care about the fishing much; I just liked to be with my big brother. When he grew up and left Baton Rouge, my heart just broke. I think maybe I fell for Jerry because he reminded me of Emerald.

MARTHA JANE

Here. I've got something to *really* stir up your memories.

(MARTHA JANE stands up and retrieves a photo album from the cupboard. Sitting down, she opens it on her lap. LAINIE joins them on the glider, and they all look at the photos.)

LAINIE

Oh, Lord! Would you look at us! I didn't know you had all these!

MARTHA JANE

I'll make you copies if you want.

PATTY

(Points.)

Is that you, Momma? What's with that hairdo?

LAINIE

That was the style! I went through a can of hairspray every week.

MARTHA JANE

And that one's your Uncle Emerald and your daddy out at Lake Charles. Weren't they a couple of handsome devils? Emerald was just back from Korea. So skinny! Took me the better part of a year to fatten him back up. I swore I'd hog-tie him before I'd let him go back into the service.

LAINIE

I was so glad Jerry was 4F!

MARTHA JANE

(Turns the page.)

Look at this! Mardi Gras, 1959.

LAINIE

Oh, my! I forgot all about this! I really do have to get some copies!

PATTY

What are you supposed to be dressed as?

LAINIE

Queen of Hearts. We're all playing cards, see?

MARTHA JANE

(Nudges PATTY.)

Your momma was seventeen in that picture, and *wild!*

LAINIE

Now, Martha.

MARTHA JANE

(Ignores LAINIE.)

Just a dancing fool! It was dawn before we could drag her away.

LAINIE

Tattletale!

PATTY

And you won't even let *me* stay out past eleven!

LAINIE

(To MARTHA JANE.)

See what you started?

MARTHA JANE

(To PATTY.)

Best part is, when we got her home, your grandpa chased your daddy round and round the house until he promised to marry her!

(LAINIE hides her face in her hands.)

PATTY

Momma! Is that true?

LAINIE

(Looks up and sighs.)

We were planning on getting married anyway.

MARTHA JANE

(Wistfully.)

That was me and Emerald's last Mardi Gras. Always meant to get back for one more; never made it.

PATTY

Why did everybody move up to Michigan?

LAINIE

It was hard to make money down South. Fishing industry practically died.

MARTHA JANE

Emerald heard about jobs up here so we packed up what we could and went. I was carrying Bobby that winter. We moved into an upstairs flat in Highland Park, and Emerald went to work at the Ford plant. Couple years later, your momma and daddy came up, too. Emerald got your daddy his job at Ford. Your momma tell you that much?

LAINIE

Of course I did.

(To PATTY.)

And we brought your Granny Faye with us. If it wasn't for your Uncle Emerald maybe none of us would have done so well.

MARTHA JANE

But we always missed New Orleans. It's in the blood.

PATTY

I'll have to get down there sometime.

LAINIE

(Pulls a cigarette out of her purse, lights it, and blows smoke.)

When you're thirty! Your daddy would have a fit!

PATTY

Momma! You promised you'd quit smoking!

MARTHA JANE

Now that's the Lainie I remember. Say, did Jerry come back to the house with you all?

LAINIE

Oh, yes. He's in there with the rest of them.

MARTHA JANE

I didn't get to say "hey" at the funeral.

LAINIE

I'm sure he'll be wanting to see you before we go.

MARTHA JANE

That boy's getting fat!

LAINIE

I've been telling him that!

MARTHA JANE
(Picks up a remote and turns on the TV.)

Well, don't rush him in here until after my soap opera. It's about to start.

LAINIE
(Sighs.)

You're just a magnet for all the cultural icons!

MARTHA JANE

Whatever that means. Are you getting thirsty? I could stand some cider.

LAINIE

You want me to get you a plate before they clear off that buffet?

MARTHA JANE

That'd be real sweet of you. Get me some of Ginny's salad mold if there's any left. And tell Hanna there's another pot of gumbo in the fridge if it's getting low.

LAINIE

All right. Patty, you want something to eat?

PATTY

No, thank you, Momma. I'm trying to diet.

(The two older women exchange a glance and laugh.
LAINIE rises and EXITS to the house.)

MARTHA JANE

Now we can *really* talk. You got a boyfriend?

PATTY

Nobody special.

MARTHA JANE

Oh, come on. You can tell *me!*

PATTY

No, really. Most of the guys I know just aren't . . .

MARTHA JANE

Worth the bother?

PATTY

Yeah.

MARTHA JANE
(Pats PATTY'S knee.)

Well, you're young. Lots of time. Soon enough you'll find yourself in front of a preacher, and I hope you'll be lucky enough to be standing there with a man good as my Emerald.

(Gazes off into the distance.)

Fifty-one years we were married. Fifty-one years and every one blessed as surely as I'm sitting here. He gave me three good boys who love us enough to stay close to home. He always worked harder than he had to and never gave me a minute's worry.

(Turns back to PATTY.)

He had a smile that lasted all day. Why, the only time I remember him without it was the day they drove Nixon out of office. And he got over that in time for Johnny Carson. You remember what I'm telling you, honey. Look for a man with a smile that lasts all day.

PATTY

Okay, Auntie, I will.

MARTHA JANE

(Gazes off again.)

Fifty-one years. All blessed. Even his death was blessed.

(Turns to PATTY.)

The night he died, we'd just gone to bed. He reached up to turn off the light, and he stopped all of a sudden. He turned and looked at me, kind of surprised. He said, "Martha, honey, I think the Lord is coming for me. Kiss me quick." And I kissed him like he asked, and he was gone. Quiet and sweet.

PATTY

Wow!

MARTHA JANE

The Lord must have loved him a lot to give him such a gentle end, don't you think?

PATTY

I guess so.

MARTHA JANE

What I think is: If the Lord loved him so much he's sure to let us be together again someday, right?

PATTY

Sounds right to me.

MARTHA JANE

Neither of us was exactly a saint, but we tried to do right, and the Lord was sure good to us. He wouldn't keep us apart for long, now would he?

PATTY

Of course not.

MARTHA JANE

(Gazes off.)

Fifty-one years he was my good man. The only man I ever had. Fifty-one years, and twenty-five of those he worked at that plant with never a fuss.

Every day he'd come home for lunch. Every day I'd give him his sandwich, and he'd give me a little loving. You can't ask for better than that. No, you can't ask for better than that.

(MARTHA JANE bows her head, weeping quietly.)

PATTY

(Puts an arm around MARTHA JANE'S shoulders.)

Don't cry, Auntie. Emerald wouldn't want you to be sad.

(LAINIE ENTERS with a tray loaded with food and drink.)

LAINIE

Well, you were right. Everybody's singing show tunes in there.

(Seeing MARTHA JANE crying, she puts down the tray. She takes MARTHA JANE'S hand.)

Oh, honey, it's just starting to hit you, isn't it?

MARTHA JANE

How can I live without him, Lainie? What am I going do? I miss him so bad already.

LAINIE

I know, honey, I know. It's hard, so hard. Have a sip of this cider . . . you'll feel better.

(Hands her a glass off the tray.)

Come on, honey, you'll have us all crying in a minute. Look at Patty. She's getting all moony-eyed.

MARTHA JANE

(Wipes her eyes.)

Did you bring some for all of us? We could drink a toast.

LAINIE

Now, that's a good idea. Why don't we do that.

(LAINIE passes PATTY a glass from the tray, and takes one herself. They all hold their glasses aloft.)

LAINIE

(Pauses, then sighs.)

Goll darn it, I can't think of a thing to say.

(LAINIE sits down.)

PATTY

I can.

(Stands and faces the older women.)

Here's to fifty-one years with a smiling man.

(Holds her glass up high.)

Uncle Emerald, here's to you.

MARTHA JANE

(Turns up the sound on the TV.)

Oh, look! My soap opera's starting.

LAINIE

(Disgusted.)

Oh, no!

PATTY

All My Children! Did Erica break out of jail yet?

MARTHA JANE

Not yet. I think they ought to keep her in there.

PATTY

Me, too. I couldn't believe it when she took Maria's baby.

LAINIE

Patricia Louise! How is it you're so familiar with this junk?

MARTHA JANE

Shhhh! I can't hear!

PATTY

(Stage whisper.)

They play it in the student commons every day at lunch.

LAINIE

Well, I suppose this is the "higher education" our tax dollars go for.

MARTHA JANE

Shhhh!

PATTY

Oh, Momma! Mind your own beeswax!

(LAINIE looks at PATTY askance; MARTHA JANE bursts into laughter.)

(Lights fade as the theme music from *All My Children* is heard. THE END.)

In this play, Nancy creates three characters who come together under a trying circumstance: a wake. At the beginning of the play, Patty, the main character, doesn't want to stay at the wake with her mother, Lainie. Her first line exemplifies this conflict: "When can we go home, Ma? I'm so bummed." But as the play twists and turns, Patty begins to enjoy being with her aunt, Martha Jane, and even comforts her on the loss of her husband, Emerald.

By the play's end, Patty and Martha Jane have bonded and found something in common, leaving Lainie "askance." As with most three-character conflicts, a change in alliances has occurred.

Acknowledgements

Baxter, Charles. "Translation from an Unknown Language" by Charles Baxter. Copyright © Charles Baxter. Reprinted by permission of the author.

Dixon, Stephen. From *The Stories of Stephen Dixon*, copyright © 1994 by Stephen Dixon. Reprinted by permission of Henry Holt and Company, Inc.

Dunn, Stephen. "The Substitute" from *Local Time* by Stephen Dunn. Copyright © 1986 by Stephen Dunn. Reprinted by permission of William Morrow & Company, Inc.

Dunning, Stephen. Adapted form "Choking on Love" by Stephen Dunning in *Indiana Review*, Fall 1993. Reprinted by permission of the author.

Dybek, Stuart. From "Nighthawks" in *The Coast of Chicago* by Stuart Dybek. Copyright © 1990 by Stuart Dybek. Reprinted by permission of Alfred A. Knopf, Inc.

Edson, Russell. "The Father of Toads" from *The Tunnel: Selected Poems* by Russell Edson. Oberlin College Press, 1994. Reprinted by permission.

Foster, Norm. "The Pitch" by Norm Foster first published 1996 by Blizzard Publishing in *Instant Applause II: 30 Very Short Complete Plays*. Reprinted by permission of the author.

Heaney, Seamus. "Blackberry-Picking" from *Poems 1965–1975* by Seamus Heaney. Copyright © 1980 by Seamus Heaney. Reprinted by permission of Farrar, Straus & Giroux, Inc.

Hegi, Ursula. "Thieves" by Ursula Hegi. This article is reprinted from *Feminist Studies*, Volume 7, Number 2 (Summer 1981) 25–29, by permission of the publisher, *Feminist Studies*, Inc., c/o Department of Women's Studies, University of Maryland, College Park, MD 20742.

Howe, Tina. "Teeth" by Tina Howe. Copyright © 1988 by Tina Howe. Reprinted by permission of Flora Roberts, Inc.

Kauffman, Janet. "How Many Boys?" from *Places in the World a Woman Could Walk* by Janet Kauffman. Reprinted by permission of Darhensoff & Verrill Literary Agency.

Komunyakaa, Yusef. "My Father's Loveletters" by Yusef Komunyakaa from *Magic City*, Wesleyan University Press, 1992. Reprinted by permission of the author.

Martone, Michael. "On the Planet of the Apes" by Michael Martone from *Third Coast*. Reprinted by permission of Third Coast.

Nye, Naomi Shihab. "The Trashpickers, Madison Street" is from *Words Under the Words: Selected Poems* by Naomi Shihab Nye; published by Far Corner Books, Portland, Oregon. Copyright © 1995 by Naomi Shihab Nye. Reprinted by permission of the publisher.

Olds, Sharon. From *The Wellspring* by Sharon Olds. Copyright © 1996 by Sharon Olds. Reprinted by permission of Alfred A. Knopf, Inc.

Oliver, Mary. "Milkweed" from *Dream Work* by Mary Oliver. Copyright © 1986 by Mary Oliver. Used by permission of Grove/Atlantic, Inc.

Plath, Sylvia. "You're" from *Ariel* by Sylvia Plath. Copyright © 1961 by Ted Hughes. Copyright Renewed. Reprinted by permission of HarperCollins Publishers, Inc. and Faber and Faber Ltd.

Soto, Gary. From *New and Selected Poems* by Gary Soto. © 1995, published by Chronicle Books, San Francisco.

Stafford, William. "Traveling Through the Dark" copyright 1962 by William Stafford from *Traveling Through the Dark* (Harper & Row). Reprinted by permission of the Estate of William Stafford.

Wilbur, Richard. "The Writer" from *The Mind-Reader* by Richard Wilbur, copyright © 1971 by Richard Wilbur, reprinted by permission of Harcourt Brace & Company.

Williams, William Carlos. "The Red Wheelbarrow" by William Carlos Williams from *The Collected Poems: 1909–1939, Volume I.* Copyright © 1938 by New Directions Publishing Corp. Reprinted by permission of New Directions Publishing Corp.

Index

A

Aborell, Nancy, 360–69
Action, 352
    culminating, 231
    dramatic, 296
    expanding narratives with, 110–12
    exploring and experimenting with,
        295–98
    fictional, 179
    parenthetical, 297–98
    rising, 344, 345
Action tag, 158
Active verbs, 93
Adjectives, 93, 135
    minimal, 95
Adverbs, 93
Analogies, 25
"Anytime" (Richardson), 56–57
The Arabian Nights, 251
"At Least It's Something" (Tooney), 316–23
"At the Bridge" (Nemesi), 38–39
Audience, identifying, 27

B

Backdrop, 217
    adjusting, 217–18
Baker, Dana, 247–49
Bauer, Todd, 77
Baxter, Charles, 101, 103–4, 108, 196
"Behind Grandma's House" (Soto), 60–61
Bell, Shannon, 223–26

Bennett, Jeff, 2
Benson, Genevieve, 40
"Blackberry-Picking" (Heaney), 81
"The Boy" (Stout), 170–73
Butzine, Sarah, 137–38

C

Camera lens view, 227
The Canterbury Tales (Chaucer), 250
"Caught in Silent Spin," 135–36
Chaffin, Nicolaus, 140–41
Characters and characterization
    dramatic, 296
        building, 339–40
        changing, behavior of, using twists
            and turns, 345–46
        exploring and experimenting with,
            255–58
        exploring and experimenting with
            strong, 291–95
        revising for consistency in, 310–15
        three-character conflict, 337–44
        two-character conflict, 298–306
    fictional, 145, 174, 227–49
        exploring and experimenting with,
            through dialogue, 152–66
Chaucer, G., 250
"Choking on Love" (Dunning), 145–49,
    152–53
Chronological order, 234
Clarity, cutting for, 135–37

Clichés, 179
Collaborative poem, 105–6
Commas, 115, 123
Commentary, inserting, 159
Comparison
    experimenting with, 46–47
    metaphors in, 45–46
        extended, 47–52
    similes in, 45
Composing and structuring in writing
    process, 2, 9–13
Conflict
    dramatic, 296, 298–306
        exploring and experimenting with
            three-character, 337–44
        exploring and experimenting with
            two-character, 298–306
        intensification of, 303
    fictional, 174
        building, from characterization, 145
        exploring and experimenting with,
            255–58
        exploring and experimenting with
            leads in establishing, 149–52
        psychological, 232–34
        resolving, 210
    poetic, narrating simple, 22–41
Conjunctions, subordinating, 126, 128
Connotation, 130–31, 242
Consistency, revising for, in characterization,
    310–15
Conversation
    creating closing, 163
    recording, 340–41
        from direct observation, 294–95
        from memory, 293–94
Copelin, David, 324
Creative writing
    as right-brain activity, 5
    writing process in, 3–20
Culminating action, 231

D
Daily life, writing from, 59–79
Daily life poem, writing, 66
Davis, Lisa, 278–81
Dennotation, 131, 242
Denstaedt, Geoffrey, 97
Details
    cutting extraneous, 135
    expanding narratives with, 110–12
    sensory, 180
    in writing description, 178

Dialogue
    dramatic, exploring and experimenting
        with, 291–92
    fictional, 109, 145, 179
        exploring and experimenting with
            characterization through,
            156–66
        reducing, 155
        tagging, 158
    poetic
        creating, 28–29
        expanding narratives with,
            110–12
Diction, revising with eye on, 92–95
Direct address
    experimenting with, 69–71
    exploring, 68–69
Direct observation
    freewriting from, 5–7
    recording a conversation from,
        294–95
Discovery, 4–9
    in drama, exploring and experimenting
        with, 348–52
Distance, maintaining, 203–4
Dixon, David, 57
Dixon, Stephen, 251–54, 255
Dodynd, Stephen, 105
Drama, 283–369
    action in, 295–98
    acts in, 298–99
    characters in, 291–95, 296
    comparison with short stories, 284
    conflict in, 296
    dialogue in, 291–95
    discoveries in, 348–52
    dramatic structure in, 298–306
    history of short, 284
    language in, 296
    playscript format in, 301–2
    resolution in, 305–6
    reversals in, 348–52
    stage directions in, 301–2, 306–8
    theme in, 296
    three-character conflict in, 337–44
    twists and turns in, 344–47
    two-character conflict in, 298–306
Dramatic situations, exploring and experi-
    menting with, 24–31
Dunn, Stephen, 120, 121, 124, 126, 131
Dunning, Stephen, 149, 150, 152–53, 156,
    157
Dybek, Stuart, 9–10

E

Editing in writing process, 2, 16–20
Edson, Russell, 101, 103, 108
"Emerald's Wake" (Alborell), 360–69
Emphasis, cutting for, 135–37
End-stopped line, 113, 115
Events, dramatizing, 27–28
Exclamation points, 123
Expanding, 7, 15–16
Exploring, 7–9
Extended metaphor, 43
    exploring and experimenting with,
        47–52

F

"The Father of Toads" (Edson), 101
Feedback, listening to, in writer response
    groups, 13–15
"Fertilizer," 186–88
Fiction, 144–281. *See also* Short stories
    adding details in, 63
    characters and characterization in,
        156–66, 227–49, 255–58
    conflict in, 255–58
    exploring leads in establishing conflict
        in, 149–52
    first-person point of view in,
        152–54
    flashbacks in, 234–41
    frame-tales in, 250–54
    imagery in, 242–47
    movement in, 180–88
    psychological conflict in, 232–34
    recurring images in, 189–93
    repetition in, 167–70, 258–69
    setting in, 177–80
    suspense in, 205–10
    tone in, 216–23
Fictionalizing, 7–9
Figurative language, 45, 179
    extended metaphors, 43, 47–52
    metaphors, 42, 45–46, 123, 179,
        243
    onomatopoeia, 94
    similes, 33, 42, 45, 179, 243
First draft
    assembling, 12, 164–66, 186–88,
        212–16, 239–41, 265–69
    weakness of beginner's, 15
First-person point of view, 10, 30, 60, 108,
    129, 144, 145, 162, 178, 196
"Fish Out of Water" (Butzine), 137–38
Fixed forms, 73

Flashbacks
    fictional, 203
    exploring and experimenting with,
        234–41
"Floater," 190–93
Focused free association, 106
Focused-lens view, 62, 64, 69, 71
Focused writing, 5
Foster, Norm, 325–36
Frame-tales, 250–54
Frankenstein (Shelley), 250
Free association, 5, 87
    focused, 106
Free-verse poem, 114
    exploring, 72
    revising to create, 73–75
Freewriting, 5–7, 28, 51, 83, 84, 87, 89,
    106–7, 130

G

Gardner, John, 227
Ghazal, 73
"Girl with Book" (Mitchell), 116
"Glass Girl" (Benson), 40–41
Golab, Susan, 98–99
"Gone Fishin'" (Dixon), 57–58
"The Good Samaritan," 168–70
Grammar, 123
    and sentence control, 123
Griffith, Brent, 39

H

Haiku, 73
"Halftime," 354–59
Halleran, Ashley, 96
Hamilton, Adam, 58
"Heading Home," 244–46
Heaney, Seamus, 81, 83–84, 89
Hegi, Ursula, 228, 235
Hooking readers, 203
Howe, Tina, 284, 285–90
"How It Should Really Feel" (Mitchell),
    194–95
"How Many Boys?" (Kauffman),
    197–200
Hugo, Richard, 100

I

Imagery, 62
    fictional
        connecting with theme, 271–78
        revising for, 242–47

in poetry
experimenting with, 63–67, 90–91
exploring, 61–63, 87–90
Images
collecting daily, 64
recurring, 189–93
Imagination, exploring and experimenting
with, 82–87, 102–7
Imagists, 87–88
"Incivility," 18–19
Information, withholding, 205–6
"Insomnia" (Dybek), 9–10
Introductory clause, 126, 128

J
The Jackie Gleason Show, 285
James, David, 105
Journal, writing in, 4, 83

K
Kauffman, Janet, 197, 201, 202, 203, 206
Komunyakaa, Yusef, 22, 25, 27–28, 33

L
Language
in drama, 296
figurative, 45, 179
literal, 45
Language threads, 105, 132
Leads, in establishing conflict, 149–52
Left-brain activity, 5–6, 17
Limerick, 73
Line breaks, 112
shaping poetry with, 114
Lines
endings and beginnings of, 72, 73–74
end-stopped, 113
length of, 72, 73
run-on, 113
Lists, 127
Literal language, 45

M
Martone, Michael, 175, 180–81
Meaning
exploring and experimenting with, 31–35
revising and developing, 13–16
Media res beginnings, 203, 341
Memory
exploring, in writing poems, 80–81, 82–87
freewriting from, 5–7
narrating, 29–30
recording conversation from, 293–94

Metaphors, 42, 123, 179, 243
definition of, 45
exploring, 45–46
extended, 43, 47–52
x is *y* formula for, 46
"Milk Bubble Ruins" (Olds), 23, 25–26,
32, 33
"Milkweed" (Oliver), 61
Milton Berle's Texaco Star Theater, 285
Minimal adjectives, 95
"Mirror" (Hamilton), 58
Mitchell, Elizabeth, 116
Mitchell, Kristen, 194–95
Modeling, 11
Movement in fiction, exploring and experi-
menting with, 180–88
"My Father's Loveletters" (Komunyakaa),
23–24, 26, 33

N
Narration, of memory, 29–30
Narrative, 250
expanding, with details, action, and
dialogue, 110–12
immediacy of, 145
Narrative poetry, 22–41
connecting with readers, 25
signal words in, 34
Narrative voice, 227
Narrator
importance of, 51
role of, 255
"The Nature Area" (Bell), 223–26
Nemesi, Kris, 38
Nordan, Lewis, 174
Nouns, 113–14
focusing on, 93
importance of strong, 130
precise, 95
Nye, Naomi Shihab, 80, 81, 84, 89–90

O
"Oak" (Chaffin), 140–41
Oates, Joyce Carol, 144
Observations, reflecting on, 65–66
Olds, Sharon, 22, 25, 27, 32–33
"Old Stories" (Swartout), 78
Oliver, Mary, 60, 62–63, 68, 72
One-act plays, 285
Onomatopoeia, 94
"On the Planet of the Apes" (Martone),
175–77, 180–81
"Oracle" (Davis), 278–81

Orler, Jill, 75
"Out Too Late" (Griffith), 39–40

P

Pantoun, 73
"Paralyzed" (Baker), 247–49
Parenthetical actions, composing, 297–98
Past-tense verbs, 30, 233
"Perched by Golden Flame" (Denstaedt), 97
Periods, 115, 123
"The Pitch" (Foster), 325–36, 337–38, 339
Place, describing a, 178
Plath, Sylvia, 43, 45, 46, 54
Plays. *See* Drama
Playscript format, 301–2
Poetic line, revising for, 112–14
Poetry, 21–141
    collaborative, 105–6
    definition of, 80
    diction in, 92–95, 130–34, 131
    direct address in, 68–71
    drawing unusual comparisons in, 42–58
    exploring dramatic situations in, 24–31
    extended metaphors in, 47–52
    free-verse, 72–75, 114
    imagery in, 61–67, 87–91
    imagination in, 102–7
    line breaks in, 112–14
    meaning in, 31–35
    memory in, 82–87
    metaphors in, 45–46
    narrative, 22–41
    prose, 54
    revising verbs to reduce wordiness in, 36–38
    similes in, 45
    stanzas in, 53–56
    third-person point of view in, 108–12
Precise nouns, 95
Prepositional phase, 127–28, 136
Present-tense verbs, 129, 233
The Princess Bride, 250–51
Proofreading in writing process, 2, 16–20
Prose poems, 54
Protagonists, 325
Psychological conflict, 231–34
Published works, experimenting with the techniques and structures of, 9–11
Punctuation, proofreading for, 16–17

Q

Question marks, 123
Quotation marks, 115, 156

R

Raw materials, generating, in writing process, 2, 4–9
Readers
    connecting with, 25
    expectations of, 104
    hooking, 203
Reading, freewriting from, 5–7
"Reading Whitman," 34–35
Rearranging, 15–16
Recurring images in revising, 189–93
"The Red Wheelbarrow" (Williams), 88
Repetition, 145
    exploring and experimenting with, 258–69
Resolution
    in drama, 305–6
    in fiction, 210
Reversal in drama, exploring and experimenting with, 348–52
Revising
    for consistency in characterization, 310–15
    in developing meaning, 2, 13–16
    diction in, 92–95
    for emphasis and clarity, 135–37
    for imagery, 242–47
    poetic line in, 112–14
    recurring images in, 189–93
    reducing wordiness by revising verbs, 36–38
    repetition in, 167-170
    stage directions, 353–60
    for theme, 270–78
    for tone, 216–23
Richardson, Laura, 56
Rising action, 344, 345
Run-on line, 113, 115
Russell, Kaitlin, 118–19

S

"Sailing to Tahiti," 114–15
Sarton, May, 43
Scenes
    constructing, 341–42
    replaying, 236–37
Second-person point of view, 108
Sensory details, 180
Sentence control, exploring and experimenting with, 123–30

Sentence fragment, 127–28
Sentence frames, 129–30
Sentences
    definition of, 121
    length of, 125, 126, 127, 128
Sestinas, 72, 73
Setting, 175
    exploring and experimenting with,
        177–80
Shelley, Mary, 250
Short stories, comparison with drama, 284
Signal words, in narrative poems, 34
Similes, 33, 42, 179, 243
    definition of, 45
"Sleep Song," 55–56
"A Sloppy Story" (Dixon), 251–54
"A Smaller Man" (Bauer), 77
Sonnets, 72, 73
Soto, Gary, 59–60, 62, 63, 68, 72
"Space, Time, and Motion" (Witkowski),
    117
Speaker tag, 158
Spell checking, 16
"Spring Training," 218–22
Stafford, William, 120, 121, 124, 131
Stage directions, 301–2, 306–8
    revising, 353–60
Stanzas, 72
    definition of, 53
    purpose of, 53
    revising for, 53–56
Storytelling, 152
    ingredients of, 8
Stout, Kyle, 170–73
Structure, discovering best for subject,
    11–13
Subject, discovering best structure for, 11–13
Subordinating conjunctions, 126, 128
"The Substitute" (Dunn), 121–22
"Summer's Call" (Halleran), 96
Suspense, 197
    exploring and experimenting with,
        205–10
Swartout, Richard, 78
Symbols, 243
Synonyms, 131
Syntax, 131

T
Tag lines, 115
Tangible writing prompts, 89
"Tapping Feet," 74–75
"Teeth" (Howe), 284, 285–90, 301

Tercets, 56
"That Way" (Russell), 118–19
Theme
    in drama, 296
    in fiction, 270–78
"Thieves" (Hegi), 228–30
Third-person limited point of view, 108,
    231, 232
Third-person objective point of view,
    exploring and experimenting with, 201–5
Third-person omniscient point of view, 10,
    108
Third-person point of view, 108, 152, 196, 227
    exploring and experimenting with,
        108–12
    narrative, 197
Thought tag, 158
Three-character dramatic conflict, exploring
    and experimenting with, 337–44
Time
    moving back in, 184
    word choice in signaling shifts in, 34
Time-sequence pattern, 12–13
"Tinting the Rainbow" (Orler), 75–76
Titles, choosing, 14
Tone, 197
    revising story for, 216–23
Tooney, Marty, 316–23
Tranforming, 15–16
"Translation from an Unknown Language:
    The Man Who Sold His Bed" (Baxter),
    102
"The Trashpickers, Madison Street" (Nye),
    82
"Traveling Through the Dark" (Stafford),
    122–23
Turning point, 344
Twists and turns, exploring and experiment-
    ing with dramatic, 344–47
Two-character conflict, 298–306
"Two Scientists," 36–37
Two-step movement maneuver, 181, 184

U
"Until" (Wisniewski), 138–39
"Up a Tree," 212–16
Updike, John, 250

V
Vaudeville, 285
Verbs
    active, 93
    of being, 36

differences in tense, 233
importance of strong, 130
past-tense, 30, 233
placement of, 115–16
present-tense, 129, 233
revising, to reduce wordiness, 36–38
in series, 155
unobtrusive, 158
Villanelles, 72, 73
Voice
creating distinct, 26
narrative, 227

W
"What We Save," 94–95
White, E. B., 27
White space, using, 164
Whitman, Walt, 35
Wilbur, Richard, 43, 45–46, 47–49, 54
Williams, William Carlos, 80, 91
Wisniewski, Tom, 138–39
Witkowski, D'Anne, 117

Word, connotation/denotation of, 130–31, 242
Word choice, 16–17, 123
in signaling shifts in time, 34
Wordiness, eliminating, 36–38, 135
Writer response groups, listening to feedback in, 13–15
Writer's block, 5
Writer response groups, 310
using, 53, 71, 112, 134, 166–67, 189, 241–42, 269–70, 352
working in, 35–36
"The Writer" (Wilbur), 44–46, 47–49
Writing process, 2
composing and structuring in, 2, 9–13
editing and proofreading in, 2, 16–20
generating raw material in, 2, 4–9
revising and developing meaning in, 2, 13–16

Y
"Yesterday's King Salmon" (Golab), 98
"You're" (Plath), 43, 45